AT THE EDGES OF STATES

Power and Place in Southeast Asia

The series examines social struggles and their connection with the particularity of places in Southeast Asia. It embraces an ecumenicity of innovative approaches within the humanities, social and political sciences, while retaining a central role for 'power' and 'place'.

Editors: Gerry van Klinken (KITLV) and Edward Aspinall (Australian National University).

VERHANDELINGEN
VAN HET KONINKLIJK INSTITUUT
VOOR TAAL-, LAND- EN VOLKENKUNDE

275

MICHAEL EILENBERG

AT THE EDGES OF STATES

Dynamics of state formation in the
Indonesian borderlands

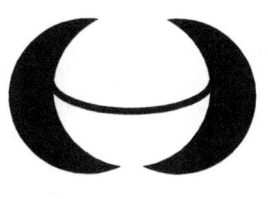

KITLV Press
Leiden
2012

Published by:
KITLV Press
Koninklijk Instituut voor Taal-, Land- en Volkenkunde
(Royal Netherlands Institute of Southeast Asian and Caribbean Studies)
P.O. Box 9515
2300 RA Leiden
The Netherlands
website: www.kitlv.nl
e-mail: kitlvpress@kitlv.nl

KITLV is an institute of the Royal Netherlands Academy of
Arts and Sciences (KNAW)

KONINKLIJKE NEDERLANDSE
AKADEMIE VAN WETENSCHAPPEN

Cover: Creja ontwerpen, Leiderdorp

Cover photo: Borderlander standing on the hilly ridge that constitutes the heavily forested border between Indonesia and Malaysia. Photo by the author 2007.

ISBN 978 90 6718 374 1

© 2012 Koninklijk Instituut voor Taal-, Land- en Volkenkunde

No part of this publication may be reproduced or transmitted in any form or by any means, electronic or mechanical, including photocopy, recording, or any information storage and retrieval system, without permission from the copyright owner.

Printed in the Netherlands

In memory of Reed Lee Wadley

Acknowledgements

I wish to thank all the people who in various ways have helped me during the research process leaving up to this book. First and foremost, I would like to thank the members of Rumah Manah and the surrounding communities in the Kapuas Hulu borderland, both for helping me with my research and letting me take part in their daily lives. In particular, I thank the families with whom I stayed for welcoming me into their homes and making me family. Thanks to Devi, Wati, and Lala for helping me through the bureaucratic labyrinths in Pontianak, introducing me to interesting people and making my stays in this bustling city pleasant and enjoyable.

In the academic arena, I wish to acknowledge the mentoring I received from Reed L. Wadley who sadly passed away before this book was completed. Reed generously shared his large knowledge of the West Kalimantan Iban and gave me excellent advice and inspiration throughout my undergraduate and graduate studies. I am profoundly grateful for his intellectual engagement and collegial support and dedicate this book to him.

I would like to thank the following people who have all read, and commented on, the articles/chapters included in this book and who have been important sources of inspiration: Christian Lund, Tania Murray Li, James Scott, Nancy Peluso, Willem van Schendel, Barbara Andaya, Derek Hall, Thomas Sikor, Lesley Potter, Michele Ford, Lenore Lyons, Keith Foulcher, Campbell Macknight, Timo Kivimaki, Ole Bruun, Nils Ole Bubandt, Mikael Gravers, Ida Nicolaisen and several anonymous reviewers. Special thanks are owed to Gerry van Klinken and Edward Aspinall editors of the KITLV Press sub-series on 'Power and place in Southeast Asia', whose support was crucial for the publication of this book. Many other people contributed immensely to this work but I cannot mention each of you by name. Your contribution is greatly appreciated.

Sections of the data presented in this book have previously been presented in various articles. The data have, however, been extended and revised. Drafts of the second part of Chapter 1 were published in Michael Eilenberg, 'Borderland encounters: a letter from Kapuas Hulu, West Kalimantan', *Review of Indonesian and Malaysian Affairs*, 42-1 (2008): pages 191-200. Parts of Chapters 3 and 4 were elaborated in Michael Eilenberg, 'Straddling the border: A marginal history of guerrilla warfare and 'counter-insurgency' in the Indonesian borderlands, 1960s-1970s', *Modern Asian Studies*, 45-6 (2011), pages 1423-1463. Parts of Chapter 5 were published in Reed Wadley and Michael Eilenberg, 'Autonomy, identity and "illegal" logging in the borderlands of West Kalimantan, Indonesia', *The Asia Pacific Journal of Anthropology* 6 (2005), pages 19-34. The essence of Chapter 6 was addressed in Reed Wadley and Michael Eilenberg, 'Vigilantes and gangsters in the borderland of West Kalimantan, Indonesia', in Alexander Horstmann (ed.), *States, Peoples and Borders in Southeast Asia. A Special Issue of the Kyoto Review of Southeast Asia* 7 (2006), pages 1-25. Finally, drafts of parts of Chapters 7 and 8 were drawn upon in Michael Eilenberg, 'Negotiating autonomy at the margins of the state: The dynamics of elite politics in the borderland of West Kalimantan, Indonesia', *South East Asia Research* 17-2 (2009), pages 201-27.

Field research conducted for this book was funded by the Danish Council for Development Research and carried out under the auspices of the Indonesian Institute of Sciences (Lembaga Ilmu Pengetahuan Indonesia, LIPI). The study was also made possible by the Department of Political Sciences, Tanjungpura University (UNTAN), Pontianak, and Professor Dr. Syarif I. Alquadrie, who acted as my academic sponsor in Indonesia and aided me in many ways. I am most grateful to these institutions for their support. Any conclusions and opinions drawn here are my own and are not necessarily shared by the above institutions. Any errors in this book are entirely my own.

Lastly, my warmest gratitude and love goes out to my partner Rikke and to my two wonderful daughters, Liva and Aja, who provided immeasurable encouragement. Without their support, none of this would have been possible.

Michael Eilenberg
Aarhus
Denmark

Contents

	ACKNOWLEDGEMENTS	vii
	List of maps and figures	xiii
	Terminology	xv
	Note on spelling and translation	xv
1	INTRODUCTION	1
	Prologue	1
	Borderland encounters	8
	Researching borderlands and illicit practices	13
	The Kapuas Hulu borderland	17
	The border advantage	24
	Structure of the book	32
2	BORDERS OF ENGAGEMENT	43
	Borders and borderlands	44
	State formation from below	49
	Decentralizing Indonesia: More room to manoeuvre	58
	Patterns of patronage and the 'border effect'	60
	Rules and norms as processes of negotiation	67
3	EVADING STATE AUTHORITY	75
	Settlements on the pre-colonial frontier	77
	Drawing borders: Colonial encounters on the frontier	83
	The wild frontier: Batang Lupar country	88
	Migration and warfare	92
	Rebellion and pacification	97
	Border outlaws: Perpetuating semi-autonomy	101
4	GUERRILLA WARFARE AND RESOURCE EXTRACTION	113
	Konfrontasi: State making on the border	114
	A time of disruption: Nationalist aspiration and state violence	119
	Operation Destruction: Counterinsurgency and anti-communism	124

| Contents

  The PARAKU: Insurgents or liberation army?   132
  Establishment of a borderland elite   144
  New Order legacies: Authoritarian rule and resource extraction   150
  Large-scale timber concessions and military rule   151
  Moulding loyal citizens and its paradoxical outcomes   159

5   PATRONAGE AND POWER   165
  Decentralization, informal networks and 'illegal' logging   166
  Towards increased regional autonomy   167
  Cooperative logging and a booming economy   169
  Negotiation and collusion: elite opportunities   175
  Cross-border patron-broker-client relations   180
  The Malaysian connection   181
  Captain of the timber industry   183
  Small border elites   187
  Cooperation and disputes   191
  Non-state forms of authority   198

6   INTERSECTING SPHERES OF LEGALITY AND ILLEGALITY   205
  Vigilantes: The usnata killing   208
  'Wild' logging and 'gangsterism'   213
  Confession of a Malaysian timber baron   216
  Shifting loyalties   223
  Illegal but licit: Circumventing the law, enforcing local norms   227
  Defying the limits of legality   230
  Shades of gray   232

7   SOVEREIGNTY AND SECURITY   235
  Security through development   237
  Grand schemes   246
  Re-militarizing the border   249
  Contesting large-scale schemes   254
  Tightening border regimes   257

8   BORDERLAND AUTONOMY AND LOCAL POLITICS   261
  Promotion of a 'North Border District'   262
  Justification for a new district   268
  Separatism: Playing the border card   271

	Ethnic sentiments	272
	Multiple levels of power struggle	274
	National and transnational networks of influence	277
9	CONCLUSION	283
	Fluid borders and fluctuating borderlands	284
	Claiming authority, negotiating autonomy	287
	Zones of semi-autonomy	290
	APPENDIX	293
	Timeline of important events	293
	ACRONYMS AND ABBREVIATIONS	295
	GLOSSARY	299
	BIBLIOGRAPHY	301
	INDEX	339

List of maps and figures

Map 1: Indonesia
Map 2: Island of Borneo
Map 3: District of Kapuas Hulu
Map 4: Colonial Borneo, 1747[1]
Map 5: Colonial West Borneo, 1895[2]
Map 6: Batang Lupar Country, 1895[3]

Fig 1: Badau border crossing (PLB), 2007
Fig 2: Labour migrants resting before crossing into Sarawak, 2007
Fig 3: Official border crossing point (PPLB), 2007
Fig 4: The town of Lanjak, 2005
Fig 5: The Lanjak -Badau road (Jalan Lintas Utara), 2007
Fig 6: The Governor's visit to Lanjak, 2007
Fig 7: The Governor's speech, 2007
Fig 8: Forest cover along the West Kalimantan-Sarawak border, 2007
Fig 9: Iban swidden fields in the border hills, 2002
Fig 10: Planting hill rice in the border hills, 2002
Fig 11: Hunters in the border hills, 2007
Fig 12: Small concrete border pillar, 2007
Fig 13: A group of Batang Lupars, 1920
Fig 14: Temporary longhouse in the vicinity of Nanga Badau, 1932
Fig 15: Batang Lupars parading at a visit by Governor-General, 1920
Fig 16: Batang Lupars in full wardress (date unknown)

[1]   One of the first Dutch maps of Borneo, dated more than a century before the colonial borders were drawn. The map shows the interior of the islands as largely unexplored and unknown (source: Jacob Keizer and Jan de Lat, 1747, 'Kaartje van Borneo' in *Weerelds Hand-Atlas*).

[2]   Section of Dutch colonial map of West Borneo dated 1895 (G.A.F. Molengraaff, 1895, 'Stromkarte von West Borneo' in *Petermanns Geographische Mitteilungen* 41, tafel 14).

[3]   Batang Loepar Landen. (source: Topographisch Bureau, 1895, 'Boven Embaloeh en Batang Loepar' in Residentie Wester-Afdeeling van Borneo; Blad XVII en XVIII. Opgenomen in 1890-1894. Topographisch Bureau, Batavia.).

| *List of maps and figures*

Fig 17: Catholic school in Lanjak (date unknown)
Fig 18: Temenggong (right) in soldiers's uniform, 1932
Fig 19: Consultant ir. G.A. de Mol and Iban headman, 1932
Fig 20: Military certificate signed by General Soeharto, 1967
Fig 21: Military certificate thanking Iban leader, 1974
Fig 22: Military certificate to Iban WANRA 'volunteer', 1988
Fig 23: Monthly honorarium to Iban member of civil defence unit, 1976
Fig 24: Letter of loyalty signed by Iban leader, 1970
Fig 25: Letter of honour to Iban leader, 1972
Fig 26: Hand painted sign on path leading to timber-cutting site, 2000
Fig 27: Mixed forest gardens, along the border, 2007
Fig 28: Logging truck transporting newly cut timber, 2003
Fig 29: Logging road along the border, 2003
Fig 30: Trucks loaded with sawn timber, 2003
Fig 31: Aphengs large sawmill on the Indonesian side of the border, 2003
Fig 32: Newly logged forest and soil erosion, 2003
Fig 33: Jalan Lintas Utara during the rainy season, 2003
Fig 34: Graffiti on a shop in Lanjak, 2005
Fig 35: Confiscated logs from up-river logging camps, 2007
Fig 36: Apheng's deserted and burnt down logging camp, 2007
Fig 37: Control post along a timber road, 2002
Fig 38: Police post close to the Sarawak border, 2007

Terminology

As an aid to the reader I will here briefly sketch the different layers of administrative structures and institutions of authority within Indonesian regional government:

Level of administration	Government officials
1. Propinsi (Province)	1. Governor (Gubernur)
2. Kabupaten (District)	2. Bupati (District head)
3. Kecamatan (Subdistrict)	3. Camat (Subdistrict kead)
4. Desa (Village)	4. Kepala Desa (Village head)
5. Dusun (Hamlet)	5. Kepala Dusun (Hamlet head)

Traditional institutions of authority

Panglima perang	Traditional war leader
Temenggong	Dayak tribal-head/*adat* leader
Patih	Deputies of temenggong/*adat* elder
Tuai rumah	Longhouse head

NOTE ON SPELLING AND TRANSLATION

Throughout the book I will be quoting my informants and including different cultural terms in the text. Communication with informants was carried out in two languages – Indonesian and Iban. When referring to cultural terms and place names I will be using Iban or Indonesian spelling but when quoting my informants I will use an English translation for the sake of readability. Modern Indonesian spelling is used in the body of the text. Where references are made to historical sources the spelling in the original is maintained. Quotations from interviews were translated as literally as possible, and significant terms (Indonesian, Iban and

| *Terminology*

Dutch) are reproduced in the body of the translation. Unless otherwise indicated, all translations of Indonesian and Dutch data (interviews, documents, reports) are my own. I would like to thank Reed Wadley for granting me access to his large and partly translated compilation of reports on West Borneo from the Dutch Colonial archives, especially the 'Mailrapporten' (reports on local/regional conditions) and 'Verbaalen' (long reports, both public and classified) from the Algemeen Rijksarchief (now Nationaal Archief), The Hague, Netherlands. Materials from the Algemeen Rijksarchief are designated with ARA. Dutch colonial quotations originally translated by Reed Wadley are marked [TransRW].

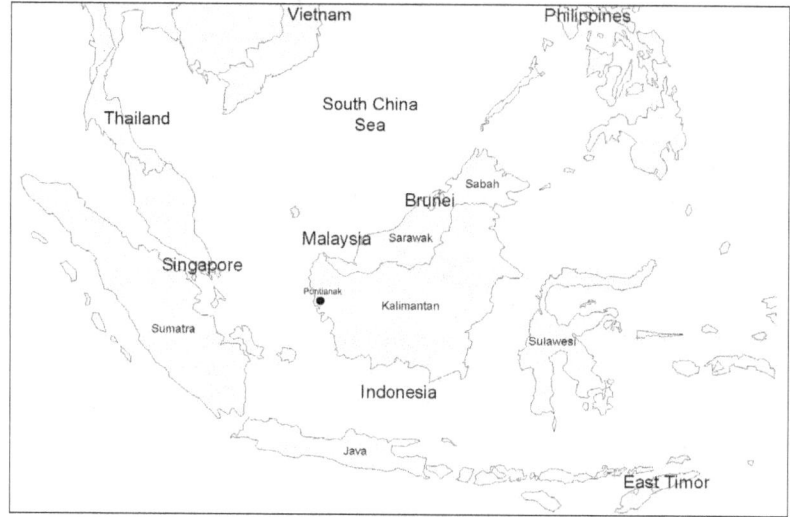

Map 1: Indonesia

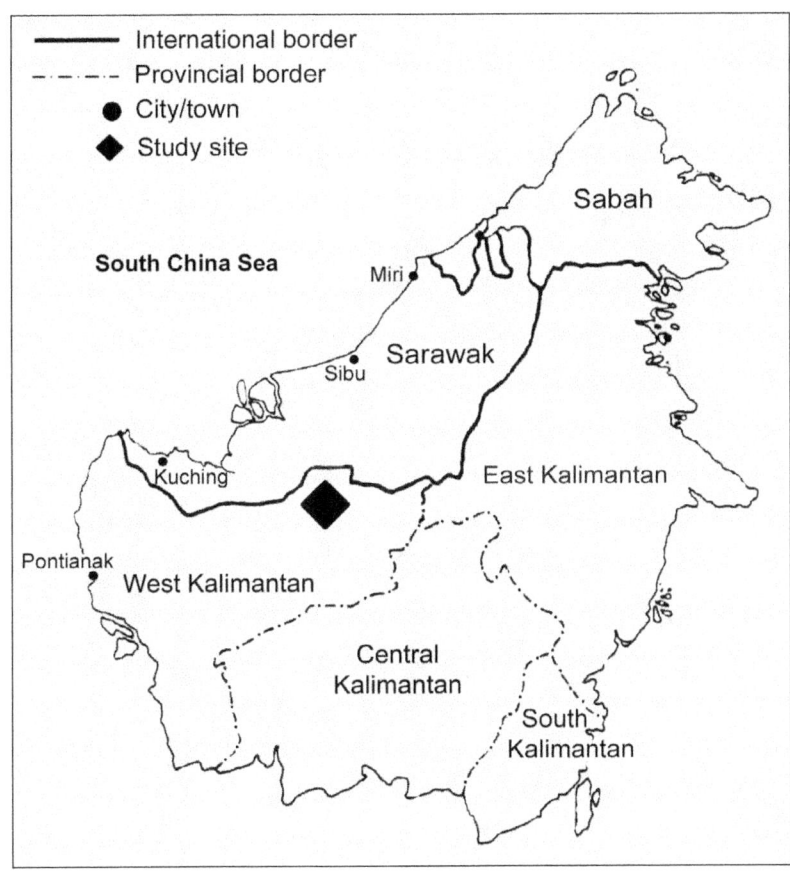

Map 2: Island of Borneo

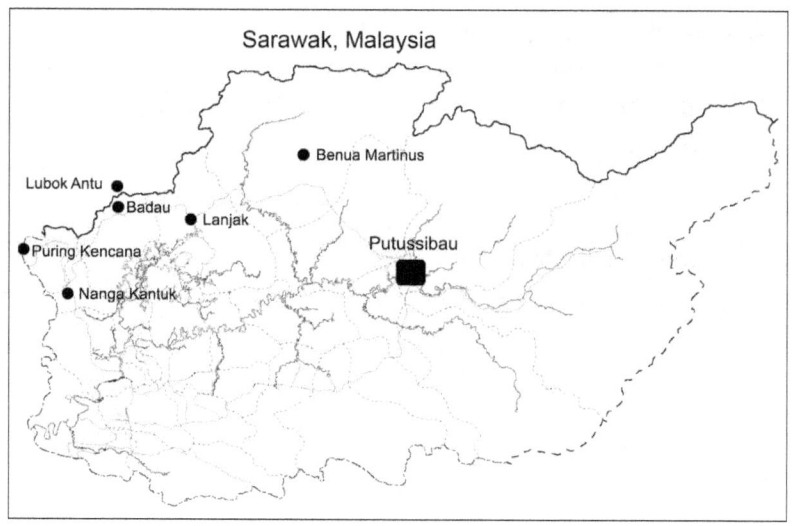

Map 3: District of Kapuas Hulu

1

Introduction

> Smuggling rings, clan and tribal relationships that have spanned territorial and/or public-private boundaries [...] have quietly put forth systems of meaning that imply boundaries quite different from those represented in the image of the state. Some have sought to change the lines on maps; others act only to minimize the importance of those lines. In both cases, they have openly or surreptitiously challenged a key element in the image of the state: its claim to be an avatar of the people bounded by that territory and its assumption of the connection of those people encompassed by state borders as a (or *the*) primary social bond (Migdal 2001:26).

PROLOGUE

The Indonesian-Malaysian borderland, 7 June 2007. Around noon a convoy of Kijang pick-ups with the Kapuas Hulu district seal accompanied by district police trucks entered the dusty border town of Lanjak. The convoy travelled the bumpy gravel road and passed the main bazaar at great speed with wailing sirens and blinking lights en route to the sub-district office close to a newly erected community hall at the outskirts of town. In great anticipation of this arrival a large crowd had assembled along the road, many coming from faraway villages situated close to the international border with Sarawak.

Surrounded by heavily armed police, the governor of West Kalimantan stepped out of the front car; flanked by his vice-governor and the district head, he walked the 50 meters towards the community hall. Nervously surveying the crowd, the police bodyguards tried to keep the crowd at bay by levelling their sub-machine guns and using their bodies to erect a defence line. According to a local spectator, this hefty show of force should be attributed to the governor's anxiety about being attacked by 'timber gangsters' and other renegades roaming the border hills. In previous years, the provincial government (at the request of Jakarta) had initiated a series of police/military raids in order to end the widespread timber smuggling along the border and restore law and order. The sudden crackdowns by the provincial and central government largely crippled the local economy and aroused tremendous local antagonism. In the heydays of 'wild' logging on the border initiated in the turbulent years after President Soeharto's fall in 1998, the small border towns experienced a boom in cross-border timber commerce. This activity attracted industrious Malaysian entrepreneurs (timber barons) from across the border, internal labour migrants from as far away as Flores and Timor, and other more regional opportunity seekers. From being a quiet backwater and isolated outpost before the logging boom, the borderland changed drastically. Small, rapidly built hotels and shop houses, restaurants and brothels popped up everywhere to cater to the numerous logging crews. The smell of sawn timber hanging thick in the air and the large amount of ready cash in circulation gave these towns a distinctly frontier atmosphere.

Then suddenly in 2005 this local economic adventure abruptly ended when large numbers of military and police personnel were stationed along the border as part of a national crackdown on illegal logging. The transformation was immense. The previously so vibrant and prosperous boomtowns along the border were plunged into economic depression and almost overnight became sleepy ghost towns. Only a shadow of their former glory remained as the timber barons were chased back across the border by national police and military. The former timber mills that had been so busy stopped operating; the endless traffic of logging trucks loaded with sawn timber and shiny pick-ups with Malaysian number plates that scuttled over the dusty potholed dirt roads between the border towns of Lanjak and Badau were replaced by the occasional motorbike and women carrying vegetables to the market. Losing the only cash-generating income in the region, the border inhabitants were once again forced to turn towards Malaysia for labour opportunities in order to make ends meet, awaiting the next major political and economic shift to affect the borderland.

In the days up to the high-profile visit by the governor, influential community leaders had been busy preparing for the arrival of this 'official guest'. The governor is not a common visitor in these remote parts of the province; on the contrary, most locals had difficulty remembering when a governor or any other highly placed state official had last visited. This was their long-awaited opportunity to present their grievances and desires. Great hopes were expressed that the governor would engage the locals in a dialogue and address the difficult circumstances of life experienced by the border population.

The official reason for the governor's visit to the border district was to open a new community hall, although the looming governor elections and the opportunity for vote-fishing seemed to be a more plausible reason for this grandly staged official visit. Border development, law and order, national security and the boisterous border population had long been hot issues in provincial and national media, and the 'brave' act of visiting the lawless borderlands would receive much needed media attention.

At the entrance of the elaborately decorated community hall the governor was greeted by a chosen group of prominent local leaders, all wearing their traditional war attire and more official regalia, as is the custom when receiving important guests. The governor and his assembly were seated on a platform in the back of the fully packed hall, where they were greeted with drinks and traditional dance. Then the governor immediately embarked on an hour-long speech about his administration's future border development plans if re-elected. (He was not.) He also praised his 'successful' crackdown on illegal activities along the border and the arrest of dangerous timber 'gangsters' that for so long had crippled development initiatives and stolen the nation's natural resources. Ironically, before the stern instructions from the president to eradicate illegal logging in the border region in 2005 the governor (and district head) himself had profited immensely from these arrangements, through unofficial taxes and private business engagements.

Having prepared their own official speeches, the community leaders were anxiously waiting for the governor's speech to end in order to get the opportunity to express their concerns about the perceived injustice that had been done them. However, their opportunity never came. After a quick photo session, and after making a generous donation for the community hall, the governor left the border district with his entourage as quickly as he had arrived. Clearly disappointed that the governor had not taken the time to listen, one of the community leaders sardonically stated:

> For more than fifty years, we have patiently waited for the centre (*pusat*) to include the border area in national development. We have protected the nation's borders against the Communist threat and shed our blood, but they are still ignorant of our needs. We would be better off managing our own affairs; the centre has little to offer us border people.

The Lanjak incident clearly demonstrates the complicated interactions between border communities and government authorities in this remote part of the West Kalimantan borderlands. This book investigates that relationship as a window for understanding the dynamics of Indonesian state formation since colonial rule. It does so by analyzing more than a century of resource struggle and the quest for increased regional autonomy along a particular stretch of the Indonesian-Malaysian border.

By examining key moments in borderland history, the book illustrates how local social-political practices and strategies are constituted in a complementary relationship with shifting state policies and institutions. As illustrated in the Lanjak incident, the borderland population has a shifting relationship with the Indonesian state. A main argument of the book is that it is a dialectic relationship, in which border communities and in particular small border elites are actively involved in shaping their borderland milieu. These interrelations between state institutions, border elites, and local communities provide clues to how everyday processes of state formation are constituted along the border. It argues that international borders are equally regulatory and restrictive and provide ample opportunities for local strategies and practices that flow into and out of state control. These creative practices often transform the meaning of 'the sovereign state' and its 'strict' territorial borders. As such, the West Kalimantan borderland is a zone characterised by varying degrees of state accommodation and subversion.

The book argues that the particular milieu generated by the borderland has a crucial impact on processes of Indonesian state formation. The borderlands can be seen as critical sites for conceptualizing the changing dynamics of state-society relations and the kind of governance that Indonesia has experienced since independence, especially in the wake of recent processes of decentralization. In their role as key symbols of state sovereignty and makers of statehood, borders become places where states most often are eager to govern and exercise their power; however, they are also places where state authority is likely to be challenged, questioned and manipulated. This is so because border people often have multiple loyalties that transcend state borders and contradict state conceptions of sovereignty, territory, and citizenship.

It has been suggested that borders and adjacent borderlands can be seen as unique laboratories for understanding how citizens relate to 'their' nation-state and how competing loyalties and multiple identities are managed on a daily basis. From an analytical perspective, a focus on borderlands is thus one way of challenging perceptions of 'the state' as a cohesive and 'faceless' unitary whole, and a way of capturing the more intricate ways in which the state intertwines with the local. Marginal populations, especially those living in remote borderlands, are not just to be seen as passive victims of state power but as actors, actively pursuing their own political goals and strategies. Although state interventions and regulatory practices in borderlands create certain constraints for cross-border movement, they also create important opportunities that often underlie economic expansion and social and political upheaval among certain entrepreneurial segments of the border people. These persons, often working in the shadows of legality, creatively exploit the nooks and crannies that border life entails.

I have chosen to focus on a certain section of local society that seemed to play an influential role as mediators across the supposed state-society divide. I call this group of people the border elite. This term embraces a large category of people holding various types of authority. What all these officials or leaders have in common is their high position within traditional institutions of leadership, and simultaneously their intricate and historically complex networks of patronage with state agents (both central and local), as well as their wider cross-border business relations. All play multiple roles as state agents, politicians, traders, and traditional chiefs at the same time. With the assistance of these networks, some of these local leadership figures have become local businesspersons and smugglers; others have pursued influence through local politics as party politicians or as local level government officials. However, more often than not these various roles are mixed in a complex dance, with elites wearing several hats at once. For example, a small handful of prominent local figures have become elected members of the district assembly (agents of the state), giving them a front row position from which to influence decisions made at the district level concerning their own constituencies along the border. At the same time, they were negotiating illicit practices through their cross-border networks. I believe that the concept of elites allows for a dynamic and multifaceted perspective on borderland dynamics. The term "elite" is not used to describe a static group, but is here used to accentuate a sense of agency, exclusivity and authority, and an apparent separation from poorer segments of borderland society. Elite in this study is thus defined as the relatively small number of people who control key economic, symbolic, and political resources. This border elite has continuously used the state apparatus to enhance their position of power while at the same time maintaining their roots within their birth communities.

The book argues that this border elite is the outcome of more than 150 years of state formation in the border region. First the Dutch and later shifting Indonesian state administrations used local leadership figures as agents of indirect rule in the remote and lawless border regions. Despite engagements with the state, which have increased their room for manoeuvre, these local leaders have continued to employ a strategy of flexible loyalties that traditionally have been well suited to the ever-changing borderland milieu. The enhanced local status of this elite is the result of their ability to creatively make use of events and opportunities derived from the waxing and waning of state authority along the border. At times they emphasized their role as guardians of national sovereignty with the complicity of state institutions like the military, while simultaneously enabling illicit trade across the border and thereby disregarding formal state laws and regulations.

The book strives to achieve two interconnected objectives. First it aims to situate processes of state formation on the border in a broad historical context and in relation to instances of state-society friction. Second it aims to investigate empirically how border communities are active agents in negotiating access to resources along the border by appropriating government rhetoric of development for local purposes while at the same time challenging state sovereignty through cross-border connections. These practices all cast doubt on the central government's ability to control its territorial border. The above aims are tied together by the assumption that in order to make sense of contemporary dynamics along these state edges, strategies and practices need to be understood in a broader historical perspective of state formation.

Ideas about the nature of the relationship between state and society are placed at the forefront of the investigation and problematized. To specify this thinking and to provide structure for the study, the following question will guide the investigation: What does a focus on borders and borderlands tell us about the process of Indonesian state formation? This larger question can be disaggregated into five inter-related questions: How have succeeding governments (colonial and post-colonial) asserted authority over people and territory along the border? What is the relationship between border communities and government authorities? How do border communities negotiate authority and autonomy within shifting political regimes? How and to what extent do these various practices contribute to or redefine the nature of state-society relations and the more general political transformations occurring at the edges of the Indonesian nation-state? Finally, if the borderland is to be understood as a productive site for the study of state formation, then what can we learn about the shaping of 'the state' from local narratives of inclusion and exclusion at the border?

Concisely put, in addressing these questions the book investigates a range of cases (in different time periods) and practices (guerrilla warfare, timber logging, vigilantism and border autonomy movements) which all use the border as a vantage point. These cases and practices help us to see the ambivalent and fuzzy relationship between state and society. In particular how multiple allegiances and strategies are parts of everyday border life. Empirically, the book argues that ever since Indonesia's founding, the modern state of Indonesia has had to expend considerable effort to control the border areas of what is now known as West Kalimantan. The means of exercising government control have changed over time (in ways that are examined below), but a constant and primary aim has been to exploit natural resources and to strengthen the modern state both in terms of physical security and national identity.

Attempts to govern the border areas have come in waves; at times state control has been strong and hard, such as during the Iban pacification in the early decades of the twenty century and Indonesian militarization in the 1960s and 1970s. At other times it was exceptionally weak and loose, as it appeared to be in the heydays of decentralization and period of illegal logging from 1999 to 2005. I argue that the shifts from relaxation of border controls to tightening of enforcement and back again play a decisive role in forming and understanding the ambivalent relations between state and society in the borderland studied. As eloquently put by Thomas Wilson and Hastings Donnan, 'Borders are spatial and temporal records of relationships between local communities and between states' (1998a:5).

BORDERLAND ENCOUNTERS

This was my first encounter. Since the onset of the dry season, a continual flow of logging trucks had been driving day and night through the longhouse area, making it extremely difficult for hunters to bring down any game. The noise from the trucks had made the game move further away from the logging roads. The local game of particular choice, wild boar, seemed to have disappeared. A group of men in the longhouse where I resided therefore arranged a three-day hunting trip to the still densely forested areas along the international border with Malaysia. They invited me to come along as spectator – a welcome opportunity to escape the intense sociality of everyday longhouse living and go on a small journey. At one time, after several days of arduous walking along twisting logging roads and through small forest streams searching for signs of game, we stopped to rest on one of the many forest-covered hills dotting the area. Casually, one of the four hunting participants pointed towards the foot of the hill and told me that just down there the Malaysian state of Sarawak began. I was taken by utter surprise; at no time had I known that we were that close to the border. No visible line marked the border, and to me the area just looked like a never-ending row of trees and underbrush. I immediately began speculating as to how many times during the last days of hunting we had crossed this invisible borderline without my knowledge. In my mind, I began to imagine the risks involved. What if we had been apprehended? I was a foreign researcher, and crossing an international border without official approval would have been treated as a serious offence. After I recovered from my initial worries and shared them with my hunting companions, they assured me that we had at no time physically crossed the border, which seemed to be a mere coincidence rather than a deliberate choice. The men did not appear particularly concerned with the physical borderline; on the contrary, they seemed to take little notice of the fact that this was the territorial line separating two sovereign nation states. Even though they were very conscious of where the border was situated (despite a few small dispersed concrete poles there were no visible signs of the border), the men spoke as if the Sarawak territory simply was an extension of the area we had just passed, and just as familiar. It became clear that for my companions, the political border was very much an artificial construct – an artifact of history, mere black lines on the map that divided them from their close kin in Sarawak. On the ground they did not feel that the other side was foreign.

Poking further into the matter of border and kinship, my companions immediately began a meticulous reading of the landscape by enumerating what seemed like an endless line of names of people, supposedly both Indonesian and Malaysian citizens, who still enjoyed customary user rights to the forest and old fruit gardens along the stretch of the border where we were standing. Among the names of still-living border inhabitants, I heard the names of numerous brave men (*urang berani*) buried on the top of the small hills, as well as place names of former longhouse settlements (*tembawai*). The longhouse settlements were abandoned during the Dutch colonial period (*musim belanda*) of forced resettling of the remote and troublesome border communities during the early twentieth century. The surrounding forest landscapes that at first appeared to be virgin wilderness suddenly became sites of fierce battles and rebellious resistance.

The senior hunters told these stories of forced movement during the Dutch period in a light-hearted manner and their old stories of the Dutch frustrations of pacifying Iban rebels criss-crossing the border were accompanied by laughter. With some indignation the hunters next mentioned a much more recent time of upheaval during the 1960s Indonesian-Malaysian Konfrontasi and subsequent Communist insurgency. Numerous border communities had once again been forced to leave their ommunity lands (*menua*), this time in order to escape 'enemy' mortar fire from Commonwealth troops across the border, and on their ownside the Indonesian military's accusations of cooperation and collusion with Communists. Paradoxically, harsh treatment by the Indonesian military led many Indonesian border communities to permanently migrate and settle across the border in Sarawak as Malaysian citizens.

The hunter who had pointed out the borderline to me responded to my puzzled expression at hearing these stories by saying in a mix of Iban and Indonesian: 'We are all Iban' (*kami semoa bangsa Iban*). Simultaneously, he pointed in both directions. From the hill we stood on, the men were able to point out a patchwork of old swidden fields belonging to kin and friends on the opposite side of the border and a maze of trails and routes that have connected the area's inhabitants for many decades. In consonance with the above statement, someone said, 'We are all related' (*Kami semoa kaban*). Those very same cross-border trails or 'mouse paths' (*jalan tikus*) pointed out by the men, I was told, were used for cross-border labour migration, trading (smuggling) of various commodities and visiting kin in Sarawak. During the colonial era, they functioned as escape routes for Iban raiding expeditions when they were fleeing Dutch and British punitive expeditions. A senior hunter animatedly described how Iban returning from raids in Sarawak (1870s) cut a wide trail across the border, which they later booby-trapped with sharp bamboo stakes to slow down their pursuers.

Even long before the ideas of an Indonesian and Malaysian nation-state were born, the Iban were quite aware of the importance of such borderlines and made strategic use of them. As we made our way home following the dusty logging roads that encroach further and further northward towards the Sarawak border, each of us with a large chunk of wild boar popping up from our rattan backpacks (*ladung*), I realized that my understanding of the immediate border landscape and its long history of movement, forced resettlement, confrontation and resource extraction had changed radically. This broadened understanding added many new dimensions to the complexities of borderland life. When talking about family relationships, labour opportunities, trade and many other subjects of everyday life, most Iban communities in Kalimantan still regard the area immediately across the border in Sarawak as a major part of their social world. Their attitude well illustrates the fact that national borders do not always coincide with the social identities of the border populations.

The above incidents occurred during fieldwork among Iban border communities in the district of Kapuas Hulu. They revealed to me some of the ways in which the political border have and still is affecting local livelihood strategies and worldviews. My first encounter with the border communities of West Kalimantan was in late 1997 during a one-month visit to the remote district of Kapuas Hulu situated at the distant head of the great Kapuas River (1086 km). This was a time of great political, economical, and social upheaval in the region. Indonesia was experiencing economic collapse, and the New Order regime of President Soeharto was ending. The strong man of Indonesian politics was losing his grip on power, and serious outbreaks of communal violence occurred in the province.

These changes did not go unnoticed in upland areas along the border. The economic collapse and the uncertain political situation created a power vacuum, which meant a loosening of security restrictions along the nation's borders, opening up the remote border regions, rich in natural resources, to cross-border investment and exploitation. Border inhabitants quickly took advantage of these new opportunities to trade across the border, and as I was later to find out, these cross-border strategies belonged to a long history of cross-border interaction that has changed continuously according to the waxing and waning of state power. This initial borderland encounter sharpened my interest in the complexities of life along the border and especially the intricate ways in which locals manage to negotiate the shifting circumstances of this area. Years later, in 2002-03, I returned to the same district in order to carry out research for my MA, and a few years later, in 2007, for my PhD degree. Unless I specify otherwise, the ethnographic present is 2007. The book is thus the outcome of a series of extended encounters over a five-year period in the West Kalimantan borderland, with a total of 17 months spent in the field.[1]

As indicated in the 'hunting' account, the border inhabitants' special relation to the border was somehow embodied in everyday practice and knowledge – something that over time had become a natural part of their lives. Daily activities and discussions implicitly involve the border in some way or another, but rarely did I encounter people discussing the border solely as an institution of exclusion. On the contrary, working in Malaysia, trading with Malaysians, marrying Malaysians, joining ethnic celebrations in Malaysia, and using Malaysian hospitals when ill are ubiquitous topics when border inhabitants tell their life stories.

Many men and (less commonly) women hold both Indonesian and Malaysian identity cards; some even have two passports, which are proudly displayed despite the fact that most have expired. What I want to emphasize here is that the border as an institution is part of everyday life, and in order to understand it one has to take part in this experience on a daily basis. Taking part in the 'borderland experience' is, however,

---

[1] Aditionally I visited the bordeland for a few months in 2004 and 2005.

not only a matter of choice. When residing in the borderland, one must relate to its ambivalent nature. I, too, as a researcher was forced into the position of being a 'borderlander' myself. The dual character of the borderland was especially apparent to me, as I, like the locals, also had to adjust to and master the duality of the border – use two currencies, live in two time zones and, not least, learn two national policies concurrently. Like the Iban, I also had to deal with 'outsiders' who were passing through the area – Indonesian government officials, Malaysian timber entrepreneurs or transnational labour-migrants. One needed a certain flexibility in order to negotiate between the often divergent agendas of these visitors, who had often been attracted by the prospect of instant riches at the frontier.

Like a majority of the Iban, I experienced the daily hardship of being situated in one of the most remote and economically underdeveloped corners of the Indonesian state. The lack of a functioning infrastructure made transportation a dangerous and time-consuming activity and reinforced the feeling of being isolated from the rest of Indonesia while looking towards the much closer regional centres in Sarawak. In 2007 the journey to the provincial capital of Pontianak took almost two days (in the rainy season even longer) of hazardous and expensive travelling. Few locals undertake such a trip. Hence Pontianak is foreign territory to the majority of locals, who have few or no social or kinship contacts there.

Furthermore, apart from a small border elite (many of whom have second houses in Pontianak), the locals usually do not have the education needed to deal with the bureaucracy. Only a small percentage of most borderland inhabitants had ever been outside their own district. However, many have visited Sarawak. Kuching, the main economic centre across the border, is less than half a day away in an air-conditioned bus on tar-sealed roads. Not surprisingly, apart from a small border elite, few people in the borderland have visited their own distant provincial capital, but many have walked the shiny waterfront of the city of Kuching in Sarawak. Most border communities' sentiments are primarily directed towards the adjacent regional centre in Sarawak rather than to their provisional or national heartland.

1 Introduction

RESEARCHING BORDERLANDS AND ILLICIT PRACTICES

The fact that my visits took place over a decade had many advantages. Besides deepening my understanding of change and continuity in the area, I was able to build up relations of trust with a range of people, including government officials, politicians, military, police, and locals. Trust based on extended visits has been imperative for asking questions in an area where the line between legal and illegal is often fluid and the suspicion of public authorities quite strong. This suspicion is without doubt a result of the shifting and often violent relationship with government authorities, especially during the highly authoritarian regime of Soeharto. In that period, military surveillance and large-scale resource exploitation went hand in hand. Many unspoken grievances from this recent past remain concealed, despite the revelations possible in the new climate of *reformasi* politics after the fall of Soeharto. Moreover, the borderland and the practices carried out there still raise emotions and often give rise to condemnation on the national level, leading to public pledges of tougher action against rule-bending border populations. A healthy suspicion towards outside authorities and prying researchers is part of the suvival strategy of the border population. I quickly learned which questions were open for public discussion and which were too sensitive and reserved for discussions in settings that were more private.

Ever since my initial visit, I have stayed for longer periods in several border communities throughout the borderland. Besides giving me a privileged position to observe many activities first hand, being visible and hanging around has, over time, meant that many informants felt less anxious about sharing their views. Carrying out formal interviews among locals has never been very successful, and most information at this level was obtained through informal conversations hitchhiking in a logging truck, joining family and ritual celebrations and hunting trips or just hanging out in the roadside coffee shops in the small border towns of Lanjak or Badau. Hanging out at strategic points, either overseeing the central markets and rows of shop-houses or on the verandas of friends along the border road, became an important means of getting an impression of the intricate movements of people and goods. Being the only researcher, or Westerner for that matter, in the whole borderland certainly makes one stand out and draws plenty of attention, not least from persons with 'shadow' qualities, such as policemen, military and other state agents at the border, but also from vigilantes, smugglers and other entrepreneurs operating on the verge of legality.

But more often than not, I experienced how these seemingly discrete groups were intimate entangled. As time in the borderland passed the distinction between formal and informal, state and non-state became increasingly blurred. This was readily noticeable when for example, public authorities like the military and police generated income by facilitating the flow of contraband across the border or when local communities took up the role of the police through acts of vigilantism.

Numerous colourful rumours about the raison d'être of my presence flourished, especially at the outset of fieldwork before the main purpose of my presence had become common knowledge. The three most common assumptions were that I was an audacious and slightly eccentric timber buyer, a central government spy, or just a bewildered conservationist. During my latest visit in 2007, after the government banned logging, locals told me that during my previous stays timber barons had carefully monitored my movements.

Overcoming suspicions demanded endless hours of courtesy visits to the various state and non-state authorities (timber barons, *adat* elders, village heads etc.) in the region explaining the purpose of my visit as a researcher and the rules of confidentiality that bound me. As one of the goals of fieldwork was to investigate the various actors' involvement in timber extraction (often carried out in the twilight between legality and illegality), one of my biggest problems was how to walk the fine line between talking with one group without losing the trust of others. In particular, a general distrust between certain public authorities – like border police and military – complicated matters. I experienced this when a less than five-minute motorbike ride once almost cost me a month of hard-earned local trust. I accepted a short courtesy ride from one of the many young police officers protecting the borderlands from the development of any illegal activities; afterwards I had to spend long hours assuring other segments of local society such as community leaders and *adat* elders of my impartiality. These young police officers are usually outsiders, from other parts of Indonesia, and widespread corruption, boredom and lack of local knowledge often lead them into conflict with the border communities.

When including illicit processes such as the illegal harvesting and trade in timber and various other border strategies into the research frame, certain precautions were necessary. Andrew Walker notes how powerful interests involved in such illegal practices make the collection of qualitative information extremely difficult (Walker 1999:xiii). Owing to the sensitive nature of this research, I have changed all names of informants and their communities and have been deliberately vague about their exact location. As other scholars have commented, research in border regions has often been hampered by the difficulty in conducting it, either because of its politically contested nature or due to the different 'secret agendas' the government might have in the area (Donnan and Wilson 1994:6-7). Thus one of the main challenges of the study was how to understand ambivalent and overlapping spheres of authority and explain the intricate and often complicated relations between state actors, cross-border entrepreneurs and members of the border communities, without doing too much violence to the complexity of the local setting, and while protecting the anonymity of informants.

Fieldwork was divided among three primary sites: the subdistrict (borderland), district, and provincial levels. Although the major part of the fieldwork was carried out on the subdistrict level, I had to work back and forth between 'studying up' and 'studying down'. This involved talking to local people (elite and non-elite), Malaysian entrepreneurs, politicians, and state officials at all levels of regional government administration (subdistrict, district and province). The involvement of a broad selection of informants in the research frame provided a wealth of information and a variety of distinct views on the research topic that could be checked and cross-checked in order to create a representative picture of the processes studied. Many key informants were part of a network of my old contacts from previous fieldwork. and they worked as gatekeepers in facilitating access to new networks within both official regional government and local institutions.

During my 2007 stay, I conducted and taped 71 semi-structured interviews lasting approximately one hour or more with various state officials, politicians and border elite members (village heads, tribal heads, schoolteachers, businessmen etc.).[2] Besides these more formal interviews, I participated in many informal conversations with representatives of villagers and illegal loggers from Malaysia. While taped formal interviews among government officials and politicians were carried out without

[2] A similar number of formal interviews were conducted during fieldwork in the period from 2002 to 2005.

much difficulty, they were certainly harder to do among local (Iban) border inhabitants. Because of the often sensitive nature of information concerning local illicit activities and internal conflict, information was gathered through key-informant interviews. Carrying out face-to-face interviews proved to be extremely difficult, not least because, as many other scholars conducting research among the Iban have noticed, private interviews in the longhouse were impossible because of the sociability of longhouse living. All interviews that did not include several people were either carried out in my private accommodation in Lanjak, in out-of-the-way farm huts (*langkau*), or during hunting trips. The interview setting and context were a crucial factor for success. If I had solely relied on group interviews, I would not have fully grasped the power dynamics between elite and non-elite. Informants were very hesitant to express their dissatisfaction in larger groups because of the multifaceted nature of personal networks and the potential consequences of spreading rumours and gossip in a region where people always could find some kinship bonds with each other despite large distances separating them. The propensity for gossip made it especially important to cross-check all information received from such sources.

Data collected also include numerous field notes, a wide range of official documents (colonial, military, and government) and newspaper clippings. The independent newspapers in post-Soeharto West Kalimantan can be extremely critical because they expose government weaknesses and provide an interesting contrast with the grand plans promulgated by the government.[3] In order to compare public with government opinion I followed debates in national and regional newspapers. After my initial visit in 1997, I created a database for Indonesian newspapers, national and regional, that covered a wide range of aspects of the borderland. The use of popular media like newspaper articles as data sources of course demands some caution as they are often inaccurate. Such sources should never be relied upon alone but must be applied in conjunction with and cross-checked with other sources such as interviews and official records. Taking these limitations into account, newspaper articles constituted a useful data source in comparing public and government opinion

---

[3] The media situation was of course quite different during the New Order period where national newspapers were under heavy government censorship. For example, newspapers articles on the 1960-1970s borderland 'Communist insurgency' were by and large military propaganda.

and attitudes. Newspaper sources also were a useful way to confirm larger-scale historical patterns.

My research was carried out primarily in five subdistricts with a special focus on the subdistrict of Batang Lupar, the place where my social networks were most developed because of former visits. I visited more than 20 Iban longhouse communities chosen for their proximity to the border at locations dispersed within all five subdistricts.[4] Furthermore I talked to members from several other communities during their weekly visits to Lanjak, the administrative seat of Batang Lupar subdistrict and a market town, which also was used as one of my two bases when in the border area.

In order to get more in-depth knowledge of specific strategies in relation to the border, I chose one particular Iban longhouse community, 'Rumah Manah', as my main locale.[5] Rumah Manah is located in the hills in the upper parts of the Leboyan River (Ulu Leboyan) within the subdistrict of Batang Lupar, approximately 20 kilometres as the crow flies from the town of Lanjak. This longhouse community consists of ten nuclear families and approximately 100 people. The number of residents varies considerably throughout the year, and in some months the in-residence population can be much smaller. Many residents (especially young men) spend a certain amount of time every year working in Sarawak. During my stay in the community, I opted for intensive participation in daily life and gained the confidence of the community, which paved the way for productive research.

THE KAPUAS HULU BORDERLAND

The stretch of border and adjacent borderland that make up the primary setting for this book is situated in the remote district (*kabupaten*) of Kapuas Hulu in the Indonesian province of West Kalimantan (Indonesian Borneo) (see Map 1, p. xvi and Map 2, p. xvii). The Kapuas Hulu district consists of 29,842 km^2 (20.33 percent of West Kalimantan) divided into no fewer than 23 subdistricts with a total population of only 209,860. It lies in the most northern corner of the province, more than 700 km from

---

4   Many of the same communities were also visited during previous fieldwork.
5   'Rumah Manah' is a pseudonym to preserve the anonymity of its residents. Other places are accurately reported, though the names of all individuals mentioned have been changed.

| *At the edges of states*

the provincial capital Pontianak on the coast (Kabupaten Kapuas Hulu 2006). To the north, the district shares the international border with Sarawak, Malaysia, while to the east it borders the Indonesian provinces of Central Kalimantan and East Kalimantan. I focussed specifically on a series of events unravelling primarily in five Iban-dominated subdistricts (*kecamatan*) within the Kapuas Hulu district on the border of the Malaysian state of Sarawak (see Map 3, p. xviii). When referring to 'the borderland' I mean these five subdistricts unless otherwise qualified.

The five subdistricts are Batang Lupar, Embaloh Hulu, Badau, Empanang, and Puring Kencana. Most of the data presented in this book was collected in the first of the above-mentioned subdistricts, Batang Lupar. The five subdistricts (covering approximately 6,296 km^2 or 22 percent of the district) make up the largest stretch of territory along the international border out of seven border subdistricts within the 'mother' district. In 2007, the population in the five was estimated to have reached approximately 37,000 (PPKPU 2007).

The principal ethnic groups are Iban, Maloh, and Melayu, with the Iban population by far the largest group. Melayu is the local term for the Muslim population in the area (compared to the predominantly Christian Iban and Maloh population). In 2007, the Iban population was estimated to account for more than 50 percent (approximately 20,000)[6] of the total population, the Maloh 30 percent and the Melayu 10 percent. This is a rough estimate based on recent district population data (BPS-KH 2006) and an ethnic census (Wadley and Kuyah 2001:720-23), but due to the unreliability of these data, numbers may differ.

The hilly forested areas along the border and fertile valleys are predominantly shared by the Iban and Maloh population while the Melayu population predominantly is occupied as fishermen in the shallow lakes at the foot of the hills. Besides the three groups mentioned, the area has periodically attracted large numbers of migrants from other parts of the province and Indonesia. This was especially the case during the different periods of heavy timber logging, when the border population increased dramatically. These migrants largely resided in wooden shacks in the administrative posts and market towns of Lanjak and Badau and the numerous surrounding logging camps and sawmills. Besides the large number of internal migrants, the local timber adventures also attract opportunity

---

[6] The Iban population is divided into 109 distinct communities, encompassing 1,843 households, plus those residing in the subdistrict seats (Wadley and Kuyah 2001:723).

seekers from across the border – for example, Malaysian Chinese entrepreneurs and their ground personnel – a mix of Chinese and Iban mechanics, lorry drivers, foremen, cooks and chainsaw operators.

The main economic sector within these five subdistricts and Kapuas Hulu as a whole has traditionally been forestry. The Kapuas Hulu economic dependency on forestry is more than twice as great as in other districts in the province (Alqadrie et al. 2003). Due to its large forests, remote location and lack of functioning infrastructure few other economic opportunities have been available. According to district statistics, between 2001 and 2005 an average of approximately 25,282 km^2 was said to belong to various categories of forest.[7] That is more than 80 percent of the total land area of 29,842 km^2 (BPS-KH 2002, 2006). In 2001 the Gross Regional Domestic Product was Rp 307,784 million, of which Rp 74,008 million (US$7,600) derived from the forestry sector.[8] According to figures from 2002 and 2003, this amount has risen even more (BPS-KH 2002; 2006).[9]

Low hills and river plains characterise the landscape of the particular section of the border encompassing the five subdistricts. Hills along the border are easily crossed and pose no physical barrier. Besides the main border roads such as the one between Nanga Badau (Indonesia) and Lubok Antu (Sarawak) (which locals have used for centuries), there are estimated to be more than 50 small back-roads, or *'jalan tikus'* (mouse paths), leading into Sarawak (*Pontianak Post* 2004h).[10] Upriver in close proximity to the border the area is dotted by small hills largely covered by tracts of secondary forest in different stages of growth – a result of generations of swidden cultivation and more recently commercial logging. Besides numerous small streams, two major rivers have their source in the hilly border area – the Leboyan and Embaloh. These feed into an extensive area of shallow lakes and seasonally flooded swamp forest and valleys at the foot of the hills. Between these tracts of secondary hill and swamp forest are large pockets of old growth forest. Two such large pieces of old-growth forest were designated national parks in 1995 and

---

[7]   Such as production forest (Hutan Produksi) and protected forest (Hutan Lindung).
[8]   Throughout the book exchange rates in US dollars are an estimate based on official rates in the year mentioned.
[9]   The actual figure is probably much higher as the income from 'illegal logging' is, of course, not reported.
[10] The sheer size and amount of traffic have made locals rename these cross-border routes as *'jalan gajah'* (elephant paths).

1999.[11] Altogether more than half of the district is classified as protected forest, thus falling under the authority of the central state. The border landscape is thus a patchwork of swiddens, forest gardens, and old-growth forest, criss-crossed by multiple logging roads and rivers.

The West Kalimantan borderland as a whole has a long history of economic underdevelopment compared to other parts of the province. A weak socio-economic infrastructure, isolated regional markets, and scarcity of large-scale investments characterise the borderland. Until recently, the borderland has been heavily militarized as a result of tension between Indonesia and Malaysia, triggered by an armed confrontation between the two nations in the early 1960s and followed by military anti-Communist operations in the mid-1960s to 1970s (see Chapter 4). This was followed by large-scale resource exploitation. Many of the former high-ranking army personnel who fought against the communists received large concessions along the border. A prominent group of local Iban received similar grants. The result of these land distributions was a sharp escalation of timber extraction. And the distributions were carried out in the name of national security. The first part of the timber extraction period was described to me by a majority of the local population as a time of corruption and nepotism.

During discussions with non-elite community members, much anger and bitterness was directed towards these former military timber cronies and the small Iban border elite who benefited along with them. At the time, little or no compensation was paid to the majority of communities for timber extracted from local forest territories, and the operation generated few local jobs. Additionally, until the early 1990s the borderland functioned as a security buffer zone facing neighbouring Malaysia. Access for civilians not residing in the borderland was largely restricted, and permits from district military and police were needed in order to enter the borderland. Consequently, the Indonesian state purposely delayed infrastructural and other kinds of development. This meant that transport was time-consuming, unreliable, and often interrupted or made impossible by seasonally restricted roads and waterways.

Furthermore, growth of the local economy has been stalled by lack of relations with and remoteness from the provincial economic centre in Pontianak, which in turn has made cross-border trade crucial. Indeed,

[11] Betung Kerihun National Park, with 800,000 ha of hill forest along the border, and Danau Sentarum National Park, with 80,000 ha of shallow lakes and swamp forest.

the borderland's closeness to major political and economic centres in Sarawak has resulted in close networks of trade (including smuggling) and social mixing across the border. Not only in terms of geographical space are the Iban more closely connected to Sarawak; it is also true in terms of time. The Iban border inhabitants, for instance, do not use Western Indonesia Standard Time (WIB) GMT+7, as does the rest of the province. Local schools and other government institutions by and large use Malaysia Time (MYT) GMT+8, which is one hour ahead of WIB, as this is more convenient considering the degree of cross-border interaction. Additionally, in many border communities all cash transactions are carried out in the stronger Malaysian currency while the Indonesian rupiah buys little of value (*Kompas* 2003b).

Under the Basic Agreement of 1967 between Malaysia and Indonesia, border inhabitants on either side were to be allowed to cross the border for short, non-work-related social visits (Agustiar 2000; Bala 2002; Fariastuti 2002). But such border crossers need a pass locally known as the red letter/book (*surat merah* or *buku merah*). Applying for a pass can be time consuming and expensive. Because of these constraints, most Iban prefer crossing the border illegally. This seems to pose few obstacles as they have an intimate knowledge of the border area and can blend into the Sarawak Iban population almost seamlessly. In addition, local authorities have long ignored border crossing without official documents along these informal routes (Edward 2007; Fariastuti 2002; Tirtosudarmo 2002).

In reality, because government surveillance at the Nanga Badau border post (Pos Lintas Batas, or PLB) is very lax, with official resources few and corruption widespread, most Iban seeking employment simply cross the border without passes (*Kompas* 1999a). The few who use the pass are mostly local non-Iban traders selling or shopping at the main bazaar in Lubok Antu, although some also obtain passes to enter Malaysia with the intention of later looking for work (see Hugo 2003:445). An Iban woman said that if she wanted to sell her farm produce or handicrafts or shop at the Lubok Antu market, she just had to promise the Sarawak border officials to be back across the border the same day, although no one is likely to notice longer stays.[12] Many Sarawak immigration officers stationed at border posts are ethnic Iban themselves and often ignore Kalimantan

---

[12] A few times a year, women from borderland communities cross into Sarawak to sell their traditionally woven cloths, which are highly sought after because of their high quality and affordability.

Iban, to whom they are frequently related. Finding some kin connection or simply common ethnicity in border crossing negotiations can open up many doors.

In connection with illegal commerce, one interesting example is the cross-border trading of shotguns and shotgun shells. The former are illegal in Sarawak, the latter are inaccessible or expensive in West Kalimantan. Hunting being an important aspect of life on both sides of the border, such items are in great demand. The Kalimantan Iban are skilled ironsmiths and make homemade shotguns to be smuggled to Sarawak and sold. The local price for these homemade shotguns was around Rp 500,000 to 700,000 in 2002-2003, while across the border in Sarawak they sold for more than twice that amount. Shotgun shells are extremely expensive in the Kalimantan borderland while the price is much lower across the border. I was told that to be able to buy shotgun shells in Sarawak, you needed to have a licence and some used shells to show for it. The empty shells were usually collected and given to Malaysian kin who had a licence, and who then bought shells in Malaysia to sell to their Kalimantan kin, who smuggled them across the border. Because of the harsh punishment if caught, only a limited number were involved in a given transaction. One example of such illicit affairs is the case of a local Kalimantan Iban man who was caught in the Malaysian border town of Lubok Antu and jailed for smuggling a large backpack (*ladung*) of shotgun barrels across the border.

In the 1980s and 1990s the provincial and district government began constructing what is known as the North Bound road (Jalan Lintas Utara) along the border in order to connect the remote border region with the rest of the district and province and thus promote development and increase security along the border (Japari 1989). This road later became part of a larger plan to open 2000 km of roads along the entire length of the Kalimantan border (*Kompas* 2005a). The national media has often indicated that the lack of good roads connecting the border area with the rest of the province is the main reason why border communities are less directed towards their own country than neighbouring Malaysia (*Kompas* 2001).

Beginning in 2007, this slowly improving infrastructure has included stretches of paved roads, electricity in many roadside communities, and cell phone towers, and has recently reduced travelling time for residents when going to town to sell cash crops, buy consumer goods, attend school, and visit government offices and clinics, as well as to cross the border to work or visit family in Sarawak. The building of a road network along the border has facilitated an increased flow of people and goods, both legal and illegal, in both directions. The Asian economic crisis and the development of regional autonomy following the fall of Soeharto's government had already accelerated these flows.[13] During fieldwork in 2007, the last stretch of road from the district capital of Putussibau to the border crossing in Nanga Badau was finally paved and subsequently upgraded to a national highway. However, the generally poor quality of construction will probably make the road highly vulnerable to heavy seasonal rains and require high maintenance expenses in coming years.

Despite these initiatives, the borderland is still seen nationally (and regionally) as both backward (*terbelakang*) and left behind (*tertinggal*) in regards to the national development and is consequently classified as an area of high poverty (*daerah miskin*) (KNPDT 2007; PKB 2005b). As pointed out by the border scholar Oscar Martínez, people living in such out-of-the-way places have, because of their weak national orientation (Martínez 1994a:18-20), often been branded as a hindrance to national development. The political centre tends to see border populations as less sophisticated and even uncivilized compared to more centrally located populations. Such prejudiced attitudes of the central government and its agents have exacerbated local feelings of alienation from the national scene and increased the popular orientation towards Sarawak. This sense of separateness and otherness seems to pervade the lives of the majority of the border population. For many, their connections over the border are often stronger than those with their own nation (Eilenberg and Wadley 2009).

Locals describe the second period of timber extraction in the borderland running from the late 1990s until 2005 as a good time, as the local economy prospered. After Soeharto's fall in 1998, all timber concessions along the border were cancelled. Although the legal status of timber extraction during this transition period was undecided, local governments and communities nonetheless invited Malaysian timber barons to come and fell their forest in return for royalties and taxes paid to local government and communities. This period of fuzzy regional autonomy

---

[13] Fariastuti 2002; Riwanto 2002; Siburian 2002.

and cooperation with Malaysian timber barons lasted until 2005, when the central Indonesia government, who viewed these undertakings in the more or less self-ruling border areas as illegal, initiated several large-scale raids along the border.

After 2005, the economic situation in the border area has been one of crisis, since the only major local income provider – logging – was stopped. Border communities are enraged and blame the central government for the local economic depression. Consequently, a local 'border autonomy movement' has received massive local support. The border population is also afraid that history will repeat itself and that the renewed government focus on the borderland is a sign that central government once again will take over control of local forest resources. Many feel that the only way to prevent this outside confiscation of local assets is to create a semi-autonomous border district.

THE BORDER ADVANTAGE

The Iban border population, who form the ethnographic starting point of this book, reside within a contested and ever-changing border environment. The populace has for centuries been involved in an ongoing effort to maintain control over, and access to, their forest resources under the fluctuating power of former colonial rule and, more recently, the Indonesian state. This attempt has involved dealing with both national and transnational interests in harvesting their forest. The Iban, like many border people, do not think of themselves as part of a large national entity and have divergent definitions of citizenship, space and place. For the majority of people living in borderlands, central government often is seen as a confining entity that restricts their everyday practices and spatial mobility. Citizens often think that the distant provincial and national centres do not comprehend the special and shifting circumstances of life in the borderland that denote a high degree of spatial flexibility. Subsequently, they consider themselves less obligated to abide by formal state laws. As ethnicity plays a major role in local self-understanding, and is strategically applied in negotiations with government authorities, a small introduction to the Iban is imperative. I introduce the basics of Iban social organization below, especially the different levels of traditional authorities that make up the power base of border elites. Because this is not a study of Iban social organization per se, this description is only sketches out the most important social units, which will be referred to throughout the book.

Categorizing a large group of people under one label can be problematic, and it is not the intention to treat 'Iban' as a natural category but rather to show how ethnicity plays a strategical role. For a detailed discussion the Iban ethnic category in Kalimantan, see Reed Wadley (2000a) and Victor King (2001). In order to avoid any confusion and to simplify the argument, the study will apply the term Iban as a common label for the Ibanic group studied. In terms of ethnic identities, at least three main types of border populations can be identified:

> (i) those which share ethnic ties across the border, as well as with those residing at their own state's geographical core; (ii) those who are differentiated by cross-border ethnic bonds from other residents of their state; and (iii) those who are members of the national majority in their state, and have no ethnic ties across the state's borders (Wilson and Donnan 1998a:14).

The West Kalimantan Iban are a good example of the second type of border population. The outlook of the Iban population in Kalimantan has been, in many ways, directed toward the much larger Iban population living in more prosperous Sarawak. Ethnic identity consequently plays a crucial role in everyday, cross-border interaction. According to Robert Alvarez and George Collier, 'ambiguities of identity in borderlands can also be strategically played upon to forge, reformulate and even mobilize ethnic identity to [an] advantage' (1994:607). Being Iban is thus not only a marker of community belonging, but also a strategic asset used in social and economic negotiations along the border. With respect to the border, Iban identity in West Kalimantan may be seen as two parts of a whole – the first being ethnic Iban and culturally connected to the larger Sarawak Iban population; the second being long-time residents of the remote border area, at the edges of the Indonesian state and at the bounds of citizenship. These two parts of Iban identity are a critically important factor in local Iban perceptions and decisions and applied appropriately to fit different times, places, and circumstances (Wadley and Eilenberg 2005).

When dealing with neighbouring Iban communities within the specific area where they live the Iban in West Kalimantan do not call themselves Iban. Rather, they identify themselves by referring to the name of the community, river, and wider area in which they live. Locality being the traditional marker of identity, the inhabitants of the community Rumah Manah in this way identify themselves as Urang Manah (people of Rumah Manah) and as Urang Emparan (people of the low-lying hills) etc. The label used to identify a certain group belonging to Iban, like other groups in Borneo, is very much dependent on the context, and on the group from whom you want distinguish yourself at a specific moment (Wadley 2000a:83-94).

The term 'Iban' becomes the prime identity marker, with which the majority of the population in the study area identify when they seek wage labour across the border and when they have to deal with ethnic kin and Malaysian government officials. However, when facing local or provincial Indonesian government officials, they often downplay ethnic affiliation and instead emphasize their national identity as Indonesian citizens (Lumenta 2001; 2005; Pirous 2002). As a district government document on border underdevelopment from the late 1980s explains frankly, one should not be surprised that people in the border areas are more familiar with officials in the Sarawak government than with those in the Indonesian government (Japari 1989:13-14).

In numerous cases, families are split in their orientation, with some members knowing almost nothing about Indonesian politics because of long-term work or schooling in Sarawak, while their siblings or children may be more 'Indonesian' after attending boarding school or university in Pontianak. For example, in the subdistricts of Badau and Puring Kencana more than 50 percent of Iban children attend school across the border in Sarawak because of lower cost and better quality.[14]

As an ethnic label, 'Iban' refers to a widely distributed portion of the population in northwestern Borneo. In the province of West Kalimantan, the Iban constitute a small minority primarily residing in the five border subdistricts, while across the border in Sarawak the Iban are the single largest ethnic group. The Iban number more than 600,000 in the Malaysian state of Sarawak, where they make up slightly more than a quarter of the population. Smaller Iban groups live in Sabah, the Sultanate of Brunei, and along the international border in West

[14] For detailed discussion on the paradoxical outcomes of schooling in the borderland, see Eilenberg 2005.

Kalimantan (Sather 2004:623). The majority of the Iban in the border area still practice traditional longhouse living, although in the 1960s and 1970s, during the period of strong military presence in the borderland, some communities were forced to abandon their longhouses and move into single-family dwellings. Government and military largely saw longhouses as primitive and unhygienic fire hazards, and considered their supposedly communal structure and organization to be ideal bases for Communist infiltration. Despite intense pressure, the majority of communities resisted and kept the longhouse as their prime organizational unit. The military was only partially successful in one area, namely the subdistrict of Nanga Kantuk (subdistrict of Empanang), where their presence and authority was especially high (McKeown 1984). Since the late 1990s, local government has encouraged longhouse dwelling because of its tourism potential. The anthropologist Derek Freeman has described the Iban longhouse community as a street of privately owned houses (Freeman 1970:5). A more popular image of a longhouse community, as seen by outsiders (government officials, migrants or tourists), is that of a single structure where the inhabitants live in one large joint community and where values such as communal ownership prevail (Dove 1982).

A longhouse consists of a set of generally closely related but individual families, living side by side in separate apartments (*bilik*). Each *bilik* is semi-autonomous and is primarily responsible for its own economic production and general welfare. They do periodically enter into loose working relationships and, if need be, receive help from other *bilik*. The separate *bilik* are often parts of larger kinship alliances, which cooperate both economically and politically. While the *bilik* is the fundamental point of belonging for the individual Iban, the longhouse is the largest unit of traditional Iban organization. A longhouse community is an autonomous entity that holds the rights over a specified tract of land that makes up the longhouse territory (*menoa*). Inside this territory, each *bilik* owns certain tracts of land. Furthermore, the longhouse communities are politically and ritually independent of each other.

Throughout history, the longhouse has proven to be a stable social unit among the Iban in the borderland, and the traditional political autonomy of longhouse communities has resulted in divergent interests between longhouses. Even after incorporation into the Indonesian nation-state, the longhouse has maintained its integrity as the primary social unit. However, in the early 1980s the Indonesian government implemented a new administrative hierarchy at the local level throughout Indonesia. Under this new system, one or two longhouses were suddenly designated hamlets (*dusun*), and several hamlets were grouped into one village (*desa*). Each village elected a village head that became an official of the district government, in charge of dividing various government subsidies and implementing development plans. In reality, this new system created a fair amount of confusion and conflict as the new status of a village head (*kepala desa*) meant that one person now had the official authority over several longhouses, which was in sharp contrast to the traditional autonomy of the longhouse unit. Hence the authority of a village head in reality is often limited. Despite the introduction of these new administrative units, the longhouses have continued to operate autonomously.

Within the *bilik* and longhouse community, each member is regarded as autonomous. Individualism is in this way one of the fundamental principles in Iban society and is assigned much symbolic capital. The Iban have an anthropological reputation of being highly 'egalitarian'; i.e., there is equality between all individuals in society (Freeman 1970; Sather 1996). It is true that no institutionalized formal social stratification systems dividing people into social categories are to be found in traditional Iban society. To say that Iban society is egalitarian is to a certain degree correct, but that does not mean that all Iban are basically equal. This said Iban and other so-called egalitarian communities in upland Indonesia have always recognized various informal levels of status or class, based on achievement and on an individual's personal ability to accumulate wealth.

In the borderland, social egalitarianism still appears to be a central principle, though not to be understood in the romantic sense that everybody should be basically equal, socially and economically, but that everybody is equal to compete and follow economic opportunities as they appear. Those who do not have the ability to compete because of their lack of needed social or economic capital largely end up as the new and increasingly marginalized rural poor, excluded from the benefits of borderland life. Conjuring up the popular idea of community solidarity can obscure how certain elite members of society exploit their less educated kin to sell the produce of forest or land to timber companies and plantation schemes.

1 Introduction

Those members of borderland society who have obtained the social and economical capital to move between the various layers of government have not been slow to take advantage of policy changes on the border and the opportunities they bring. They have managed to position themselves as what some spectators have called 'small border kings', whose authority is not based on raw physical power but on their ability to create alliances and negotiate influence within multiple settings.

The Iban recognize differences between individuals, which, among other things, are expressed in the relationship between the sexes, level of education, wealth, and age. Individual agency is highly honoured. Strong values of personal autonomy and achievement permeate Iban society and influence the way they deal with the outside world. Because of those values, however, substantial material and political differences can exist between households within the same longhouse – an occasional source of resentment and disdain in internal relations. As such, there is a general: '... tendency towards measuring decisions according to the relative advantages that the Iban anticipates' (Sutlive 1988:111).

Traditionally an Iban longhouse has no chief who can exercise power over the other inhabitants of the longhouse. Instead, they have an elected person (*tuai rumah*) who acts as spokesperson and mediator in internal or external disputes but who does not enjoy any authority other than what the community grants him. The relations between members of a longhouse community are mediated by the traditional law system of *adat*, which is made up of a set of rules of conduct that touch upon every aspect of life. *Adat* prescribes the way of maintaining equilibrium in society. In the border area, *adat* still plays a crucial role in conflict settlement, which is why the Iban population seldom makes use of official Indonesian courts. Disputes between local communities in the Iban-dominated border subdistricts are largely handled by a tribal head or *adat* leader, *temenggong*, and deputies, *patih*, who are a group of influential senior members of society.[15] This system was originally introduced by the Dutch colonial administration and was later officially recognized by the Indonesian state as an alternative to its own courts (Harwell 2000b:49; Kater 1883; Wadley 1997).[16]

The traditional economic foundation of the Iban communities is

---

[15] Each of the five subdistricts has its own *temenggong* and *patih*.
[16] For an example of how *adat* is employed in local resource management in the area, see Harwell 1997.

subsistence agriculture and forestry, its fundamental component being rice farming in hill or swamp swiddens. Very few have official deeds on their lands, which for centuries have been passed from generation to generation through intricate systems of rights (Wadley 1997). As a supplement to rice farming, the Iban engage in hunting, fishing and collecting different kinds of forest products. Iban rely heavily on their forests for swidden rice farming and numerous non-timber forest products. One study determined that Iban purchased only nine percent of their foods; the remainder came from fields and forest (Colfer et al. 2000). To further supplement the household economy, be able to buy consumer goods, and pay for children's schooling, people engage in wage labour across the border in Sarawak.[17] Although the Iban are dependent on subsistence rice farming, the flexibility of Iban social organization has made it possible for Iban men especially to seek wage labour in neighbouring Sarawak for certain periods during the year. Such flexible household economies have been shown to be successful life strategies in the ever-shifting borderland milieu.[18]

The transborder Iban as a whole have a long history of migration and a well-established network of trade, communication, and kinship dating back to pre-colonial times. After both Malaysia and Indonesia achieved independence in the mid-twentieth century, the old colonial borders of Borneo, as with many former colonial territories, continued to demarcate the new post-colonial states, and the Iban subsequently became Indonesian and Malaysian citizens. Yet, in almost all West Kalimantan Iban communities, every family in one way or another is closely related to people living on the opposite side of the border. A middle-aged Iban informant explains:

> My grandmother has 12 sisters and brothers, and she is the only one who lives in Indonesia. Other grandchildren from my grandmother's sisters and brothers live in Batang Lanjang, Batang Lupar, Semenggang, Miri, Bintulu, and Limbang (all Sarawak place names). Therefore, I can definitely say that we have much family over there.[19]

[17] See Eilenberg and Wadley 2009; Wadley 1997, 2000b.
[18] Sturgeon notes a similar diversity and flexibility of production among the ethnic Akha in the Thai-Burma-China borderlands and claims that it constitutes a strength when engaging with shifting political regimes (Sturgeon 2005:7).
[19] Personal interview, Lanjak, 23-3-2007.

These relationships are strategically used to engage in various border-crossing activities. Well aware of their special 'border advantage', the Iban continually exploit state inconsistencies on both sides. Indeed, border residents find it difficult to imagine life without the special opportunities that the border gives them. In addition, having been absorbed into two very different nation-states, the two Iban populations have been exposed to different political-economic regimes. As a large percentage of the Sarawak population is ethnic Iban, the Iban language is widely spoken and understood throughout the state. Iban culture, in various forms, permeates Sarawak society because of their sheer numbers, and the Iban are widely recognized as having played a key role in the state's history. Not only were they centrally involved with the early British Brooke kingdom, but they later became important political players after Malaysian independence (Jawan 1994; King 1990). The Sarawak Iban have enjoyed greater freedom of cultural expression than their cousins in West Kalimantan, a freedom of which the latter are often envious.

In Sarawak, Iban culture is on display everywhere, from posters advertising Iban pop and traditional music to banners from the Malaysian Tourism Board promoting 'exotic' Iban culture as a major tourist attraction. Many young Iban interviewed emphasized that the Iban in Sarawak are respected and that life is easy and full of possibilities for them. In contrast, Kalimantan Iban are still poor people (*orang miskin*). In addition, when discussing the difference between Sarawak and Kalimantan, they often described the former as a place of 'order' where things functioned properly, thanks to a strong government, while the latter was a place of 'disorder' where nothing functioned, corruption was widespread, and the government was weak. Such idyllic images of Sarawak as the land of honey, both culturally and economically, were commonly expressed among all generations in the borderland.[20] Although the partitioned Iban groups on either side of the border are strongly connected by social, cultural, and economic ties, the inhabitants experience the border in profoundly different ways. In his study of the coastal Malay village of Telok Melano in Sarawak, situated on the tip of the border with West Kalimantan, Noboru Ishikawa (2010), observes a similar strategic use

---

[20] Although the living standards of Sarawak Iban have generally been better than that of their Kalimantan relatives, Sarawak Iban, like other indigenous and non-Muslim groups there, have enjoyed less of Malaysia's rapid economic development than the dominant Malay and Chinese populations (King and Jawan 1996).

of ethnic identity and cross-border networks among the border dwelling Malay communities. However, as is the case among the Iban, the flow of Malay people and their trade commodities is most often directed across the border towards wealthier Malaysia.[21]

The duality experienced by the Kalimantan Iban and other border communities on Borneo is in keeping with the identity of border communities elsewhere (Martínez 1994a; Ominiyi 1997). As in many borderland situations, it is often the minority portion of the partitioned population that exhibits this identity complex. Whether among Italian Swiss or Kalimantan Iban, contradictory identities are felt, while their kin on the other side of the border do not face a similar ambiguity (Leimgrubber 1991). Indeed, Sarawak Iban, even those living close to the border, do not show the borderland 'mentality' that their cousins across the border do. They may cross the border to visit kin in order to engage in a casual cockfight (a legal pastime in the Kalimantan Iban-dominated border area, but illegal in Malaysia), or to marry one of the 'gentle' and hard-working Kalimantan Iban women. However, they feel no attraction from Kalimantan to be something other than Iban and Malaysian. Whenever the Malaysian Iban speaks of the Indonesian side, he or she most often exhibits fear of the Indonesian state stemming from the various military confrontations along the border, and a sense of superiority with respect to their 'rustic' Kalimantan kin.

STRUCTURE OF THE BOOK

The book is divided into three sections beginning with an introduction to the main argument of the book and the central theoretical discussions framing this argument (Chapters 1-2). This is followed by a broad historical introduction (Chapters 3-4) and a series of in-depth case studies divided into four analytical chapters (Chapters 5-8). Finally, the book concludes by wrapping up the main arguments (Chapter 9).

Chapter 1 sets out the research agenda and introduces the contextual backdrop of the study. Chapter 2 draws attention to border areas as critical sites for exemplifying the changing dynamics of state-society interactions and the art of governance that Indonesia is experiencing in the

[21] For a similar arrangement among the related border populations of Kelabit (Sarawak) and Lun Berian (East Kalimantan), see Amster 2005a.

wake of the last decade of political transformations. The chapter applies the insights drawn from the anthropology of the state to the realm of the borderland. Within this theoretical framework, a special focus is placed on the burgeoning literature appearing on states, borders, and local agency in Southeast Asia and elsewhere. In addition, the analysis is grounded in regional discussions on the relationship between frontier peoples, the state, and the struggle over access to natural resources. These discussions problematize in various ways how the Indonesian rural uplands have been transformed, imagined, and (attempted to be) controlled by the Indonesian state. By discussing these processes, I contribute to broader attempts to grasp the political orders and the scrambles for resources that are emerging in the wake of the 1999 decentralization processes.

Chapters 3 and 4 outline the particular historical formation of the border and adjacent borderland studied. First, they provide an account of border formation in the pre-independence period and shows how the Iban-inhabited border area gained a large degree of autonomy under the Dutch. Second, they provide a detailed discussion of the undeclared border war and subsequent 'Communist insurgency' in the 1960s and 1970s and the onset of resource extraction in the Soeharto New Order period in the 1980s and 1990s. The historical perspective will illuminate the long-term flow of people and commodities across this border. The main aim of these chapters is to explore the changing regulatory regimes and practices in the borderland.

Chapter 5 presents a series of case studies on how border communities reacted to the uncertainty during the political transformations in a decentralizing Indonesia after 1998. I focus on cross-border logging operations carried out in cooperation between border communities, district government, and Malaysian timber barons from 2000 to 2005. These cases illustrate the long-term configuration of patronage relations that involve local collaborations with different state authorities (border military and district officers) and cross-border relations (Malaysian timber barons and ethnic kin). Special attention is given to locally based elites and their general role as mediators between state institutions and local communities as well as their more specific manoeuvres to position themselves as patrons to certain villagers, thereby controlling access to forest resources.

Chapter 6 discusses the intersecting spheres of legality and illegality in the borderland. It explores how local strategies are often perceived

| *At the edges of states*

locally as acceptable (licit) while deemed illegal by state rules, even while state authorities at different levels take part in these strategies. The book here discusses cases of 'gangsterism' and 'vigilantism' that demonstrate the fair amount of local autonomy the border population enjoys in handling local matters, especially how these small zones of autonomy have been created in the borderland – zones in which state regulations are negotiated and interpreted locally according to the 'special circumstances of border life'. The cases show how local strategies along a politically contested border often take a 'shadow' or 'twilight' character and are therefore perceived nationally as signs of disloyalty towards the Indonesian state.

Chapter 7 examines perceptions government authorities and the borderland population hold vis-à-vis each other, especially how the various government authorities (central or regional) conceptualize the borderland and its population. It attempts to answer the question, through what actions are government authorities trying to integrate the borderland and its population into an Indonesian nation-state, and how do those actions fit or collide with local needs? The book here touches upon the often-divergent perceptions of citizenship, territoriality, and their implications for the relations between state and non-state actors. The overall argument of this chapter is that central government imaginations of borderlands in relation to development plans, security and territorial control, are far from monolithic. Government regulatory practices along the border are here understood as entangled with those of border communities. The outcome will depend on the manner in which they are interpreted and put into play by lower-level government employees, elected representatives and others. Uneasy relationships and contradictory ties and commitments among state authorities coexist at various levels of government and in various departments.

Chapter 8 analyzes an ongoing local claim for border autonomy through the attempted creation of an administrative border district. This final case feeds into the previous cases and illustrates local border elites' long-term attempt to claim authority over a stretch of the Kalimantan-Sarawak border by 'formally' creating their own autonomous border district, enacted within the legal (but fuzzy) framework of recent administrative decentralization reforms. This case will illuminate how the state is understood creatively and how national loyalties are claimed at the state edges by appropriating state rhetoric of development and good citi-

1 Introduction

zenship. The focus here is the creation of nationhood along state edges. Chapter 9 concludes by summarizing the main arguments of the book and discussing their theoretical and empirical implications.

Fig 1: Badau border crossing (PLB), 2007 (Photograph by author)

Fig 2: Traders and labour migrants resting before crossing into Sarawak, 2007 (Photograph by author)

Fig 3: Official border crossing point with immigration and customs facilities (PPLB), 2007 (Photograph by author)

Fig 4: The town of Lanjak, 2005 (Photograph by author)

Fig 5: The Lanjak-Badau road (Jalan Lintas Utara), 2007 (Photograph by author)

Fig 6: The Governor's visit to Lanjak, 2007 (Photograph by author)

Fig 7: The Governor's speech, 2007 (Photograph by author)

Fig 8: Forest cover along the West Kalimantan-Sarawak border, 2007 (Photograph by author)

Fig 9: Iban swidden fields in the border hills, 2002 (Photograph by author)

Fig 10: Planting hill rice in the border hills, 2002 (Photograph by author)

Fig 11: Hunters in the border hills, 2007 (Photograph by author)

Fig 12: Small concrete border pillar, 2007 (Photograph by author)

2

Borders of engagement

> Territorial boundaries may vary even though the formal lines on maps remain unchanged; the meaning attached to those boundaries in the image of the state may be challenged in a variety of ways (Migdal 2001:26).

This book attempts to incorporate several bodies of literature that all, in various ways, focus on making sense of the ambivalent relationship between state authority and local authority along state edges – in this case literal state borders and its borderlands. Such a framework aims to encompass macro and micro interactions between the local agency of border populations and the regulatory structures of state governance. In order to identify the special milieu (or social field) where local agency is enacted, the book discusses the various ways state borders and adjacent borderlands are conceptualized within recent scholarly debates. The book will pay special attention to ongoing debates concerning Southeast Asian borderlands. Within these debates, the idea of 'the state', as seen from the borderland and its population, inevitably takes a central position. Afterwards the book elaborates on the value of applying a process-oriented approach as an overall frame for understanding the complexities and social dynamics in the borderland setting.

The extensive literature on border studies is spread across many disciplinary fields, and there are just as many ways of approaching the subject. The approach of this study is primarily inspired by anthropological studies that embrace different attempts to theorize on the dynamics of state borders, adjoining borderlands and their populations. Here state borders are not merely lines drawn on maps where the nation-state enforces its outer territorial sovereignty and imposes its strict authority,

| *At the edges of states*

but also places of intricate local agency.[1] The object of this research is not the border itself, that bold line drawn on maps, but the practices and opportunities for local agency it fosters.

BORDERS AND BORDERLANDS

Studies on the political and economic aspects of border regions within the social sciences have traditionally taken a top-down approach, mostly focusing on state-level activities, especially on the ways in which states deal with borders and their populations by exercising control and exerting power. The emphasis of these studies has generally been centre-periphery approaches. Here the periphery was portrayed as passive, and relationships between border communities and the centre were analyzed within the rhetoric of resistance and domination.[2] Scholars paid little attention to the local practices of populations living in close proximity to state borders and how these communities negotiated with state authority and shaped the borderland environment (Campbell and Heyman 2007).

There has been a pronounced tendency within social sciences to marginalize these border regions and their populations (Haller and Donnan 2000; Van Schendel 2005). According to Hastings Donnan and Thomas Wilson, 'These local border communities are not simply the passive beneficiaries or victims of world statecraft' (Donnan and Wilson 1994). Because of this failure to appreciate the everyday subtleties of state-society interaction, border regions are often stereotypically displayed as places of strict regulation. Such narrow views do little justice to the intricate ways of local lives.[3] Views of an imagined distant 'state' somewhere asserting its regulative power at its borders are of course useful and tell important stories about repression, domination and power, but as this study shows they tell only a partial story.[4]

Since the mid-1990s state borders and borderlands have been subject

---

[1]   See, for example, anthropologists Alvarez 1995; Baud and Van Schendel 1997; Donnan and Wilson 1994 and 1999; Haller and Donnan 2000; Rösler and Wendl 1999; Wilson and Donnan 1998a.

[2]   For a critique of the state-centric, centre-periphery approach, see Donnan and Haller 2000:10; Walker 1999:5.

[3]   I am aware of the shortcomings in using the binary distinction between state and society, but for the sake of clarity, I will stick with these categories for now and explain their shortcomings as my analysis proceeds.

[4]   For a comprehensive review of border studies within anthropology, see Alvarez 1995; Donnan and Wilson 1999; Wadley 2002a; Wilson and Donnan 1998a.

to growing interest within the social sciences, not least among anthropologists who have begun to redress the one-sidedness of state-centred studies by recognizing border regions as laboratories of social and cultural change (Baud and Van Schendel 1997:235).[5] This perspective has been referred to as 'the anthropology of borders' (Rösler and Wendl 1999:61; Wilson and Donnan 1998a:3) or 'the anthropology of borderlands' (Alvarez 1995).

Following these research trajectories, this study attempts to turn the argument around and to promote an understanding of borderland processes and state formation from the point of view of local agents living there. By approaching international borders and borderlands from below, as structures of opportunity, the study show how borderlands are places where people and ideas meet, new things come into being, and complex socio-political change occurs, despite the apparent rigid control and rules of government bureaucracy. In an attempt to conceptualize the distinctiveness of border regions and move beyond static perspectives of the hegemonic and repressive state, several 'border' scholars began developing the concept of borderlands, which has become of central importance in order to create a common foundation for studying the dynamics unravelling along state borders. They argue that the functions of borders are basically similar everywhere; they separate national territories and control and regulate the flow of people and goods between these territories (Rösler and Wendl 1999). Although still a heavily debated concept, broadly speaking, what characterises a region as a borderland is the close proximity to a state borderline and the direct and significant effect economically, socially and politically this border has on life in the region. This follows the definition by Robert Alvarez that considers 'the borderlands as a region and set of practices defined and determined by this border' (Alvarez 1995:448).[6]

Discussing borderlands as a common term for a certain region implies that these borderlands have something in common from place to place, some similar characteristics. In his efforts to show the universality of border phenomena and to create a conceptual framework to under-

---

[5] International or state borders have traditionally been the study subject of the political sciences (Bath 1976; Prescott 1987) and political geography (Grundy-Warr 1990; Minghi 1963), who generally have analyzed the subject of borders from the outset of the nation-state and based on descriptive and historical analysis of border demarcations. Here border studies became rather static and deterministic.

[6] For similar definitions, see also Baud and Van Schendel 1997; Martínez 1994b; Rösler and Wendl 1999; Van Schendel and Abraham 2005.

stand these, Oscar Martínez has argued that ' the determining influence of the border makes the lives of border peoples functionally similar' (Martínez 1995a:xviii).[7] He has proposed several key characteristics, which when combined constitute and shape what he calls the overall 'borderlands milieu' (Martínez 1994b:8). These characteristics are meant to be very general because of the infinite borderland variations and the heterogeneity of borderland contexts.

In the following, I have chosen briefly to elaborate on a few such characteristics, which are all relevant when discussing most Southeast Asian borderlands and in particular the West Kalimantan borderland. It is important to note that the characteristics presented by Martinez are based on studies of the highly unsymmetrical Mexican-US borderland, a context that resembles the Indonesian-Malaysian context. The main similarities are that both the Mexican and Indonesian (weaker) states border wealthier (stronger) states, the United States and Malaysia. This economic disparity inevitably results in an asymmetrical flow of people and resources between the two states. However, such asymmetrical characteristics might be less obvious in a European context, for example, where state authority along borders is usually much stronger, and the economic and political differences between bordering states are less pronounced. The reality is that not all border communities are divided by the border in the same way (Wilson and Donnan 1998b:14).

Located at the edge of a nation-state close to a foreign country, the borderland is situated in a transnational atmosphere, creating certain possibilities and opportunities for local populations that are often unavailable to populations farther inside the countries. Border populations are largely affected by, and participate in cross-border interaction, be it economic, social, or cultural interaction. Transnational interaction materializes in many different ways. For the border population studied here, interaction such as cross-border trading, smuggling, labour migration, socializing, and visiting friends and kin on the opposite side are main characteristics of their daily transnational lives. Further, a high degree of ethnic or cultural similarity among people of adjacent borderlands is found throughout Southeast Asia and plays a crucial role in understanding local borderland strategies (Skeldon 1999:9). For example, Iban connections to similar ethnic populations on the other side of the

[7] Several other border scholars recognize a similar shared 'border experience' among border people (Donnan and Haller 2000:15; Donnan and Wilson 1999:12).

border enhance transnational interaction and create alternative possibilities for cross-border activity, which often circumvents official state rules (Martínez 1994a:10).

Because of their geographical location, borderlands are especially vulnerable when disputes with neighbouring countries occur. Struggle over territory or politics can end up turning borderlands into battlefields, often meaning that local populations become subject to attacks from both their own co-citizens and foreigners. Caught in the struggle between two conflicting parties, these populations are often forced to choose to be loyal towards one party, leading to violent repercussions from the other (Martínez 1994a:13). Another general characteristic that permeates local lives in the borderland is the sense of being pulled in several directions at once, both from within their own state, in which they reside, and from the neighbouring state, with which they are often economically and socially connected. From which side of the border the pull is stronger depends on the degree of interaction and relationships, economic, social and cultural (Martínez 1994b:12). For a majority of border populations connections across the border often seem stronger than those within their own national heartland, which often results in weaker national self-identification. Politically, these populations belong to a state that demands their unswerving loyalty, but economically, ethnically and emotionally they often feel part of another, non-state entity (Baud and Van Schendel 1997:233).

According to Martínez, the border populations with the weakest loyalty towards their own state are often those with the strongest cross-border ties (Martínez 1994a:19). This is very much the case in connection with the Iban in Kalimantan, whose strong ethnic and kinship links across the border in Sarawak determine their direction of relationship. Their sentiments are primarily connected to the social and economic processes in the adjacent Sarawak state rather than to their own distant provincial or national heartland. While such cross-border attachment is most evident among the Kalimantan Iban their kin on the Sarawak side of the border do not show such strong attachment towards Kalimantan. On the contrary, the Sarawak Iban living just across the border seems to display a strong identification with Sarawak and feel much more integrated into the Malaysian state.

The sense of otherness in connection with the national state, as experienced by some border populations, is further increased because

| *At the edges of states*

of their often diverse and conflicting interests. Many do not think of themselves as part of a large national unity and often feel that a distant political centre does not understand the special circumstances of living in a borderland. Subsequently, they may feel less obligated or bound to follow national laws. Often border populations continue their cross-border economic links, although doing so may subvert national rules and policy through such actions. In many cases, they do not have any other option because their national government has not succeeded in integrating the borderland into the larger national economy (Baud and Van Schendel 1997:229). Therefore, there may be a tendency to bend, ignore and breach laws that they feel are interfering with their interests and special way of life. Government regulations at state borders, which in different ways at least formally attempt to put restrictions on cross-border interaction, may lead to different kinds of conflict and rule bending (Martínez 1994b:12). To breach trade and immigrant regulations is, for example, a common and, by border populations, acceptable praxis (Flynn 1997). The border, by its very nature of dividing two separate nation-states with their often different administrative and regulatory regimes, generates a kind of opportunity structure that invites illicit actions such as smuggling and illegal immigration (Anderson and O'Dowd 1999:597). Smuggling and illicit trade is often described as the borderland occupation par excellence (Rösler and Wendl 1999:13).[8]

This distinctive environment of the border is characterised by its ambivalent nature of being both uniting and dividing. Borders can be viewed as an economic opportunity whereby a two-way flow of goods and workers brings development. It can also be 'abused' for economic gain through import and export, such as the smuggling of timber over the border to Sarawak from West Kalimantan. The illegal processes taking place at borders have been referred to as a subversive economy. Donnan and Wilson note how such a second economy provides an important livelihood for many border populations and is sometimes the most important economic factor of the border region (Donnan and Wilson 1999).

As indicated above, life in the borderland seems to generate common interests among people living there that promote transnational practices (such as timber smuggling) that by the local population itself

---

[8] For a similar statement, see also Baud and Van Schendel 1997:230-1; Driessen 1999:117.

are considered acceptable (licit), but, more often than not, declared illegal by their states (Galemba 2008:21). Investigating such an apparent conflict of perceptions between border people and powerful state interests is a useful point of entry into exploring the limitations of top-down perspectives of 'seeing like a state' along national borders.[9] In order to cast light on the logic behind state interventions, the practice of governance and the power relations entangled in such within the borderland setting, discussions of state governance and its various configurations on the border become central aspects in the analysis. This will also aid in the understanding of the exercise of governmental rationality as imposed by the various authorities entering the borderland who attempt to govern border people in the name of development (see Chapter 7). This analytical frame also underscores the fact that governmental interventions do not always achieve their goals and often have unintended effects as they are transformed through local social, cultural and economic processes.

Within this overall approach to borderlands, there is a shared understanding that borders create certain unique physical, political, and economic circumstances not seen in areas farther removed from the border. These circumstances give rise to cross-border strategies and interaction that among border populations often result in ambivalent attitudes towards their nation-state. Here the primary focus has shifted from the state level and issues of state-related security and sovereignty, to a focus on the practice of border people and their dialectic relationship to shifting government authorities.

STATE FORMATION FROM BELOW

> [...] There is no neat dichotomy of formal/government on the one hand, and informal/non-government on the other. Reality is messier (Lund 2006a:699).

Besides these more general interests in conceptualizing borders and borderlands within anthropology and social sciences in general, there is

---

9   See Heyman 1999a; Van Schendel and Abraham 2005; Scott 1998.

a burgeoning ethnographic literature on Southeast Asian borderlands.[10] Building on the above insights, these studies take the vantage point of border narratives in finding new ways to re-conceptualize the concept of 'the state' and emancipating themselves from state centrist views.[11]

Matthew Amster, in his studies of the borderlands of Malaysia and Indonesia, has (among other scholars) pointed out the helpfulness of meticulous ethnographic case studies in highlighting localized processes through which mechanisms of state control are articulated, reaffirmed, resisted, and manipulated (Amster 2005b:24).

The main emphasis is here put on state definitions as negotiated and contested. This approach offers a conceptual framework with which to imagine how we might loosen the tight grip of 'the state'. This view of the state fits well into another line of recent studies within anthropology and international studies. Although not necessarily taking borderlands as their analytical departure point, these studies have taken up the challenge of conceptualizing the state as a series of effects rather as an *a priori* homogenous whole.[12]

According to Joel Migdal (2001), scholars within social sciences, predominantly political science, have long stressed the idea of the state as an autonomous unit. Inspired by a rigid reading of the 'ideal state' of Max Weber, these scholars focussed on the state as a unit that could be studied apart from society, an organization with 'extraordinary means to dominate'. Migdal notes that it was never Weber's intention that his definition of the 'ideal state' should be taken as a normal state; rather, it was to be understood as an heuristic 'ideal type state' (Migdal 2001:8-15). Despite this, the above conceptualizations of the state have largely become inherent within popular and academic discourses. They have been adopted readily and appropriated by state leaders to promote the idea

---

[10] Studying international borders in Southeast Asia is a recent practice, and up until the late 1990s, little attention was paid to this approach among anthropologists (and other scholars) of the area (Horstmann 2002:2). Most regional studies of international borders have concentrated on the Americas (Martínez 1994a; 1994b), Africa (Asiwaju 1990; 1993; Nugent and Asiwaju 1996) and Europe (Anderson and O'Dowd 1999; Donnan and Wilson 2003; O'Dowd and Wilson 1996; Wilson 2005).

[11] Amster 2006; Cooke 2009; Horstmann and Wadley 2006b; Ishikawa 2010; Schoenberger and Turner 2008; Sturgeon 2005; Tagliacozzo 2005; Walker 1999. Within these studies the margins are not only to be understood as a geographical locale but also as an analytical category, echoing Anna Tsing's definition that margins are to be understood as a: 'conceptual site from which to explore the imaginative quality and the specificity of local/global cultural formation' (Tsing 1994:279).

[12] See Das and Poole 2004b; Ferguson and Gupta 2002; Gupta 1995; Hann and Dunn 1996; Hansen and Stepputat 2001; Lund 2007; Migdal 2001; Sharma and Gupta 2006; Wilson and Donnan 2005a.

of the state as a strong and coherent entity. This idea has strengthened the illusion that their respective governments are representing 'the state'. Thus the state often becomes synonymous with government institutions and the perception blurs the fact that state representatives have multiple statuses and relationships. A good example is the New Order 'state' of former Indonesian President Soeharto. Much literature on the relationship between state and society during Soeharto's Indonesia took a state-centred approach. This approach had a tendency to take for granted the idea of a strong, solid and oppressive state and thereby to overestimate state power.[13] As mentioned by Gerry van Klinken, many scholars were: 'blinded by the solid state' (Van Klinken 2001:265). The idea of an overly repressive state that dominates every aspect of local society has been widely debated during the post-Soeharto period and deemed to be simplistic. The breakdown of Soeharto's regime in 1998 clearly showed the fragmented character of the state and the more dynamic relationship between state and society.[14]

With a point of departure in state 'margins', Veena Das and Deborah Poole (2004) have suggested that we should distance ourselves from images of the state as bounded and imbued by an inherent rationality, detached from local practice. Instead, we should analyze how the regulatory practices of the state are embedded in and shaped by local practice (2004:2).[15] Das and Poole note that state borders, as 'spaces of exception', are especially illustrative expressions of such state margins. Here they illuminate the pluralization of regulatory authorities (Das and Poole 2004:18-19). Likewise, Aradhana Sharma and Akhil Gupta (2006) point out that an analytical approach to state formation as culturally embedded avoids assumptions that the state stands at the 'apex of society' and is the source of all power (2006:8-9). As Wilson and Donnan put it, the state is no longer treated as 'an actor just off stage whose face is never seen but who has the ability to constrain or enable the actions of others' (Wilson and Donnan 2005b:2).

While we can learn much by seeing the state as grounded in everyday practices, it is still important to take into account that the idea of the unitary state still plays a major role as a potent symbol of power in local

---

[13] For good examples of this tendency among scholars on New Order Indonesia, see Budiman 1990.
[14] For an overview of these early debates on state-society relations in Indonesia, see Van Klinken 2001.
[15] Their analytical starting point is that the 'margins' of the state can be either the conceptual or literal territorial margins such as state borders (Das and Poole 2004a:3).

| *At the edges of states*

imaginations (Gupta 1995:390; Hansen and Stepputat 2001: 5). In the West Kalimantan borderland, one commonly hears state authorities and community members mention that 'the state' imposes its control and power from above on local matters. State authorities widely employ the rhetoric of the state locally in legitimizing various acts of governance, but also as pretext for not acting at all. They may claim that 'this is not a district government matter but a matter of the central state; therefore our hands are tied'. At the same time, local communities often use the state rhetoric of development to justify acts of economic advancement through 'illegal' activities. To creatively employ and play with the rhetoric and symbols of the state is common practice and often used for local advantage (Das and Poole 2004a:20).

The concept of the state as an entity is continually reinforced and fortified (especially along borders) through various practices, images, symbols and rituals: territorial maps, border posts and markers, passports, military ceremonies and flag rising. See, for example, Migdal (2001:18) and Donnan and Wilson (1999:63-87). A central motivation for this book is to disaggregate this popular ideal of the unitary nation-state with its perceived fixed and regulated borders, territorial integrity, national control over national resources, bureaucratic and legal coherence, obedience to rules and laws, and loyal citizenry. I argue that all these elements that 'ideally' would make up a fully formed 'state' are always in 'formation'. Therefore, the fully formed state never is completed. Instead, state formation is a historical continuum, a fluid process of negotiation and contestation. This book attempts to show that borderland dynamics throw each of the above elements of the ideal state sharply into question.

In a paper on the difficulties of studying the state, Philip Abrams suggests that the state is best understood as 'an idea'. He proposes that it is more an ideological construct to be employed in exercising and legitimizing power than a real entity (Abrams 1988:75-6). As such, there are two interrelated aspects of the state: the state as constituted in local everyday practices, and the state as an idea visualised as a potent, monolithic source of power. Migdal elaborates on this point by noting the importance of analysing the state as a contradictory entity that is understood best on two levels – one that recognizes the powerful image of the state as a unified entity with clear boundaries and territory, and one that reunifies the state as bundles of loose fragments. He shows how the ill-defined boundaries between these fragments and other groupings working inside and outside literal state borders are 'often promoting conflicting sets of rules with one another and with "official" law' (Migdal 2001:22). In the words of Migdal, the state possesses an inherent paradox of simultaneously being: *a part* of society and *apart* from society' (Migdal 2004:18).

What makes these process-oriented approaches especially beneficial and useful as a framework for analysis is the way they help us to understand the diffuse and slippery concept of the state by studying it in conjunction with the everyday practices of negotiation and contestation between local-level state officials and local actors (Gupta 1995; Migdal 1994 and 2001). Migdal has very tellingly named this way of grasping state-society relations as the state-in-society approach (1994, 2001). Conventional dichotomies of state and society are breached, and the static image of the state as the all encompassing entity and the singular source of power is replaced by an approach that sees the state as bundles of everyday institutions and forms of rule. Here the reference is to the multiple ways the state is configured and practiced in the local milieu (Corbridge et al. 2005:5-7). The attempt in this book is to show the forms of these negotiations and contestations as they are worked out over time and affect borderland lives and livelihoods.

Before proceeding further, I must emphasize that although I highlight the importance of local agency I still acknowledge the immense importance of central state regulations and institutions in shaping local borderland lives. I acknowledge the profound inequalities of power and tremendous risks attached to borderland livelihood strategies (Chalfin 2001:133). The main point is that such top-down regulations and laws are often reshaped to fit local realities, and the outcomes differ from what was expected by policymakers in Jakarta. Migdal notes that state laws and regulations have to compete with many other and different forms of normative behaviour, 'often with utterly unexpected results for the societies that states purport to govern – and for the states themselves' (Migdal 2001:12). Additionally, some fragments of the state, such as the military, have often colluded with non-state actors to achieve their goals. Such alliances have acted to promote certain rules and orders that often differ widely from the official rules and regulations of the state. These alliances, coalitions, or networks contradict the portrayal of strict territorial and social boundaries that the state attempts to establish, 'as well as the sharp distinction between the state as pre-eminent rule maker and society as the recipient of those rules' (Migdal 2001:20).

Having arrived at perceptions of state power as fragmented and state formation as continually evolving thorough local-level negotiations with authority, I find it helpful to introduce the concept of authority. In particular, I want to ask how we should understand the relationship between state (government) and non-state forms of authority (authority exercised by local border elites) in arenas like the borderland where state authority at times either is largely absent or openly challenged.

Christian Lund (2006b) proposes an analytical strategy that focuses on such ambivalent arenas and the various institutions within them that exercise *de facto* 'public' authority but are not the state and as such manoeuvre in the twilight between state and society. These groupings he terms 'twilight institutions' (Lund 2006a:676-8).[16] These 'twilight' institutions make it particularly difficult to draw a fine line between what is state and what is not. Within this framework Lund defines authority as 'an instance of power which seeks at least a minimum of voluntary compliance and is thus legitimated in some way' (2006a:678). As elaborated by Willem van Schendel and Itty Abraham, the absence of a strong state does not necessarily imply 'a state of disorder' but most often entails the presence of non-state and competing forms of authority with their own moral order (Abraham and Van Schendel 2005).

The Iban border elites and their networks of patronage are a vivid example of such non-state 'institutions' that exercise a kind of *de facto* authority as alternatives to the lack of functioning central state institutions. Local state officials often legitimize these institutions while the central state is less accommodating with what they term 'local' attempts to contest their authority. Further, as asserted by Lund, the local recognition of 'public' authority takes different forms and is often associated with the affirmation of control of a particular geographic area, in this case the borderland (2006b:694-5).

For example, local acts of vigilantism (see Chapter 6) are common in situations where the Iban population considers state institutions ineffective or inconsistent with local ways of life. Locals often express their claims of legitimacy by emphasizing their deep roots in the borderland. In that way they claim the right to profit from the border's advantages

---

[16] Although Lund's analytical points are based on research in Africa, the dynamics he mentions are applicable to and relevant for a Southeast Asian setting.

(Flynn 1997). They perceive the distant central state as an authority that does not understand the particular circumstances of life in the borderland and therefore the special practices it necessitates. This is especially so during periods of borderland history in which the politics of the central state have been experienced and portrayed as distinct and remote from the 'local arena' (Lund 2006b:688).

In their attempt to place local agency in the forefront of the study of Southeast Asian borderlands, Alexander Horstmann and Reed Wadley (2006b) mention the importance of recognizing that there are two sorts of narratives along state borders, one promulgated by the state and one by the border population. In accordance with the aforementioned studies on state and state formation, I will argue that these narratives are not necessarily disconnected as noted by Horstmann and Wadley but more often than not are intertwined and overlapping. This study assert that the intense focus on local agency within the new debates on borderlands has had a tendency to overemphasize the resistance of oppressed marginalized population along borders and to a certain degree neglected investigations into the question of how these local populations also engage in networks of collusion and other potentially rewarding relationships with various state authorities. Thus, it is not my intention to celebrate the 'weapons of the weak' but instead recognize that local relationships with the state should be understood as more than merely contentious (Horstmann and Wadley 2006a:17).

The borderland should not be seen solely as an arena of struggle between state and local communities – a place state power is a given, somehow suspended above local society. I instead propose to examine how state and local authorities are formed in tandem at the border. As such this study takes a slightly different approach from the majority of studies of borderlands mentioned above. I draw substantial regional inspiration from studies on Southeast Asian borderlands, like those of Andrew Walker (1996, 1999, 2006a) and Janet Sturgeon (1997, 2004, 2005), that enumerate many of the dynamics that I see to be similar to and of particular relevance to the study of the West Kalimantan borderland.

In his work on the borderlands of Laos, Thailand, China, and Burma, Walker provides an appealing regional perspective on how state regulatory practices are entangled with those of local communities. He shows how the outcome of what he refers to as 'technologies of rule' depend on the manner in which they are interpreted and put into play by lower-level government employees, elected representatives and others (Walker 1999). Walker highlights how various members of these 'frontier' communities often actively participate as collaborators in the regulation and maintenance of borders (1999:111-112). He argues that these collaborations are 'fluid and volatile' and that state officials should not be seen as [...] robotic agents of a hegemonic state (1999:112).

Walker's study accords well with Sturgeon's work on local 'border chiefs' and their engagement with state authorities in the borderlands of Burma, Thailand, and China. Sturgeon approaches these relations through historical analysis of control of access to resources and the means by which such relations take special configurations because they are enacted along an international border.

While differently argued, Sturgeon's work, like Walker's, takes a critical stance towards the series of border studies that emphasize a basic conflict between border communities and state officials. Instead of making presumptions that accentuate the state as exclusively restrictive of local cross-border strategies, she argues for much more complementarity in these relations (Sturgeon 2005:30). She discusses how state officials and border elites like village heads are joined in a 'complicated dance designed to meet the needs of each'. Here state official do not necessarily wish to eliminate local cross-border networks, be they legal or illegal, but instead collaborate with locals to take advantage of the opportunities and benefits these networks provide.[17] The bargaining power of border elites and well connected entrepreneurs increases under circumstances where the access to resources is largely under their control and can lead to tacit tolerance by state agents of their 'criminal' activities as long as its suits these agents' needs (Smart 1999).

While Walker in his study portrays the strategic advantage of borderlands in a rather optimistic tone as zones of expanding economic opportunity, Sturgeon paints a somewhat murkier portrait of local opportunities.[18] She highlights the success of well-connected border elites (small border chiefs) and how they position themselves as patrons negotiating access to valued resources through their lucrative relations with

---

[17] Sturgeon 2004:466; 2005:32.
[18] Walker later notes that his initial view of local community interaction with the state within the borderland studied might have been 'overly benign'. He confesses that he had paid insufficient attention to issues of class and ethnicity (Walker 2009:106).

state officials and cross-border networks. Simultaneously, she underlines how the non-elite population (poor hill farmers) experience increasing marginalization and poverty. She refers to this phenomenon as 'predatory patronage' (Sturgeon 2004:482). A somewhat similar scenario of increasing inequality is seen in the West Kalimantan borderland, which stresses the fact that borderland communities are far from homogenous. Sturgeon contends that borders 'are nodes for the collection and distribution of resources, and the role of small border chiefs is implicated in and even produced by state-making (2004:466).' As stressed by Sturgeon, I believe that the examination of resource access and how it is negotiated between state authorities and local authorities provides an especially good starting point for understanding everyday forms of state formation in the resource-rich borderlands of Southeast Asia. In these marginal regions, natural resources are often the focus of negotiations between local authorities and the state.

In line with the more general debates on borders and the regional debates on Southeast Asian borderlands in particular, the book thus advocates a more benign approach to understanding the relationship between state institutions and local populations along borders. Such an approach does not solely portray borderland populations as resisting state intrusion but captures the intricate ways in which state and local factors are intertwined. Thus, these relationships can be both beneficial and constructive as well as negative and destructive for the actors involved. On the other hand by recognizing local strategies in exploiting the 'nooks and crannies' of the border, this study does not want to discard the importance of internal inequality within the borderland and the larger regulatory powers of the state. State regulatory powers along borders are in constant flux, and they can be suppressive and signify inequality for some segments of local society, but they can also constitute rewarding opportunity structures for others. What makes borderlands intriguing is the manner in which people living there both subvert and support their state. At times they fall victim to state power, while at other times they see the state as a means of gaining authority and wealth (Haller and Donnan 2000:12). The anthropological study of the everyday lives of border communities thus simultaneously becomes the study of the daily life of the state (Wilson and Donnan 1998a).

DECENTRALIZING INDONESIA: MORE ROOM TO MANOEUVRE

Building on the basic propositions of states, borders, and borderlands, this study has wider implications for the debates on regionalism and local politics within a decentralizing Indonesia. Decentralization generally refers to the process in which central government relocates political, administrative and economic authority to lower-level regional governments like districts. The process is said to make government more transparent and accountable to its local constituencies and to result in better governance.[19] However, debates indicate that decentralization processes in Indonesia are more complex and do not necessarily result in heightened transparency as originally envisioned by policymakers.[20] Obviously, processes of decentralization are general phenomena throughout Indonesia, but as will be elaborated, the configuration of the borderland gives the phenomena a unique shape here.

The drastic changes in the wake of the economic and political crisis and President Soeharto's fall from power in 1998 quickly changed the dynamics of local politics in the borderland. In an attempt to distribute political and economic power more evenly and give authority back to the districts, a reckoning with more than thirty years of highly authoritarian and centralized system of governance under Soeharto, several new and shifting Indonesian 'reform' governments began initiating national programs of decentralization. Regional autonomy became the main topic, and new legislation resulted in a series of reforms that gave local districts increased autonomy over government sectors such as forestry. One of the initial intentions behind this strengthening of regional autonomy was to diminish separatist movements in previously marginalized resource-rich regions and thereby prevent a possible break-up of the country.

I will not here venture into the more technical discussion of decentralization laws and the various reforms they entail, but rather I will briefly point out a few developments within this transformation process that stand out as particularly interesting for the borderland case. First, within the Indonesian context, a large body of work has focussed on how these political transformations have affected the control of access to various resources in the marginal and resource-rich regions, especially

---

[19] The Indonesian decentralization reforms have been portrayed as among the most radical worldwide (Aspinall and Fealy 2003a).
[20] See Aspinall and Fealy 2003b; Schulte Nordholt and Van Klinken 2007b.

highlighting the role of locally entrenched elites.[21] Second, and linked to the above, is the creation of new administrative districts often headed by local elites motivated by their desire to enhance their authority over valuable local resources.[22]

What seems to be the overarching touchstone within these discussions is that decentralization has had profound effects on the configuration of state-society relations. While decentralization has resulted in the state becoming more personal and tightly embedded in local society and has empowered local people's participation in decision making, the shift has also engendered a great potential for enhanced collusion among well-connected border elites, district officials and entrepreneurs. Lines of authority to a certain degree have been rearranged, but there are still considerable continuities with former arrangements of informal networks and alliances. Referring to the distinct patrimonial patterns of the former Soeharto regime, Schulte Nordholt and Van Klinken consider it misleading to view this regime as 'an integrated set of institutions operating primarily apart from society'. They instead argue for a critical re-evaluation of the distinctions between 'state' and 'society', 'formal' and 'informal' that are often invoked when referring to the New Order period in Indonesia (Schulte Nordholt and Van Klinken 2007a:8).

One can cite numerous examples of how regional elites who colluded with the former Soeharto regime have maintained their networks and still retain their roles in local polities in the post-Soeharto period of decentralization. In fact, these elites often have enhanced authority because of the increased local autonomy and the ability to bypass central state authorities. As noted by Schulte Nordholt and Van Klinken, 'Decentralisation comes into this world not as a *deus ex machina* but as a rearrangement of existing force fields' (2007a:2). In short, what these studies ultimately show is the continuity in informal networks as well as the way the reshuffling of authority has sharpened the struggle over resources on the local level since decentralization was introduced.

I have argued that borderlands create particular opportunities for local agency to arise and that processes of decentralization in Indonesia have created new opportunities for local (border) people to exercise their authority and influence formally (and informally) through political

---

[21] See Casson and Obidzinski 2002; McCarthy 2004; Morishita 2008; Resosudarmo 2003; Van Klinken 2008a, 2008b; Wollenberg et al. 2006.
[22] See Duncan 2007; Roth 2007; Vel 2007.

engagement. Consequently, the distinction between local and state in the borderland studied is becoming further complicated, with local Iban entering government institutions, each with their own political agenda.[23] It can be argued that the decentralization processes in Indonesia initiated in the late 1990s have created mass incentives for some segments of local society to capitalize on their newfound authority, especially those with a large network of influence reaching beyond the immediate local level. As demonstrated by Schulte Norholdt and Van Klinken, the rise of localism or regionalism set off by the decentralization process after the collapse of Soeharto's authoritarian regime, 'invites us to abandon the concept of the strong centralized state in favour of a model that offers room for a more fragmented polity' (2007a:3). They point out how such transformations: 'made certain hidden aspects of the state more explicit as it revealed the extent to which local actors used the state for their own interests' (2007:24).

PATTERNS OF PATRONAGE AND THE 'BORDER EFFECT'

Patron-client ties can be seen to arise within a state structure in which authority is dispersed and state activity limited in scope. ...(Weingrod 1977).

Michiel Baud and Willem van Schendel suggest that in order to understand the historic and social dynamics of borderlands we need to focus on the 'triangle of power relations' or overlapping networks between the state, regional elites and local people (Baud and Van Schendel 1997:219, 225). This 'triangle' of power is best understood by focusing on the perspective of patronage networks and alliance making on the border. [24] More precisely, the book investigates how strategic access to the control of resources (in this case forest) is negotiated with various officials of the state and cross-border networks. In addition, by analyzing these relationships over time this study will take a historical approach that shows how the authority of border elites is the result of ongoing

---

[23] See also Nancy Peluso's discussion of the conflicting demands faced and different roles played by local-level state officials in the struggle over access to forest resources on Java (Peluso 1992).

[24] The literature on patron-client relationships is too broad to be displayed here and it is beyond the scope of this study to engage in a larger theoretical discussion of the phenomena. For a more detailed discussion, see for example Eisenstadt and Roninger (1984, 1980), Gellner (1977) and Schmidt et al. (1977).

negotiations and fraught relations with various state officials. In line with Schulte Nordholdt and Van Klinken, it is agreed that such 'networks of influence' are a useful entry point for analyzing the 'more personalized paradigms of state-society relations' (Schulte Nordholdt and Van Klinken 2007a:20).

It is important to note that the concept of patronage as applied in this book is somewhat different from the classic formulation that has been used in Southeast Asia and elsewhere. In their classic sense, patron-client dependency relations were mostly seen as static, exploitative and unsymmetrical. They were supposedly based on strict dependency relations between a patron and his clients, the patron often being a powerful landlord and his clients being landless peasants. According to James Scott, these kinds of 'feudal' patron-client relationships have since lost legitimacy and changed considerably to involve vertical links such as those between peasants and politicians (Scott 1972:6; 1977:125). Scott concludes that the structure of patron-client relationships in general is probably best understood as one that expands or contracts over time (1972:13). Furthermore, discourses related to extreme forms of exploitation and inequality have since been moderated to involve some degrees of reciprocity and the acknowledgment that 'weaker' peasants had certain 'weapons' of resistance; see, for example, Scott's analysis of landlord-tenant relations in a Malay village (Scott 1985). Scott demonstrates that the conditions in Southeast Asia in general were quite favourable to the formation of patron-client relationships. However, the classic perspectives of patronage relations that emphasize extreme asymmetry and unbalanced bargaining power are not directly adaptable to the borderland context. Here patronage relationships function somewhat differently. I believe that seeing patron-client relations as merely asymmetrical 'dyadic ties' is too simplistic and does not account for the often very complex local bargaining positions and broader social and economic arrangements involved. While early studies of client-patron relations emphasized such dyadic relations, recent studies of patronage have taken an analytical shift and focussed on networks, factions, and coalitions.

As noted by Joel Kahn (1999) in his study of patronage relations in the uplands region of East Kalimantan, it is not possible to draw such clear distinctions between patrons and clients as local relations are much more egalitarian in regard to land distribution and social structure (compared to the often more stratified low land communities). A distinct class of landlords is difficult to recognize. The strictly asymmetrical view of patronage relations matches very poorly to the real-life categories of these upland populations. Here the border élites more often than not draw their authority and status from relationships and networks with powerful others such as state officials and wealthy entrepreneurs, not as large landlords (Kahn 1999:94-5). Hence one can see clear and important distinctions in the extent of restraints involved in a patron-client relationship.

Moreover, in the Iban case, the high value placed on personal autonomy and achievement has made such hierarchical dependency relations less obvious. As noted by Scott, certain marginal and upland regions of Southeast Asian states have only been 'intermittently subject to central government control' and operate with relative autonomy (Scott 1977:133). Although there are significant internal differences in wealth and status, no formal or traditional 'class' hierarchy or political organization exists within the Iban border communities. Only during Dutch colonialism were official hierarchies of 'tribal chiefs' introduced in order for the Dutch to influence authority indirectly over its inland subjects. Today local identity is mainly based on kinship ties. In pre-colonial West Borneo, small inland Malayu kingdoms did engage as patrons with various non-Malay communities, exchanging vital goods and services, although the kings were not landlords in a classical sense as their power was measured in the amount of followers not land ownership. However, the Iban was never part of this kind of asymmetrical patron-client relationship. Milne (1973:898-9) draws similar conclusions in reference to pre-colonial Iban communities living in Malaysia.

The Iban elite largely derive their position as brokers or patrons by their greater access to knowledge and personalized networks. Thus they become 'gatekeepers' (or brokers) as they link local communities with the outside world. They cannot directly exert power on local communities. In this context the relationship between patrons, brokers and clients is much more complementary as local communities (the clients) obtain a certain amount of bargaining power, although the relationship is still based on a certain degree of inequality.

Two basic analytical characteristics usually attributed to patronage networks are their inherent informality and seemingly illegal or semi-legal nature of relationships opposing official laws (Eisenstadt and Roniger 1980:50-1). The emergence of patronage networks is generally seen as a result of dysfunctional or absent strong state institutions. This view revolves around the assumption that when the state fails to provide basic services and social security, people seek such services through informal networks of reciprocity. Networks of patronage therefore appear most clearly entrenched at the edges of the state. Moreover, as will be demonstrated in the following chapters, such patronage relations are highly vulnerable to the challenge of countervailing socio-political forces, as they are not fully legitimized.

In an attempt to comprehend the recent booms of illegal timber logging in marginal regions of Indonesia after the onset of decentralization in the late 1990s, several authors have suggested that we look at the role of patronage networks.[25] Krystof Obidzinski argues that the study of such dependency relations is thought to be important for understanding the misuse of political power and the structuring of the flow of resources in Indonesia (Obidzinski 2003:14-6). The studies mentioned here differ in that they are more localized and take a more benign approach. Many former studies emphasized the fraught relationships among higher-level political elites and neglected the more localized forms of patronage relations.

In his studies of the informal networks involved in illegal logging in Sumatra, John McCarthy (2007, 2006, 2002) points out that understanding such often very personalized relationships is imperative for understanding the complexity behind these practices. He argues that informal networks become especially significant in marginal regions where formal institutions of the state are weakly constituted; central state rules that are imposed often are inconsistent with local traditions and lack local legitimacy. In these regions one detects a latent need for informal alternatives that can provide various services and fulfil needs normally delivered by the state (McCarthy 2006:14-7).

Patronage networks are developed to achieve certain goals in situations of public institutional uncertainty. The goals more often than not relate to access to valuable resources and benefits derived from these. In such circumstances, members of border elites (at the village and district level) often assume leadership positions and act directly as patrons either in a strict sense or through their influence as brokers between local villagers and higher-level patrons, or through a combination of both roles. In

---

[25] See Casson and Obidzinski 2002; McCarthy 2006; Obidzinski 2003; Wollenberg et al. 2006.

the case of forest exploitation, border elites usually lack sufficient capital to undertake large-scale operations on their own, and they need financial and technical backup and support from higher-level patrons, including local and state officials (police, military etc.) and wealthy outside entrepreneurs (timber barons).

These relationships merge into what McCarthy calls 'clientelist coalitions' (or patron-broker-client bonds) (McCarthy 2002:81).[26] The person acting as client is not only expected to make specific resources available to his patron but must also accept the patron's complete control over access to markets and over his capacity to convert resources. Similarly, the patron's position is not entirely solid or guaranteed. The patron's position is never fully legitimized and is therefore vulnerable to attack by social forces and by the competition of other patrons and brokers. Due to these constant threats, patrons are compelled to rely on their followers to solidify their position. The patron must also give up some short-term gains to protect public claims and to boost images of power and reputation. Sometimes this earns him the right to determine the basic rules of the social relationships. In return, the client is protected from social or material insecurity and is provided with goods, services, and at times social advancement (Roniger et al. 2001). Thus the mechanisms by which patronage work involve rules of reciprocity whereby the various actors engage in binding, although not legally enforceable, obligations of exchange, such as the flow of wealth, favours and support.[27]

This follows the perspective taken by another study on illegal logging in the province of East Kalimantan. Obidzinski (2003) notes how long-term, deeply entrenched patronage relationships there have changed from more traditional forms of patron-client relationships that involved highly asymmetrical power relations in which the client was highly dependent on his patron to something that more resembles 'cooperative, symbiotic, quid-pro-pro exchange relationships where individuals involved act as partners' (2003:18). According to Obidzinski local engagement in these patronage relationships was largely an attempt to meet certain localized economic subsistence and political needs (2003:33).

[26] The related terms clientelism and patronage are often used interchangeably. Clientelism often describes the logic of social exchange and the character of trust within patron-client relations, and patronage calls attention to the support granted by the patron to his followers and clients (Roniger et al. 2001:11118).

[27] In recent studies of Indonesian party politics the concept of clientelism has been employed as a way to understand the institutional complexity of politics after decentralization.

In line with Obidzinski I believe that local engagement in networks of patronage should be analyzed as a localized coping strategy based on mutual respect and trust enacted in response to the shifting and unpredictable political and economic situation in the borderland. Although the prime mechanisms driving most parties within the networks are cost-benefit calculations, and the main interest is economic advancement, their methodology is very much determined by local norms and values.

The face-to-face character of these relationships creates bonds of mutual trust and even friendship, which further enhance personal ties (Scott 1977:126). Such bonds of trust or interpersonal loyalty were developed in an extreme sense in the borderland in the 1970s when Iban elite figures 'adopted' Indonesian military officers as 'blood brothers' and three decades later similar bonds of trust were created with Malaysian timber barons. S.N. Eisenstadt and L. Roniger mention how such loyalty or solidarity can be closely related to local conceptions of honour and obligations (Eisenstadt and Roniger 1980:50). While this is very true in the borderland setting, I will also later spell out in greater detail how these bonds of trust often are of an ambivalent nature.

The Iban case clearly shows the persistence of these bonds. In the borderland, the Iban elite have for long acted as brokers or mediators between villagers (the clients) and various other actors, be they state officials, military or non-state individuals like powerful cross-border entrepreneurs (the patrons). In some relationships the border elite act as the patrons, being holders of, for example, logging concessions, while in other circumstances they are themselves clients to higher-level patrons. It is important to note that the redistribution of resources taking place in these networks involves a certain amount of inequality. In their role as brokers, border elites seem to secure their own personal interests and that of their nearest kin, while the degree of benefits reaching the village level is often limited. However, border elites, which include village heads, do not engage in patron-client relations solely for personal gain. For example, village heads must balance the expectations of them among close kin and needs and demands of the larger community. These patronage relationships spell out certain contradictions. They are characterised as being based on a combination of inequality/exploitation, mutual trust/solidarity and voluntary cooperation.

What makes these border elites especially adept in taking on the mediating role is their capacity to move confidently between the village

| *At the edges of states*

level, the regional level of district and province, and the transnational level. These networks build upon their multiple and strategic positions as local traditional leaders, district politicians, local-level entrepreneurs and their shared kinship ties extending across the border. Knowing the 'rules of the game' puts them in an ideal negotiating position with regard to the control of access to local resources. The extra-local network of these elites further makes such patronage systems extremely dynamic and easily adapted to sudden change in the local setting. Iban elites, for example, have been quick to take advantage of the uncertainties arising from recent political transformations of decentralization and to venture into relationships with local government and Malaysian entrepreneurs. Previously, their relationships had built upon ties with central state-based institutions like sections of Soeharto's military elite whose authority since the onset of decentralization dwindled in the borderland.

The book argues that the historically based networks of patronage on the border, based on illicit flows and the skill of strong and entrepreneurial men, may tell us interesting things about the advancement of Indonesian state formation. According to Thomas Gallant, the activities of such illegal networks largely facilitated the advancement of capitalism into remote border regions of the early modern state (Gallant 1999). Illegal socio-economic networks encouraged hinterland marketization and provided a venue for local upward economic mobility. The presence of these illegal networks often led by 'military entrepreneurs' (be they bandits, pirates, rebels, or ethnic chiefs) who 'literally and figuratively lived on the edge of society' has compelled national governments to sometimes violently intervene in an attempt to force their control on the border.[28] These processes have largely facilitated the incorporation of these remote border regions into national polity – an outcome that Gallant terms the 'border effect' (Gallant 1999:48). The idea of the 'border effect' is useful in thinking the waxing and waning of state power on the West Kalimantan border.

The following chapters, for example, illustrate how border rebels, war chiefs, timber barons, gangsters, vigilantes, ethnic elites, and not least (predatory) military entrepreneurs worked the border, and how these 'men of prowess' in various ways contributed to the demarcation of the

---

[28] Gallant (1999:26-7) does not refer to the formal institution: 'national army' when using the term 'military entrepreneurs'. Instead, he wishes to stress the tendency of these entrepreneurial men to 'take up arms' and apply the 'threat of violence' in their activities.

territorial state. In particular, how they contributed to the continuous reproduction of the border through their ambivalent and shifting engagements with central state institutions. These engagements continuously fluctuated between processes of cooperation, collusion, and pacification and the outright defiance of central state authority. But most importantly, these processes show that such 'men of prowess', whose activities most often are deemed illegal, are not the antithesis of modern state formation but instead an integral part of it. As Gallant plainly stated, 'Bandits helped make states and states made bandits' (Gallant 1999:25).

RULES AND NORMS AS PROCESSES OF NEGOTIATION

What seems to connect the theoretical discussions cited above is the processual character of state-society relations and state formation in particular. Norms and rules are continuously shaped and reshaped in the contact between actors inside and outside the state apparatus. As a 'meta' analytical frame of this book, the insight of Sally Falk Moore's process-oriented theory is applied. Moore's concept of 'semi-autonomous social fields' is particular fruitful in explaining the dynamics of state-society relations in the borderland setting.

According to Moore, ethnographers should focus on change-in-the-making, such as process and events, and not assume an *a priori* existence of social structure and systems. For Moore change is a fluid process marked by unintended consequences that are difficult or impossible to estimate. She therefore questions whether 'a focus on regularity and consistency should not be replaced by a focus on change, on process over time, and on paradox, conflict, inconsistency, contradiction, multiplicity, and manipulability in social life?' (1975:217). Based on her study of local politics in Tanzania, Moore presents the assumption that 'indeterminacy' is a basic aspect of social life. In that regard, the underlying qualities of the organization of social life are basically 'temporary, incomplete, and contain elements of ambiguity, discontinuity, contradiction, paradox, and conflict' (1978:48-9). Socially generated rules and norms are in a process of flux as inconsistencies constantly are being questioned and manipulated.

In her process-oriented approach, Moore differentiates between 'processes of regularization' and 'processes of situational adjustment'.

Accordingly, social life is undergoing a constant struggle between pressures of establishing or maintaining order and regularity, and the underlying messiness of social organization. This initially makes social life unsuited to complete ordering and regulation (Moore 1978:39). The situational or instance-by-instance use of rules permits the kind of reinterpretation, redefinition, and manipulation connected with so-called processes of situational adjustment.

By emphasizing the processes of regularization, situational adjustment, and the basic postulate of indeterminacy as an underlying quality of social life Moore attempts to explain the movement between efforts at establishing total or partial control and the unmanageable social forces that affect the first two. Furthermore, within this process-oriented approach the concept of a semi-autonomous social field takes a central position. By developing the notion of a 'semi-autonomous field', Moore attempted to advance an analytical perspective in understanding legal systems in particular and social change in general. While the study of law was a dominant factor in her studies, her analytical framework was not solely about 'law', but rather about normative fields in general (Moore 1978:55). Moore's idea of 'semi-autonomous fields' was at the time a contribution to a new and burgeoning approach within anthropology concerned with the interaction between different and often colliding legal orders and norms, an approach often referred to as 'Legal Pluralism'. According to Moore, a 'semi-autonomous social field' is not to be understood as a discrete organizational unit but as a network of social relationships.

A social field is semi-autonomous in the sense of being affected on one side by a 'larger social matrix' but also being able to draw on this matrix for its own ends on the other side. By introducing the notion of semi-autonomy, Moore attempts to mediate between notions of the state as all compassing and the existence of completely autonomous social fields. Neither of the two states of affairs seems to be applicable to social settings studied today. Moore investigated the extent to which social fields generate and enforce their own rules and the ways in which these fields influence and, in turn, are influenced by forms of regulation such as state laws. Sally Engle Merry notes that 'the outside legal system penetrates the field but does not dominate it; there is room for resistance and autonomy' (Merry 1988:878). The semi-autonomous social field is thus a limited social arena where strong social groups of interdependent actors with the capability to generate their own rules and norms often have more power than state laws and regulations. That situation resembles the borderland dynamics studied here.

Moore argues that state legislation or other attempts to change social habits often fail to achieve their intended purposes; even when they succeed wholly or partially, they frequently carry with them unplanned and unexpected consequences: 'This is partly because new laws are thrust upon social arrangements in which there are complexes of binding obligations already in existence' (1978:58). This perspective directs focus to the dialectic and mutually constitutive relations between state law and other normative orders, and, more importantly, emphasizes the interconnectedness of social orders.

The borderland as a social field brings together many different actors who engage in multiple and overlapping relations that generate their own rules and customs internally but are also affected by larger outside forces and rules surrounding it (Moore 1978:55). The borderland, or more precisely the whole complex of relationships portrayed in local patronage networks that it encompasses, can be considered as a semi-autonomous social field. What constitute this semi-autonomous social field are the processes through which state rules and laws are being continuously negotiated and challenged in the shifting relationship between state actors and border communities. This book argues that the process of 'mutual adjustments' between state rules and local norms, the ongoing negotiation over authority and definitions of legality and illegality makes the concept applicable to the borderland setting.

Omar M. Razzaz has, for example, identified several ways in which actors operating within a semi-autonomous social field may evade conforming to state laws and authority. First, actors within a social field can produce their own internal rules that could hinder the penetration of external rules. Second, they can avoid state laws by taking advantage of loopholes in the laws or inconsistencies in the enforcement procedures (Razzaz 1994). As will be demonstrated in the following chapters, the borderland has been shaped by a number of external forces but at the same time the borderland and its population have managed to maintain a certain amount of 'legal' semi-autonomy.[29]

Focusing on recent efforts to theorize that the concept of the state

---

[29] This is the concept applied by Fernanda in analyzing the semi-autonomous social field of a Ladakhi village (Fernanda 2006).

that highlight its fragmented character, some argue that international borders provide an exceptionally good arena for studying state formation processes and the creation of nationhood along margins. This framework indicates that the region on the territorial border of state control brings certain qualities of the state into view that counter the popular idea of the state as an all-encompassing and unitary structure. By applying this framework, with its focus on process and networks, to the Indonesian setting, I hope to provide the means of overcoming the conceptual straitjacket of the state. As we shall see in the next chapter that discusses colonial encounters on the border, the relationship between state and local actors in the Indonesian borderlands has continuously shifted between processes of accommodation and resistance.

Fig 13: A group of Batang Lupars, 1920 (Photo courtesy KITLV, Leiden)

Fig 14: Temporary longhouse (dampa) in the vicinity of Nanga Badau, 1932 (Photo courtesy Koninklijk Instituut voor de Tropen, Amsterdam)

Fig 15: Batang Lupars parading at a visit by Governor-General Limburg van Stirum, 1920 (Photo courtesy KITLV, Leiden)

Fig 16: Batang Lupars in full wardress (date unknown; probably early twentieth century) (Photo courtesy Koninklijk Instituut voor de Tropen, Amsterdam)

Fig 17: Catholic school in Lanjak (date unknown; probably early twentieth century) (Photo courtesy Koninklijk Instituut voor de Tropen, Amsterdam)

Fig 18: Temenggong (right) in soldiers's uniform, Batang Loepar Kampong Rongga, 1932 (Photo courtesy Koninklijk Instituut voor de Tropen, Amsterdam)

Fig 19: Consultant ir. G.A. de Mol and Iban headman on the border between Dutch West Borneo and Sarawak, 1932 (Photo courtesy Koninklijk Instituut voor de Tropen, Amsterdam

3

Evading state authority

> The status of borders has been contingent on varying historical circumstances, rather than being immutably rock-like. Borders shift; they leak; and they hold varying sorts of meaning for different people (Migdal 2004:5).

This chapter and the subsequent Chapter 4 are a critical reading of key moments in borderland history, ranging from the latter part of the Dutch colonial period (1850s) to the end of the New Order period of former President Soeharto (1998). An underlying objective is to show the historical development of the Kalimantan Iban as a border people, in particular, the way the borderland, and more specifically the strategies of border inhabitants, have been shaped in relationship to colonial and postcolonial states and their regulative border policies. I here demonstrate that states and their borders are not static or permanent structures, separating territories and excluding people as originally intended by colonial state planners, but are the result of dynamic historical processes. The chapters unravel the continuities between these periods, describe the long-term social and economic interactions across the border, and finally discuss the implications of these historic legacies of the past for the consolidation of authority among local border elites.

In order to locate the borderland in time, the historical account is divided into two chapters, each dealing with a specific period in borderland history (pre- and post-independence). Each period illuminates the ongoing ambivalent relationship between local communities and government authority (the Dutch colonial administration or the Indonesians state). The chapters argue that this ambiguity is an outcome of the particularities of life at the border, of being situated between two divergent nation states and of the continuously shifting character of the border. This first

| *At the edges of states*

chapter briefly introduces the pre-colonial setting in order to situate the Iban communities, as long-time residents, in the region. The focus then immediately moves to the Dutch colonial intervention in the borderland beginning in the mid-1800s, where the first Dutch effort to establish an officially recognized territorial border was initiated through a complicated negotiation with the British colonial administration. Here a special emphasis is placed on Dutch attempts to pacify the autonomous border Iban by interdicting their migration between the two colonial territories. I highlight how the Iban population gradually adjusted to the new colonial territorial divisions by using these arbitrary borderlines to their own advantage.

The second historical chapter (4) makes a short leap in time to the early decades after Indonesian independence and the period of modern state formation.[1] Analyzing the post-colonial period of confrontation and militarization along the border in the 1960s and 1970s, I provide a detailed account of how the Indonesian state attempted to establish its authority over people and territory along its national borders through strict military control. I demonstrate how border communities were caught between the various conflicting parties and their ambivalent engagement with these, which led either to great rewards or to severe punishment. Importantly, the elite configurations that will be discussed in the following chapters were partly formed by the political transformations and border militarization during that period. The foundations of a border elite power base and its networks of influence were in many ways laid in the early 1960s, when the borderland was plunged into an armed conflict with the newly established federation of Malaysia. The third section of the chapter briefly deals with the period immediately after the border confrontation, which marked the onset of state- sanctioned resource extraction that continued until the fall of the Soeharto regime in the late 1990s. Here the focus is on both the conflicting relationship between a majority of border communities and logging companies and on border elite collusion with the same state-sponsored companies. Overall, these chapters provide a historical framework for situating the contemporary processes of negotiating local border autonomy.

The data presented in Chapter 3 draw on a combination of primary

[1] Data on West Kalimantan and the borderland in particular is very scarce for the period of the early twentieth century until Indonesian independence in the 1950s. Japanese bombing of the provincial capital during World War II destroyed various archives, and much information was lost.

and secondary sources such as Dutch colonial records, other scholarly literature and oral history collected during and after fieldwork.[2] History plays an important role in local historical placement and ethnic consolidation in the border area, and past events are generally recalled with great pride. Iban historical narratives can be divided into two levels: the present and recent past (*diato'*) that is still within the memories of living individuals, and the ancestral past transmitted from generation to generation (*kelia dulo'*). Iban connections to the ancestral past are kept alive through an intricate system of tracing one's ancestry (*tusut*). Most Iban in the border area are able to remember and trace their descent for as many as five generations back in time.[3] Comparing such 'family histories' with colonial and other government accounts provided an interesting picture of past state-local relations and was especially important because the past is continuously employed locally to justify current affairs and reasoning.[4]

SETTLEMENTS ON THE PRE-COLONIAL FRONTIER

Several Borneo scholars have pointed towards the middle Kapuas basin[5] in West Kalimantan as the site of early Iban settlement. They say that ancestors of the Iban originated several centuries ago in this area, and

---

[2] In the meticulous records kept by Dutch officials on eighteenth-century territorial boundary making in West Borneo, a special emphasis was placed on the border region inhabited by the Iban – a population that seemed to be of special concern to the colonial authorities. Generally, this early period in borderland history is well documented, while the records on the subsequent period of Indonesian state formation are scantier. Official data on the period of militarization in the borderland from the early 1960s until late 1970s was particularly difficult to locate. Even now, several decades later, this period is still a sensitive matter in the province.

[3] These narratives include a mix of family histories involving migration and raiding.

[4] Data collected on the colonial period and parts of the post-colonial period were partly generated from local oral narratives about the past. There are several problems and weaknesses associated with this data collection technique. Firstly, one faces the issue of authority. I was inevitably guided towards certain local 'experts', mostly senior *adat* and community leaders and other grand orators considered knowledgeable of local history. These people, as members of border elites, often had their own agenda in mind when formulating their stories. Knowledge of local community dynamics became crucial for deciphering their discursive strategy. It is here important to note that historical claims can be used to legitimise certain claims such as property rights, territorial rights, resource claims, or leadership positions. For example, three ethnic groups in the borderland, Iban, Maloh, and Melayu, have become increasingly interested in their own history as competition over land has increased. Historical narratives are being used to validate local inter-ethnic resource claims.

[5] The Kapuas is the longest river in West Kalimantan, stretching approximately 1,145 km from its source at Gunung Cemaru in the upper Kapuas Mountains to the coast at the provincial capital of Pontianak.

the Iban themselves generally accept this statement. Evidence based on Iban oral history show that some time prior to the nineteenth century, the Iban migrated out of the Kapuas basin and spread across the border into what is known as the upper Batang Lupar river system (*Ulu ai'* in Iban) in Sarawak and, from there, further afield.[6] Dating this migration more precisely is problematic, because the history of the settlement of the Iban in the borderland and wider Kapuas area is based entirely on local oral histories, and much specificity has been lost over generations.

Nonetheless, although early records on Iban settlement in the area are scarce, oral accounts paint a picture of Iban interaction with other inhabitants of the area that was characterised by a mixture of raiding and trading (Sandin 1967). Iban accounts of their prehistoric arrival in the area are largely contradictory. Some accounts describe how the hilly area along the border was uninhabited prior to their arrival, while others claim that the area was occupied by groups of forest gathers known as the *orang bukit* (literally 'hill people'), who supposedly fled from early Iban intrusions (or became incorporated within Iban communities). Still other Iban accounts tell of scattered Maloh settlements in the area prior to Iban arrival, assertions that largely are supported by Maloh oral accounts (King 1976b:96).[7]

Oral accounts emphasize the shifting Iban relationship with the small (Muslim) Melayu kingdoms/states in the upper Kapuas. Although the Iban were never under the direct rule of these kingdoms, they frequently engaged in trade and alliances with the Melayu.[8] The kingdoms allied with the Iban against other groups whom they wanted to suppress and bring under their authority (Bouman 1924:187; Kielstra 1890:1104). The Malayu rulers did not measure their power in terms of territorial possessions, but the by number of people who paid them tribute. By refusing to pay tribute, the Iban were known as the 'free Dayaks'[9] (*mardaheka dayaks*), or 'those who were under nobody's authority but their own',

[6]   See Freeman 1970; Pringle 1970; Sandin 1967, 1994; Sutlive 1989; Wadley 2000c.
[7]   In the climate of increased resource struggle and interethnic conflicts since the late 1990s, these oral accounts of prehistorical settlement have come to play an important role in legitimizing ethnic claims to land ownership.
[8]   Many other ethnic groups in the area, like the less numerous Maloh and Kantu, frequently paid tax and tribute to these rulers (Wadley 2000c).
[9]   The term 'Dayak' is an umbrella term referring to all non-Muslim populations living in the interior of Kalimantan, with the Iban being just one of many ethnic groups named Dayak (such as Iban Dayaks). The Dayaks living along the border were later referred to by the Dutch as 'border Dayaks' (*grens-Dajakhs*) (Kater 1883).

while the '*serah dayaks*'[10] were the Dayak groups who paid tribute to the Melayu kingdoms (Enthoven 1903; King 1976b; Van Kessel 1850). This analysis fits well with Scott's more general statement concerning how control of people was more important than control of land throughout pre-colonial Southeast Asia (Scott 1998:185).[11] Although such 'peaceful' cooperation was common, what seems to be the most common state of affairs within this relationship was that of mutual exploitation, such as continuous Iban raiding of Melayu settlements and counterattacks by the Melayu rulers.[12]

Generally, the significant Iban migrations were a result of several contemporary processes, prompted by need for new land, regional politics, disputes within longhouse communities, and not least a result of warfare and raiding with other ethnic groups and internally among themselves. These movements mostly consisted of individuals and sets of families (joining relatives or kin already settled in the specific areas) and, more seldom, whole longhouse communities searching for new land to farm or escaping headhunting raids (King 1976b:88; Wadley 1997:43). The early period of migration was one of intense instability and flux. There was a constant shifting of the population, not just for the Iban but for all the peoples of the interior of Borneo (Eghenter 1999). Since the onset of these early Iban migrations, several similar back and forth movements have taken place on the hilly watershed that later came to signify Dutch and British territories and today forms the international border between Indonesia and Malaysia. Although the nature of such movements has changed considerably since, due to modern state policies imposed at these borders, it were within this context of constant movement and warfare the Iban communities were first introduced to the European idea of fixed territorial borders and the wider politics of colonial boundary making.

---

[10] '*Serah*' is a kind of forced trade where the exchange rate was to the advantage of the Malay ruler.
[11] Control of land first became a major concern after the introduction of rigid mapping regimes of the later colonial powers.
[12] See Bouman 1924, 1952; Enthoven 1903; Pringle 1970; Sandin 1967.

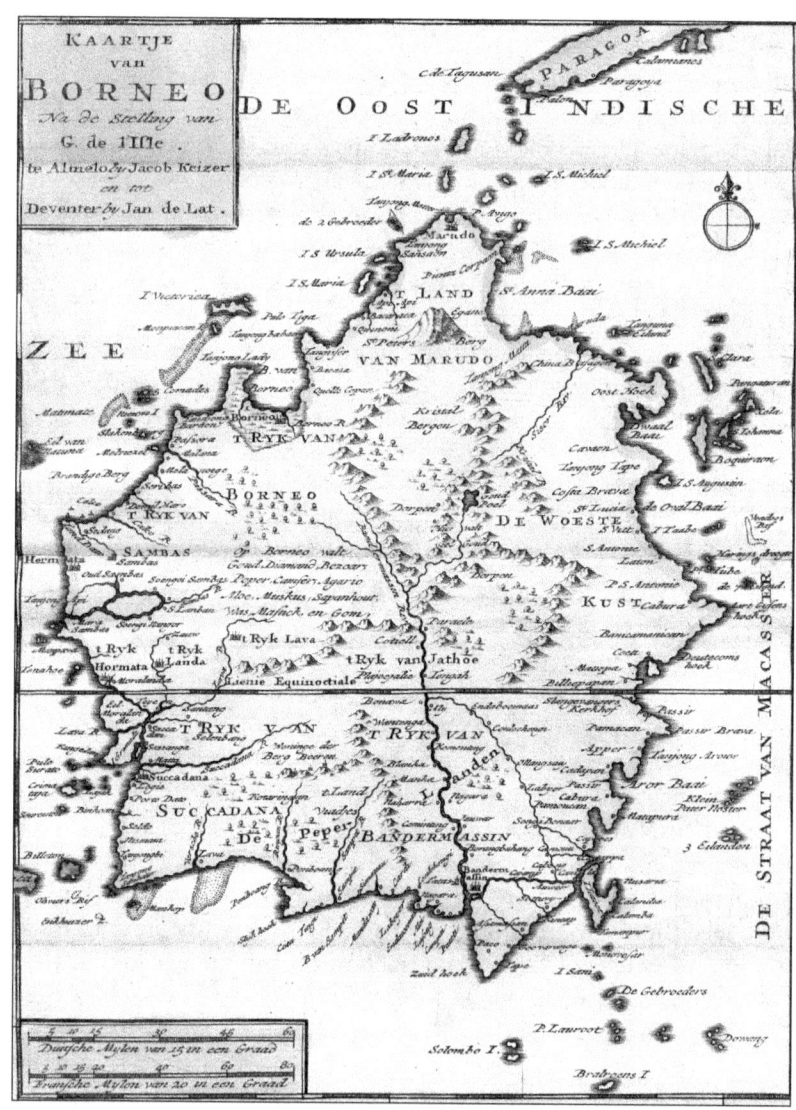

Map 4: Colonial Borneo, 1747

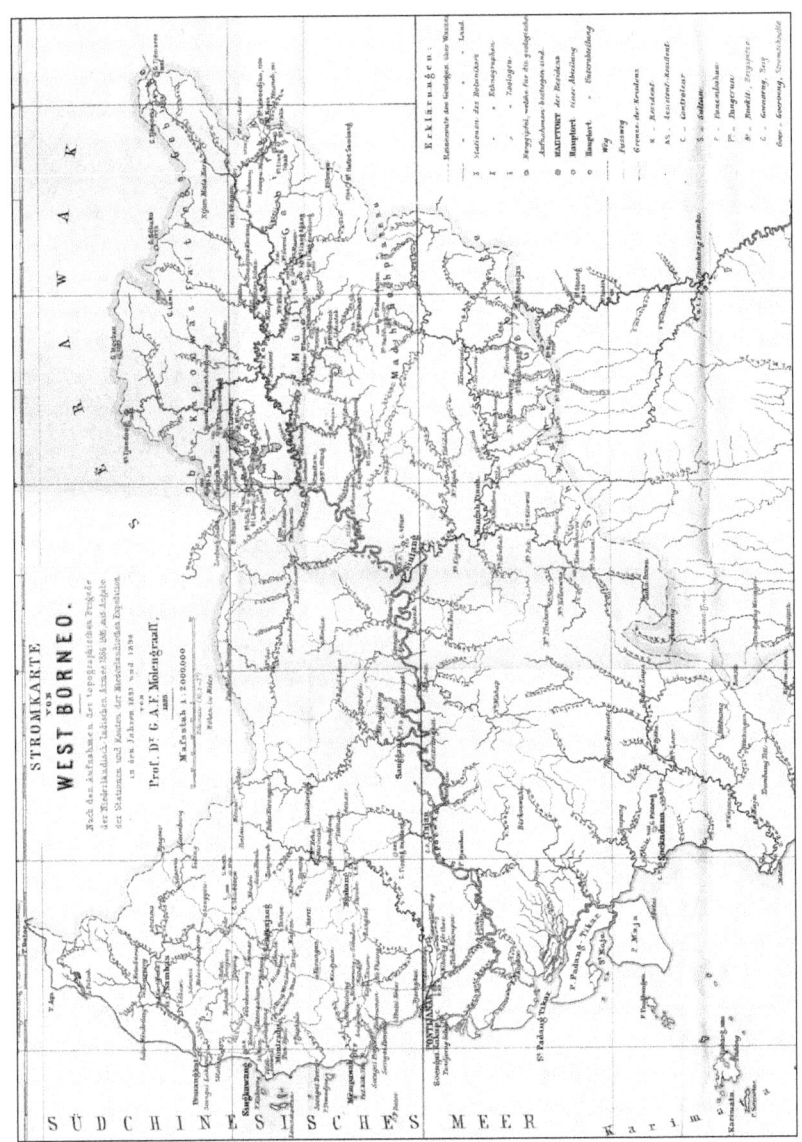

Map 5: Colonial West Borneo, 1895

Map 6: Batang Lupar Country, 1895

3 *Evading state authority*

DRAWING BORDERS: COLONIAL ENCOUNTERS ON THE
FRONTIER

All boundaries are artificial. They are human impositions on the continuous tissue of nature (Strassoldo 1989:392).

National borders are political constructs, imagined projections of territorial power. Although they appear on maps in deceptively precise forms, they reflect, at least initially, merely the mental images of politicians, lawyers, and intellectuals (Baud and Van Schendel 1997:211).

As stated in the citations above, the idea of modern international borders, as we understand them today, is a historic product of European state building and of the subsequent rise of nationalism starting in the eighteenth century (Anderson 1991). The drawing and creation of territorial borders became essential for the creation of a national identity and nationhood. Baud and Van Schendel (1997:214-5) argue that borders became markers in two ways: First, as a demarcation of state territories in order to put an end to territorial disputes. Territorial borders helped the respective states to distinguish their own citizens from those of the neighbouring state, making it easier to exercise control and collect taxes. Second, borders became the ultimate markers of the reach of state power.

The demarcation of borders as a state function in Europe was a long process that took centuries. In Southeast Asia, as in other regions under former colonial rule, this process was accelerated because of European colonialism and the struggle over people, land, and natural resources (Tagliacozzo 1999).

In March 1824, an Anglo-Dutch treaty was signed that divided the Malay world down the Strait of Melaka and assigned the right of influence on each side to the Dutch or the British. This treaty arbitrarily divided the island of Borneo into two parts, although the actual borderline was officially negotiated much later (Trocki 2000). In the period between 1886 and 1895, the Dutch government sent out several surveying teams led by Captain J.J.K. Enthoven.[13] The main purpose of these 'expeditions' was to map the entire province of West Borneo. The

---

[13] Captain J.J.K. Enthoven was the head of the Topographic Survey of the Dutch East Indies (Topografische Dienst [TD]) from 1897 to 1909. The TD became an independant military unit in 1907. See Ormeling 1996.

| *At the edges of states*

task was accomplished in nine years, and the results were published in a two-volume (900-page) book that meticulously described geographic and ethnographic features of the province (Ent-hoven 1903) (see Map 5, p. 81).

From a Dutch perspective, the border, through its dividing effect, had the function of preventing smuggling, migration and raiding, while it promoted colonial control and facilitated the collection of taxes. Although the Dutch from the very outset of their presence in the area had been determined to delimit the exact borderline between Dutch Western Borneo and British Sarawak, not until 20 June 1891[14] was a formal treaty signed in London between the two nations. And not until 1912 was the exact borderline fixed along the hilly and mountainous watershed, demarcating Dutch territories in the south and British territories in the north of the island.[15] This treaty was later followed by treaties and conventions in 1915 and 1928.[16]

On a map, these borderlines might have created clarity but, on the ground, local response to these new divisions of the landscape was seldom in line with colonial understanding. Referring to the West Kalimantan borderland under colonial rule, Wadley has noted that:

> Like other European colonial powers, the Dutch were obsessed with exclusive borders, both external and internal, in their South East Asian possessions. Externally, 'proper' borders restricted undesirable elements (namely smuggling and migration) and defined citizenship for taxation and development (Wadley 2003:93).[17]

The ordering of social and political space by creating borders was applied by European colonial administrations all over the globe. The co-

---

[14] See 'Staatsblad van Nederlandsch-Indië, Batavia: Landsdrukkerij', 1892, No.114, pp 1-7. See also 'Kaart van een gedeelte van Borneo met aanwijzing van de grens tusschen het Nederlandsch gebied en dat van het Britsche protectoraat', 1891, Ministerie van Koloniën: Kaarten en Tekeningen, No. 628, ARA.

[15] 'Convention respecting the further delimitation of the frontier between the States in Borneo under British protection and the Netherlands territory in that island. Signed at The Hague, March 26, 1928'. London 1930, Treaty Series Number 335.

[16] See 'Staatsblad van Nederlandsch-Indië, Batavia: Landsdrukkeri'j, 1916, No.145, pp 1-6 and 1930, No.375, pp 1-9.

[17] Ishikawa (2010:78-80), for example, notes how the smuggling of commodities like rubber from Dutch West Borneo into Sarawak became endemic along the lower parts of the border (Sambas-Lundu border area) in the early part of the twentieth century. These cross-border smuggling networks were often headed by Chinese entrepreneurs (*towkay/taukey*) living on both sides of the border.

lonial legacy of borders is largely similar worldwide, characterised by its tendency to divide ethnic groups and to ignore already existing ethnic boundaries. This tendency to divide ethnic groups when drawing borders and the consequences of such actions have been described in detail in an African context by A.I. Asiwaju (Asiwaju 1985). In colonial Africa, little attention was paid to kinship ties, existing economic relations, well-established lines of communication, or shared socio-political institutions when drawing borders. Similar ethnic separation took place in Borneo among the Iban when the Dutch and British colonial administrations divided the island between them. The colonial Borneo border cut through a rather homogenous area, and individuals suddenly found family members on the other side of the border and incorporated into a different colonial territory. In this way, the two Iban groups (Kalimantan and Sarawak Iban) were placed under different political regimes and consequently exposed to vastly different political, economic and social circumstances. Moreover, after independence, as was the case in many former colonial territories, the historic colonial borders of Borneo were used as borders demarcating the new post-colonial nation-states; the Iban subsequently became Indonesian or Malaysian citizens. Like the former colonial administration, the new nation-states officially embraced the same notions of borders as clear and exclusive lines of separation.

Although these arbitrary borders were drawn on maps and imagined in the minds of the colonial administrators as sharp lines and impenetrable barriers separating colonial territories, the actual picture on the ground was and is often that of continued interaction between the divided ethnic groups. As Asiwaju has pointed out in his work on colonial African borders, people divided by such artificial borders often continue their normal activities, ignoring the line of separation (Asiwaju 1985:3). Scott for example, emphasizes how the creation of strict borders became part of 'seeing like a state' and that such visions of the world often did not coincide with local perceptions. One can cite many examples of people separated by artificial colonial borders who find ways to manipulate, circumvent or simply ignore such borders.[18] People seem to take ad-

---

[18] Among many similar examples from Borneo of colonial borders cutting through an ethnically distinct population is the case of the ethnic Kelabit, who are divided by the border between Sarawak and East Kalimantan (Bala 2001; 2002). Also, the ethnic Kayan-Kenyah were divided by the East Kalimantan-Sarawak border (Eghenter 2007, 1999), and the ethnic Lun Dayeh were divided by the border between Sabah/Sarawak and East Kalimantan (Ardhana et al. 2004).

vantage of borders in ways that are not intended or anticipated by their creators (Baud and Van Schendel 1997:211). The Iban in the borderland discussed here are a vivid example of such a separated people who, ever since their separation, have continued their socio-economic relations with kin and family across the border. They have largely maintained a social understanding of belonging that does not easily correspond with the political borders of the nation-state.

The two bordering areas, today known as West Kalimantan and Sarawak, were in the nineteenth century divided into Dutch West Borneo, or the Residency of the Western Division of Borneo (*Westerafdeeling van Borneo*),[19] and the Brooke (British) Governance in Sarawak. Subsequently, the Iban groups living in each area were divided by a formally recognized border and administrated by the Dutch and Brooke, respectively. The considerable variations of politics and practices between the two administrations have since had a profound effect on the Iban population on each side and shaped their lives differently.

Despite its strategic position in the South China Sea and its wealth of natural resources, the island of Borneo, compared to insular Southeast Asia, captured the European colonial interest rather late in the course of colonial conquest of the region (Irwin 1955). In the mid-nineteenth century Dutch colonial interest in Western Borneo first wakened. Dutch presence in this part of Borneo had previously been sporadic and concentrated along the coast. For the most part, colonial resources were directed towards the more fertile volcanic island of Java. Dutch intervention and growing interest in Western Borneo was, among other things, a counter response to the increasing expansion of the British powerbase in the adjacent region of Sarawak and reflected the Dutch desire to strengthen its general sphere of influence in its sparsely populated outer regional possessions (Irwin 1955:151). The upriver interior in Western Borneo was especially little known and was represented by blank areas on colonial maps (see Map 4, p. 80). However, it was widely known among the Dutch that the interior was rich in natural resources, and that their access to these resources was under immediate threat by the British expansion. From 1841 on, Sarawak was governed by an independent British colonialist and adventurer named James Brooke, known as the 'White Rajah' (White King). Brooke first arrived in the area in 1839 and helped the Sultan of

---

[19] A large part of the archipelago today known as Indonesia was former known as the colonies of the Netherlands East Indies. The Residency of the Western Division of Borneo was established in 1848.

Brunei to put down a local rebellion. For his assistance in ending this rebellion, Brooke was made the sovereign ruler of Sarawak. A few years later, in 1845, he was appointed British agent in Borneo (Irwin 1955: 103). The Brooke family administered the area for several generations until it was passed on to the British crown after World War II.[20]

The Brooke administration in Sarawak had, before Dutch consolidation of power in the area; begun initiating various trade contacts with local Melayu rulers in Dutch West Borneo. The Dutch feared that the communities living along the edge of their territory would eventually be swept into the Brooke sphere of influence.[21] In the 1840s and 1850s, a series of concerned letters about James Brooke's intrusion into the lower and upper borderlands was sent from the Resident of Dutch West Borneo to the Governor General of the Netherlands East Indies (GGNI) in Batavia (Jakarta) and from there to the minister of the Colonies. These letters requested additional officers to be posted near the border with Sarawak in order to check the influence exerted by James Brooke on the border-dwelling Dayaks.

Salt and firearms were among the illegal trade items of most concern to the Dutch. Trade in firearms was a military threat, while the salt trade was an economic threat as it reduced local Dutch tax revenue. These two trade items could be purchased considerably more cheaply in Sarawak than through Dutch trade channels.[22] The Dutch were very uneasy about the Brooke government's lax attitude towards its citizens, especially by the fact that Brooke officials often ignored Sarawak traders breaching the boundary line into what the Dutch claimed as part of the Netherlands East Indies territory. They were particularly concerned about Brooke's moral influence and authority over the border population living in Dutch territory, with whom he traded, and whom he periodically fined and punished without involving Dutch authorities. Such meddling in the affairs of Dutch subjects was seen as a serious border offence that showed outright disregard of Dutch sovereignty. Border skirmishes further convinced Dutch officials of the importance of firm border control and establishment of the authority of the Netherlands

---

[20] Brooke 1990 [1866]; Pringle 1970; Wagner 1972.
[21] See, for example, Geheime Verbalen. 1847 No. 49, 255, 335 and Openbare Verbalen. 1859 No. 30, Ministerie van Koloniën, ARA.
[22] Extract van het Register der besluiten van den Nederlands-Indie Governor-General, 11-1-1855. Geheime Verbalen, 11-1-1856. No. 15, ARA.

| *At the edges of states*

East Indies in West Borneo. As stated by the Dutch Resident[23] Cornelis Kater in Pontianak: 'In order to solve the disputes with our Sarawakian neighbours, it is necessary for strict government regulation along the border (*grensregeling*)'.[24]

THE WILD FRONTIER: BATANG LUPAR COUNTRY

Already in the 1850s, several Dutch delegations were dispatched up the Kapuas River in order to make contact with local rulers and to establish a firm Dutch presence in its most northern district, the *Boven-Kapoeas* (Kapuas Hulu, Sintang and Melawi districts). Here the colonial administrators directed a particular focus on the hilly region inhabited by the Iban that bordered the British possessions in Sarawak (Kater 1883). Despite a common agreement that this hilly watershed represented the border, several attempts were made by the Dutch in subsequent years to officially delimit the border between the two colonial administrations. However, Dutch efforts in the area were not merely concerned with its territorial borders. In addition, the shifting and overlapping internal boundaries between the various ethnic groups were in need of clarification. In order to make the landscape more manageable, the Dutch put considerable effort into dividing natural resources and ethnic groups into what they defined as fixed and ordered boundaries. This vision of the landscape was based on the logic that one group or ruler had rights to a well-defined territory and its resources.[25] This vision of the landscape was continually disputed, as it did not fit well with local Iban claims over resources. Among the Iban, resource claims generally were not based on land ownership per se but on rights to a particular natural resource, like a patch of fruit trees, or fishing rights in a lake or river.

A vivid example of this expanding Dutch territorialization in Western Borneo was the effort to pacify 'rebellious' Iban communities. Under the Dutch administration the Iban were referred to as 'Batang Lupar Dayaks', and the area they lived in as 'Batang Lupar country' (see Map 6, p. 82). When the Dutch first arrived in the upper Kapuas area, some Iban com-

---

[23] The Resident was the highest colonial authority on the provincial level.
[24] Letter to Nederlands-Indie Governor-General from Resident Kater, 7-8-1868, Pontianak. Geheime Kabinetsverbalen, 30-9-1870 J13 No. 37, ARA.
[25] Van Kessel 1850; Van Lijnden and Groll 1851; Veth 1854.

munities from the Batang Lupar River in Sarawak had begun to migrate back into the upper Kapuas area and settle down along the main rivers, such as the Leboyan and Embaloh Rivers. These instances of Iban migration from Sarawak convinced the Dutch that the Iban were newcomers to their side of the border. The Dutch believed that the Iban originated in the Batang Lupar River system in Sarawak (Batang Ai). Consequently, the Iban were named the 'Batang Lupar Dayaks' or 'Batang Lupars' (*de Batang Loepars*) (Bouman 1924:174; Kater 1883:2). However, as mentioned previously, these migrations were only a later stage in a long and complex history of Iban movement in Western Borneo.

The Dutch arrival in the interior areas of the island in the mid-1850s was mainly an attempt to make their presence felt and prevent any encroachment by the Brooke administration into what they regarded as their territory. However, they often portrayed their role as that of peacemakers who would put an end to centuries of warfare between the various ethnic groups. As mentioned by the Dutch Resident:

> Without the detestable headhunting we would now have in the Batang Lupars a peaceable (*rustige*) people of perhaps 5000-6000 souls, which could cover the costs of administration amply, while at present we spend thousands to protect our peaceful subjects (*rustige onderdanen*) against the headhunting of that tribe [Iban] (Kater 1883:3).

The Dutch first encountered the Iban in 1854 at a meeting with all the customary Iban leaders in the border area (Niclou 1887). During the meeting, the Iban leaders made a vow of allegiance to the Dutch in which they promised to stop what the Dutch saw as undesirable acts, such as warfare and smuggling:

> These leaders were presented with gifts and a sort of uniform, while various matters were arranged. They would stand outside any intermediate government of Malay sultans but would be immediately under the authority (*gezag*) of the Netherlands Indies Government, restrain themselves from hostilities and headhunting, pay no direct taxes to the government but perform some services such as chopping wood and supplying ironwood shingles. By establishing these services, our principal aim was not to increase our fund with such scanty amounts but to have our authority acknowledged (*ons gezag te doen erkennen*) (Kater 1883:3).

| *At the edges of states*

Van Schendel, for example, notes that the very existence of smuggling along borders is of much state concern, as it undermines the unitary image of the state and its authority as the sole enforcer of law and order within its bounded territory, a concern that becomes most evident in the following chapters (Van Schendel 1993:189).

In an attempt to consolidate their power, the Dutch began bestowing traditional positions of authority to elected representatives of the Iban communities, who were designated *temenggong* (tribal leaders) with deputies named *patih*. These appointed tribal leaders were either chosen by the Dutch or by local communities themselves, but they were ultimately subject to Dutch authority.[26] The official role of the *temenggong* and *patih* was to act as mediators between the Dutch and local communities, resolve various disputes and collect taxes.[27] This system was part of a Dutch strategy of indirect rule applied throughout West Borneo and other possessions (Harwell 2000b:49; Kater 1883:8).[28]

Despite Dutch efforts, the *temenggong* never became fully trusted and loyal intermediaries, as was the original purpose. The *temenggong* more often than not took the side of kin rather than that of the Dutch. For example, in the 1860s a local Iban named Rentap was appointed the position of *temenggong* but soon proved a troublesome subject. In 1876, Rentap's son carried out headhunting raids in the upper Kapaus River. Refusing to hand over his son to Dutch officials, Rentap's son was forced to escape across the border into Sarawak. He later resettled on the Dutch side and gave himself up to authorities. Not trusting Rentap, the Dutch attempted to replace him as *temenggong*, but the united Iban community informed the Dutch that they would not accept another candidate (Wadley 2001b:1844). Rentap's brother, Simpe, was directly related to the leading family in the longhouse community of Rumah Manah (the main locale of fieldwork) and the first Iban given the title of *temenggong* in the district of Batang Lupar.

Although different from traditional Iban political organization that was based primarily on kinship networks and had no recognized leaders

---

[26] These were originally honorary titles likely bestowed by Malayu rulers on Iban allies long before Dutch arrival in the area. Not only Iban but also Dayak groups in general were given these titles (Wadley 2000c:47).

[27] For similar Dutch arrangements among Dayak populations in Central Kalimantan, see Van Klinken 2004.

[28] Like the appointed Iban leaders, the Melayu rulers were also given official titles such as '*pangeran*', a term borrowed from the honorifics of Javanese nobility.

besides those who demonstrated outstanding combativeness (*tuai serang*) during raids, the Dutch system of elected tribal leaders has endured until the present and has become the highest authority within Iban society. Despite bringing the traditional positions of *temenggong* and *patih* under their supreme authority, the Dutch generally kept their Iban subjects free of bureaucratic control, and they regained a considerable degree of autonomy. As stated by Francis McKeown, 'In its dealings with the border Iban, the Dutch were concerned almost solely with their international relations with Sarawak and made no attempt to exploit the labour force or agricultural production of the Iban (McKeown 1984:510).[29]

The Sarawak administration likewise invented new titles of leadership among their Iban subjects, the highest being that of *penghulu*, a leader who acted as the extended arm of the government out in the districts (Pringle 1970:157). Frustration over the lack of reliable leadership institutions among the border Iban was, for example, expressed in a letter to the Dutch from Charles Brooke in 1905: 'This Dayak community [Iban] seem almost to be without leaders or anyone who they obey or who has influence over them'.[30]

In the decades to come, the Dutch extended their presence in the border area and experienced their first difficulties in handling the Iban, and the Dutch subsequently named the Iban '[...] the terror of the Kapuas (*de schrik der Kapoeas*)' (Kater 1883:4). As reflected by a anonymous Dutch military official:

> Of all our Dayak tribes the Batang Loepars with their headhunting are the most troublesome. They come from the Batang Loepar River, live in perpetual struggle with the Kantoek tribe and the punitive expeditions of the NI Government and the Rajah of Sarawak. They are in truth a natural nation that loves liberty.[31]

---

[29] In contrast, Ishikawa (2010) in his fine-grained historical account of the lower parts of the border, for example, demonstrates the early attempts of the Colonial Sarawak government in moulding a sense of 'Sarawakian' identity into its border inhabitants by domesticating the frontier surroundings. This was done through heavy taxation, resource exploitation regimes, and the development of agricultural zones. In Sarawak, the focus was on the control of resources and people, while attempts at demarcating the territoriasl border weres more relaxed.

[30] Letter to Resident de Neve from Raja Brooke, 16-5-1905, Sarawak. Behoort in Verbaal. 17-4-1906 No. 33; Mailrapporten 1904 Nos. 861 and 865, 1905 No. 888. Politieke Verslagen en Berichten uit de Buitengewesten van Nederlands-Indië, 1898-1940. Ministerie van Koloniën, ARA.

[31] Anonymous (1928) Militaire memorie van de afdeeling Sintang, 10-11-1928. Memorie van Overgave, Koninklijk Instituut voor de Tropen 994, ARA.

MIGRATION AND WARFARE

As indicated above, two aspects of Iban life in the colonial era that were especially often mentioned in the Dutch colonial archives – warfare and migration.[32] The Dutch experienced much frustration as their territorial divisions with Brooke's Sarawak were constantly defied and resisted by the Iban population's cross-border activities. Before the colonial intrusion into Western Borneo, the Iban had a long history of migration and movement and a well-established network of trade, communication, and kinship ties. The creation of the colonial borders did not mean an end to the interaction between the closely related Iban communities on each side of the border; on the contrary, the border was at times ignored or in several ways used to their advantage when it suited their needs. I do not want to imply that the Iban had no understanding of the importance of this political boundary. The Iban were quite aware that the border was of great importance to the Europeans, and that the watershed defined this new borderline. For example, they referred to the Dutch side as *ai Belanda* (*ai* being the Iban name for watershed or river and *Belanda* the Bahasa Indonesian word for 'Dutch') and the other side as *ai Sarawak*. However, the fact that the terrain along the border was predominantly low hills meant that there were no physical barriers that prevented or made border crossings difficult.

Iban raids were often directed against other ethnic groups, but interIban raiding was also normal. Iban raiding parties attacked communities in both Dutch and Brooke territories. These warriors were often referred to as 'Urang Kampar',which is an Iban term for men who wander, trade or fight outside their own territory (Pringle 1970:229). As an immediate result of these continuous raiding campaigns, the two colonial administrations began patrolling the border on a regular basis and initiated several military counter-attacks on rebellious Iban. As a tool of pacification, they burned down longhouses, cut down fruit trees, and destroyed rice fields (*kampong werd verbrand en de ladangs werden omgehakt*) (Niclou 1887:50). When Iban raiding parties sought refuge from their enemies or from Dutch and Brooke punitive expeditions, they exploited the division of authority on the two sides of the border. When Iban from Sarawak en-

---

[32] Not only did the Iban defy colonial authority; elsewhere, in Central Borneo, the ethnic Kelabits, in a similar way raided across the border provoking punitive expeditions by the Brooke administration (Bala 2002:63).

tered Dutch territory for raiding, they could afterwards retreat over the border without the Dutch being able to follow them. The border was also used by the Sarawak Iban to escape taxes imposed by the Brooke administration. Today, as then, a network of old trails and routes cross the border and connect the two partioned Iban groups (King 1976b:101; Pringle 1970:229). 'Raiding was the order of the day (*Sneltogten waren aan de orde van den dag*)' the Dutch Resident proclaimed in a December 1872 monthly report.[33] Although Iban on the Dutch side were active in raiding, the main Dutch frustration was with the more frequent raids conducted by Sarawak Iban.

In the early years of Dutch presence in the border area, the Dutch used Iban mercenaries on several occasions to suppress Malay and Dayak rebellions elsewhere in their West Borneo territory (Bouman 1924:187). Iban mercenaries were also widely used by the Brookes in Sarawak. The Iban themselves seemed to welcome this opportunity to take part in officially sanctioned punitive expeditions because it gave them the chance to raid and take heads (King 1976b:101). The Dutch quickly abandoned the use of Iban mercenaries, however, because they believed that the practice encouraged more raiding. The Brookes on the other hand choose to continue the practice, as it was much cheaper to use the Iban mercenaries than regular soldiers (Pringle 1970:241). Charles Brooke justified his use of Iban mercenaries by asserting that only Dayaks can kill Dayaks, and that it was better to leave such matters in their hands:

> It is my firm belief that if left to themselves there will be a prompt and lasting settlement brought about, but on the other hand if there is interference from our Governments, inexperienced as they must be concerning the real feelings of the people, there will be an imbroglio which may last for years.[34]

Instead of using local mercenaries, the Dutch erected permanent military posts manned by officers and regular soldiers. One such post was

---

[33] Kort verslag der Residentie Westerafdeeling van Borneo over de maand December 1872. Mailrapport 1873, No. 50. Ministerie van Koloniën, ARA.
[34] Letter to Nederlands-Indie Governor-General s'Jacob from Rajah Brooke, 25-9-1882, Sarawak, in Letter to Charles Brooke from Nederlands-Indie Governor-General s'Jacob, 31-10-1882 (Buitenzorg). Mailrapport 1882, No. 1066. Ministerie van Koloniën, ARA [TransRW].

established close to the border in Nanga Badau.[35] According to an 1880 report to Commandant van hot Leger from the Pontianak regional Military Commandant Tersteeg, the military force stationed at the Nanga Badau border post consisted of the following: one first lieutenant as commander, one second lieutenant or adjutant (*onderofficier*), one European Fourier, two European sergeants, two native sergeants (*inlandsche*), one European corporal, two native corporals, ten European fusiliers, 40 native fusiliers, and one European corpsman. The main aims of this border patrol were, according to the commandant, to provide protection to the Resident on his expeditions among the Batang Lupars, to force the submission of hostile Batang Lupars, and to retrieve severed heads.[36] But as mentioned by Resident Kater, the Nanga Badau military post was not only to protect 'our citizens (*onze bevolking*)', but also to see that the border was respected and to keep 'our Batang Lupars' (*onze Batang Loepars*) from headhunting.[37] The stationed soldiers consequently began patrolling the border on a regular basis, a strategy that turned out to be more effective than the former use of mercenaries (Niclou 1887:51).

Not particularly pleased with a large Dutch military presence on the border with Sarawak, Brooke wrote several letters to the Dutch Governor General complaining that he doubted the effectiveness of such a show of force (*machtsvertoon*) and was not entirely clear about its main purpose. As a subtle warning, Brooke stated that such a heavily armed border patrol: 'might also be considered somewhat as a menace to the state of Sarawak'.[38]

The different approaches in dealing with Iban cross-border raids resulted in several controversies between the two colonial administrations, and they usually ended up giving each other the blame for the continuing cross-border raiding (Pringle 1970:217-8). The Dutch were particularly agitated by the continuous violation of the border and acts of indiscriminate headhunting (*koppensnellen*), which they blamed on the Brooke administration's alleged lack of control over its undisciplined

---

[35] The Dutch also established smaller native posts staffed by government-paid Malays. One such post was established in the Ulu Leboyan at Jejawe.
[36] Report to Kommandant van het Leger N.I. from Militaire Kommandant Tersteeg, 30-1-1880, Pontianak. Mailrapport 1880, No. 196. Ministerie van Koloniën, ARA.
[37] Letter to Nederlands-Indie Governor-General s'Jacob from Resident Kater, 6-3-1880. Mailrapport 1880, No. 250. Ministerie van Koloniën, ARA.
[38] Letter to Nederlands-Indie Governor-General s'Jacob from Charles Brooke, 25-9-1882, Mailrapport No. 1066, Ministerie van Koloniën, ARA.

3 *Evading state authority*

Iban mercenaries and wider Iban citizenry (Kater 1883).³⁹ Meanwhile, the Brookes blamed the Dutch for being too lenient in their handling of the Iban (Pringle 1970:218). In 1882, Charles Brooke, the second ruler of Sarawak, actually offered to take the Kalimantan Iban under his firm control and suggested that it would −

> lead to a more settled state of affairs if the whole tribe of Batang Lupar Dyaks, some of whom are living in Kapuas waters, were put under the control and direction of the Sarawak Government − even if a certain portion of the land adjoining the frontier where these Dyaks are located were transferred to the Sarawak rule ... it is not my wish to seek for enlargement of territory, or gain of any kind. ⁴⁰

The Brooke administration emphasized that, with the exception of this specific part of the border (inhabited by the border Iban), the rest of Sarawak was in a state of peace, advancement, and prosperity. The Dutch Governor General bluntly rejected Brooke's suggestion, as he did not see the advantage of such a solution. He believed instead that the best means to solve the Batang Lupar question was cooperation between governments.

The cross-border raids peaked in the late nineteenth century. The Dutch attempted to pacify the rebel Iban by sending military expeditions up the Leboyan River, but without much success, as the Iban again used the strategy of escaping across the border where the Dutch could not follow them. These military expeditions were not only an attempt to stop cross-border raids; the inter-ethnic feuding between the Iban and their neighbours the Maloh and Kantu was also of great Dutch concern. Prevention of Iban raiding of the more peaceful Maloh communities was given especially high priority.⁴¹ The strategy of criss-crossing the border used by Iban settled on both sides later triggered what was to be known as the Kedang Expedition (Niclou 1887:60-7).⁴² A Dutch official in 1885 wrote:

---

39   In the period between 1870 and 1890 there was an intensive mail exchange between the Dutch and Brooke.
40   Letter to Nederlands-Indie Governor-General s'Jacob from Charles Brooke, 25-9-1882, Mailrapport No. 1066. Ministerie van Koloniën, ARA [TransRW].
41   See, for example, Mailrapport 1882 No. 720. Letter to Nederlands-Indie Governor-General from Resident van Zutphen, 25-6-1882. Ministerie van Koloniën, ARA.
42   The Kedang Range runs along the part of the border inhabited by the Iban.

> The Rajah of Sarawak, C. Brooke, suggested starting an extermination-war (*verdelelgings-oorlog*) against the rebellious Batang-Loepars as he does not regard it possible to find a peaceful solution (*vredelievenden weg*) to the conflict (*geschillen*) with the Batang-Loepars at the border along our area (*ons gebied*). The war should be started by us (Dutch), by Sarawak or together, though in the last case it should not be simultaneously, but at different periods (Niclou 1887:29).[43]

The Iban name for the expedition was *Serang Rata*, meaning 'the attack that struck everywhere' (Wadley 2004:609). Charles Brooke described the borderland situation leading up to the expedition as follows: 'The Kedang Range is supposed and is practically the boundary line, as near as can be roughly estimated, and the Dayaks living on it drink both Sarawak and Kapuas waters' (Pringle 1970:218).

Although the Dutch did not agree on the approaches used by the Brookes, in 1886 they allowed a Brooke military expedition to cross the border in the Kedang hills to punish rebellious Iban in certain specified areas.[44] With a force of 10,000 to 12,000 men consisting of Iban loyal to the Brooke administration, the expedition burned down around 80 longhouses on both sides of the border, 41 of which were located in Dutch territory. The Dutch were very unsatisfied with the manner in which the expedition was carried out, especially the rampant raiding and looting conducted by the Iban mercenaries and their attacks on several Iban longhouses that the Dutch regarded as friendly. Based on oral accounts from contemporary Iban, Wadley, for example, describes how longhouses were systematically plundered and destroyed. The period up to and after the expedition made such a large impact on people's lives that it was referred to as the 'time of war' (*musim kayau*) (Wadley 2004:622-8).

In the period after the expedition, in an attempt to handle the Iban problem, the Dutch created a new district (*Onderafdeeling Batang-Loeparlanden*) in the borderland, where they permanently stationed a Dutch district officer (*controleur*). They further increased the number of soldiers at the border post in Nanga Badau. Iban leaders on both sides

---

[43] See also Mailrappport 1885, No. 664. Letter to Nederlands-Indie Governor-General from C&M Authority Haga, 5-10-1885. Ministerie van Koloniën, ARA.
[44] Mailrapport 1886, No. 293. Letter to Nederlands-Indie Governor-General from Resident Gijsberts, 18-4-1886, Pontianak. Ministerie van Koloniën, ARA.

of the border subsequently tendered their submission to the Dutch and the Brookes respectively. The Dutch gave the Iban on their side two conditions for submission. First, they had to pay a fine as a promise to stop raiding and second, all longhouses upriver affected by the expedition had to move away from the border into specific territories further down-river (Wadley 2001c:634-5).

REBELLION AND PACIFICATION

Where two countries like Sarawak and Netherlands Indian Borneo territory meet, with a thickly afforested and sparsely populated borderline, the difficulty of arresting criminals [referring to border inhabitants] before they have had time to pass into the neighbouring territory is very great, especially in cases where, as in Sarawak proper, the distance to be covered is not very great.... Persons who find it politic to hurriedly shift from one side of the border to the other can hardly be considered as valuable citizens of either State. In the interests of the security of both life and property we shall always be glad to know that mutual accommodation of these matters is practiced to the benefit of peaceable inhabitants and to the discomfort of the criminal classes.[45]

This *Sarawak Gazette* quote from 1895 clearly elucidates the border dilemma as experienced by the two colonial powers concerning their 'unruly' Iban. Along with raiding and migration, the collection of taxes was one of the most frequent reasons for conflict between the Iban and their colonial administrators, the Dutch and the Brooke. The Brooke administration introduced a regular 'door tax' or tax on each Iban family (Pringle 1970:160-4). When the Dutch first arrived in the Iban area, they also imposed taxes, although they did not appear to collect them on a regular basis. Under the Dutch, taxes were raised several times in the effort to pacify the raiding Iban. The Dutch purpose for taxing the Iban is made clear in the following statement by the Dutch Resident Cornelius Kater: 'The Dayak recognizes no authority than that to which he brings taxes (*de Dajaks erkent geen gezag dan dat waaraan hij belasting opbrengt*)' (Kater

[45] Quote from *Sarawak Gazette* (1-10-1895) in Report from Assistant Resident A.A. Burgdorffer, 2-12-1914, Verbaal 20-8-1915 No. 41, Politieke Verslagen en Berichten uit de Buitengewesten van Nederlands-Indië (1898-1940). Ministerie van Koloniën, ARA [TransRW].

1883:3). As both Pringle and Wadley point out, the taxation of the Iban was not just carried out in order to increase government revenue, but to a considerable extent as an attempt to demonstrate authority over the Iban, who were considered especially recalcitrant by the Dutch and British. Furthermore, when the Iban refused to pay taxes they at the same time denied colonial authority and signalled rebellion (Pringle 1970:164; Wadley 2004:615).

In the time after the Kedang Expedition and the following (forced) peace agreement, the raiding seemed to cease, and a short period of stability began, but trouble broke out again a few years later. Bantin, a renowned Iban war-leader from the Delok River, got into a conflict with the Brooke administration by refusing to pay taxes and resettle away from the border.[46] In an 1897 letter to the Dutch resident, Brooke requested that the Dutch prevent their Iban from aiding Bantin, who in preceding years had moved back and forth across the border. In a reply to Brooke's letter the Dutch resident agreed to talk with his Iban citizens about the matter, but also explicitly stated that no Sarawak punitive expedition would be allowed to cross the border:

> However Sir, in the event of your directing a *bala* [large raiding party] to punish the rebels, Your Highness will highly oblige me by strictly forbidding Your Dyaks to pass the frontier, as this would be unnecessary and dangerous. Unnecessary because I dispose of sufficient means to prevent criminals from hiding within our territory, dangerous because of the possible consequences of some misunderstanding easily to be conceived.[47]

Bantin was generally on good terms with the Dutch, and the Dutch ignored Brooke's requests to treat Bantin as an outlaw. The Brooke frustration concerning the Dutch attitude towards Bantin and his followers is clearly outlined in the following statement by a Sarawak official:

> As long as Bantin and his people know that they are not treated as enemies by the Dutch authorities I am convinced they will continue to give trouble to Sarawak Dayaks (Quote in Pringle 1970:230).

---

[46] Bantin was at the time one of the most feared Iban warriors in Sarawak (Pringle 1970:220).
[47] Letter to Resident Tromp from Raja Brooke, 14-8-1897, Kuching. Openbaar Verbaal, 11-8-1898, No. 43. Ministerie van Koloniën, ARA [TransRW].

Additionally, Brooke stated in a letter dated 12 April 1903 to the Dutch Resident de Neve in West Borneo:

> Bantin seems to have no power, if indeed, he has the wish to do so, to prevent his people from making marauding expeditions, and these people rely upon their vicinity to the frontier for protection and for the necessities of life. They are careful to keep on good terms with the NI government officials, police, and Chinese traders across the border. It is known that Dutch Batang Lupars are involved in Bantin's raids [...]. Pronounce Bantin and his follower's enemies and forbid any Dutch subjects from having any relations with them. They should be declared outlaws and be dealt with severely and any measures taken against them, even to their being attacked, will not call any official notice from me, so long as they continue in the lawless state.[48]

The Dutch Resident de Neve replied to Brooke in a letter dated 29 April 1905:

> Owing to the fact however that Bantin and his followers have never made marauding expeditions nor committed any hostile act on Dutch territory and are even, as Your Highness states, anxious to be on friendly terms with the Netherlands officials, I do not feel justified to declare them outlaws and to attack them by force of arms.

In the same letter, the Resident further asked whether Brooke had any objections 'to Bantin and his own people establishing themselves after submission on Dutch territory under the special control of the Dutch officials'.[49]

In the period 1902 to 1908, the 'criminal acts' of Bantin and his troubled relationship with the Brooke colonial administration was repeatedly mentioned in the Simanggang Monthly Reports of the *Sarawak Gazette*.[50]

---

[48] Letter to Resident de Neve from Raja Brooke, 12-5-1905, Singapore. Behoort in Verb. 17-4-1906 No. 33; Mailrapporten 1904 Nos. 861 and 865; 1905 No. 888. Ministerie van Koloniën, ARA [Trans-RW].

[49] Letter to Raja Brooke from Resident de Neve, 29-4-1905, Pontianak. Behoort in Verb. 17-4-1906 No. 33; Mailrapporten 1904 Nos. 861 and 865; 1905 No. 888. Ministerie van Koloniën, ARA [Trans-RW].

[50] See Simanggang Monthly reports, 1902-09, *Sarawak Gazette*, Sarawak Museum Library (SML).

| At the edges of states

For example, it reported, 'The N. I. Dyaks were fined for disturbing the border and fines were also imposed upon the Ulu Ai and Engkari [Iban]. The Sarawak Dayak refused to pay and in March Bantin attacked Ulu Sremat (below Lubok Antu) killing three Dyaks and wounding two.'[51]

In October 1902 Brooke launched a large force (approximately 12,000 men) of government-friendly Iban against Bantin on his side of the border.[52] Unfortunately, this expedition was severely diminished by disease (cholera) and was repulsed. Several other major expeditions were carried out in 1903,[53] but it was not until 1908 that the Brooke administration managed to subdue the rebels and put a stop to Bantin's raiding in Sarawak territory. Resident D.J.S. Bailey of the Batang Lupar District (Sarawak) notes how he burnt down the house of Bantin and that of several other rebel leaders in a successful September 1908 government expedition against the rebels in the Ulu Ai. A total of 22 longhouses was destroyed.[54] In a statement on the Bantin problem made in July 2008, a few months before the expedition, Resident Bailey asserted,

> I am certain that until these people are dealt with there will be no peace in the Ulu of this river. All the other people are insignificant compared with these notorious head takers – Bantin, Ngumbang, Alam, Rangga [Bantin's son] and others, whose houses are near the border in Ulu Delok, on Bukit Katupong.[55]

Not welcome in Sarawak territories, Bantin fled back and forth across the border, and in 1909 he eventually took refuge and permanently settled in the Ulu Leboyan area with his followers, who numbered approximately eighty families (King 1976b:103; Pringle 1970:220-33).

---

[51] Quote from Simanggang Monthly Report, 3-3-1903, p 51, *Sarawak Gazette*, SML.
[52] Simanggang Monthly report, 3-3-1903, pp 50-1, *Sarawak Gazette*, SML.
[53] 'The Batang Lupar expedition' and 'Report on the Batang Lupar expedition', 1-5-1903, pp 65-7, *Sarawak Gazette*, SML. See also Letters to Nederlands-Indie Governor-General from Resident de Neve, 1903, Pontianak, geheim. Behoort in Verb. 26-8-1906 No. 39; Mailrapporten 1903 Nos. 418 and 567. Politieke Verslagen en Berichten uit de Buitengewesten van Nederlands-Indië, 1898-1940. Ministerie van Koloniën, ARA.
[54] 'Expedition against Dayak rebels in the Batang Lupar', 1-10-1908, pp 244-6, *Sarawak Gazette*, SML. See also Kort verslag over September 1908, Resident van Driessche, 30-10-1908, Pontianak. Behoort in Verb. 7-5-1909 No. 44; Mailrapporten 1908 Nos. 512, 649, 799, 1057, 1319, 1532, 1701, 1849. Ministerie van Koloniën, ARA.
[55] Simanggang Monthly Report, 1-9-1908, p 223, *Sarawak Gazette*, SML.

BORDER OUTLAWS: PERPETUATING SEMI-AUTONOMY

As an informative case of the troubled relationship between the Iban and their colonial masters I will briefly describe the oral accounts of one particular longhouse community, Rumah Manah in the Ulu Leboyan. The leading families of this contemporary Iban community trace their origins back to the warrior Bantin and his followers, just as do many other Iban communities in this part of the border area. The older generation of Rumah Manah still tells stories with great pride about how Bantin and his warriors used the borderland as a starting point and refuge for conducting raids into Sarawak and areas down-river in Dutch territories (Burgemeestre 1934).

Despite the fact that he was on good terms with the Dutch, Bantin's continuing violation of the Dutch prohibition against raiding and the threat of more punitive expeditions by the Brookes caused the Dutch to send troops into the Ulu Leboyan in early 1917 to pacify Bantin. The outcome of this largely peaceful Dutch show of force was the relocation of as many as 300 Iban households down-river away from the border (Bouman 1952:83-4). This movement was carried out under the threat of force, and although no fighting took place, several Iban men were jailed for resistance, weapons and severed heads were confiscated, and longhouses and fields were burned. The Iban were warned that if they did not comply with Dutch authority they would be expelled across the border to Sarawak. After some resistance, Bantin and his followers took an oath of allegiance to the Dutch and settled permanently along a small stream in the Ulu Leboyan. Bantin died in 1932 and was buried on a hilltop close to of the Rumah Manah longhouse, as was the custom for war heroes (*urang berani*) (King 1976b:104-5).

Old longhouse settlements (*tembawai*) have since been abandoned in favour of locations closer to the Leboyan River, the main artery of transport at the time. The families of these old longhouse settlements have since erected several 'new' longhouses in the Ulu Leboyan area, Rumah Manah being one. Although partly covered by secondary forest and old growth fruit gardens, old settlements close to the border still play a crucial role in the local imagination of a glorious past with brave warriors and fierce battles. The people in the Ulu Leboyan still remember the names of many brave men such as Ngumbang, Asan, Ajun, Emba, Enjak, Simpai and Belaiung, to mention a few. Every *bilik* member in

Rumah Manah, young or old, is very conscious of his or her roots of origin. During an interview, one of the junior members of the longhouse, Ningkan aged 14, proudly told me about his famous descendant: 'My family descends from brave people (*Keluarga saya adalah keturunan orang berani*)'.

The cultural landscape is very rich with stories about Iban and Dutch confrontations. When I accompanied locals on trips around the area, they constantly pointed out to me locations of fierce battles and strongholds against the Dutch and the Brookes. The landscape of the Ulu Leboyan is spattered with locations of confrontation from Iban rebellions in the late nineteenth and early twentieth century. These locations have become symbols of how the Iban courageously fought the Dutch and Brooke colonial regimes. An example of such a location is a large flat rock where many of the former Iban settlements were located. The people of Rumah Manah call this rock *Batu Bangkai* (literally the stone of corpses), referring to the fierce fighting that took place in the 1870s and 1880s between the Iban and the Dutch on that location (Niclou 1887:50). Nearly all Dutch reports on 'the Batang Lupar issue' from that period mention the Iban communities at Batu Bangkai as especially resistant towards colonial authority. The Dutch Resident Kater mentioned how the isolated and almost inaccessible Batu Bangkai 'gradually became a hide-out for all with whom we had a score to settle (*rekening hadden te vereffenen*)' (Kater 1883:10).

In 1879, patrol Commandant Lieutenant Schultze reported on a military expedition up the Leboyan River accompanied by an attachment of 55 men. Arriving at Batu Bankai, an Iban stronghold, he sent emissaries to the Iban in order to seek their surrender and arrange for their resettlement away from the border. Not receiving any response from the Iban, Schultze decided to burn down two longhouses and destroy fruit gardens and swiddens. Nothing was spared (*Van dezen werd overigens niets bespaard*).[56] In a letter dated 7 June 1880 to the Dutch Resident Kater, Brooke stated the importance of ruthlessly subduing rebellious Iban along the border. This was specifically directed towards those rebel Iban at Batu Bangkai, who were particularly hostile outside the control of colonial power. He further claimed that these Iban were

---

[56] Report of Patrouille Kommandant 1st Lt. Schultze, 24-9 to 28-11-1879, 15-12-1879. Mailrapport 1880, No. 196. Report to the Kommandant van het Leger N.I. from Militaire Kommandant Tersteeg, 30-1-1880, Pontianak. Ministerie van Koloniën, ARA.

so savage and inaccessible that peace, even among themselves, was hopeless.[57]

Bantin and his group of followers were not the only Iban rebels from Sarawak to seek refuge in Dutch territories over the border; there are several similar examples (Pringle 1970:216-8). Ever since Bantin and his followers settled down in the Ulu Leboyan in the early twentieth century, when the international border was created, there has been an ongoing movement of people back and forth across the border. According to Dutch figures, the total number of Iban or 'Batang Loepars' living in Dutch Western Borneo territory was approximately 6780 individuals in 1921 (Bouman 1924:192). The inhabitants of the present Rumah Manah are a mixture of the families of the original founders and kin from Sarawak who, over time, have joined the community.

For example, one of the founding fathers of the present Rumah Manah has since immigrated across the border to Sarawak, joining family there. Although resident in Sarawak and now a Malaysian citizen, he still enjoys the inactive rights to large tracts of land around the longhouse of Rumah Manah. According to Iban *adat*, moving away means giving up one's rights to fallow lands, but one still retains rights to fruit and honey trees on such land. However, as noted by Wadley, such relinquished rights are easy to regain by moving back (Wadley 1997b:101). A daughter of this former inhabitant of Rumah Manah has since moved back to the longhouse and claimed the rights of her father's land. Thus, over time, there has been an ongoing shift in and renewal of the Rumah Manah inhabitants, which shows that the community has always been in a stage of flux and taken advantage of cross-border strategies. For the inhabitants of Rumah Manah and other Iban communities in the borderland, this long history of raiding and migration has in several ways affected their outlook on life when dealing with contemporary social, political, and economical processes – an issue I will discuss in more detail later on.

In half a century, from July 1868 to August 1917, Dutch and Brooke forces carried out approximately seventeen documented punitive expeditions against Iban inhabiting the Dutch side of the border. Six of these were directed against communities in the Ulu Leboyan. During this

---

[57] Letter to Resident Kater from Rajah C. Brooke, 7-6-1880, Mailrapport 1880 No. 1030. Letter to Nederlands-Indie Governor-General from Resident Kater, 15-10-1880, Pontianak. Ministerie van Koloniën, ARA.

period, 115 longhouses were destroyed (Wadley 2007:117-9).[58] Dutch efforts to pacify the Iban seemed to have had an effect and but a Dutch colonial officer mentions how the Iban on their side of the border were still restless after the pacification (*de Batang Loepars aan onzen kant der grenz roerig geweest....* (Bouman 1924:187).

Even after pacification of the Iban border communities, the colonial governments treated the Iban with caution in order not to antagonize them. For example, Iban on both sides of the border paid fewer taxes than other native peoples – in Sarawak because they were obligated to serve on government expeditions, and in Dutch West Borneo probably to keep things on a par with Sarawak's practice. Dutch government commissioner A. Prins stated that the Iban should not pay any considerable taxes in order to make it increasingly in the Iban interest to side with the Dutch.[59]

From the 1930s until the Japanese occupation in the 1940s, only sporadic raiding took place in the borderland. Because of World War II, the Dutch left the area in 1942. In addition, the system of Dutch-appointed leaders, *temenggong* and *patih*, became increasingly autonomous over time, particularly during the political transition of the 1940s and 1950s, when the borderland and its population was largely left alone. The short period of Japanese occupation did not greatly affect the lives of the West Kalimantan Iban compared to the devastating effect it had on the coastal population in the province (Heidhues 2003:197-210). In the borderland, the Japanese occupation (*musim Jepun*) was generally associated with a lack of all necessities such as salt and cooking oil and depicted as indeed a difficult time (*masa pemerintahan Jepun susah sekali*).[60] One finds only a few accounts of Kalimantan Iban involvement in fighting against the Japanese, although a large group of local Iban took part in an attack on a Japanese military camp across the border at Engkilili, Sarawak, where they suffered great losses because of Japanese superior weaponry (Lumenta 2005:13-4; Wadley 1997:48). After World War II and the sur-

---

[58] Also back home in the Nederlands, reports of the 'vicious' Batang Lupars in the West Borneo possessions reached local newspapers. For example in March 1912 *Utrechts Nieuwsblad*, a Dutch daily, published an article with the heading 'Headhunters' that depicted how a band of Batang Lupars in November 1911 had beheaded several friendly Dayaks in the Lanjak area and how the culprits had escaped the Dutch military patrol by crossing the border to Sarawak.
[59] Letter to Nederlands-Indie Governor-General from Gen. Sec. and Govt. Com. Prins, 19-5-1856, Openbaar Verbaal, 22-9-1857 No. 9. Ministerie van Koloniën, ARA.
[60] Personal interviews, Lanjak, 3-3-2007.

render of the Japanese, the Dutch once more tried to regain control of the Indonesian islands. The last mention of the Iban border communities in the colonial archives appeared in a small note in 1947 mentioning how a military patrol was sent out to the *Batang Loepar-landen* in response to a rumour about an Iban headhunting trip planned along the border.[61] Confronted with widespread Indonesian nationalism, the Dutch formally withdrew from the province in 1949. The Indonesian struggle for independence subsequently resulted in the creation of an Indonesian State. In 1953, the Indonesians took control of West Kalimantan and created their own government administration, and in January 1957, the region received provincial status (Layang 2006).

Many scholars have portrayed borderlands as being outside state influence and as zones of anarchy where identities are flexible, loyalties ephemeral, and state authority largely evaded. Depicted by state administrators as outlaws and rebels roaming the border hills, the populations inhabiting these peripheral areas of states further seem especially resistant towards officialdom because of their involvement in practices of questionable legality and their apparently heightened sense of autonomy. As 'non-state spaces', the stretch of the Dutch West Borneo-Sarawak border inhabited by the Iban in many ways resembles what Scott has termed 'the last enclosure'. Zones of refuge in which state authorities are relatively weak and populations openly resistant to state political and administrative pacification and standardization (Scott 2008, 2009).

For many border people, these borders were and still are as much a basis of opportunity as they are a barrier. By contrasting local narratives with colonial records in the border regency of *Boven-Kapoeas* in Dutch West Borneo in the mid-nineteenth century, I have shown how regionally renowned rebel leaders did their best to take advantage of the differing terms and conditions that colonial rule offered on either side of the border and as a result openly challenged colonial authority. The border-dwelling Iban became increasingly accustomed to considerable autonomy in dealing with local matters and have not hesitated to challenge attempts to reduce that autonomy. A late nineteenth-century Dutch official referred to them as '*een levendig en strijdlustig volk* (a lively and

---

[61] Algemeen Overzicht, Res. West-Borneo, 1-15-4-1947. Geheim Mailrapport 1947, No. 1160. Rapportage Indonesië 1945-50. Ministerie van Koloniën, ARA.

| *At the edges of states*

pugnacious people)'.[62] Although one should be cautious about drawing overly simplified conclusions like this one, it does account for a certain cultural vitality and confidence that has been fostered, in no small part, by the unique relationship the Iban on both sides of the border have crafted with changing governments over the past century and a half. Not coincidentally the Iban-inhabited stretch of the border between Dutch West Borneo and British Sarawak produced the most continuous border tensions between those colonial powers in the nineteenth and early twentieth centuries. The Iban were demonstrably difficult to contain and pacify.[63]

Rebel defiance of colonial power and accompanying border tension convinced colonial administrators that they needed to impose strict control among the Iban-inhabited stretch of the Dutch West Borneo-Sarawak border. One could argue that the numerous Iban rebellions and consequent Dutch attempts to establish law and order largely contributed to the territorial demarcation of the colonial state and later Indonesian state. Accompanying punitive military expeditions and administrative pacification of the rebel Iban thus significantly contributed to the strengthening of the border and larger processes of state formation. Hence, the struggle with the Iban rebels simultaneously became a struggle over territorial borders. As Gallant concluded, 'Boundaries took on concrete form in space through the interactions between border guards and bandits who seized upon the jurisdictional ambiguity of these liminal zones as cover for their depredations' (Gallant 1999:40). Despite the determined efforts of the colonial state, the Iban were not easily subdued; they remained largely autonomous in dealing with local affairs and continued their ambivalent relationship with state authorities in post-colonial Indonesia.

---

[62] Letter to Nederlands-Indie Governor-General from Resident Tromp, 10-6-1891, Openbaar Verbaal, 12-6-1894 No. 13. Ministerie van Koloniën, ARA.
[63] Letter to Nederlands-Indie Governor-General from Resident Tromp, 4-4-1894, Openbaar Verbaal, 6-6-1895 No. 12. Ministerie van Koloniën, ARA.

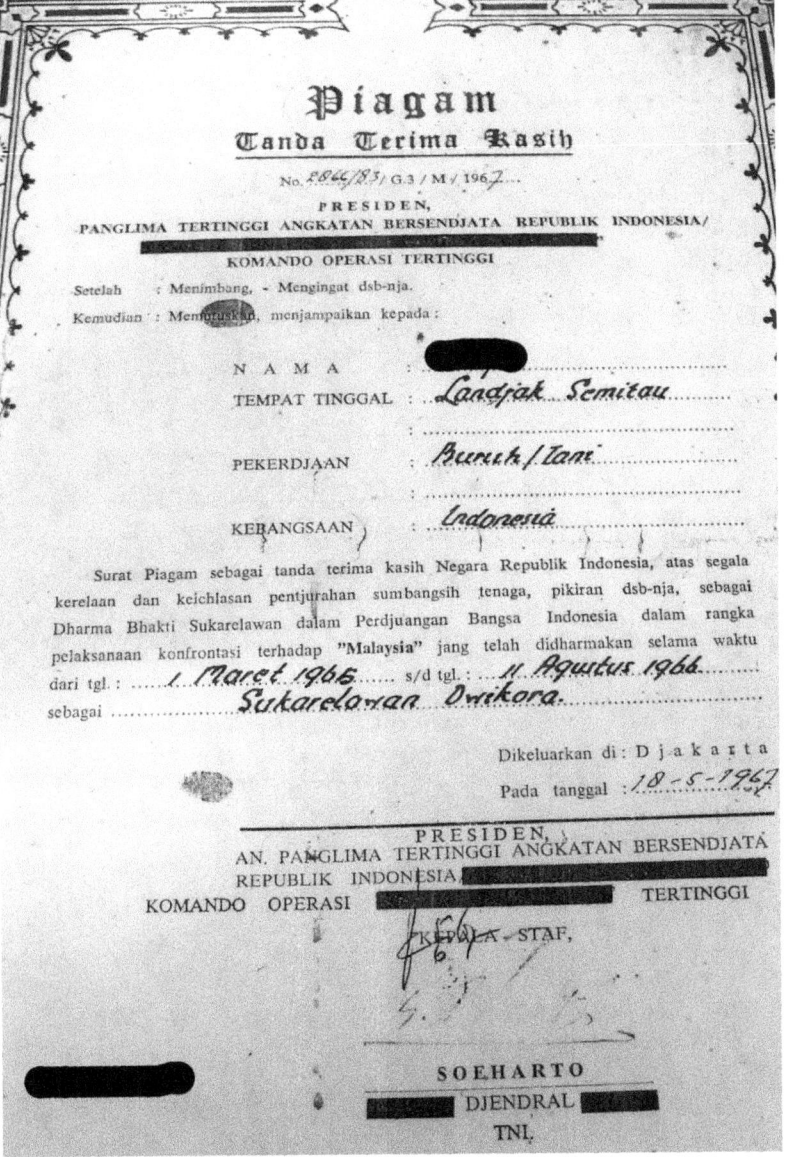

Fig 20: Military certificate issued to an Iban volunteer signed by General Soeharto, 1967 (Photograph by author)

Fig 21: Military certificate from Battalion Infantry 327 Braddjawidjaja thanking Iban leader for his help during the anti-insurgency, 1974 (Photograph by author)

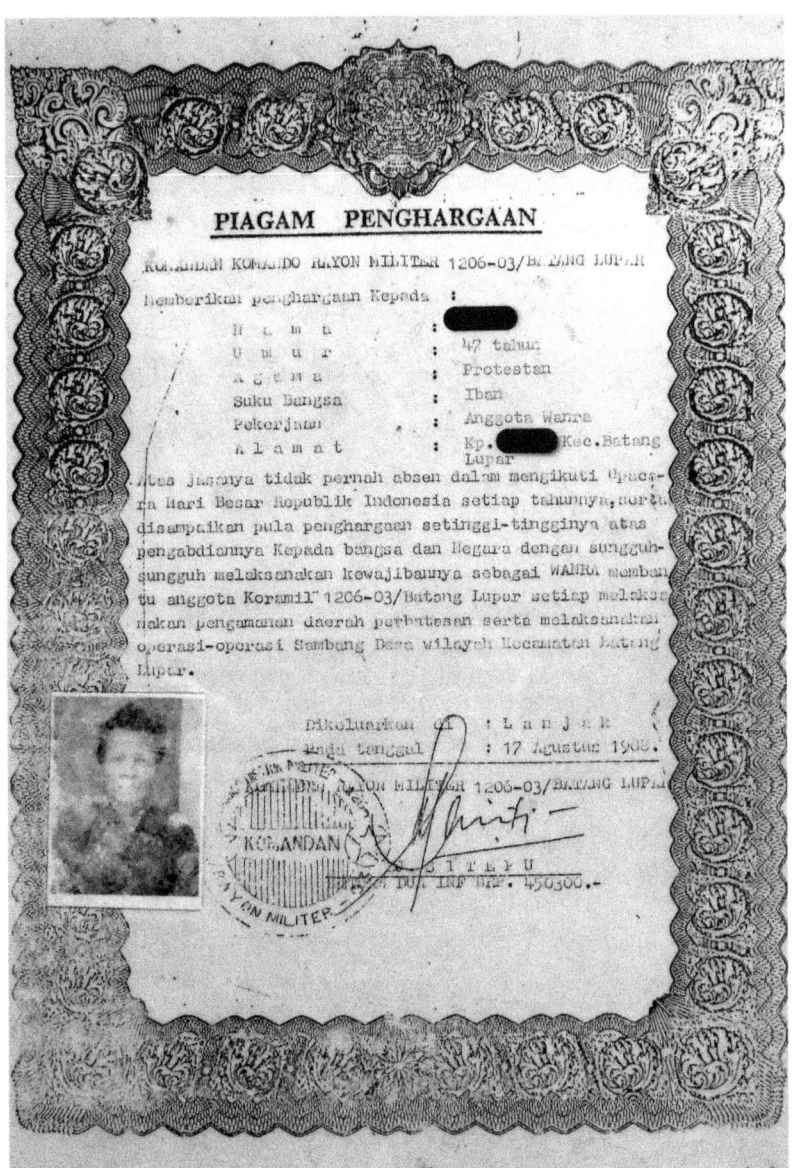

Fig 22: Military certificate to Iban WANRA 'volunteer', 1988 (Photograph by author)

MARKAS DAERAH PERTAHANAN SIPIL XII
KALIMANTAN BARAT

JALAN CEMARA NO. 1   TELEPON NO. 675.

Mengingat : 1. U.U.D. 1945 ;

2. Surat Keputusan Presiden R.I.No.132 tahun 1967 tanggal 9 Nopember 1976, tentang pokok-pokok Organisasi dan Prosedure bidang Pertahanan/Keamanan yang disempurnakan dengan Surat Keputusan Nomor.79 tahun 1969 tanggal 4 Oktober 1969 ;

3. Surat Keputusan Menteri Pertahanan/Keamanan No.Kep/A-/323/1967 tanggal 9 Nopember 1967, tentang penyempurnaan Organisasi Pertahanan Sipil ;

4. Surat Keputusan Presiden R.I.Nomor.56 tahun 1972 tentang pelimpahan Pembinaan Organisasi Pertahanan Sipil dari Menteri Pertahanan/Keamanan kepada Menteri Dalam Negeri ;

5. Instruksi bersama Menhankam/Pangab dan Mendagri No.Instruksi/B/34/VIII/1973 No.18 tahun 1973, tentang pelimpahan Organisasi Pertahanan Sipil dari Departemen Hankam kepada Departemen Dalam Negeri ;

MEMUTUSKAN

Menetapkan :

Pertama : Memberikan honorarium bulanan kepada :

DAN TON Hansip Kampung ████ ████, Kecamatan Batang Lupar, Kabupaten Kapuas Hulu, karena jasa-2nya membantu ABRI dalam rangka menumpas PGRS/PARAKU/Komunis didaerah perbatasan Kalimantan Barat dan Serawak(Malaysia Timur) ;

Kedua : Honorarium setiap bulannya sebesar Rp.3.500,-(tiga ribu lima ratus rupiah)ditambah dengan beras 25(dua puluh lima) kg.

Ketiga : Pengeluaran yang berhubungan dengan Surat Keputusan ini dibebankan kepada Mada Hansip XII Kalimantan Barat atas Pos Bantuan Umum biaya Routine.

Keempat : Dengan ketentuan bilamana terdapat kekeliruan dalam Surat Keputusan ini akan diadakan peninjauan dan pembetulan seperlunya.

Kelima : Surat Keputusan ini mulai berlaku pada tanggal 1 Juli 1976.

Keenam : Kutipan Surat Keputusan ini disampaikan kepada yang bersangkutan untuk diketahui dan seperlunya.

Dikeluarkan di- : PONTIANAK.
Pada tanggal : 29 AGUSTUS 1976.-

TEMBUSAN:Kepada Yth.
1. MENDAGRI CQ.DIRJEN SOSPOL DI JKT.
2. KAPUSCADHAS DI JKT.
3. PANGKOWILHAN I SUM/KALBAR DI MDN.
4. GUBERNUR KDH.TK.I.KALBAR.
5. PANGDAM XII/TJPR.
6. KADAPOL XI/KALBAR.
7. KEJAKSAAN TINGGI KALBAR.
8. DAN SIGNAL DI PTK.
9. DAN LANU SUPADIO DI PTK.
10. BUPATI/WALIKOTA KDH/KA MARES HANSIP 1201 S/D 1207.

Fig 23: Monthly honorarium to Iban member of civil defence unit, 1976 (Photograph by author)

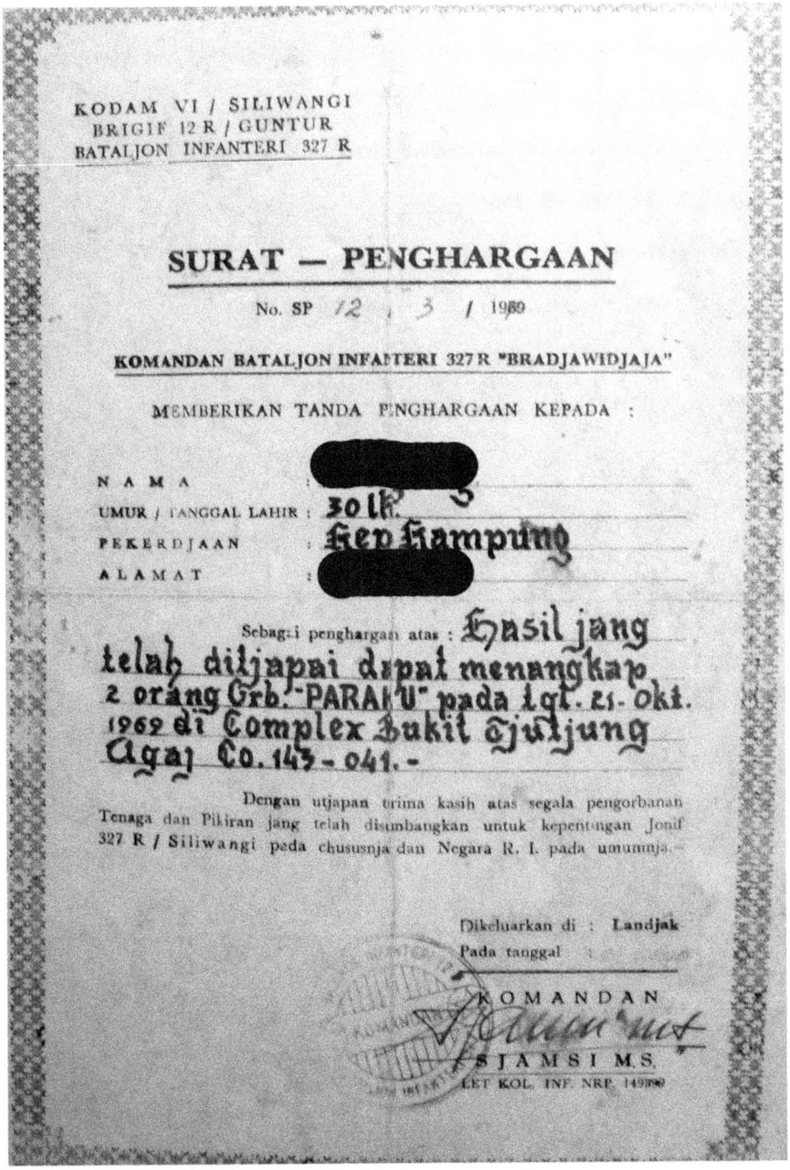

KODAM VI / SILIWANGI
BRIGIF 12 R / GUNTUR
BATALJON INFANTERI 327 R

SURAT — PENGHARGAAN

No. SP 12 / 3 / 1969

KOMANDAN BATALJON INFANTERI 327 R "BRADJAWIDJAJA"

MEMBERIKAN TANDA PENGHARGAAN KEPADA :

николаNAMA : ▓▓▓▓▓▓
UMUR / TANGGAL LAHIR : 30 th
PEKERDJAAN : Kep Kampung
ALAMAT : ▓▓▓▓▓▓

Sebagai penghargaan atas : Hasil jang telah ditjapai dapat menangkap 2 orang Grb. "PARAKU" pada tgl. 21- Okt. 1969 di Complex Bukit Tjutjung Agaj Co. 145-041.-

Dengan utjapan terima kasih atas segala pengorbanan Tenaga dan Pikiran jang telah disumbangkan untuk kepentingan Jonif 327 R / Siliwangi peda chususnja dan Negara R. I. pada umumnja.

Dikeluarkan di : Landjak
Pada tanggal

KOMANDAN

SJAMSI M.S.
LET KOL. INF. NRP. 14959

Fig 24: Letter of honour to Iban leader for his help in apprehending two PARAKU rebels, 1970 (Photograph by author)

```
KOREM 12/TANJUNG PURA
ALAMBANA WANAWWAE
DETASEMEN TEMPUR SWJ-I
----------rz----------
```

SURAT PERNYATAAN/ PERJANJIAN

I. YANG BERTANDA TANGAN DIBAWAH INI :
   N a m a   : ███████
   U m u r   : 30 tahun.
   Bangsa/Suku   : Indonesia/Iban.
   A g a m a   : Animisme.
   Tempat tinggal : Kampung ███ Kecamatan Lanjak Kab.
                     Kapuas Hulu.

II. Dengan ini saya membuat pernyataan dan perjanjian sesuai dengan sumpah Adat dan Kebulatan tekad yang diadakan pada tanggal 11 Oktober 1970 di Kampung Seriang di hadapan Panglima KodamXII/TANJUNG PURA.

III. Bahwa saya benar2 akan mengabdi membantu Pemerintah R.I. setiap saat dimana diperlukan.

IV. Tidak akan membantu gerombolan Paraku dengan dalih apapun.

V. Bila mana ternyata perjanjian saya ini tidak ditaati/di langgar maka saya bersedia dituntut dengan dasar hukum yang berlaku.

VI. Demikian Surat Perjanjian ini saya buat dengan sadar/tidak ada paksaan apapun.

MENGETAHUI
KOMANDAN
b.
PASI-I DEN PUR SWJ-I

M A R T O N O
LETDA INF NRP 333480.-

DIBUAT DI : L A N J A K.
PADA TGL : 15 - 12-1972

YANG BERJANJI.

Fig 25: Letter of loyalty to the Indonesian government signed by Iban leader, Lanjak 1972 (Photograph by author)

4

Guerrilla warfare and resource extraction

Post-independence ethnic minorities inhabiting the Southeast Asian borderlands were willingly or unwillingly pulled into the macro politics of territoriality and state formation. The rugged and hilly borderlands delimiting the new nation-states became spaces of confrontation between divergent political ideologies. In the majority of the Southeast Asian borderlands, this implied catastrophic disruption in the lives of borderlanders that came to affect their relationship to their nation-state.

The politically muddled and wrenching processes of nation-building that took place along Indonesia's longest land border in the 1960s and 1970s provide a vivid example of the ambivalent relationship between ethnic minorities, like the Iban, and the central Indonesian state. This is particularly so with respect to the deep anxiety concerning ethnic minorities' susceptability to Communist infiltration. This government anxiety created an often strained and violent relationship. The idea that 'backward' ethnic minorities were especially prone to Communist influence and subsequent engagement in subversive acts of insurgency against pro-Western governments was a general fear among Western powers and allied states throughout Southeast Asia (CIA Intelligence Report 1970, 1973). Here borderlands often became key battlefields in preventing the spread of communism and 'saving' Southeast Asia from falling into the hands of communist regimes.

One aim of this chapter is to unravel the little-known history of how the Iban segment of the Indonesian border population became entangled in the highly militarized international disputes with neighbouring Malaysia in the early 1960s and in subsequent military cooperative 'anti-communist' 'counter-insurgency' efforts by the two states in the late 1960s and 1970s. What follows brings together facets of national belonging and citizenship within the borderland context largely based on local narratives.

Throughout the highly authoritarian New Order regime of President Soeharto (1965-1998), the fight against the perceived Communist threat impinging on its national border, on the island of Borneo, was popularly portrayed as a grand success that induced great national pride. State rhetoric stressed how stern military actions effectively subdued and drove out the Communist insurgents from their hideouts in the hilly, heavily forested borderlands. These military deeds were supposedly executed with the support of the 'patriotic' borderland populations. While such state rhetoric played an important role in maintaining the idea of the Unitary State of the Republic of Indonesia (NKRI), local narratives tell a rather different and less flattering story of state violence and broken promises of development assistance.

Another purpose of the chapter is to show how today's border elite power base and its networks of influence were, in many ways, established in the early 1960s, when the borderland was plunged into armed conflict with the newly established federation of Malaysia. Much has been written about this period of militarization as it unfolded in the lower and middle part of the West Kalimantan province and how it affected ethnic Chinese communities, but there is a general lack of research on how this violent period affected the communities further inland along the border in districts like Kapuas Hulu.

KONFRONTASI: STATE MAKING ON THE BORDER

The early period of Indonesian state formation and nationalism went largely unnoticed in the remote borderlands until the early 1960s, when the Malaysian Federation, protected by its former colonial masters, the British, was is the process of being established (Jones 2002; Mackie 1974; Subritzky 2000). The Malay Peninsula became independent in 1957 as the Federation of Malaya. Subsequently, in 1961, the Malayan Prime Minister suggested an enlargement of the federation to include Singapore, Sarawak, British North Borneo, (the current Sabah) and Brunei.[1]

[1] Singapore and Brunei decided not to become part of the federation and instead created their own independent states.

Political turmoil and the spread of communism in the region greatly induced the former British colonizers to maintain their authority in the region, by giving strategic support to a Malay pro-Western federation. At that time, the new Indonesian republic, under the leadership of President Soekarno, reacted strongly towards this suggestion of creating a Malaysian nation-state, which from the Indonesian side was seen as no less than a neo-imperialistic threat to its interests in the region. Soekarno had a vision of a united Borneo under the administration of Indonesia and believed that the formation of a Malaysian federation was a British attempt to shore up its power base in the region, which Soekarno termed the *Nekolim* (neo-colonialists-imperialist) threat (Easter 2005).

In an attempt to undermine the hatchling Malay Federation before it could develop, Soekarno's left-wing government gave its support to a leftist militant group, the North Kalimantan National Army (TNKU) by providing training and arms.[2] The TNKU was formed from the remnants of a 1962-failed rebellion against the British-protected Sultanate of Brunei and the British Crown Colonies of Sarawak and North Borneo. One should keep in mind that there is no one standard view of the motivations behind Soekarno's confrontational policy. His military served a range of ideological, strategic and political purposes. Several scholars for example explore Soekarno's ambition to see that Indonesia take control of the region and assume leadership of an alliance including Malaya, the Philippines and Indonesia to be known as 'Maphilindo', as one such motivation. A strong British presence in the region was seen as a major impediment to the creation of Maphilindo (Gregorian 1991). Others mention that the domestic power struggle going on at the time led to Soekarno's allegations of neocolonialism as a smokescreen for engaging the military in the conflict, thereby keeping it occupied (Sodhy 1988).

Under the heading 'Mission: Liberation – Armed Indonesians on the march', *The Borneo Bulletin,* a Brunei weekly newspaper, published a front-page story 26 May 1962. The story described how Sarawak tribesmen had seen about 1000 men trekking through the jungle towards the Indonesian border. According to the newspaper, these men, a mix of Malay, Iban and other 'races', were on the way to Kalimantan to be trained for an Indonesian-led Borneo 'Liberation Army', which would

---

[2] For a detailed account of the TNKU and the Brunei rebellion, see Mackie 1974.

| *At the edges of states*

return to 'liberate' the three states of Brunei, Sarawak and British North Borneo (Sabah) from the Sultan and the British colonizers (Brackman 1966:140; Majid 2007:76-7). A few months later, on 8 December 1962, an armed uprising broke out in the British-protected Sultanate of Brunei and in several nearby towns of the British Crown Colonies of Sarawak and North Borneo (Mackie 1974:117).[3] The armed revolt was a result of a long conflict between the Brunei left-wing party named Ra'ayat (People's Party) and the government (the Sultanate and the British), and it later came to be known as the Brunei Rebellion.[4] The Ra'ayat opposed the British idea of creating a Malaysian State and preferred that the federation cede Sarawak and its eastern neighbour Sabah. The Ra'ayat Party drew its inspiration from Soekarno's Indonesia, and they wanted to unite all Borneo territories and form their own independent state – the North Kalimantan Unitary State (Negara Kesatuan Kalimantan Utara, or NKKU) (Stockwell 2004). At the onset of the rebellion, the British military command in Singapore quickly dispatched a few thousand troops to fight the rebels in Brunei and the neighbouring Crown Colonies. The troops were a mixture of British Commandos and Gurkhas (Harold and Sheil-Small 1971). The uprising was led and organized by a group of hard core insurgents who had military training from West Kalimantan (Fujio 2005). Despite its strong local support, the rebellion was badly planned, and the British soldiers defeated the rebels in two weeks. However, one group of rebels escaped and retreated to the border area between Sarawak and Kalimantan, where they initiated guerrilla warfare against Malaysian soldiers and mixed brigades of British, Australian and New Zealand Commonwealth troops (Dennis and Grey 1996; Pugsley 2003). In 1964 as many as 30,000 British soldiers were reportedly employed in this undeclared war, one of the largest British military operation since World War II (Tuck 2004:93).[5]

Under the pretext of supporting the TNKU's armed struggle against

---

3   In 1946, Sarawak became a British crown colony.
4   The leader of the rebellion was a Brunei politician, A.M. Azahari, who was originally educated in Indonesia where he also was active in the Indonesia independence struggle against the Dutch (Stockwell 2004:793).
5   In the years leading up to the British military involvement on the Indonesian border the British government was reluctant to apply direct military force. They thought that military involvement should be a last resort in order to maintain diplomatic and commercial relations with Indonesia. However, as the Indonesians were not 'up for compromise', the only solution envisioned was to bring Indonesia to its 'knees by a prolonged process of attrition'. See 'Cabinet: Policy towards Indonesia', 6-1-1964, Cabinet papers CP (64) 5, British National Archives, Kew, Richmond, Surrey.

the creation of a Malaysian federation, President Soekarno's left-wing government dispatched Indonesian volunteers (*dwikora sukarelawan*) to help. The term *dwikora* (Dwi Komando Rakyat/People's Twin Commands) became the slogan for this anti-Malaysia campaign, encouraging the engagement of the 'people' in the fight. The volunteers were recruited among local Indonesians supportive of the cause, especially among those with sympathy to the Indonesian Communist Party (PKI). Many of these were ethnic Chinese and Javanese, although Iban and other Dayaks from both sides of the border were also recruited (Porritt 2004:89).[6] A man from Lanjak tells how he was recruited to the TNKU in 1963:

> In 1960, I went abroad (*merantau*) to Sarawak, tapping rubber. Then a few years later the dispute between Indonesia and Malaysia broke out and because I am Indonesian I was detained in Semanggang for one month and repatriated across the border together with 130 other Indonesians. Across the border, we were quickly approached by the RPKAD (Resimen Para Komando Angkatan Darat, Army Para-Commando Regiment),[7] who asked if we wanted to be volunteers (*sukarelawan*) of the TNKU. They said now you must register. I kept quiet but those of us who were young and fresh were chosen anyway... for three months we were trained by the RPKAD and a lieutenant from Battalion 642/Tanjungpura in handling weapons. Afterwards we marched to Hulu Kantuk with soldiers from Battalion 305 Siliwangi [Sundanese from West Java] from where we went into the jungle and attacked targets on the Malaysian side like at Batu Lintang [Sarawak].[8]

Another border inhabitant 'persuaded' by the RPKAD to join the TNKU as a volunteer recollected:

> I told them that I was illiterate (*buta*). They [the RPKAD] said 'we don't care whether you are illiterate as long as you can be trained to shoot a weapon and hide from the enemy (*berlatih nembak berlatih menghilang*). This doesn't need advanced education. The most important thing is that you

---

[6] On the Malaysian side, these volunteers went under the less flattering name of Indonesian Border Terrorists or IBTs (Harold and Sheil-Small 1971:60).
[7] A Special Forces unit locally known as the Red Berets (Berat Merah) that later evolved into the notorious Kopassus elite force.
[8] Personal interview, ex-TNKU, Lanjak, 23-7-2007.

can shoot.' After being trained in Hulu Kantuk [Empanang subdistrict] together with Malaysian volunteers [Sarawak and Kalimantan Chinese] we went to the border. We were 45 persons, 25 were given weapons, and the other 20 just had grenades. Our first battle was at the Setikung River; here we were attacked by Ghurkhas and many of us died, as we didn't know how to engage in combat (*belum tahu perang*).[9]

In reality, the main actors on the Indonesian side of the border in this undeclared war were Indonesian volunteers, members of the **TNKU** and Indonesian army troops. Two companies from the **RPKAD** Battalion 2 were deployed to West Kalimantan in 1963, one in Nanga Badau and one in Senaning. They were employed to stage raids into Sarawak together with the TNKU. However, the raids could not be staged as a regular Indonesian military campaign and were therefore disguised behind the TNKU banner (see Conboy 2003:96). Besides the RPKAD brigades, units from the Marine Commandos (Korps Komando Operasi, **KKO**) Air Force Paratroops/Fast Mobile Force (Pasukan Gerah Tjepat, **PGT**) and the paramilitary Police Mobile Brigade (Brigade Mobil, **BRIMOB**) from the Indonesian National Police also took an active part in the fighting (Pugsley 2003).

Later in 1963, the Indonesian army units together with these volunteers and rebels began making incursions across the West Kalimantan-Sarawak border, as part of Soekarno's 'Crush Malaysia' (*Ganjang Malaysia*) campaign. The first incident is recorded in a Malaysian Government White Paper:

> 12 April 1963. The first series of armed raids in Sarawak took place when a party of some 75 armed men in uniform attacked a police station at Tebedu in Sarawak three miles from the Indonesian border. They killed a corporal and wounded two soldiers. The attackers came from and withdrew to Kalimantan (Indonesian Borneo). They spoke an Indonesian form of Malay Language. A belt left behind by one of them had Indonesian army markings and two envelopes dropped by them were addressed to persons in Pontianak in Indonesian Borneo. Indonesians had previously been inquiring into the strength of the security forces in Tebedu (KPM 1965:1).

---

[9] Personal interview, ex-TNKU, Lanjak, 07-7-2007.

4 Guerrilla warfare and resource extraction

The incursions developed into what is known as the Indonesian-Malaysian Confrontation (*Konfrontasi*) (Brackman 1966; Mackie 1974). Despite initial Indonesian efforts to prevent the new federation, in September 1963 Malaya merged with the Borneo territories and became an independent nation-state, although at this stage it was not formally recognized by Indonesia. Another motive for the Indonesian government's heavy militarization of Kalimantan and stationing of thousands of troops both during the latter part of Konfrontasi and the subsequent Communist uprooting was to subdue regional separatist aspirations. In the late period of Dutch colonialism and just after Indonesian independence, ideas about a pan-Dayak identity were emerging in Kalimantan.[10] For example, in 1945 Iban leaders from both sides of the border met to discuss ideas of separatism and their possible role in an independent Pan-Dayak state (Wadley 1998:82). Moreover, in the 1950s the *bupati* of Kapuas Hulu (1951-1955) was a Dayak called Y.C Oevang Oeray who in 1960 was elected governor of the province. Oevang was one of the main figures in the pan-Dayak movement at the time. He was later removed from his post as governor and replaced by the Military Colonel Soemadi (1967-1972). Until 2008, the province was ruled by a succession of governors with military backgrounds. Jamie S. Davidson gives a detailed discussion of early Dayak elite consolidation (2003a and 2003b).

A TIME OF DISRUPTION: NATIONALIST ASPIRATION AND STATE VIOLENCE

The primary Indonesian tactic during the Confrontation was to carry out small raids into Sarawak, attacking longhouses and terrorizing Iban and other Dayak communities in an attempt to provoke a native rebellion against the new Malaysian Federation.[11] The tactic largely failed because of the nearly complete lack of genuine support among most of the border population (Mackie 1974:212-3; McKeown 1983:103-5).

---

[10] See Davidson 2003b; Peluso and Harwell 2001; Thung et al. 2004.
[11] For a discussion of the effects of the Konfrontasi period on communities elsewhere along the border, see Ishikawa 2010.

6 June 1963. A group of eight Indonesian terrorists raided a village shop and a longhouse in Ensawang near Lubok Antu, the second division of Sarawak. One Iban was killed and one Security forces sergeant was wounded in this incident. The terrorists fled across the border into Indonesian territory (KPM 1965:1).

17 June 1963. A party of 30 border raiders crossed into Sarawak and surrounded a longhouse at Wong Panjoi (near Lubok Antu) but dispersed when a Defence aircraft flew over the area. From subsequent investigations, three of the raiders were recognized as having come from Badau in West Kalimantan, which is a known base for border raiders (KPM 1965:2).

Iban communities on both sides of the border were drawn into the conflict. On the Sarawak side, well-trained Malaysian soldiers assisted by British soldiers, Gurkhas and Australian troops patrolled the border using Iban and other border-dwelling Dayaks as scouts. The Iban were greatly favoured by British army patrols and often employed as trackers known as the 'Border Scouts' (a Dayak vigilante corps). Their reputation as former headhunters and fierce fighters made them valuable allies. As mentioned earlier, the Brookes had often employed Iban for the same purpose. Iban trackers were also brought over from Sarawak to the Malaysian peninsula to help track down Communists during the anti-communist Emergency campaigns in the 1940s.[12] Sarawak Iban were not the only trackers; a large group of Kalimantan Iban from the Lanjak area also joined the fighting. After the end of the Emergency campaign on the Malay Peninsula, most of these men remained in what later became the new Malaysian Federation but retained their cross-border connections.

During the early 1960s, the Malay and Commonwealth troops, with the help of their Border Scouts, carried out numerous 'hot pursuit' operations code-named 'CLARET' across the border.[13] Unofficially, they were permitted by high command to venture 2000 yards into Kalimantan in order to counter the TNKU and Indonesian Army cross-

[12] See Dennis and Grey 1996:259; McMichael 1987:107; Pringle 1970:213.
[13] The CLARET operations were kept secret by the Commonwealth forces even after the end of Confrontation. Afraid that it would strain its relations with Indonesia, Australia, for example, first recognized its involvement in these secret incursions on Indonesian territory as late as 1996 (Forbes 2005).

border incursions, as long as the operations left no traces and were kept off the record. The Commonwealth countries did not want to be accused of violating Indonesian territory (Pugsley 2003). A similar strategy of recruiting local scouts was applied by the Indonesian military across the border in Kalimantan (Dickens 1991; Pirous 2002). Despite the fact that most Kalimantan Iban had no particular interest in the conflict, a group of Iban from the Lanjak area were 'recruited' (by force) as scouts. These unwilling scouts did their uttermost to prevent clashes between the different border patrols, Indonesian and Malaysian.

Former Iban scouts in Lanjak recount how they purposely led the Indonesian military patrols in circles around the Malaysian patrols in order to prevent clashes. In doing so, they avoided being forced to fight Iban kin employed as scouts by the 'enemy'. One very common strategy employed by Iban trackers was to use different kinds of signals to warn the oncoming Iban trackers employed by the enemy. For example, they imitated animal cries or simply wore their caps backward as a signal that regular soldiers were following close behind. The ability of the Iban to cross the border and easily blend with ethnic kin, who were also recruited by the fighting parties, was highly valued. The commanding officer of the Commonwealth forces stationed across the border in Lubok Antu recounts how he employed Kalimantan Iban 'agents' to provide intelligence on the exact location of the Indonesian Army bases in the Badau area. In many instances, the opposing troops were stationed only a few kilometres apart. Malaysian and Commonwealth troops erected army camps in Batu Lintang, Lubok Antu and Jambu across the border in Sarawak just opposite the Indonesian camps (Gurr 1995:106-7).

The Iban (and other Dayaks), trapped between the two sides and feeling no special commitment to fight, tried to protect themselves by betting on both sides in the conflict.[14] During interviews, senior Iban relate how they attempted to appear neutral in the conflict, despite their strong kinship bonds with Iban communities in Sarawak. This bond posed a dilemma as several Iban tribal leaders from the Sarawak border region vocally expressed their anti-communism. For example, in 1963 two ethnic Iban leaders were appointed to strategic positions in Sarawak

---

[14] See Mackie 1974:213; McKeown 1984:105.

politics as chief minister of Sarawak, Stephen Kalong Ningkam,[15] and federal minister of Sarawak affairs, Tun Jugah Anak Barieng. Both these men were strong anti-communists who actively resisted Soekarno's Konfrontasi. Tun Jugah in his role as the principal chief of the Iban in Sarawak was highly respected in Kalimantan where he had close kinship relations. For the Kalimantan Iban, however, it was a wise strategy to avoid openly acknowledging admiration for one's Sarawak kin.

Senior inhabitants of Rumah Manah describe the years of Confrontation as a period of restrictions. The tense situation along the border made contact with relatives across the border difficult and dangerous. For many generations, crossing the border to visit family and to work or trade had been largely unhindered; now suddenly the border was patrolled by military on both sides. Consequently the border was officially 'closed' for several years. Nevertheless, with help from relatives across the border, several inhabitants from Rumah Manah continued their cross-border business throughout the Confrontation, although at considerable risk of being caught in the line of fire. Furthermore, several families took the radical decision to permanently immigrate (*pindah*) and join their Sarawak kin. This was largely done without permission from the Indonesian government. Almost all Iban longhouses I visited during my fieldwork had families who emigrated to Sarawak during the Confrontation. The Iban who moved across the border did not see themselves as running away, but as returning to an area from which their family had migrated a few decades ago. The Iban used the word '*pulai*' to describe this movement, *pulai* being the Iban word for returning home.

A senior Iban, originally from Rumah Manah but today a Malaysian citizen, conveyed during a visit to Kalimantan how after emigrating to Sarawak he was employed by British soldiers to fight the Indonesian army. Ironically, he was later awarded honorary military insignia by the Malaysian state for his courage in the fighting.[16] Iban fighting for the

[15] Stephen Kalong Ningkam was an influential politician and leader of the Sarawak Nationalist Party (SNAP). He was of mixed Iban/Chinese descent and from the Katibas region in Sarawak just opposite the border. He held the position as Chief Minister from 1963 to 1966 and drew his main support among Iban communities in the First and Second Divisons. His younger brother, a police sergeant stationed at the 18th-Mile Police Station along the Kuching-Serian Road, was killed in a 1965 cross-border raid by a group of TNKU guerrillas from Indonesia (Tan 2008:14-6).

[16] See also Christine Padoch, who has noted similar emigration of Kalimantan Iban from the upper Kapuas River into Sarawak during the Confrontation in order to escape harassment by members of the Indonesian military (Padoch 1982:31).

Indonesian army received similar honorary insignia and documents. For example, in Rumah Manah, four men were given medals of bravery (*pala berani*) by the local army commandant, but despite such recognition of their national loyalty, they have all since migrated and settled in Sarawak.

Communities situated close to the border were particularly vulnerable to the fighting. Brigadier Robert Gurr, the commanding officer of a company from the New Zealand Commonwealth forces stationed across the border in the Lubok Antu area (Second Division of Sarawak) reported:

> Those who lived in proximity to the border were sandwiched between hostile forces. Mistaking the identity of groups of Dayaks was always a problem, particular those who ran the gauntlet of border crossing. [...] (Gurr 1995:109).

Several longhouses in the Badau and Lanjak area were hit by mortar fire from the Commonwealth forces, and the Indonesian army relocated entire longhouse communities further away from the border (just as the Dutch had attempted to do a century earlier). Senior inhabitants in the area tell how the heavy British bombing of the Indonesian encampments in the border hills largely prevented locals from going to the forest and harvesting their hill rice. This led to a scarcity of food and subsequent hunger.[17] The military further employed many locals as forced labourers for carrying supplies of rice and ammunition from camp to camp along the hilly front line. Such incidents hardened local sentiments against military and government. As recounted by two senior Iban:

> Soldiers patrolled the border, and as Indonesian citizens, we had to help our forces carry the soldiers' rice, their bullets (*angkut beras angkut peluru*) and other supplies. We suffered deeply (*sangat menderita*); we could not go to our rice fields, could not make gardens, could not do anything.[18]

> Day and night, the British bombs hit our fields at Perayung hills trying to hit the [Indonesian] army dugouts in the hills. Almost 300 bombs

---

[17] For detailed accounts of the numerous clashes between the Indonesian army and Commonwealth troops in the Badau-Lubok Antu area see Gurr 1995:85-102.
[18] Personal interview, Iban *patih*, Lanjak, 23-3-2007.

| *At the edges of states*

were dropped in this area, which made it impossible to clear the land for making fields.[19]

What characterised these years of Confrontation was an unrelenting atmosphere of insecurity. Combatants from each side of the border continuously carried out armed raiding back and forth across the forested boundary line with local communities caught in the middle. While the relationship between the Indonesian military and the border population often were strained and violent, the Commonwealth troops on the opposite side of the border developed a more benign approach to win the 'hearts and minds' of every border community by supplying food provisions and medical services (Smith 1999:7).

OPERATION DESTRUCTION: COUNTERINSURGENCY AND ANTI-COMMUNISM

These low-impact cross-border incursions lasted until 1965, when General (later President, 1967) Soeharto came into power after crushing a failed coup attempt by leftist troops from Soekarno's presidential guard.[20] The new right-wing Soeharto regime quickly began to establish relations with Sarawak and initiated a new strategy of 'peaceful confrontation' (Weinstein 1969). An official ceasefire was agreed upon in early 1966, and a memorandum of understanding was signed in August 1966 in Jakarta. A joint boundary committee was formed with members from both sides. The main purpose was to define the exact borderline between the two countries. A year later, the work of the committee culminated in the signing of the 1967 Basic Agreement between Malaysia and the Republic of Indonesia that formally recognized the border between the two nations. Additional meetings were held in 1972 in Kuala Lumpur and again in 1973 in Jakarta to plan joint survey operations.

The Soeharto regime quickly established a firm military presence in West Kalimantan, including the remote borderlands of Kapuas Hulu.

---

[19] Personal interview, Iban headman, 22-6-2007. See also Pugsley (2003:314-5) on the Commonwealth troop build-up on the Sarawak side of the Perayung hills and their bombing across the border. The hilly borderland is still scored by trenches and littered with unexploded bombs.

[20] The ambiguous manoeuvering behind this coup attempt that later led to the overthrow of President Soekarno is still highly controversial.

4 Guerrilla warfare and resource extraction

Consequently, all Indonesian military support of the TNKU was withdrawn. As stated by a former TNKU veteran living in Lanjak:

> The Malaysian soldiers sent us a letter saying 'we are not looking for war but peace' (*bukan cari peperangan tapi cari damai*). So we went to the border in the Kedang area for a meeting with the Malaysians. Afterwards all the volunteers were called (*dipanggil*) to Semitau, and in 1965 all volunteers were dismissed (*sukuan dinyatakan bubar*). Those who still felt strong went straight into (*teruskan ke tentara*) the army as regular soldiers or joined other groups fighting the Sarawak government. The rest of us were given a letter of passage and could return home.[21]

After Soeharto took power, Indonesian politics altered course, resulting in the launching of an anti-Communist campaign, and an uprooting of what the military labelled 'Communist insurgents' along the border.[22] Subsequently, from the mid-1960s until well into the 1970s, guerrilla warfare took place in the West Kalimantan borderland between Communist guerrillas (former allies of Soekarno's war against Malaysia) and the Indonesian army.[23]

The Indonesian army initiated a series of so-called 'counterinsurgency' operations along the border known by the overall name of 'Operation Clean Sweep' (Operasi Sapu Bersih) (Rachman et al. 1970:239-301). To begin with, military operations were mostly concentrated in the lower district of the province with its large Chinese population. In the late 1960s and early 1970s the military focus first shifted towards the more remote and rugged inland border areas like that inhabited by the Iban.[24] The inland district of Kapuas Hulu (together with those of Sanggau and Sinang) were labelled the 'eastern sector' by the military command (Soemadi 1974:94). As part of the 'Clean Sweep' campaign, the military in 1968 embarked on 'Operation Destruction' (Operasi Penghantjuran) in the eastern sector, the purpose of which was, as the name implies, a

---

[21] Personal interview, ex-TNKU, Lanjak, 23-7-2007.
[22] The term 'insurgents' is here deliberately place within quotation marks, as it is important to remember that the term carries a negative conation. It labels the rebels 'cause as illegitimate, whereas the rebels themselves see the government authority itself as being illegitimate.
[23] This was part of a larger coordinated military campaign against the 'Communist insurgents' launched by the Indonesian and Malaysian security forces.
[24] This major military operation was carried out in three periods, Operasi Sapu Bersih I (1967), II (1967-1969) and III (1969-1970). See Soemadi 1974.

total annihilation of insurgent activities in the borderland. The part of the sector inhabited by the Iban was given special attention (Rachman et al. 1970:295-7). The same year the Indonesian military commander in West Kalimantan, Brigadier General Witono, claimed that as many as 5,600 regular troops were engaging the insurgents in the province (Kroef 1968:263).

The Indonesian New Order government saw indigenous minorities, especially borderland communities like the Iban, as a possible conduit for the infiltration of foreign ideologies such as communism into the country. As a result, the military operations were carried out on two fronts. Besides direct military action against so-called insurgents, attempts were made to win over the hearts and minds of the Iban and make them into compliant citizens. The Iban long-term orientation towards Sarawak, their low level of education and lack of religion were of particular military concern.

As indicated in a historical account of the Regional Military Command in Pontianak (KODAM XXI/Tanjungpura), military leaders were well aware of the strong kinship bonds between Iban in Kalimantan and those in Sarawak and their ongoing socio-economic interaction (Rachman et al. 1970:295). This interaction was acknowledged as partly a consequence of historical processes and shared ethnicity, but also a result of the particularly low level of development on the Indonesian side of the border. Military accounts emphasized how compared to Sarawak the Iban in Kalimantan were still relatively backwards (*terbelakang*), both materially and intellectually. As stated in one military account:

> Iban awareness of political engagement is not yet developed (*belum madju*), the necessities of daily life are more primary for them, they therefore easily fall under the influence (*pengaruh*) of the Chinese communists (*Tjina komunist*) and they are easily influenced by agitation and manipulation (*dihatut dan diperalat*) of their (the communists') politics (Rachman et al. 1970:319).

According to the military, one consequence of the above-mentioned circumstances was that the majority of Iban communities generally took an uncooperative stance towards the Indonesian military operations in the area (Rachman et al. 1970:295, 319). The Indonesian military was aware of the possibility of Communist infiltration among the border Iban, as coordination meetings in September 1969 with Sarawak's Special Branch (security police) – now allies of the Indonesian army, conveyed information that several Sarawak Iban had already been influenced by Communist propaganda.[25]

The KODAM XXI accounts stated that the main objective behind Maoist/Communist warfare strategy was to infiltrate the common people. As in Sarawak, also in Kalimantan: the Iban and Chinese communities had a long tradition of socialising, trade and intermarriage; consequently, the Iban were particularly prone to Communist infiltration and not to be underestimated (Rachman et al. 1970:320-1; Soemadi 1974:96). This also included the ethnic Chinese communities who largely were labelled as Communists and seen as a potential security threat. Unable to achieve the status of Indonesian National Citizens (Warga Negara Indonesia, WNI,) they were seen as foreigners (Warga Negara Asing, WNA) and were especially vulnerable to military harassment and forced expulsion (*Tempo* 1974a, 1974e). Many ethnic Chinese civilians were living along the border in towns like Nanga Badau and Lanjak, and the Indonesian Army was supposedly afraid that these communities would support the insurgents with supplies. In order to prevent these Chinese communities from siding and interacting with the Communists, the Army in 1970 relocated approximately 70,000 ethnic (Hakka) Chinese, removing them from the border districts of Sanggau, Sintang, and Kapuas Hulu (Soemadi 1974:91). In other parts of the province (especially the lower Sambas and Bengkayang districts), the military directly encouraged local Dayaks to engage in violent expulsions of Chinese farmers; this led to massacres. Jamie Davidson and Douglas Kammen note how the 'Dayaks' were encouraged by the Indonesian military authorities to engage in violence and headhunting (*ngayau*) (Davidson and Kammen 2002:17-8). Such violent outbreaks against ethnic Chinese, however, did not take place in the borderland inhabited by the Iban.

Five years previously, a similar attempt to relocate (Hakka) Chinese communities situated on the Sarawak side of the border was carried out by the Sarawak government. This operation was code named 'Operation Hammer' and resulted in the resettling of more than 8,000 Chinese

---

[25] The Sarawak Special Branch was originally created in 1949 in order to collect intelligence on various subversive activities and secessionist movements including those inspired by Communism. This special unit of the police later came to play an important role in curbing the spread of Communist 'propaganda' in the 1960s and 1970s (Porritt 2006).

to temporary, wire fenced 'security concentration centres' away from the border in so-called 'controlled areas' (Siburan, Tapah and Beratok) (Yong 2006). Like the Indonesian government, the Sarawak government believed that among the ethnic Chinese communities were subversive elements that were actively supporting the 'Communist terrorists' in their cross-border raids (Tan 2008:24-5).

Although much military effort was put into countering the Chinese influence, through relocation on both sides of the border, less militaristic attempts were carried out in order to shift the loyalty of the Kalimantan Iban communities. In 1971 Brigadier General Soemadi, a leading military general from the provincial Military Command stationed in the border area, emphasized that Communist infiltration among the border communities could not be solved without immediate action to develop the area. According to Iban statements, Brigadier General Soemadi often expressed sympathy for the difficult situation of the border population. His long presence in the border area resulted in various closer relationships with the Iban. A highly placed member of the local Iban elite claims that Major General Soemadi, while stationed in the border area, even married a close cousin of his from Merakai Panjai (now Puring Kencana).

In a 1971 interview with the Indonesian news magazine *Tempo magazine*, Soemadi stated that the border area was very underdeveloped (*sangat terkebelakang*), the local farming techniques were still that of swidden agriculture, and people's health condition and education were very weak (*sangat rendah*). Furthermore, the problem of cross-border shared ethnicity (*hubungan darah*, literally 'shared blood') made it extremely difficult to control the movement of these populations and to determine their exact nationality, as many were born across the border in Malaysia (*Tempo* 1971a).[26]

In order to solve the problem of underdevelopment (*problema pembangunan*) and lack of national consciousness, the military implemented several measures intended to help raise the local standard of living (Soemadi 1974). In 1974, a team from the National Development Planning Agency (BAPPENAS) visited the border region to assess future development initiatives; they found six areas in special need of development projects (*proyek khusus*), two of which were Nanga Badau and Nanga

---

[26] Bear in mind that newspaper and magazine articles dealing with the 1960s and 1970s 'Communist insurgency' were by and large military propaganda.

Kantuk in the Iban inhabited part of the borderland.[27] According to Governor (Colonel) Kadarusno, approximately Rp24 billon (US$58 million) was to be used on border development in the next five years (*Tempo* 1974c, 1974d). As stated by Nancy Peluso and Emily Harwell, such development programs were a well-integrated strategy in military counter-insurgency tactics (Peluso and Harwell 2001).

In the Lanjak area, the military invested much energy in developing areas for irrigated rice fields or wet rice (*sawah*) cultivation as an alternative to swidden cultivation in the hills, which was perceived as destructive and primitive (Soemadi 1974:140-5; *Tempo* 1971a). Furthermore, by encouraging the growing of irrigated rice in the valleys, the military hoped that Iban communities would move away from the hilly areas closer to the border and settle out of reach of the insurgents. This only partly succeeded, and most communities remained in the hills. Davidson and Kammen, for example, describe how the Indonesian government invested large sums in similar projects throughout the province as part of what was known as the 'road and rice' campaign (Davidson and Kammen 2002:25). Only a few Iban embraced this new possibility as it meant leaving their customary land, over which they had traditional user rights, and moving to areas already occupied by other Iban and Maloh communities.[28] In the 1920s the Dutch had used a similar tactic and constructed irrigated rice fields in the plains, meaning that the communities who were forcibly moved at that time already claimed most land suitable for this kind of cultivation.[29] In addition, the land converted by the military was generally not suited to extensive wet rice cultivation, and the yield quickly fell to below what was produced through swidden farming.

The military were convinced that in order to improve Iban sentiments towards Indonesia, programs of social education in loyal and appropriate behaviour were needed in addition to development projects (Soemadi 1974:96-9). Social education programs included everything from learning catchwords, symbols, and acronyms associated with the nation to courses in health promotion and appropriate lifestyle (discouraging longhouse living, for example). The Regional Military Command

[27] The four other areas were Sajingan (Sambas district), Balai Karangan (Sangau district), Senaning and Sungai Antu (Sintang district) (*Tempo* 1974d).
[28] Growing hill rice plays a vital role in Iban social and spiritual life, and many of the more conservative Iban are extremely reluctant to give up this form of rice cultivation.
[29] See W.H.E. Scheuer, Memorie van Overgave van de afdeeling Sintang, Juli 1932, Koninklijk Instituut voor de Tropen, No. 997. ARA.

| At the edges of states

stated that: 'Their (the Iban) national attitude (*sikap nasional*) is indeed very low (*tipis sekali*), you could even say it is not there at all' (Rachman et al. 1970:295). In an attempt to heighten national loyalties and promote state ideology, the military began to construct schools and undertook mass education (*pendidikan massa*) (Soemadi 1974:104). Several hundred soldiers were posted as teachers along the border (Davidson 2002:198). Recalcitrant Dayaks like the Iban who were classified as particularly 'difficult' subjects (*klasifikasi berat*) were forced to endure 'mental education' (*pendidikan mental*) in order for them to choose the 'right' side and oppose the enemy (Soemadi 1974:124). The Iban were taught the national ideology of Pancasila[30] in order to develop their understanding of the unified nation-state (*Kesatuan Negara*).[31] Threatened with being labelled unpatriotic, the Iban were persuaded to proclaim their allegiance to the Indonesian state ideology. As recollected by a senior Iban:

> I was still young and there were no real schools in the area [Ulu Leboyan] at the time. I remember how the officers from the military camp across the river came to the longhouse every day in the evening when people returned from their fields. They brought books, and we all had to sit on the open veranda (*ruai*) and listen so we could become good citizens (*warga negara*). I did not learn to speak Indonesian (*Bahasa Indonesia*) before the soldiers arrived.[32]

The first principle in the national ideology states the importance of religion, or more specifically, the belief in one God (monotheism). As an Indonesian citizen, you are required to be a member of one of the five state approved religions (Islam, Catholicism, Protestantism, Hinduism or Buddhism). As stated by Brigadier General Hartono: 'I don't care what religion they have; the main point is that they have a religion (*beragama*)' (*Tempo* 1974b).

This posed another problem for the Iban. The more conservative Iban living in the hills along the border had been very reluctant to adopt the preaching of the early Christian missionaries and, unlike other

---

[30] Pancasila relies on five principles; 1) Monotheism (*Ketuhanan*), 2) Humanism (*kemanusiaan*), 3) The unity of nationalism (*kebangsaan*), 4) Democracy through representative government (*kerakyatan*), 5) Social justice (*keadilan social*).
[31] For a more detailed discussion of national schooling in the borderland and the paradoxical outcomes, see Eilenberg 2005.
[32] Personal interview, Ulu Leboyan 30-5-2007.

4 Guerrilla warfare and resource extraction

groups such as the Maloh, they had felt no need to convert. In 1908, Dutch Capuchin missionaries set up missions in the Iban-dominated town of Lanjak at the border.[33] These missions were expected to have a 'civilizing' *(beschaving)* influence on the Iban, lifting them up to a higher living standard *(menschwaardig bestaan)* (Anonymous 1921:58). The missions were temporarily closed in 1915 and completely abandoned in the 1920s as the Iban refused conversion, and the missionaries consequently moved to the ethnic Maloh stronghold in Benua Martinus (Buil 1921).[34] As reported by the Capuchin Father Ignatius. 'The Iban were not yet mature enough for schooling' *(De Ibans zijn nog niet rijp voor school)*. Ignatius here indicated that he thought the Iban had not yet reached a sufficiently advanced stage of intellectual or emotional development.[35] The lack of success was also placed squarely on the shoulders of the government *(bestuur)*, despite the efforts of the missionaries.

> They (the missionaries) would have succeeded among the Batang Lupars if the government had given more support. The government is taken to task; a thorough and wise government brings betterment and progress, but a weak and vacillating one does not lift the poor Dayak up. It is hoped that a new Resident will support the mission more.

Ignatius goes on to say that earlier on the Dutch government pushed for the mission to begin work in order to help the government with its efforts of pacification, but at present their help is not needed and the government advises the mission to leave the task of civilizing the Iban to the government. At the time the mission was set up, the military still had little influence on the Iban, and the mission had to come and help among that murderous people *(dit moordzuchtige volk)*. There were many severed heads being brought in then *(Menig gesneld hoofd werd in die dagen nog in triumf binnengehaald)*. He asks rhetorically, why did the then-government officer provide protection and an armed guard when the first missionaries ventured among the notorious *(beruchte)* Iban? In answer, the unnamed goverment official knows it was not advisable to go alone and unarmed

---

[33] See 'De vestiging van de nieuwe missiepost te Landjak, Zondagsblad 1909', No. 2741, Verzameling Losse Archivalia, Katholiek Documentatie Centrum, Nijmegen.

[34] See also Kroniek over de Missie van Borneo, samengesteld door Valentinus, 27-1-1954. Kapucijnenarchief, Archivum Capucinorum Hollandensis (ACH), 's-Hertogenbosch, Netherlands.

[35] Letters from Lanjak 1908-17, to Pater Provinciaal. 30-9-1912, P. Ignatius. Kapucijnenarchief, Archivum Capucinorum Hollandensis (ACH), 's-Hertogenbosch, Netherlands.

amongst that people (*dit volkje*). But, he says, our missionaries are apostles of peace and did not rely on the power of weapons. He adds that the missionaries went unarmed to the heathen (*heidensche*) headhunters, trusting only in help from Above (Anonymous 1921:59-60).

At the onset of militarization in the 1960s, the majority of the majority of the Iban still retained their traditional beliefs and were consequently portrayed by state authorities as lacking religion. This was of special concern for the military, as it was believed that the Iban, like other conservative Dayaks lacking a recognized religion, would be especially susceptible to the teaching of the godless Communist insurgents and therefore more at risk of joining the Communists. In order to avoid military accusations of Communist collaboration, many Iban felt forced, at least formally, to convert to either Protestantism or Catholicism. For example, in Lanjak the military erected churches and carried out missionary work. Battalion 308 stationed in the area at the time played an especially important role. That battalion consisted primarily of Protestant Christians from the Batak region in North Sumatra. Such military involvement in civil matters was formalized in the 1980s, as the government introduced an official program of direct military development intervention called AMD (*ABRI masuk desa*) or 'ABRI (the Indonesian military) enters the village'. In the border area the AMD programs involved military personnel who engaged in projects such as teaching, developing rice-production schemes and the like. Although development was the official rhetoric behind the AMD programs in the borderland, it was primarily an attempt to prevent the local communities becoming influenced by foreign ideologies.

Despite considerable efforts by the military to win over the minds (and souls) of the recalcitrant border communities, reorientation of national sentiments was never successful among the Iban. Iban attitudes towards the Indonesian state remained ambivalent, partly due to military brutality and partly to the long Iban history of autonomy and close cross-border ties.

THE PARAKU: INSURGENTS OR LIBERATION ARMY?

During both Konfrontasi and the subsequent Communist uprooting, the majority of border communities avoided direct involvement in the conflicts. However, a group of locals (mostly Iban) were drawn into the conflict between ABRI and the left-wing rebels (predominately Communist). The rebels active in the Kapuas Hulu borderland were known as the PARAKU, an acronym for the North Kalimantan Peoples' Army (Pasukan Rakyat Kalimantan Utara).[36]

The PARAKU consisted of a mix of former TNKU rebels, Sarawak Chinese Communists, and a small number of Iban and other Dayaks (Soemadi 1974; Sulistyorini 2004). The large majority of the PARAKU was Sarawak Chinese, many from the Sarawak Communist Organization (SCO), which had supported the TNKU since the Confrontation in the early 1960s. Several Iban interviewed in Lanjak further recounted how a small group of Sarawak Iban actively joined the PARAKU ranks. One Iban man in particular, Ubong from the Rejang area in Sarawak, was described as main figure and deputy commander of the PARAKU rebels in the Kapuas Hulu area. According to Fujio Hara, Ubong was appointed deputy commander of the PARAKU rebels in the late 1970s (Hara 2005:502). Ubong supposedly brought both his wife and children with him across the border. Ubong's jungle skills and bravery quickly made him a local legend in the borderland. Moving like a shadow in the forest, killing many Indonesian soldiers without being shot or captured himself, he was believed to possess supernatural powers (*sakti*).[37]

The PARAKU rebels were a mix of mostly young men and women, often husband and wife, fighting side by side.[38] Their prolonged stays in the border region often cut off from supply lines in Sarawak meant that many of the PARAKU units began making camps that were more permanent. Here they engaged in the cultivation of rice and vegetables in garden plots in the remote upriver interior along the border. Growing their own rice and vegetables played a major role in the endurance of the rebels. However, by clearing fields in the forest they also became more vulnerable to bombing by Indonesian planes cruising the border hills.

The main ideological goal of the PARAKU was, like that of the former TNKU, to liberate Sarawak from the Malaysian state. Consequently,

---

[36] The rebels were divided into two groups concentrating on different parts of the West Kalimantan-Sarawak border. PGRS/Paraku (Pasukan Gerilya Rayakat Serawak/Pasukan Rakyat Kalimantan Utara) (Davidson and Kammen 2002:3).

[37] Personal interview, Lanjak, 23-3-2007.

[38] Lumenta (2005:15) notes how the female Communist rebels were known as *Pasukan Amoy* (Amoy troops among the locals. '*Amoy*' is an Indonesian form of address given to a Chinese girl (in some regions only). In its original meaning, 'Amoy' denotes a Chinese dialect.

fighting was primarily oriented towards Sarawak, but the military cooperation between Indonesia and Malaysia and the heavy engagement of the Indonesian army in the border area meant that the PARAKU was forced to fight them as well.[39] Many of these PARAKU rebels, originally volunteers during the previous period of Konfrontasi, were trained and armed in the early 1960s by the Indonesian Special Forces, RPKAD, in camps along the border. The PARAKU therefore found it advisable to establish guerrilla base camps in the rugged and heavily forested Kalimantan borderland, from which they could launch attacks into Sarawak.

In an interview with a former RPKAD captain named Untung Suroso, Conboy describes how three RPKAD military trainers in the early 1960s were parachuted into the border village of Nanga Badan (misspelling of Nanga Badau) in West Kalimantan. These three soldiers supposedly trained 300 locals in guerrilla warfare. This group of volunteers was later divided into two groups lead by two army lieutenants named Kentot Harseno and Mulyono Soerjowardojo (Conboy 2003:95). As recounted by an Iban *patih* in Lanjak:

> In 1962, I was still in school but I remember I saw them [TNKU] practice together (*latihan sama-sama*) with the RPKAD Special Forces. In Lanjak, there were three military posts and three barracks and the Chinese from Sarawak and the volunteers was given weapons and food by the Indonesian government. I remember the TNKU commander in that times his name was General Peng. He was from RRC (Republic Rakyat Cina/People's Republic of China, he wore a broad hat with 'Peng' written on it, and there was a red picture of Mao. He was a smart person (*orang pintar*). On every August the 17th [Indonesian Independence Day] he held a ceremony and gave a speech (*ceramah*) of encouragement to his people (*anak buahnya*). General Peng was fluent in Indonesian, English, and Iban.[40]

Whether the above statement is entirely accurate is difficult to assess; local rumours say that instructors from the RRC entered Kalimantan during this period, but it is more likely that the General Peng mentioned here was a Sarawak Chinese trained in China. A 1973 classified CIA

---

[39] For a detailed description of the general political dynamics in West Kalimantan during the era of militarization, see Davidson 2002.
[40] Personal interview, Iban *patih*, Lanjak, 23-3-2007.

intelligence report states that Peking provided moral support to the insurgents, although there was no confirmation of Chinese military personnel taking an active part in the training of the insurgents within Kalimantan or Sarawak (CIA Intelligence Report 1973). Like the PARAKU, many of the TNKU soldiers used an alias. However, in his account of the military involvement in fighting the PARAKU, General Soemadi mentions the 1971 surrender of a rebel leader named Sim Kiem Peng from the PARAKU Unit Satuan 330 who operated in the Lanjak area (Soemadi 1974:130-1).

During military training, socializing between the volunteers and Iban inevitably occurred. At that time, the army actively encouraged Iban communities to provide supplies of rice and meat and logistical support in form of longboats to transport the volunteers and their supplies upriver to the 'front' along the border.

The sudden change in Indonesian politics from being pro-Communist under Sokarno to anti-Communist under Soeharto deeply confused many Iban, and they became increasingly unsure about who was friend and who was enemy. As an elderly Iban informant in Lanjak put it:

> Old allies suddenly became enemies when the Communists were forced into the jungle in 1965 by Soeharto and returned as the PARAKU a few years later. The PARAKU were well trained (*melatih*), because those who trained them were Indonesian Special Forces (Pasukan Khusus, RPKAD). But after being trained they separated (*pisah*), friends became enemies (*kawan jadi lawan*). This is the problem (*ini masalahnya*).[41]

Another peculiar twist adding to this confusion erupted in 1969 when Brigadier General Witono put forward allegations that some segments within the West Kalimantan Army Command supposedly supported the PARAKU. In the subsequent period, several Army officers were arrested (Kroef 1970:49).

Caught in the struggle between the two conflicting parties, the Iban were often forced to choose to be loyal towards one, leading to violent reprisals from the other. Some Iban men developed friendships with PARAKU rebels (several of whom were Iban) who came to their villages asking for supplies, which were often provided in return for helping out

---

[41] Personal interview, Lanjak, 23-3-2007.

in the rice swiddens. If detected by the Indonesian army, such interactions with the 'enemy' were severely punished. Meanwhile, other Iban men were employed as scouts for Indonesian army patrols to track down the very same people, or served as intelligence gatherers at the village level.

Senior inhabitants of Rumah Manah describe the shifting relationships with both the ABRI and PARAKU in the borderland during the 1970s. One of these, Mandau, who at the time of the PARAKU was in his mid-thirties, speaks of how Chinese Communists often visited his longhouse, asking for food.[42] Not having any grudges against these people, who often spoke Iban very well, the Iban often provided the food. The PARAKU further entered into different kinds of relationships with the Iban, such as trading medicine and buying domesticated pigs and chickens from the longhouse inhabitants.[43] Furthermore, Mandau tells how several people in the longhouse were cured of illnesses by the use of acupuncture administered by the PARAKU:

> If the PARAKU came to the village [longhouse], we would give them food, because we are human beings, are we not? If we gave food, the government suspected us (*dicurigai*) of being Communist collaborators, but it was not our intention to be disloyal to the government. We felt squeezed (*terjepitlah*) in between the two [Indonesian forces and PARAKU].[44]

In many instances, the insurgents enjoyed a closer relationship with the local population than the Indonesian military did. The latter relationship was more troubled because the military often forced the locals to perform unpaid labour (Davidson and Kammen 2002:30). An article from a 1971 issue of *Tempo* magazine describes how the PARAKU operations in the border area were made possible through the PARAKU's extensive knowledge of the border area, its population, language, and customs (*Tempo* 1971b).

During military operations against the PARAKU carried out by the Malaysian forces, various documents were obtained, such as Communist publications in the Iban language, Iban dictionaries and notebooks. These documents were indications that the PARAKU were actively try-

---

[42] Personal interview, Ulu Leboyan, 13-11-2003.
[43] See also Soemadi 1974:94.
[44] Personal interview, Iban farmer, 10-4-2007.

ing to learn Iban (Porritt 2004:164; Rahman 1972:15). One extract from captured letters reads:

> Regarding what we need, please get me some Mao badges, Mao's Quotations, Mao stamps, and so on. We also need Iban books, an Iban dictionary, a Chinese dictionary, the various new and old laws and ordinances of the puppet regime, materials concerning the history, geography and people of North Kalimantan, and shotgun cartridges (Rahman 1972:15).

The Malaysian government's anxiety concerning the so-called expanding 'Communist threat' in Sarawak is most evident in a White Paper published in 1972 (Rahman 1972). The White Paper quotes a document of the Sarawak Communist Organization (SCO) dated December 1967 that supposedly details the SCO plan for armed struggle:

> In view of the disadvantageous political situation in Indonesia, our Organization quickly withdrew our comrades to the border area in two batches; one retreated to the West and the other to the East. [...] By going to the border area, we will be able to set up bases with excellent topographical conditions and launch a long-term guerrilla war. We will gradually penetrate into the country with the border area as the stepping stone and then surround the cities from the rural areas, occupy the whole country and finally take over the power of Government' (Rahman 1972:2). [45]

While the Iban acknowledge some interaction with the PARAKU, Mandau, cited above, also talks about young Iban men earning a salary by helping the Indonesian military track down these same insurgents.[46] One example was that of an Iban man from the Lanjak area who worked as an intelligence-gatherer under the cover of *ngayap*, an Iban term for young men engaged in finding a wife. Such courtship pursuits often involve the bachelor visiting many different communities, which is a good cover for gathering intelligence. Similar examples of Iban involvement in the uprooting of the PARAKU have been noted by other scholars like

---

[45] It is important to remember that this White Paper was part of the Malaysian government's anti-Communist propaganda.
[46] For similar statements about Iban communities in the subdistrict of Empanang, see McKeown 1984:105.

Pirous (2002) and Lumenta (2001, 2005) in their research on the Iban living along the Embaloh River.

Adding to the ambiguousness of this case, two local men who during Konfrontasi were hired by the military to become TNKU volunteers were later employed by the same military command to track down the PARAKU (several of whom were former TNKU). One group of local scouts mostly consisting of former TNKU volunteers was stationed in Lanjak and assisting the military to track down the PARAKU.[47]

> The Javanese soldiers who came to the border could not find their way (*tidak tahu jalan tidak tau apa*) in the forest where the PARAKU were operating. They did not know anything. We were always brought as guides to show the way although many did not want to help the soldiers. My company was named 'White Bear' (*Bruang Putih*) and when we guided the soldiers, they never met the PARAKU, but when the soldiers went alone they often clashed. The soldiers were confused (*heran*) and asked why is it that when we go by ourselves we meet them (the PARAKU) by chance, but if you join us we never meet. Maybe you have some kind of magic (*mungkin Bapak punya Ilmu*) the soldiers said.[48]

> This is a well-known secret (*rahasia*). Before, the people who are now called PARAKU used to be together with us (the former TNKU), but then we were separated (*berpisah*) in 1965 and1966. After they left us and went to the jungle, they sent us a letter saying 'my friends we leave you all because Sarawak is now part of a independent Malaysia, but we will stay in the jungle and keep fighting, and if you are our friends join the soldiers but do not shoot at us. We will not bother you either; this is our promise'. They kept their promise (*janjinya*); we were never shot, although the soldiers walking behind us sometimes were fired upon from the jungle. When we arrived at a PARAKU camp they had just left and we only saw their wet footprints on the stones (*bekas PARAKU di batu masih basah*). The PARAKU knew the jungle (*pandai masuk hutan mereka*); they had already been here for a long time. Think about that (*cobalah*).[49]

---

[47] In the Lanjak area, several army units used Iban 'scouts,' such as Battalion 323 (Galuh), 324 (Siluman Merah), 327 (Brajawijaya), and 642 (Kapuas). For examples of military certificates given to local Iban recruited as 'scouts' see Figures 21, 24 and 25.

[48] Personal interview, local scout 23-7-2007.

[49] Personal interview, Lanjak, former local scout, 23-7-2007.

Iban involvements with the Indonesian army have later been recognized by local and central government as examples of acts of loyalty towards the Indonesian State (Japari 1989:11). War veterans further received official certificates signed by President Soeharto and were promised a lifelong war pension:[50]

> After the insurgency, we were acknowledged (*diakui*) as war veterans (*anggota veteran*) but never received our pension. Several times we went to the Kodim office [District Military Command] but we never got an answer. Some of us even went to Pontianak and Jakarta but it was no use. We were very disappointed, as no one seemed to respect those of us who went to war to defend the country (*membela Negara*). We were not even given one cent in reward (*tidak ada satu pun, sepersen pun imbalannya*).[51]

The flexible attitude towards the two fighting parties was not without a certain risk. If cooperation with the Communists was detected by the military, it could have serious repercussions for the Iban communities. There are several examples of how the military bombed longhouses as punishment for such arbitrary loyalties (Lumenta 2005; Pirous 2002). Afraid of military punishment, many families moved to Sarawak, including entire longhouse communities. Close to Rumah Manah was a longhouse of thirteen families who moved to Sarawak overnight in 1968 leaving everything behind, even treasured heirlooms (*pusaka*) such as old brass gongs. Rice was left on the plates, pigs and chickens still roamed under the house. The group followed the Leboyan River until they reached Sarawak and never returned to get their belongings. The community supposedly decamped in order to escape severe military punishment for harbouring PARAKU insurgents. As one Iban informant stated, 'they cannot return permanently because they are now [citizens] under another flag (*mereka sudah bendera yang lain*)'.[52]

Just across the border in Lubok Antu, several Iban leaders was arrested and accused by Malaysian Forces of supplying food and intelligence to the PARAKU. In 1968, ten Iban headmen were arrested in Lubok Antu (Porritt 2004:164). In the subdistrict seat of Lanjak, there were several cases of Iban being tortured or executed for their alleged

---

[50] See Figure 20.
[51] Personal interview, Lanjak, Iban war veteran, 23-7-2007.
[52] Personal interview, Lanjak, 14-7-2007.

cooperation with insurgents. Many stories of military brutality against civilians still flourish in the borderland, some better substantiated than others. Two episodes that were verified by all my informants were the accounts of Rantai and Ranau. These accounts in many ways stress the difficult situation that the Iban leaders were confronted with especially in their ambivalent position between the military and the PARAKU.[53]

In 1966, a group of heavily armed PARAKU rebels ambushed an Indonesian army patrol near Lanjak. The patrol was taken totally by surprise, and several soldiers were instantly killed, while only one rebel was hit before the PARAKU again withdrew towards their hideouts in the forest. One Iban man named Rantai was subsequently arrested and accused of being involved in the attack by supplying the PARAKU with intelligence. Rantai was taken back to Lanjak, where he was executed and hung in a tree in a rattan cage. The cage was shot full of holes and left on display.[54]

Ranau was the headman of an Iban longhouse near Lanjak. Since the early encampments of the PARAKU in the borderland, before the strong military presence, Ranau had engaged in a working relationship with the PARAKU. They helped him in his rice fields, sowing and harvesting, and did other kinds of manual labour in exchange for food and shelter in his field huts. This relationship evolved into friendship, and Ranau became blood brothers (*bekempit darah*) with two PARAKU men operating in the area. According to Iban customary law, taking a blood oath means that you are mutually responsible for each other's safety; you are friends until death (*teman sampai mati*). As the military presence grew stronger in the early 1970s, rumours of Ranua's relationship with the PARAKU went from mouth to mouth (*dari mulut ke mulut*) and finally reached the ears of the Indonesian military commander. Ranau was consequently arrested and tortured (*disiksa*) in public. He was submerged in the small river running through Lanjak for hours and beaten with rifles. The commander of the military company stationed in Lanjak supposedly announced in public that 'if he [Ranau] can catch the PARAKU, behead (*memenggal kepala*) them and bring their heads he will be free to go, if not he will go to jail until he dies'. Ranau supposedly felt there was no other way out than to follow this command; along with two other Iban,

[53] The military policy of intimidation and violence was also widely felt among other Dayak communities living along the lower parts of the border . See, for example, Peluso 2005:120-1).
[54] Personal interview, Lanjak, 9-6-2007.

armed with military rifles, he went to the forest and after a week he returned with the heads of two PARAKU rebels. Both of these men were working under the command of the General Peng mentioned earlier. The two PARAKU rebels were not killed by Ranau but by two of his followers, although he was the one who gave the order. Ranau was later given the rank of local war commander and received a military pension for his deeds.[55] This incident created great internal condemnation, as breaking a blood bond is a great sin (*berdosa besar*) that was and still is among the greatest Iban taboos. Several senior inhabitants of Lanjak said, 'He [Ranau] has a bad soul. It is not neutral (*tidak netral jiwanya*)'. During the former periods of continuous headhunting, internally and with other ethnic groups, fear of losing one's head was constant among the Iban; one way of solving this uncertainty was to make sacred pacts with other (hostile) groups. The pact was made binding when the leaders of both groups attended a blood ceremony and became one another's adopted brother. Ultimately this meant that the groups were obliged not to engage in hostilities against each other (Wadley 2001a).

These difficult years are locally referred to as the time of disruption or disturbance (*musim kacau*).[56] For example, in 1970 ABRI initiated a massive military campaign in the Kapuas Hulu border area by having the air force bomb supposed Communist strongholds in the hills and dropping platoons of paratroopers to hunt down the PARAKU (Davidson and Kammen 2002: 31). Besides using Iban scouts, the military created so-called 'people's resistance' units, WANRA (Perlawanan Rakyat),[57] whose main purpose was to form a local border defence. These groups were subject to military codes and laws.[58] They mostly accompanied the soldiers, acted as forced porters on weeklong operations, and were forced to walk in front of the soldiers as shields against enemy fire. According to several informants, some WANRA members were equipped with rifles and ammunition and further received special food rations, although the majority had to do with homemade shotguns, swords and spears. The military supposedly were hesitant to arm the Iban because of their

---

[55] Personal interview, Lanjak, 8-6-2007. This incident is also noted in General Soemadi's 1974 account of the PARAKU period (Soemadi 1974:130-1).
[56] Wadley has noted that the same term was used to describe the period of raiding and punitive expeditions during colonial times (Wadley 2004a:62).
[57] The WANRA were a kind of local civil defence unit (*Pertahanan Sipil* or *Hansip*) (Sundhaussen 1982:192-3).
[58] See also Presidential Decree No. 4 of 15-3-1965.

shifting loyalty. According to former WANRA members interviewed in Lanjak and Nanga Badau, each person was given a certificate in the 1970s by the military allowing them a salary of Rp3,500 (US$8.40) and 25 kilos of rice every month.[59]

Each village had its own WANRA unit that was expected to guard the village and keep it free of enemy incursions and Communist teaching (McKeown 1984:384-5). According to locals, there was a strict agreement with the military that if any regular soldiers were killed while stationed in the village area, the village head would be held solely responsible and executed.[60] The function of the WANRA units on the Indonesian side of the border was in many ways similar to that of the Sarawak Border Scouts created by the Malaysian military. The Border Scouts was a semi-military unit of local volunteers (Dayaks) from the immediate border area. The unit's main purposes were to protect the local community and provide intelligence to the military (Bala 2002). But unlike the WANRA units, the Border Scouts became an effective tool in fighting the PARAKU. One reason for this was that they were genuine volunteers, well armed, and highly respected by the regular military, while the WANRA units were based on military coercion and intimidation. Generally the border population in Kalimantan had a much more strained relationship with their military than their Sarawak neighbours had with theirs.

As during the time of the Confrontation, this period of militarization of the borderland also severely affected local lives. Everyday routines were disrupted, transportation was dangerous, and limited and basic essentials were difficult to obtain. In an attempt to seal the supply lines of the insurgents, the military heavily increased its surveillance and restrictions on border trading, which had a 'dislocating effect on the border economy' (Kroef 1963:255). A five-mile-wide 'free zone' was established on both sides of the border, and only persons with special military approval could trade within this zone (Porritt 2004:157-8). The Iban, being extremely dependent on cross-border trade (especially now that the remote borderland was empty of basic goods), were severely affected:

[59] See certificates shown in Figures 22 and 23.
[60] Personal interview, Badau, 19-3-2007.

In the 1970s every time we wanted to visit communities in other areas in the district or bring produce back and forth across the border we had to pass military posts. We were not free to move around; we were anxious (*ketakutan*); our backpacks (*ladung*) were checked (*diperiksa*). There were many restrictions. For example, we were only allowed to carry 5 kilos of rice, 1 kilo of sugar, and 5 matches. If we had more than that, we were accused of supporting the PARAKU. No batteries were allowed. If we were caught carrying one battery, the fine was one year in jail. Sometimes we were forced to leave everything to the soldiers. If the soldiers wanted to eat chicken, they took your chicken. They were free (*mereka bebaslah*) to do want they wanted. If people resisted, they were beaten. This created a feeling of hatred (*rasa benci masyarakat*) among communities towards the soldiers.[61]

Many people began to smuggle (*semukil*) [loan word from the Dutch '*smokkelen*', to smuggle] goods like sugar and batteries over the border but if detected they were directly accused (*langsung dituduhlah*) of feeding the PARAKU in the forest.[62]

Despite the heavy militarization along the border, the Iban still maintained a certain degree of autonomy on certain local matters and did not hesitate to assert their interest and authority, even in potentially dangerous situations. For instance, at the end of the military uprooting of the PARAKU the Iban were ordered to hand in their shotguns. More or less every Iban family in the borderland was in possession of one or two shotguns, predominately used for hunting. Many of these guns were homemade, and shells were smuggled from across the border where they could be purchased at a low price. The Iban rejected this military confiscation demand outright and, led by their *temenggong* and *patih,* a group of several hundred men in full ritual regalia descended on the army headquarters. They said that they would only hand in their shotguns if the military promised to post soldiers in their swidden fields to protect them against marauding forest pigs and monkeys. The military command consequently decided not to carry out the confiscation of guns for fear of stirring up local sentiments and provoking violent confrontations. Today the five subdistricts dominated by the Iban are the only places

[61] Personal interview, Badau, 21-3-2007.
[62] Personal interview, Badau, 19-3-2007.

in the district, and perhaps in the entire province, where citizens are allowed to keep their shotguns at home and not register them at the local police station (Wadley and Eilenberg 2006).

Such incidents of Iban-military confrontations convinced some factions of the military that the Iban issue was to be handled with care in order not trigger a major local uprising that would be to the advantage of the PARAKU (Soemadi 1974; *Tempo* 1971a). The head of the subdistrict military command[63] in Lanjak outlined the delicate situation of the time in the following way:

> One day my superior, a military Captain named Pak Suma, ordered me to arrest a group of local Iban who allegedly were helping the PARAKU. The Captain had a list of 60 people from many different longhouses. These people were selected based on statements from two PARAKU insurgents captured in Lubok Antu. However, I was not convinced that the information was valid enough and told the Captain that I was afraid to suspect and beat up the wrong people, because then later we would have to fight the whole community. If one Iban gets hit it could raise a war (*perang*) between the Iban and the soldiers, because the Iban think differently, if one gets hurt they will unite and take revenge. I suggested that it was better if we used the strategy of indoctrination first (*induktrinasi dulu*), and the use of force second, by explaining the PARAKU problem to the communities.[64]

The head of the Koramil later married an Iban woman from Lanjak and settled in the area. Several (Javanese and others) soldiers stationed in the area settled in the border area after the counter-insurgency. Some became civil servants, others entrepreneurs and storekeepers, but all became incorporated into the local border elite.

ESTABLISHMENT OF A BORDERLAND ELITE

Although a majority of the Iban kept their distance from both sides, not all Iban took such an arbitrary stance; some vigorously joined the Indonesian military anti-PARAKU campaign. Several openly expressed

[63] Komando Rayon Militer, or KORAMIL.
[64] Personal interview, Lanjak, 9-4-2007.

their anti-Communist sentiments by directly engaging in the fighting on the side of the military and today proudly recall their involvement in the heavy jungle warfare.

Although their shifting relationships with the fighting parties meant that Iban loyalty was often questioned by Indonesian authorities, a small handful of loyal Iban, especially those who managed to obtain good military connections, were appointed to the military rank of *panglima perang* (often translated as commander, but with connotations of honour and power), a position created especially for the situation. These 'commanders' came to represent local communities in their dealings with the military. They received a small salary from the government, and in return they were expected to uphold security and resolve conflict situations.[65] Each subdistrict had its own *panglima perang*, who in turn appointed his own 'intelligence assistants' (*pembantu intelijen*) to keep him up to date with developments in his area. Wearing official military uniforms, the Iban commanders were given their new titles of *panglima perang* and certificates signed by Soeharto on 17 August 1970 during a public ceremony of Indonesian Independence Day. According to one of the Iban *panglima perang*, Brigadier General Soemadi supposedly said,

> You have worked hard to fight the PARAKU even though you were not given a salary, so this is your salary' and he pointed towards the forest. Although we were not given any letters of proof, we still remember his words.[66]

Another *panglima perang* recalled:

> Every time a new military commander was stationed in the border area we [*panglima perang*] were forced to take a pledge or customary oath (*perjanjian adat*) saying; 'We as the people of Indonesia do not help PARAKU, but Indonesia' (*kami rakyat Indonesia, tidak membantu PARAKU, membantu Indonesia*). This was said while stabbing a pig, as is the customary way of the Iban.[67]

---

[65] See also McKeown 1984:388; Effendy 1995; Lumenta 2005:17.
[66] Personal interview, Embaloh Hulu, 12-6-2007.
[67] Personal interview, *Panglima Perang*, Lanjak, 9-3-2007.

In order to instill a sense of national loyalty in local leaders, a chosen few of the *panglima perang* were taken to Jakarta where they were given medals of honour for good service in fighting the rebels and given an audience with the President (Soemadi 1974:163). These potent state symbols were later used as signs of authority in negotiations with various state authorities over benefits from resource exploitation.

Besides using the *panglima perang*, the Indonesian army also took advantage of the system of tribal chiefs, the *temenggong*, originally invented by the Dutch decades earlier. Like the Dutch, the Indonesian army appointed several loyal anti-Communist Iban as *temenggong* who could support the *panglima perang* in keeping Communists at bay. Since the 1960s, a local government council named MUSPIKA (Musyawarah Pimpinan Kecamatan) consisting of the subdistrict head, police and local military command began appointing the *temenggong*, although local communities were still allowed to nominate candidates (Lumenta 2005:17).

As I will detail later, some of these *panglima perang* and *temenggong* were eventually awarded forest concessions in the area in return for their help in uprooting the PARAKU. Today it is these men and their followers who form the base of the border elite. Besides controlling their own concessions, these Iban came to play a prominent role as points of liaison between local communities and various national and transnational logging interests. In the process, they managed to channel considerable resources their way, investing in things such as schooling for their children and various small-scale businesses ventures like shops, restaurants, and hotels. Furthermore, high-ranking military officers who after returning to Jakarta were appointed to various strategic positions within military and government circles became powerful allies for these elites.

Several of the Iban *panglima perang* had 'adopted' young military officers as their 'foster sons' (*anak angkatnya*). For example, one Iban *panglima perang* made the young military officer Mohamad Basofi Sudirman, who later in the 1990s became Governor of East Java, his adopted son, while another Iban *panglima perang* adopted a young man named Kentot Harseno. Harseno arrived in West Kalimantan in the early 1960s and became commander of a platoon in Battalion 602. In the 1970s, he joined the Army Para Commando Regiment (RPKAD). Harseno was one of the two young army lieutenants mentioned previously who was parachuted into the border town of Nanga Badau in the early 1960s in order to train locals in guerrilla warfare. The fate of the other lieutenant

4 Guerrilla warfare and resource extraction

Mulyono was quite different. In 1965, post-Soekarno, he was executed by the military, accused of being a prominent sympathizer of the PKI and implicated in the so-called Communist coup (Conboy 2003:148).

After serving in the borderland and other places, Harseno became President Soeharto's military adjutant (1978-1981), commander of the Jakarta military garrison, and later Inspector General of Development (Irjenbang, 1990s). Besides these two extremely well-connected 'adoptive sons', several other prominent figures were involved in the anti-PARAKU operations in the Lanjak area. Names such as Colonel Soemadi (Governor of West Kalimantan from 1967 to 1972),[68] Aspar Aswin (Governor of West Kalimantan from 1993 to 2003) and Yogie S. Memet (former governor of West Java from 1985 to 1993 and minister of the interior from 1993 to 1998), as well as several others are often mentioned in local conversations (Lumenta 2005:15).

In the early 1990s, two *panglima perang* and one local Iban member of the district assembly for the Golkar party went to Jakarta to gain support for the development of a border road. Using their military contacts, they managed to get an unofficial audience with General Mahmud Subarkah and eight other military persons in the Dharma Putera Hotel in Kebon Sirih, Jakarta. The general was a member of the People's Consultative Assembly (MPR) and one of Soeharto's advisers at the time. The Iban district assembly member claimed that he had known Mahmud Subarkah previously when the general was stationed in Putussibau. According to the Iban representatives, the General's reply to their inquiry about road development was to say, 'do not be disappointed, my brother, but there is no use for a road in the border area. It is too sparsely inhabited; there are more monkeys than people (*banyak monyetnya daripada orang*)'. The Iban answer was, 'So, General, how do we make people's living better than that of monkeys (*Bagaimana manusia itu kehidupannya lebih bagus daripada monyet*)?' Despite such harsh comments, the General supposedly promised to send more development funds to the border area.[69]

The Konfrontasi and subsequent anti-PARAKU operations thus became an important factor in deciding the later power relations along the border. Networks established during this period of militarization are important for an understanding of current loyalties and the roots of border

---

[68] Colonel Soemadi is not to be confused with Brigadier General Soemadi mentioned earlier.
[69] Personal interview, Lanjak, 23-3-2007.

elite authority. As noted by Baud and Van Schendel in their theorizing on the historical dynamism of borderlands:

> The role of the state [along borders] was...] determined by its relationship with regional elites. When borderland elites were well integrated into networks of state power, they could become important allies of the state in its effort to control borderland society. ... However, borderland elites retained an independent power base and were in a position to oppose state policies (1997:217-8).

As further noted by Sturgeon in her study of Akha village heads and their involvement in controlling local resources on the Burma, Thailand and China border,

> With their role enhanced by state approval, small border chiefs [village heads] have reworked patronage practices, serving larger state interests while controlling local resource access and increasing their own wealth and influence (Sturgeon 2004:466).

Like the ethnic Akha elite, the Iban borderland elite have also claimed loyalty towards the unitary state of Indonesia while simultaneously engaging in and maintaining cross-border connections and loyalties. Sturgeon reports that 'by manoeuvring among multiple affiliations in more than one state, border chiefs have in fact constituted the border' (2005:32). But as mentioned by Peluso, in the Kalimantan context it would be misleading to: 'assume a level of elite machination and absolute power that has little historic basis among any Dayak subgroups' (2008:49). Although some local Iban figures attained certain favourable positions, these elite have never obtained absolute authority over local border communities and decisions taken; rather, their authority lies in their wide networks, high level of schooling and roles as intermediaries between the local level and the government bureaucracy.

The militarization of the borderland has continued until recently and there are still unfounded rumours circulating about Communists hiding deep in the forest. During the early days of my field research, I was told never to walk far away from the longhouse on my own, because there was a risk of stumbling into armed men, a reference to the PARAKU. It is difficult to pinpoint the exact year the PARAKU left the border area, as the records differ considerably. In October 1973 in the town of Simanggang one of the insurgent leaders, Bong Kee Chok, officially signed the so-called 'Deklarasi Sri Aman' (Sri Aman declaration),[70] a memorandum of understanding and peace agreement with the Sarawak government. The PARAKU were subsequently given amnesty. But factions within the PARAKU saw this surrender as a mistake and restored their bases in West Kalimantan a few years later (Fujio 2005:502). Moreover, after withdrawing from Kalimantan in 1985 the insurgents continued their guerrilla warfare in Sarawak until another peace agreement in 1990 (*Sarawak Tribune* 1990).

Officially, the Indonesian government declared their anti-PARAKU efforts ended in the early 1970s by a total annihilation of the PARAKU rebels. However, according to Fujio Hara and locals interviewed in the borderland, the insurgents were present in the upper part of the border area until the mid-1980s.[71] For example, Davidson and Kammen mention how in 1982 an ethnic Chinese man was arrested in the Lanjak area and accused of being involved with the PARAKU (2002:33). The 1982 incident fits well with local accounts of how an ethnic Chinese PARAKU rebel named Pecin in the early 1980s surrendered to a local *panglima perang* in Lanjak.[72] Lumenta further notes that several PARAKU surrendered to the Iban in the upper part of the Embaloh River as late as 1986 (2005:20). Iban who worked for the military tell how the Indonesian army in 1982 gave orders to hang flyers or letters on rocks and trees in the forest telling the PARAKU to surrender. According to an Iban informant the PARAKU once did reply by leaving a letter on a rock along the Embaloh River. The letter supposedly revealed that the PARAKU still had more than 200 men in the area dispersed in 82 camps along the border.[73]

The episodes discussed here affected the Iban inhabitants in different ways. Certain historic parallels can be drawn between the times of raiding during the Dutch and the Brookes regimes and the period of armed confrontation along the border in the 1960s and 1970s. The pragmatic practice of betting on two horses at the same time in order to deal with

---

[70] 'Sri Aman' is a Malay phrase for 'peace', and after signing of the memorandum the town of Simanggang was renamed 'Sri Aman' to commemorate the agreement. However, the Iban still use the former name of the town.
[71] For similar claims see also Japari (1989:11-2). (Japari was *bupati* of Kapuas Hulu from 1985 to 1995.)
[72] Personal interview, Lanjak, 23-7-2007.
[73] Personal interview, *panglima perang*, Embaloh Hulu, 12-6-2007.

often conflicting outside demands is a strategy often applied among the ethnic communities in the borderland. In a region where state power and cross-border involvement fluctuate over time, this approach is understandable. In what follows, I will build on these legacies of the past by examining the subsequent period of resource control and struggle.

NEW ORDER LEGACIES: AUTHORITARIAN RULE AND RESOURCE EXTRACTION

When General Soeharto came to power in 1967, a key principle in his New Order regime[74] was the idea of a strong unitary state: Negara Kesatuan Republik Indonesia, or NKRI. In this the military came to play a dominant role as the ultimate upholder of national unity. The military developed the 'dual function' (*dwifungsi*) doctrine that emphasized the role of the military as both guardian of state sovereignty and political, economic, and ideological overseer of the state. Under Soeharto, the military became entrenched in civil affairs, and they had a number of permanent seats in the parliament. Military officers also held top positions within all levels of government, district, and province, and played key roles in state-owned and private business corporations. For example since the mid-1960s nearly all governors and district heads in the province of West Kalimantan, have had some sort of military background. Promoting the 'national myth' of a unified state through the militarization of Indonesian politics was Soeharto's attempt, as commander in chief, to retain strong central control of the Indonesia nation. Instead of completely prohibiting political parties, the New Order government merged most parties into a single party known as Golkar (Partai Golongan Karya). The borderland of Kapuas Hulu has long been a Golkar stronghold, especially because of the large military presence. As numerous Iban informants describe the situation, 'if your community wanted any subsidies from the government or if you wanted your children to pass their exams, you had to vote Golkar'. Local Golkar supporters often accused other parties like the Democratic Party of Indonesia (PDI) of being a 'Communist' party made up of remnants of the banned PKI (Indonesian Communist Party) and PARAKU. Local elites were

---

[74] Soeharto applied the term New Order (Orde Baru) to imply a transition in politics from former President Soekarno's Old Order rule (Orde Lama).

generally strong supporters of Golkar and were actively engaged in party rallying during various elections.

As touched upon previously, the military presence in the borderland during the New Order era had a dual function: it defended the territorial borders of the nation, but it also defended national unity through its role as disseminators of the national ideology, Pancasila. As I will outline in the following paragraphs, military activities in the borderland were not only about defence and indoctrination, but also about economic gain.

LARGE-SCALE TIMBER CONCESSIONS AND MILITARY RULE

Until the late 1960s, little effort was put into harvesting the border area's extensive forest resources, partly due to the area's remote location and partly due to various political restraints. During the Dutch colonial period large-scale harvesting of timber in the remote parts of West Borneo was seen as unprofitable and not worth the investment needed. Consequently, little was done to control land and forest. As discussed earlier, the main issue at that time was the establishment of claims on the territorial border with Sarawak (Vandergeest and Peluso 2006:49-50).

In 1967, as a direct result of the anti-PARAKU campaign, the immediate border area was put under strict military control by the Indonesian state and categorized as a green 'safety belt' (*sabuk pengaman*). The establishment of the DOM (Daerah Operasi Militer) set the stage for major resource exploitation along the border. With the Basic Forestry Law No. 5 from May 1967,[75] the central government could now assert authority over all state forest lands, without taking into account local people's claims to these lands.[76] As part of his national development program, Soeharto consequently designated most of Kalimantan's forest as state forest (*hutan negara*). The government monopoly on all forests, and areas classified as such, created many problems for local populations, such as the loss of traditional rights to land and the use of natural resources.

In the province of West Kalimantan, President Soeharto divided widespread forest areas along the border into large timber concessions (Hak Pengusaha Hutan, HPH, or Commercial Forest Concession) that

---

[75] Undang-undang Pokok-pokok kehutanan.
[76] The Basic Agrarian Law of 1960 made this possible by formally categorizing all customary forest land (*hutan adat*) as state forest.

provided the concession holder with the exploitation rights for a specific area for up to 20 years.[77] Logging licences were in many instances awarded to military officers and border elites who had served along the border during the anti-PARAKU fighting in the 1960s and 1970s. In return for awarding the military this opportunity for economic gain, Soeharto received military support in upholding strict conformity to the New Order politics in the peripheral regions of the nation. Military involvement in the business sector was also a way to compensate for inadequate budgets and wages (Brown 1999; Human Rights Watch 2006). Since the 1960s, all the governors in the province of West Kalimantan have had a military background, as have many of the district heads.

In the West Kalimantan border region, Soeharto in 1967 (through the Ministry of Agriculture)[78] allocated huge tracts of forest (843,500 ha)[79] to a foundation created by the Indonesian armed forces named 'Yayasan Maju Kerja' (PT Yamaker Kalbar Jaya).[80] In the 1960s the military began, creating various foundations (*yayasan*) that handled their many business ventures such as logging. These foundations were exempted from paying taxes and benefited greatly from government monopolies on various sectors such as forestry. The Yamaker foundation was heavily linked to the Ministry of Defence and Security (Departemen Pertahanan dan Keamanan or Dephankam) (Human Rights Watch 2006; *Jakarta Post* 1999).

Despite being the principal permit holder, Yamaker possessed little forestry experience and did not have the knowledge and financial resources needed in order to carry out productive logging. Therefore, it often leased out its concessions to various timber contractors, both Indonesian and Malaysian.[81] Interestingly, taking the anti-Chinese sentiments of the PARAKU time into consideration, the logging activities in the study area were often carried out in cooperation with ethnic Chinese entrepreneurs from the provincial capital Pontianak. These entrepreneurs possessed the technical expertise and economic investments

[77] See Government Regulation 21/1970.
[78] Decree of the Ministry of Agriculture, 1-11-1967 (HPH No. Kep/79/11/1967).
[79] The Yamaker concessions were later extended in 1989 (SK Menhut No. 1355/Menhut-VI/89).
[80] Yamaker was also given 224,000 ha of forest in neighbouring East Kalimantan, which combined with the concessions in West Kalimantan totalled more than one million hectares. For more information on Yamaker's activities in East Kalimantan, see Obidzinski et al. (2007).
[81] PT Yamaker coordinated, worked together with, or provided security to several logging companies operating in the area during this period such as PT Rimba Ramin, PT Benua Indah, PT Mekanik, PT Militer and PT Tawang Maju.

necessary for such large-scale operations and allegedly cooperated with Malaysian Chinese companies in marketing the timber.

PT Yamaker combined economic exploitation with national security concerns, and its operations encompassed a stretch of border from Tanjung Datu, the most western tip of the province on the coast, to the upper part of the Leboyan River and Embaloh River in the east, approximately 400 km in length.[82] The main activity of the foundation was logging to generate income for the armed forces, although in return for the HPH concessions, the company was officially required to improve the socioeconomic welfare of the border communities by promoting various rural development programmes.

In the late 1970s, three Iban war veterans accompanied by prominent community leaders travelled to Jakarta to address the board of the Yamaker Foundation and lobby for their part of the border region to be opened up to logging. They argued that logging would bring prosperity to local communities, but it was the vast forest resources, and to a lesser degree the need to keep external threats (Communists) at bay, that quickly convinced PT Yamaker of the area's potential. In October 1980 the head of the Yamaker board (*pengurus*) in Jakarta, Major General R. Soebiantoro, issued a letter of declaration acknowledging Yamaker support of the request for local development made by these leading members of the border community. The letter stated that:

> The community representatives have declared that the forest environment where they reside is still intact (*utuh*). This forest territory conforms (*sesuai*) to – Decree of the Minister of Agriculture No. Kep 79/11-1967 – and is part of the Yamaker forest concession (HPH), and until this moment there has been no company activity (*kegiatan*) in this area. In accordance with the statement of the [Iban] representatives, the local community truly hopes that Yamaker will soon commence operating (*dapat operasi*) in their area, in order for the community to receive [economic] benefits (*manfaatnya*), and their safety from the PARAKU can be secured (*dijaga*). When the HPH is up and running, they [the representatives] request that some of the living requirements of the local people (*penghidupan rakyat*) be provided such as the construction of schools and community halls, and that the local community be provided jobs in the logging operations.

[82] The entire length of this international border between Indonesia and Malaysia is circa 1200 km (BPS-KB 2006).

Yamaker agrees that if it starts operating in the area this request will be granted (*permohonannya akan dipenuhi*) – Jakarta, 21 October 1980.[83]

Logging activities were initiated, and alongside the major role played by PT Yamaker, the Iban elite were granted licences to run their forest concession, PT. Lanjak Deras. It is here important to note that it was only a chosen few among the war veterans who received such great rewards for their help in fighting the PARAKU. Other veterans who actively took part on the side of the Indonesian military only received documents acknowledging their status as veterans and a promise of a pension that never materialized.

Consequently, these few Iban, empowered by military authority and their position as community leaders, opened up several community-forest territories for timber extraction on behalf of the wider Iban community. Not having the needed investment to start up logging themselves, they made financial support agreements with Malaysian Chinese and Iban from Sibu, Sarawak. A crucial instrument in attracting these external investors was the strong military backing. The concession was dubbed an 'Iban concession', although benefits ended up in the pockets of a few men (Harwell 2000b:94-5). As noted by Harwell, the granting of an 'Iban concession' is quite unique during the New Order period, as most other concessions was given to military officers and other powerful cronies of Soeharto. Harwell suggests that the granting of this local concession most likely was a reflection of the 'state's deep anxiety' about Communist infiltration in the borderland (2000a:95). The concession can therefore be understood as an attempt by the military to gain sympathy and loyalty among local leaders.

According to one informant, these negotiations were carried out without the knowledge (*masyarakat kecil tidak tahu*) of the larger non-elite community in the borderland.

> The community did not know that certain leaders (*wakil masyarakat*) went to Jakarta and asked for the forest to be open for the welfare of the local community (*kesejahteraan*). Actually, it was not done for community welfare. They [the representatives] got duped (*ditipu*) by the entrepreneurs (*pengusaha*) in Jakarta and the leaders duped the community. The commu-

---

[83] Surat Keterangan, Dewan Pengerus Yayasan Maju Kerja, No. 165/Kep/P.Y/X/1980.

nity didn't know that the company was coming but could just stand and look with their eyes wide open (*lihat dengan mata terbuka*).[84]

This informant and several others claimed that one man who held the position of *temenggong* and *panglima perang* at the time (he has since passed away) had particularly strong ties to the ruling elite in Jakarta. He supposedly met with both Soekarno and Soeharto on several occations in his position as a *panglima perang* and veteran from the Konfrontasi and anti-PARAKU operations in the 1960 and 1970s.

During the subsequent period of resource extraction, little or no compensation was normally awarded to the majority of non-elite inhabitants for timber extracted from local forests. Yamaker did not fulfill its promises of developing the area and providing local jobs . For local communities the benefits were few, and even today, most people recall the logging operations of the 1980s and 1990s with indignation. As a local Iban farmer in the Lanjak area stated:

> Only those [companies] who had HPH [forest concessions] permits (*punyai ijin*) benefited. The communities did not receive any benefits (*untung*) from forest cutting. They instead became traumatized (*masyarakat diibaratkan traumalah*).... We just received pocket money for buying sugar – we were sweet-talked (*untuk gula saja*) and eventually the revenue from logging was not spread equally (*hasilnya tidak merata*) generating social jealousy (*cemburu sosial*). Only the bold and the brave (*berani*) were favoured.[85]

Traditional forest claims were largely disregarded, resulting in a certain degree of bitterness towards the timber companies and some of their partners within the border elite. Despite the initial promises of job creation implied in the company's name (*Maju Kerja*, or 'Advancing Employment'), the PT Yamaker workforce consisted largely of workers brought in from Java, and development efforts were generally half-hearted (*Sinar Harapan* 2005b). In spite of community bitterness towards PT Yamaker's broken promises, there were only a few occasions during the 1980s and 1990s when local communities showed their discontent with the timber companies through direct actions such as erecting roadblocks

[84] Personal interview, Lanjak, 24-6-2007.
[85] Personal interview, Lanjak, 24-6-2007.

and claiming compensation. Their animosity mostly went unspoken in public, as timber companies enjoyed the protection of powerful military interests and were sanctioned by border elites and central state authorities. Wadley, for example, has noted how, during meetings between locals and company agents, the Iban elite (that is, *temenggong* and *patih*) directly discouraged the local communities from bringing grievances against companies (Wadley 1998:79).

With all forest land in the border region, as elsewhere in the province, now belonging exclusively to the centralized Department of Forestry, local communities had little legal ground for receiving compensation for trees cut on what they perceived as their traditional forestlands. Operating under broad state-supported authority over the forest granted to them, companies felt little commitment to reinvest resources in local development. In their dealings with local communities, company agents often talked about gaining permission from locals to carry out logging. However, locals were generally aware that the companies did not need permission from the communities, as they already had been granted permission by the central government. In order to prevent major local unrest that could end up affecting company business, most companies gave token assistance to communities affected by the logging activities. Most commonly, the companies helped build access roads to longhouses, gave rides on logging trucks, and supplied gasoline for generators and various other handouts. Compensations were also paid for damage to fruit and rubber trees during logging and the construction of logging roads. Formally the Indonesian Forestry Law obliged the companies to pay some compensation for destroyed property, and as most logging roads ran through locally claimed forest rubber and fruit tree orchards communities saw this as a possibility to benefit from the logging. Locals therefore attempted to claim ownership of felled trees and receive compensation (Wadley 1998). The local elite negotiated the amount of compensation. Besides representing the communities, the elite also received their own honoraria from the timber companies. Significantly, the *temenggongs* and *panglima perang* at the time were largely appointed by the government or military, and some were concession holders themselves.

Despite the split loyalty of local leaders and heavy military presence, some local communities maintained a certain degree of autonomy. For example, in the late 1980s when Yamaker began extending its logging operations in the Ulu Leboyan, the community of Rumah Manah began negotiating with the company. Besides compensation for destroyed forest gardens and graveyards, a special (written) contract was made stating, among other things, that Yamaker had to provide ironwood timber for a new longhouse. Despite several requests from the community headman, the company supervisors delayed fulfillment of their part of the agreement. Consequently, in the early 1990s armed members of the community confiscated all logging equipment from the main Yamaker timber camp located opposite the longhouse across the Leboyan River.[86] After several failed attempts to negotiate with the company on site, a delegation of five community members travelled to Pontianak to visit the main Yamaker office to state their grievances. According to the community members, the manager of the Pontianak office, Mr. Akiang, refused to talk with the delegation, as he denied knowing anything about an agreement with the community. Not taking a 'no' for an answer, the delegation camped outside the company office for several days. They informed Mr. Akiang that the community of Rumah Manah would instantly stop all collaboration and make it difficult for the company to operate in the Ulu Leboyan. Not wishing to slow down its logging operations and to engage in potential violent confrontations with the community, the company agreed to provide the timber requested. Although little cash compensation was paid to the inhabitants of Rumah Manah, a logging road connecting the area with the main road to Lanjak was built, enabling motorized access to and from the area.

In the early 1990s, this road had passed the longhouse into the Ulu Leboyan and by 'accident' ran through an Iban cemetery where Bantin, the famous rebel, was buried. Having disturbed the dead, the company had to bring in the local *temenggong* from Lanjak to perform ritual expiation before the road construction could be continued. After this ritual involving the sacrifice of a goat and pig (at the expense of the company) was performed, the *temenggong* strongly advised the inhabitants of Rumah Manah to support the company and warned them not to engage in any more acts of vigilantism.

PT Yamaker concessions along the entire border were terminated in May 1999 by the Habibie government (1998-1999) because of gross mismanagement. Yamaker had already ended its logging operations in the Ulu Leboyan in 1994 due to lack of capital. The company was poorly

---

[86] The same location was used as base camp for the Indonesian military during the anti-PARAKU fighting.

managed and was not able to continue logging in the hilly area due to the heavy costs of building and maintaining roads and bridges on the steep slopes. The terminations of the Yamaker concessions were furthermore an attempt by the new government to make a political stand against Soeharto's former cronies. After disclosing that Yamaker was involved in large-scale timber smuggling across the border,[87] Minister of Forestry and Plantations Muslimin Nasution issued a decree transferring logging rights along the Malaysian-Indonesian border from the military-controlled PT Yamaker to the government-owned company PT Perhutani.[88] The minister announced that contracts were originally given to Yamaker because the forests along the border were considered a security zone, and it was thought prudent to have a military-linked timber firm manage the area. He further announced, 'Our decision shows that the government will not hesitate to revoke licenses or contracts of disobedient companies no matter who owns the companies' (*Jakarta Post* 1999).

Even today the Yamaker Foundation has apparently still failed to repay Rp3 billion (US$309,000) received in Forest Resource Provision funds and Reforestation funds (*Sinar Harapan* 2005b).[89] Like PT Yamaker, PT Perhutani also largely mismanaged its concessions and generated little local support.[90] The company consequently suspended its logging operations in the area.[91] By contrast, the Iban-headed concession PT Lanjak Deras was granted a ten-year contract extention after its leaders emphasized the concession's crucial role in the development of the area (Wadley 2006:117). PT Lanjak Deras was later in 1999 renamed PT Lanjak Deras Jaya Raya as it became a subsidiary of the company PT Benua Indah. The large Benua Indah possessed the needed capital to sustain logging in the area that PT Lanjak Deras lacked.[92] Despite central government's revocation of Yamaker's logging rights, the military continued to impose its authority in the border area, but instead of

---

[87] Allegations of Yamaker engaging in illegal cross-border timber smuggling together with Malaysian Chinese had been made already in the mid-1980s (*Tempo* 1987).
[88] Decree of the Ministry of Forestry and Plantations, 27-5-1999 (No. 376/Kpts-II/1999) and 16-8-2000 (No. 1007/Menhutbun-II/2000).
[89] Forest Resource Provision funds (Provisi Sumber Daya Hutan, PSDH) and Reforestation Funds (Dana Reboisasi, DR).
[90] According to local statements, PT Perhutani was also engaged with the military, which provided security for the company.
[91] Decree of the Ministry of Forestry, 31-12-2002 (No. 10344/Kpts-II/2002) concerning the revocation of Decree No. 376/Kpts-II/1999.
[92] SK Menhutbun No. 844/Kpts-VI/99, 7-10-1999.

doing so directly, the military allegedly indirectly cooperated with the Indonesian and Malaysian companies who entered the borderland after 1998. As noted by the Iban head of an environmental NGO working in the area:

> The rights of Yamaker were withdrawn (*dicabut hak*), were taken away. Actually, the generals are still in the game (*jenderal pun masih bermain*). They are involved in all processes of those illegal activities; in fact, those were not illegal because they got permission of some generals who were involved themselves (*beberapa jenderal juga yang terlibat dalam permainan ini*). We just cannot prove it (*tidak bisa membuktikannya*).[93]

MOULDING LOYAL CITIZENS AND ITS PARADOXICAL OUTCOMES

As illustrated in the previous chapters, the creation of the territorial borderline dividing the island of Borneo in two has played a crucial role in moulding local Iban lives and strategies. In what follows, I will show that the contemporary dynamics cannot be fully understood without reference to the overall borderland experience and without taking into account these dynamic historic processes and long-term ethnic links. A meticulous investigation into different borderland practices as experienced by the inhabitants themselves is decisive in understanding the borderland milieu.

Here the historically conditioned affinity the Iban border populations have developed for neighbouring Sarawak plays a crucial role. Not only are the Iban a minority group within their own province, partitioned from a much larger population in a visibly more prosperous country across the border, but also successive colonial and national governments on both sides of the border have given them special treatment. This has allowed them considerable space to develop a strong sense of autonomy, heightening the sense of separateness that appears ubiquitous with border populations. Nevertheless, this sense of autonomy has also led to shifting and ambivalent relationships with various levels of government bureaucracy. After independence, the partitioned Iban population along

---

93   Personal interview, Pontianak, 2-3-2007.

the border continued its arbitrary relationship with government rule, now with 'the state' taking the form of the new Indonesian Republic.

While the borderland was largely left alone as an autonomous entity in the first decade after independence, nationalist aspirations towards neighbouring Malaysia swiftly made the borderland into a combat zone of intense militarization and, decades later, major resource extraction and struggle. These initial Indonesian attempts to (violently) impose a sense of national consciousness among their border citizens resulted in paradoxical outcomes. The attempt to mould loyal citizens and to disseminate the message of nationalism was only partially successful. While a small segment of the borderland population vividly expressed their strong nationalist loyalty by voluntarily joining the fighting and in return gained some rewards, the nationalist indoctrination largely failed among the majority of the border population. This majority never came to develop a strong sense of belonging to a united Indonesian nation-state, primarily because of strong cross-border links, military violence and lack of immediate genuine rewards. Ironically, and despite government intentions to win its allegiance, the border population instead strengthened its orientation towards neighbouring Sarawak, Malaysia, both economically and socially. The long-term militarization of the borderland and a general exclusion from national development during the early stages of Indonesian state formation quickly destroyed any growing 'patriotic' feelings among the border communities and is today locally understood as a prime indicator of the Indonesian state's indifference towards its marginal citizens.

By confronting inherent assumptions of a strong and united state lying dormant within Indonesian national history, local counter-narratives often provide alternative histories. In this case borderland narratives provide meaningful insights into how national borders have been constructed in tandem with central state actors and border communities and not least how Cold War politics played out at the edges of the Southeast Asian states. Another important aspect of this early period in Indonesian state formation was the fact that the Konfrontasi and following counter-insurgency effort contributed in a major way to the consolidation of a strong and powerful Indonesian military elite. During these few decades of jungle warfare young military entrepreneurs proved their loyalty towards the nation and were later rewarded with key positions in the New Order regime.

As we shall see in the next chapter, the events unfolding in the bor-

4 Guerrilla warfare and resource extraction

derland following the Asian economic crisis of 1997 and the fall of the authoritarian Soeharto regime in 1998 are perhaps not very surprising, especially given the critically important historical precedent discussed in the above chapters.

Fig 26: Hand painted sign on path leading to timber-cutting site, 2000 (Photo courtesy Reed Lee Wadley)

Fig 27: Mixed forest gardens, swiddenfields and logged forest along the border, 2007 (Photograph by author)

Fig 28: Logging truck transporting newly cut timber down to the border timber mills, 2003 (Photograph by author)

Fig 29: Logging road twisting through the low-lying hills along the border, 2003 (Photograph by author)

Fig 30: Trucks loaded with sawn timber moving towards the border, 2003 (Photograph by author)

Fig 31: Aphengs large sawmill on the Indonesian side of the border, 2003 (Photograph by author)

Fig 32: Newly logged forest and soil erosion, 2003 (Photograph by author)

5

Patronage and power

> Cross-border economic and commercial activities are often based on pre-existing networks of kinship, friendship, and entrepreneurial partnership that span both sides of the border (Baud and Van Schendel 1997:229).

This chapter focusses on the period right after Soeharto's fall from power in 1998 and the subsequent termination of the military logging concessions. Through several interconnected cases I show how border communities and border elites swiftly adjusted to the new shift in power and politics following new reforms of administrative decentralization. In particular, I demonstrate how the change from authoritarian to post-authoritarian rule created novel opportunities for local negotiations of authority over resources, through collusion and patronage networks with local government and cross-border entrepreneurs. One purpose of this chapter is to examine state-society relations in a time of decentralization, where central state authority appears especially weak compared to the previous period of strict military surveillance and 'strong' state authority in the borderland. According to Sally Falk Moore, within semi-autonomous social fields local norms can supplant or dominate those of official state law. However, as depicted in this chapter, while local norms and rules diverge from those of central government, they are inherently, and often ultimately, subjected to it. The chapter further looks into how local strategies and networks applied during this period of increased autonomy can be traced back to the period of confrontation and anti-PARAKU fighting and how they once again seem to challenge the effort to differentiate between the controls imposed by governments on either side of the Indonesian-Malaysian border.

DECENTRALIZATION, INFORMAL NETWORKS AND 'ILLEGAL' LOGGING

In early 2000, on the Indonesian side of the international border between West Kalimantan and Sarawak, Malaysia, trucks loaded with sawn log blocks (*balok*) lined the heavily rutted road as they made their way toward the crossing into Sarawak. The logs, considered by the central Indonesian government to be illegally harvested and exported, came from numerous cutting sites along the border road in forests within the territories of Iban communities of the Kapuas Hulu district. At the head of one path leading to a cutting site, with *balok* piled on the side for collection, stood a hand-painted sign which read: 'CV Munggu Keringit Sdn Bhd'.[1] At first glance this sign signifies little, but examined more deeply it represents an important local perspective that must be taken into account for a more complete picture of the rampant 'illegal' logging in Indonesia generally and the borderlands of West Kalimantan specifically to emerge. 'CV'[2] stands for 'limited partnership' in Indonesia, while 'Sdn Bhd'[3] means virtually the same thing across the border. 'Munggu Keringit' simply referred to a nearby hill and the scene of action. Such a designation had no legal standing and was intended as a joke, but it very effectively summed up the ambivalent position held by borderland residents engaged in cooperative logging with Malaysian timber entrepreneurs. The writing on the sign expresses an awareness among border communities of the dual position that life in the borderland entails, and the sensible strategy of securing one's livelihood by looking towards both sides of the border, as the locals have done continuously since the border's creation more than 150 years ago (Wadley and Eilenberg 2005). 'Illegal' is here deliberately placed within quotation marks because the central Indonesian government and international organisations regard much timber harvesting as illegal, whereas local communities see the timber coming from their own traditionally managed forests as part of negotiated agreements with loggers.

---

[1] Reed Wadley initially observed this incident during field research in April 2000 (Wadley and Eilenberg 2005).
[2] The abbreviation can be traced back to the colonial Dutch and means 'Commanditaire Vennootschap'.
[3] 'Sendirian Berhad' in Malaysian.

TOWARDS INCREASED REGIONAL AUTONOMY

The drastic political changes that took place in the wake of the Indonesian economic crisis (*krisis moneter* or *krismon*) in 1997 and Soeharto's resignation from power the following year, quickly altered the dynamics of logging in the borderland. In an attempt to distribute political and economic power more evenly and to return authority to the districts, in the years after 1998, Indonesia's successive central governments began initiating national programs of decentralization. The first post-Soeharto government under the presidency of B.J. Habibie (1998-1999) came under immense pressure to take a stand against the authoritarian government structure of former President Soeharto and to take concrete steps towards enhancing the administrative powers of the districts. Regional autonomy became the main topic for policymakers, and new legislation resulted in a series of reforms that gave local districts greater autonomy over sectors such as forestry (Perdu 1999). Laws regulating the decentralization of authority (Law 22/1999)[4] and the fiscal balance (Law 25/1999)[5] between central and regional governments were passed by Indonesia's national parliament in 1999 and officially implemented in January 2001. The new regulations largely circumvented provincial governments and gave district governments authority to deal with most local affairs, including forest resource management.[6] The formerly all-powerful Ministry of Forestry suddenly lost parts of its authority over forestry management in West Kalimantan, along with the large amount of revenue this authority generated (Yasmi et al. 2006). Districts were now entitled to a much greater share of revenues produced by local timber extraction.[7]

The new legislation was often inconsistent with already existing laws and therefore created a great deal of confusion and ambiguity in relation to the right to control forest resources. The potential for conflicts over resources and environmental degradation was a persistent worry resulting

---

[4]   Undang-undang Republik Indonesia Nomor 22 Tahun 1999 tentang Pemerintah Daerah.
[5]   Undang-undang Republik Indonesia Nomor 25 Tahun 1999 tentang Perimbangan Keuangan antara Pemerintah Pusat dan Daerah.
[6]   Besides natural resource management, the districts were also given authority over industry, agriculture, trade and investment, health and education.
[7]   Law 25/1999 on fiscal balancing specifies that provincial and district governments should receive 80 percent of the Forest Resource Rent Provision (*Provisi Sumber Daya Hutan*, PSDH) and that district governments would receive 40 percent of the Reforestation Fund (*Dana Reboisasi*, DR).

from the disorderly way in which regional autonomy was implemented.[8] The distinction between what was considered legal and illegal timber extraction became increasingly blurred as central and district authorities often interpreted the laws differently.[9] A few years after the outset of the decentralization reforms, the *ad hoc* manner in which the decentralization of the forestry sector was managed sparked a fierce contest for authority between the centre and the districts.

Even though the formal implementation of regional autonomy (*otonomi daerah* or *otda*) did not take place until 2001, the chaotic period of unstable and changing governments and numerous political reforms following the fall of Soeharto quickly led to a kind of *de facto* regional autonomy in most of West Kalimantan. District officials seized the opportunities presented by the political and economic uncertainties associated with the transition period and immediately began to implement their own regional reforms and regulations, officially 'legalizing' local timber logging without the final blessing of the central government. Widespread corruption developed. Although the legal status of timber extraction during this transition period remained undecided, the district government in Kapuas Hulu and local border communities nonetheless took advantage of their proximity to neighbouring Sarawak to invite Malaysian timber barons to harvest what they considered their forest, in turn receiving royalties (*retribusi*) and locally derived revenue (Pendapatan Asli Daerah, PAD) from local timber.[10]

These arrangements boosted local district tax income and transformed the small and sleepy border towns of Badau, Lanjak and Nanga Kantuk into prospering boomtowns. Nearly all of the regionally generated income (PAD) of the district originated from forest resources. From being heavily dependent on central government grants before 1999, the Kapuas Hulu district PAD income rose sharply in the ensuing years. During this period, several Sarawak-based logging companies, such as the Sibu-based Grand Atlantic Timber Sdn. Bhd, entered the border-

---

[8] *Indonesian Observer* 2000; *Jakarta Post* 2000b; *Kompas* 2000a; *Media Indonesia* 2000a; *Pontianak Post* 2000b; *Tempo* 2001a.
[9] See Casson and Obidzinski 2002; Fox et al. 2005; McCarthy 2004.
[10] These arrangements not only unfolded in the Kapuas Hulu district, but also in other border districts like Sambas, Bengkayang, Sanggau, and Sintang where local populations also had long-term relationships with Malaysian Chinese timber entrepreneurs. For similar arrangements taking place in the borderland between East Kalimantan and Sabah. See, for example, Obidzinski et al. 2007.

land.[11] According to local timber workers, the district government and border communities had (unofficially) agreed to this arrangement in order to help boost the local economy in a time of economic crisis. Only the Malaysian companies possessed the necessary capital, equipment, and technical knowledge to restart logging in the area. It is important to note that these companies were operating entirely without official permits from the central government. Decentralization and new fiscal arrangements pushed the districts to become more self-reliant financially, and one way of generating much-needed local revenue was through timber harvesting carried out in the grey area between legality and illegality.[12] The companies' engagement in logging across the border can be seen as an outcome of several factors: the economic and political climate in the borderland and in Indonesia as a whole; the increase in international demand for timber; easy access to the area from across the border; and finally, pre-existing kinship and business ties between locals and Sarawak timber entrepreneurs. A local Iban resident described the situation in the borderland at the onset of regional autonomy as follows: 'The only thing on people's minds right now is the timber business (*bisnis kayu*)'.[13]

COOPERATIVE LOGGING AND A BOOMING ECONOMY

In West Kalimantan, as in other provinces rich in natural resources, the period following the fall of Soeharto provided a welcome opportunity for district governments and the border elite to take control of the formerly state-managed logging business (Yasmi et al. 2006). The formal implementation of regional autonomy after 2000 only heightened tensions, as provincial-level government was sidestepped in favour of increased authority for *bupati* at the local level. With respect to logging, between 2000 and 2002 the *bupati* had the authority to issue permits for small-scale forest concessions of 100 hectares located within state controlled forest (Kawasan Hutan), locally referred to as HPHH or community

---

[11] See *Jakarta Post* 2000c; *Kompas* 2000b; *Suara Pembaruan* 2000.
[12] Personal interview, timber broker, Lanjak, 15-10-2002.
[13] Personal interview, Lanjak, 03-11-2002.

cooperatives.[14] In this two-year period the district governments in West Kalimantan altogether issued over 900 such HPHH licences, and the district of Kapuas Hulu alone counted for more than 335 of these (Dinas Kehutanan Kalimantan Barat 2004; Kartodihardjo and Putro 2004). In several instances, these HPHH concessions overlapped with already existing concessions (*Sinar Harapan* 2001). In 2003 this number had risen to 450 (Dermawan 2004). Besides these small-scale concessions, the government regulations also allowed the *bupati* to issue large-scale concessions of up to 50,000 ha known as IUPHHK (Timber Product Utilization Permit/Izin Usaha Pemanfaatan Hasil Hutan Kayu) that replaced the old HPH large-scale concessions of the Soeharto period. The district of Kapuas Hulu issued nine such IUPHHK, covering an area of 142,800 ha (Dinas Kehutanan Kalimantan Barat 2004). Several of these concessions, such as PT. Benua Indah, PT. Lanjak Deras and PT. Rimba Kanyau, were placed within the borderland (Kabupaten Kapuas Hulu 2006) and allegedly cooperated with Malaysian Chinese entrepreneurs (Sinar Harapan 2008).

Like most other regulations and decrees issued by central government at the time, the guidelines for implementing the HPHH concessions were extremely unclear. Regulation of these concessions was more or less up to the *bupati*'s own interpretation. This led to interpretations that often far exceeded the legal rights prescribed in the regulations. The Kapuas Hulu district government, for example, issued its own decrees concerning how to obtain permits and regulate these new forest concessions. These district regulations were also an attempt to generate local revenue through various district taxes. The legal standing for issuing local taxes was mentioned in Law 22/1999 and 34/2000. But instead of waiting for the local legislature to prepare a detailed decree (*perda*) as stipulated in the laws, the *bupati* in 2000 instead persuaded the district assembly to produce a recommendation for him to issue a temporary decree so he could immediately begin issuing HPHH permits (*Kalimantan Review* 2001; KepBKH 2000b, 2001). The increased authority of the *bupati* made the locals refer to his position as that of a 'small king' (*raja kecil*).

---

[14] See 'Regulation No. 6/1999 on Forest Utilization and Forest Product Harvesting in Production Forest' and 'Ministry of Forestry Decrees No. 310/Kpts-II/1999 and No. 05.1/Kpts-II/2000' on guidelines and criteria for issuing HPHH licenses. These regulations and decrees provided authority to all districts across Indonesia to issue licences for small-scale timber extraction on less than 100 ha (Hak Pemungutan Hasil Hutan (HPHH)).

5 Patronage and power

The HPHH concessions were issued to so-called multipurpose community cooperatives (Koperasi Serba Usaha, or KSU). The KSUs in the borderland were often made up of several communities who worked together with an outside entrepreneur, usually Malaysian. Their supposed aim was to empower local communities by facilitating different kinds of joint development projects, but the only activity carried out under their auspices in the borderland was logging.

Although vaguely outlined, the process of obtaining HPHH permits, as stipulated in the decrees, involved several stages. First, applicants had to initiate a survey of the area to be logged by mapping the forest resources available and identifying partners with the needed capital and knowledge to carry out the actual logging. In addition to the survey, signed recommendations and letters of support were needed from sub-district and village heads. Secondly, the proposal and a work plan had to be submitted to the *bupati* office for approval and various taxes had to be paid. For example, the Kapuas Hulu district decree number 8/2001 stated that cooperatives had to pay Rp 25,000 (US$2) per hectare of forest in Forest Concession Liaison Fee (Iuran Hak Pemungutan Hasil Hutan, IHPHH) (KepBKH 2001). During this period, nearly all of the regionally generated income (PAD) of the district originated from production forest resources, especially from DR/IHH (rehabilitation fund/forest products payment), PSDH (Forest Resource Rent Provision) and IHPHH (Forest Concession Liaison Fee). From being heavily dependent on central government grants before 1999, the Kapuas Hulu district PAD income rose drastically in the following years. Out of the total budget, the PAD went from 0.7 percent in 2000 to 11.5 percent in 2002 (BPS-KH 2002, 2003; Dermawan 2004:45).

Finally, if a proposal was successful and the various taxes paid, the *bupati* office granted a one-year logging permit open to extension (KepBKH 2001). The cost of gaining permits and establishing a coop was very costly according to local standards; Dermawan (2004:43) mentions the cost as being more than Rp 10 million, but according to my data the cost was closer to Rp 20 million (US$2,200) (*DetikNews* 2004). In the case of the borderland, such high capital input was often sought through cooperation with outside moneymen and entrepreneurs from Malaysia. Although these district decrees on the regulation of HPHH concessions stipulate various criteria for the regulation of concessions, such as the type of forest to be cut, equipment to be used, and the replanting of logged areas, the actual activities taking place on the ground were another story. The new concessions issued often overlapped with existing concessions previously allocated by the central government, and some extended over the boundaries of protected forest and national parks (*Jakarta Post* 2002b). Despite the stipulated criteria, the district government did not put any effort into monitoring or enforcing compliance.

The outcome of the new district regulations soon attracted the attention of central and provincial government. Already under the Presidency of Megawati Soekarnopoetri (2001-2004) the central government began to display resistance towards the decentralization process, especially to the extent of autonomy gained by the districts over the management of local natural resources. Consequently, in 2002, the central government issued a new government regulation (to take effect beginning in 2003) that revoked the authority of districts to issue HPHH logging permits. The centre thus attempted to reassert its authority over forest resources.[15] The formal argument was that district governments were mismanaging the nation's forest resources, leading to an increase in illegal logging and corruption (Perdu 2002). However, the *bupati* of Kapuas Hulu largely ignored this new regulation, which he claimed was in conflict with the laws of regional autonomy and would lead to the loss of more than 34,000 jobs (*Pontianak Post* 2003c). In defiance of this attempt by central government to recentralize forest authority by constraining the allocation of HPHHs and permits, the *bupati* further withheld the share of timber taxes that he was supposed to pay the central government (*Kompas* 2004e; *Sinar Harapan* 2003a). The overall argument of the *bupati* for continuing the logging business was its contribution to empowerment of local border communities and the promotion of their general well-being. According to the *bupati*, never before had local communities received such a large share of revenues from the harvesting of local forest resources. By selling directly to Malaysian entrepreneurs, these communities received a much larger share than they had during the former HPH concessions (*Pontianak Post* 2004j). At this time, most of the logging operations taking

---

[15] Just before leaving office in 2004, President Megawati replaced the 1999 decentralization laws with yet a new law (No. 32/2004) on regional autonomy. The law, among other things, reaffirms the status of provincial government, and it gives far-reaching authority to the central government to control district governments, such as supervision of various regulations, decisions or policies approved or favoured on the district level (Barr et al. 2006).

place along the border were unauthorized by the central government and considered illegal.

During my fieldwork in 2002 and 2003 and at the time of a return visit in 2004, much of the logging taking place in the Kapuas Hulu borderland was carried on by community cooperatives (KSUs) in locally arranged agreements with Sarawak timber entrepreneurs as 'partners'. In order to harvest as much timber as possible, these Sarawak companies were involved with several cooperatives (sometimes more than ten) at the same time; in this way they were able to exceed the 100-hectare limit of forest allowed to be cut. However, more often than not, the 100-hectare limit was simply ignored. Furthermore, all the logging involving Sarawak entrepreneurs was carried out with the use of heavy equipment brought from across the border, and no reforestation took place. No effort was made by district government to exercise control and ensure that the operation adhered to the regulations.

In the particular stretch of the border discussed in this study, Sarawak logging companies were largely owned by a handful of Sarawak Chinese timber entrepreneurs, locally known as *tukei* (or *tauke*).[16] Such logging entrepreneurs are known elsewhere in Indonesia as *cukong*. In his research on Sumatra's rainforest frontier, McCarthy defines *cukong* as the entrepreneur with capital and *tauke* as the *cukong*'s broker who negotiates logging agreements (2000:5-6; 2006:142). In the Iban-dominated areas of West Kalimantan borderland, *tukei* are usually the entrepreneurs. The timber logged through the cooperatives by these companies was obtained very cheaply and sold for substantial profit across the border. Already in early 2000, there were no less than twelve Sarawak entrepreneurs operating along the border from Lanjak to Badau, and their numbers continued to grow until 2004. At least six *tukei* built substantial sawmills near the main government road (Jalan Lintas Utara) (Wadley and Eilenberg 2005). According to local informants, some Sarawak companies were initially invited by the *bupati* in 1998, at the onset of the economic crisis, to help develop oil palm plantations in the borderland; later they did become directly engaged in logging. As elaborated upon later, the largest and most dominant entrepreneur or *tukei* was operating in the Ulu Leboyan.

Many locals realized that the *tukei* paid regular monthly bribes to important officials and civil servants, such as local district and subdistrict

---

[16] In Sarawak, the term used for these Chinese entrepreneurs is often spelled *towkey* or *taukey*.

officials, police, military and immigration officials at the border crossing, in order to have their businesses run smoothly. In exchange for bribes, officials ignored the logging and the smuggling of timber across the border. The *bupati* of Kapuas Hulu even imposed his own local unofficial export tax of Rp 50,000 (US$6) on every truckload of logs taken across the border (*Pontianak Post* 2003a). In one year, from 2001 to 2002, the district office collected approximately Rp 6 billion (US$600,000) solely from these locally imposed taxes.[17] Besides these taxes the Sarawak companies supposedly had to pay a fee of Rp 50 million (US$5,500) a month to the district customs office at the border in order to bring their illegal timber across the border (EIA 2001). Local communities along the Lanjak-Badau road also constructed toll gates and levied a charge of RM10 to RM20 (Malaysian ringgit)[18] on each truck passing through (*Pontianak Post* 2004g).

According to civil servants in the district office, this locally imposed tax was an attempt to generate revenue for the underdeveloped district. The rationale was, that if central government did not have the capacity to live up to its obligation to regulate the international border trade, then it was up to the district to enforce such regulations for the common good of the border population. When asked about the purpose of these taxes, the *bupati* answered: 'We just please the communities, that's all (*tolong masyarakat saja*)'.[19] In addition, at least one subdistrict office has issued some *tukei* with Indonesian identity cards (KTP or Kartu Tanda Penduduk) so they could operate more freely in the province (*Kompas* 2003e). There were even reports of several *tukei* using false documents with the signature of the Indonesian president in order to persuade local communities to cooperate in opening up a new road crossing the border from the district of Kapuas Hulu to Sarawak. This endeavour involved more than 100 Sarawak citizens and 50 bulldozers, and the main purpose was to open a new route for timber transport. According to local press, they succeeded in one month in smuggling timber across the border worth US$1 million.[20] During field research in 2002-2003, around 500 trucks loaded with lumber traversed the government road from Lanjak towards the border point in Badau each week; this number

[17] Personal interview, Putussibau, 14-3-2007.
[18] Malaysian ringgit per US$ was approximately RM3.8 in 2004.
[19] Personal interview, Pontianak, 22-08-2007.
[20] *Media Indonesia* 2004; *Sinar Harapan* 2004b; *Suara Pembaruan* 2004b.

had decreased to between 150 and 200 a week by 2004.[21]

Huge amounts of money were at stake in cross-border logging at the time. When the timber crossed the border, it was 'legalized' by paying fees of RM2 per m^3 and by obtaining official papers at the border checkpoint of the Sarawak-state-owned Hardwood Timber Company (Hard Wood *Sendirian Berhads*) in Lubok Antu. Thereafter the timber was considered legal and ready to be sold and exported.[22] The Sarawak side of border has figured as a free trade zone since the 1990s, meaning that the import and export of trade goods including timber is very loosely regulated (Tirtosudarmo 2002). A team of researchers from the school of forestry at a provincial university in Pontianak (Tanjungpura University) estimated that 80 percent of the raw timber supply in the Malaysian province of Sarawak at the time came from West Kalimantan (*Jakarta Post* 2003). Sarawak has largely exhausted its own forest resources and therefore searches for timber elsewhere to feed its large timber-based industry.[23]

NEGOTIATION AND COLLUSION: ELITE OPPORTUNITIES

In the attempt to exercise a certain degree of control of their forest and deal with both regional and cross-border interests, the ambivalent position of the Iban border population surfaces again and its dual identity comes into play. Nearly all Iban communities in the area welcomed the presence of the Sarawak companies for several reasons: first, there is the existence of intimate cross-border relations. Many Iban men in the area have at some point during their lives worked for logging companies in Sarawak run by ethnic Chinese. Based on these past experiences the Iban knew the efficiency with which these operations were run and the better working conditions and salaries they provided. The *tukei*, for their part, had learned to appreciate the honesty and stamina of the Iban. Second, cultural similarities that span the border played an important part in local cooperation. Having carried out logging operations in Iban

---

[21] *Kompas* 2003d; *Pontianak Post* 2003a; 2004a; 2004l; *Sinar Harapan* 2004d.
[22] *EIA* 2001; *EIA/Telepak* 2004; *Toyoda* 2002.
[23] Sarawak-owned companies crossing the border in search of cheap timber were not unique to the West Kalimantan borderland. Along the Sarawak border with East Kalimantan, similar activities took place (Obidzinski et al. 2006, 2007).

areas in Sarawak for decades, the *tukei* and their associates had an excellent knowledge of Iban customs and ways of life, and, in the case of the Sarawak Companies operating along the border, the *tukei* and a majority of his Sarawak crew spoke Iban. Many were Iban themselves. When negotiating an agreement of cooperation, both parties used this mutual knowledge of each other strategically.

The companies used Sarawak Iban intermediaries in negotiations and attempted to appear respectful of local customs, while the local Iban used their knowledge of logging operations in Sarawak to push for higher commissions and fees. Therefore, the Iban welcomed the Sarawak companies. While the locals generally were aware of the large profit the companies made from harvesting their timber in comparison with their own modest share, they felt that the benefits they received were much better than those that were on offer during the New Order period. This gave them the incentive to cooperate. Although the commissions were small, considering the value of the timber, they represented a considerable sum for the cash-poor non-elite population. Furthermore, these local communities wanted to gain as much from the current situation as possible, since, as one resident commented, 'You never know when the situation will change (*perubahan*), so for now we take as much as we can (*mengambil sebanyak*)'.[24] These words reflected a general concern about what might happen to local forest resources in a politically uncertain future. The commissions received by the majority of Iban communities for timber harvested in their forest were approximately one percent of the profit earned after the timber had been sold across the border in Sarawak (Wadley and Eilenberg 2005).[25] The communities were not passive and entirely content with the compensations received. On the contrary, they continually tried to negotiate and optimize their situation within the constraints put upon them from the more powerful players.

Local rumours suggest that several of the Malaysian Chinese logging entrepreneurs were using the knowledge of ethnically Chinese former PARAKU rebels in their logging operations along the border and even directly employing PARAKU veterans. As expressed by an Iban man from the Ulu Leboyan:

---

[24] Personal interview, Lanjak, 20-10-2003.
[25] Once taken across the border, however, the lumber is exported beyond Malaysia, with potential profits to Malaysian lumber exporters averaging US$340 per m^3 in 2000.

The elderly Chinese who worked in the logging company (*kerja kayu*) up here [the Ulu Leboyan] all knew their way around the area. They could easily find their way through the forest into Sarawak just by following the many small rivers. They had all operated (*petugas*) here before during the PARAKU time, they told me.[26]

Locals often explain the *tukei*'s intimate knowledge of the forest areas along the border by referring to the PARAKU link. Moreover, several *tukei* logging camps were situated in the same locations as former PARAKU rebel camps, and according to locals at least one *tukei* operating in the area was involved with the PARAKU in the 1970s. Several senior Iban timber brokers further acknowledge that they still are in contact with surviving former PARAKU members now living across the border in Lubok Antu, Sibu, and Sri Aman. In his historical account of Chinese politics in Sarawak Chin Ung-Ho mentions how several timber *towkay* (*tukei*) from Sibu in 1973 were arrested by Sarawak authorities in 'Operation Judas' for their alleged financial and material support of the Sarawak Communist Organization (SCO) the political arm of the PARAKU (Ung-Ho 1996:130-1). Although allegations of such links between the PARAKU and cross-border logging are largely unfounded, they may have some role in explaining the effectiveness of the *tukei* operations in the immediate border area. However, a more likely explanation is that the various Malaysian Chinese *tukei* have decades of experience carrying out logging operations in Iban-dominated areas in Malaysia. A long tradition of labour migration to the timber camps across the border in Malaysia has furthermore resulted in various business relationships between Malaysian Chinese logging operators and Kalimantan Iban (Eilenberg and Wadley 2009). There is no doubt that centuries of close-knit relations and mutual respect between Iban and ethnic Chinese communities have contributed positively to the intricate patronage relations described here.

Agreements to establish the semi-legal cooperatives were largely mediated by locals who had existing relationships with the *tukei* and well-established ties at different levels of local, regional, and provincial government. Such patronage relations between local communities, elites, district officials, and Malaysian *tukei*, played an important role the mixed, local economic strategy along the border. The brokers, who were often

---

[26] Personal interview, Lanjak, 16-03-2007.

part of the same border elite that had cooperated with the New Order logging companies, such as PT Yamaker, used their connections (often close relatives) in district government to facilitate the process of getting HPHH licences. After obtaining the licences, they directly negotiated commissions for the various communities involved in the cooperatives, for which they received fees locally referred to as 'premiums' (*premi*). In their role as 'gatekeepers', the border elite controlled the flow and size of commissions and other benefits flowing into the communities. Communities' lack of knowledge of timber prices made them vulnerable to exploitation, since they had no ability to evaluate the benefits received. While the size of fees paid to the elite was a well-kept secret, the fees caused local speculation and envy, as members of the border elite made little effort to disguise their new wealth. Many purchased large four-wheel-drive trucks and other luxury goods. They also invested in property in both the district and provincial capitals and sent their children to schools and universities in Pontianak and Jakarta. Although this extravagant display of wealth created resentment among the less fortunate majority, few expressed resentment openly, as some benefits of the booming timber economy trickled down to everybody and the ability of elite networks to attract wealthy entrepreneurs seemed to overshadow concerns about inequitable distribution. One local Iban farmer commented:

> Before, during the New Order period, most local people got nothing out of it [profit from logging] (*tidak dapat apa-apa*), we were only spectators (*penonton saja*) and local community involvement in the logging business today (2003) grew out of past disappointment (*berangkat dari kekecewaan*). Now, there are people like the *tukei* who want to buy our timber directly. I think now with regional autonomy the longhouses have a much higher bargaining position (*posisi bargainnya cukup tinggi*) than before. Now we decide ourselves and can negotiate. If there is a *tukei* from Malaysia who wants to work, he may work, but there are requirements, we say please build longhouses; provide clean water, like that. I guess the communities are brave to fight for their livings rights. ... even though I know that certain people have become contact persons between *tukei* and community and they do not feel responsibility (*tanggung jawab*) towards all communities and take benefits for themselves (*untung sendiri*).[27]

[27] Personal interview, Lanjak, 27-10-2003.

The local brokers can be divided into two groups depending on their level of authority and commissions received. Firstly, there are the well-educated lower-level community leaders such as the administrative village heads (*kepala desa*), the administrative sub-village heads (*kepala dusun*), and other lower-level leadership figures. These persons use their knowledge of the area to identify commercially valuable forest that could be logged. They further use their kin networks in district government to obtain licences and negotiate benefits and community commissions with *tukei* representatives. They handle the day-to-day communication and coordination. Furthermore, these persons often work at the *tukei* sawmills and keep track of the amount of timber cut within the territory of the community cooperatives. In return for these services, they receive modest commissions.

The role of the second group of brokers is more indirect and consists of persons not necessarily permanently resident in the communities, although all have some kind of kinship relations to the involved communities. These higher-level brokers include *temenggong, patih, panglima,* local businesspersons, politicians (DPRD II), and district civil servants who often have close and intimate family ties with the *tukei* in Sarawak. These brokers monopolize access to the *tukei*. Through their contacts at various levels of government, they also provide access to information and guarantee the smooth running of logging operations and the safety of the *tukei* by securing collaboration among local military commands, police, and forestry regulatory agencies. The relationships between these brokers and the *tukei* are much more secretive, and the fees received much higher. Adding to the intimacy of these relations, several Sarawak Chinese have married local Iban and settled permanently in the border towns of Lanjak, Badau and Nanga Kantuk. One should remember that prior to the anti-PARAKU uprooting in the 1960s and subsequent forced resettlement of possible Communist sympathizers (Chinese) away from the border, there was a sizeable ethnic Chinese community living in the border area that for centuries had cooperated with neighbouring Iban communities. By the early twentieth century, the first ethnic Chinese traders had settled in the border town of Lanjak (Buil 1921).

CROSS-BORDER PATRON-BROKER-CLIENT RELATIONS

In order to show the intimacy of the patronage relations taking place during this period, I will in the following paragraphs offer a detailed account of these processes as they unfolded between one specific Sarawak entrepreneur (patron), a group of Iban elites (brokers) and several Iban communities (clients).

In the Ulu Leboyan area, a large Sarawak-based company originating from the Sibu area, Grand Atlantic Timber Sindirian Berhad (Sdn. Bhd) Limited, hastily took over logging where former Indonesian-run companies (like PT Yamaker) had operated until a few years earlier. Furthermore, several small-scale logging operations were scattered along the logging road in the Ulu Leboyan. They were mostly community-run and very low-tech, using chainsaws and transporting the logs out of the forest on bicycles. The logging crews in these small-scale operations were highly specialized loggers from Sambas (West Kalimantan), a border district in the far west of the province, hired on short-term contracts. In the Leboyan area, the Sambas crews were either hired directly by local communities or by one of the *tukei* who had long-standing family business ties with Sambas Chinese largely in control of the Sambas logging business. These small operations mostly supplied timber to the large sawmill owned by Grand Atlantic Timber Sdn. Bhd.

According to inhabitants of Rumah Manah and four other longhouses in the area, the company *tukei* began negotiations with local brokers and the wider Iban communities in early 2000, already having the initial go-ahead from the district government. In 2001, logging operations in the Ulu Leboyan were modified to satisfy the new regulations of HPHH and render them 'semi-legal', although timber was still 'smuggled' across the border using the same procedure as before. Grand Atlantic Timber had already been operating down-river and in other areas of the district and province since the onset of the economic crisis and now wanted to extend its operations into old-growth forest in the Ulu Leboyan along the border in the vicinity of the Betung Kerihun National Park. In order to accommodate the large volume of timber being harvested, the *tukei* built a large sawmill along the Lanjak-Nanga Badua road. According to local informants working in the sawmill, this mill processed approximately 100 to 120 tons of timber a day.[28] A close examination of this particular *tukei* and his arrival in the borderland will be helpful here.

THE MALAYSIAN CONNECTION

In late 1998 the *bupati* of Kapuas Hulu, Jacobus Frans Layang (1995-2000), an experienced politician and industrious businessman of Iban and Maloh descent born in Sarawak assisted the plantation company PT Plantana Razindo[29] to open up land in the subdistrict of Badau close to the Sarawak border for a new oil palm plantation of 30,000 ha.[30] Layang was a well-educated and well-connected politician originally from one of the border subdistricts. During the Indonesian-Malaysian Confrontation and the PARAKU period, he was actively engaged in the conflict as a local volunteer (*dwikora sukarelawan*) and cooperating with the military. After his Indonesian military service, he pursued a career as a government civil servant and rose quickly within provincial power circles. In the 1980s he was employed in the provincial Department of Agriculture (Dinas Pertanian), and in the early 1990s, he worked in the Law Bureau (Biro Hukum) at the governor's office. In between, he lectured in the Faculty of Law, Tanjungpura University in Pontianak. Finally, he was elected *bupati* of Kapuas Hulu in 1995.[31]

As both Golkar politician and chairperson of the Dayak Adat Assembly, Jacobus was a *bupati* candidate supported by both government/military and Dayak communities. The Malay community, however, was not pleased about his election and showed their discontent with this 'Dayak' candidate through several demonstrations in Putussibau. Speculations at the time of his election suggest that he was elected as an attempt by the Golkar party to gain support among the Dayak population in the 1997 national election. Layang was the only Dayak to become *bupati* during Soeharto's New Order regime (Tanasaldy 2007:360-1).

In his position of *bupati*, Jacobus used his connections within govern-

[28] Personal interviews, Lanjak, 14-2-2003.
[29] This company was already granted a location permit in 1996 of about 500,000 ha but because this permit overlapped with another active timber concession, it was reduced to 40,000 ha in 1998 (Wadley 2000d:389).
[30] Plantation permit SK Pelepasan Menhut No. 899/Kpts-II/99. Tanggal 14-10-1999 (Kepmenhut 2004:21).
[31] Personal interview, Pak Jacobus Frans Layang, Pontianak, 26-2-2007.

ment and military circles to clear the way for the PT Plantana Razindo Company, which was a joint venture between the Indonesian holding company the 'Razindo group', a Malaysian oil palm company (Hak Corporation Berhad), and the Yamaker Foundation. The company had close ties with the military and was officially supported by a former minister of defence and the governor of West Kalimantan at the time, H. Aspar Aswin, who also had a long military career behind him (Wadley 2000d). The PT Plantana Razindo Company was thus an alliance between the military, the *bupati*, and Malaysian companies. Ironically, despite the fact that the military had officially lost its logging licences along the border in 1999, the same individuals now appeared as shareholders in the PT Plantana Razindo Company.

As the area was widely forested, PT Plantana Razindo hired a Sarawak-based company, run by a Malaysian Chinese named Apheng, to carry out the actual land clearing and to apply for an IPK land conversion permit (Izin Pemanfaatan Kayu, IPK) (*Pontianak Post* 2005b; *Sinar Harapan* 2005a). Obtaining these permits was a long and potentially expensive process, as all government agencies involved demanded a considerable 'fee'. According to local informants, Apheng never managed to get the official permit as he supposedly refused to pay the large fees required, but he still ended up spending a large amount of company funds in the process and suffered a loss of Rp 9 billion (US$1.1 million). At that time, he had apparently already worked 13 months for PT Plantana overseeing initial land clearings and managing the timber harvest without being paid himself. According to local informants, the company owned by the military and *bupati* was cheating him. Frustrated by the outcome, Apheng gave up his ties with PT Plantana and instead directly approached the Iban communities who claimed customary rights to the forest. He consequently negotiated his own logging agreements, without the backing of PT Plantana.[32]

The land concession of PT Plantana Razindo involved several local Iban community forest tracts. After the break with Apheng, the company experienced significant problems in gaining access to part of the land within their concessions. They had difficulty coming to an agreement with the communities, forcing the company to suspend its operations in the area, and local communities burned company buildings. Local resi-

---

[32] Personal interview, Lanjak, 29-3-2007.

dents claim the company only wanted to clear the particular plots within the concession that contained the largest, most valuable trees. Locals in Badau belived that the company was not really interested in creating oil palm plantations but only wanted to extract any valuable timber.[33] In April 2000, Abang Tambul Husin was elected as *bupati*. He was in favour of cooperating with the *tukei*. In the name of regional autonomy, he immediately began granting HPHH concessions to local community co-operatives and their Sarawak partners. Having already established close ties with a network of local communities and leaders, Apheng seized this opportunity to semi-legalize his business under the formal authority of district government. Being well connected on both sides of the border, Apheng was in a unique position to capitalize on the uncertainty of the situation. From 2000 onwards the Ulu Leboyan area was considered to be under the sole authority (*kekuasaan*) of Apheng.[34]

CAPTAIN OF THE TIMBER INDUSTRY

Goh Tian Teck, alias Ng Tung Pheng, alias Apheng, 'mentioned above' is a former member of the Royal Malaysian Marines and the youngest of three brothers who run Grand Atlantic Timber Sdn. Bhd, part of an international business empire specializing in timber extraction and plantation development with an office in Sibu, Sarawak. Among multiple aliases, 'Apheng' is the name most widely recognized by the border communities in West Kalimantan. At the height of timber boom in the borderland in 2002-2003 Apheng was in his mid-forties, married to an Indonesian, and a highly experienced timber contractor whose main area of expertise was logging in old-growth forest. He specialized in logging in remote and demanding regions outside formal control of the legal apparatus of the central state. He obtained his experience in the heyday of the Sarawak timber industry from the 1970s until the 1990s when he worked closely with local Iban communities along the large rivers in the Sarawak interior.[35]

---

[33] Personal interview, Badau, 19-3-2007.
[34] Besides Apheng, two other Chinese Malaysian timber entrepreneurs named Hengking and Robbin also operated in the area.
[35] Personal interview, Lanjak, 19-3-2007. Sarawak Chinese timber entrepreneurs and their Iban workers have, for example, been arrested conducting illegal logging in West Papua (*Jakarta Post* 2004a).

Kalimantan Iban from the borderland acknowledge familiarity with Apheng's companies from working in the Sarawak timber business across the border during the logging boom. The Sibu area in particular was a favoured destination for labour migration due to its high salaries (compared to the meagre salaries in the Indonesian timber business) and because of the high concentration of Iban communities in the region, many being close kin.[36] Besides, Apheng was familiar with work across the border in West Kalimantan. Even before 1998 Apheng claimed that his family clan had been working on and off in the province as timber contractors for large HPH concessions going back to the period of anti-PARAKU operations in 1972.[37] However, his career was not confined to Borneo; Apheng's experience and efficiency was also highly sought after in other timber-rich regions of Indonesia and Southeast Asia such as West Papua, Vietnam, Cambodia, and Thailand. He even worked as timber contractor in equatorial African countries like Cameroon and the Congo (*Sinar Harapan* 2005a). One small incident during fieldwork in 2002 that confirms these global connections was the visit of a businessman from Cameroon who stayed several days in the borderland inspecting the company's operations in the Ulu Leboyan. According to local Iban working in the company sawmill, the businessman was negotiating with Grand Atlantic Timber Sdn. Bhd in order to have them come and harvest timber in his home country.

In general, Apheng became an extremely popular figure among the majority of borderland residents and completely surpassed the popularity of the *bupati*. As portrayed by a local Iban timber broker, Apheng was an astute politician and businessman:

> The presence (*kehadiran*) of Apheng brought new colour in life (*membawa warna baru lah dalam kehidupan*) as Apheng could offer something different (*yang berbeda*) than the Indonesian HPHs. The HPHs did not contribute anything to the communities who own the forest. I know that the relationship with Apheng was also not equal (*tidak merata*), but this time every village received some compensation from logged forest. In my opinion

[36] The ethnic Chinese communities in Sarawak, and especially in the Sibu area, have a long tradition of close relationships politically, economically, and socially with especially the Iban; see, for example, Milne (1973). The ethnic Chinese (Foochow) communities in the Sibu area arrived in Sarawak from southern China during the reign of Charles Brooke in the nineteenth century.

[37] For example, an article in *Tempo* mentions a timber contractor named Apheng operating in the Kapuas Hulu district as early as the 1980s (*Tempo* 1989).

Apheng was a smart and brave man (*cerdas dan berani sebenarnya menurut saya*), a magnificent mafia (*mafia yang luar biasa*). He read situations very fast (*membaca situasi dengan cepat*), he is a brain man (*otaknya*).[38]

Apheng's great successes were partly due to his ability, as a patron, to get things done and provide needed services where the former concessions (and central government) had failed. Besides creating local jobs in his sawmills and timber camps, he maintained the local networks of (dirt) roads and more generally sustained a booming border economy. As the non-farming population had expanded, locals developed daily vegetable markets where women from nearby communities sold their produce. Shops, cafes, bars, and hotels proliferated in the market towns of Lanjak and Badau, and prostitutes from outside the area who catered to the loggers were now ubiquitous. Besides the smuggling of logs across the border, various kinds of luxury contraband such as electronics and cars crossed the border from Sarawak to Kalimantan. For example, from 2003 to 2005 a large number of Malaysian cars without number plates cruised the Lanjak area despite the fact that there were only a few kilometres of paved roads that could be used by these small city cars (*Kompas* 2004f). The smuggling of stolen and second-hand cars from Lubok Antu to Badau was, according to Sarawak media, carried out by sections of the Sarawak police, among others (*New Straits Times* 2005).

Not without some truth Apheng was depicted in national news media as the de facto king (*raja*) of the Kapuas Hulu border area (*Kompas* 2004b). He was definitely the principal economic force during this period. Originally invited by the former *bupati* and welcomed to stay by the *bupati*, Apheng felt extremely self-confident and secure operating in the area. Despite several provincial government arrest orders hanging over his head, he did not attempt to hide or conceal his operations.[39] Furthermore, all vehicles used in logging activities, be they heavy logging-trucks, fuel-trucks, bulldozers, or jeeps, were equipped with Sarawak license plates and had the name of the actual company written in large letters on the side. Another example of his self-confidence was the erection of a large and fully equipped sawmill on the Indonesian side

---

[38] Personal interview, Lanjak, 2-3-2007.
[39] Several times during fieldwork in 2003 unfounded rumours circulated that Apheng supposedly had paid about Rp 1 billion (US$120,000) to the Indonesian minister of forestry to have the minister ignore illegal logging in the border region.

of the border along the government road between Badau and Lanjak. This sawmill represented a huge investment and built to last.[40]

Besides being closer to the timber source, placement of a sawmill on the Indonesian side of the border also allowed Apheng to circumvent legal restrictions in Sarawak, where the government did not allow raw logs to be imported. At this sawmill, the harvested timber could be processed immediately and sawn into export-friendly lumber to avoid such restrictions. In 2002, this sawmill and a major timber camp in the Ulu Leboyan employed more than 700 people. The major timber camp, named 'Sebabai', was where the freshly cut logs were stored before they were transported to the sawmill along the border road. The camp was a major investment and resembled a small town (*kota kecil*). It was situated close to the border with numerous feeder roads going in all directions. The camp was made up of more than 20 buildings, workshops, offices, shops and sleeping quarters accommodating timber workers and their Chinese foremen, many of whom had brought along their families.

Apheng himself claimed that his sawmills and timber camps throughout the border area employed altogether more than 2,000 people (*Tempo* 2005c). The sawmill was not the usual poorly constructed structure as seen other places in the province but was strongly built with large living quarters to accommodate hundreds of workers, several canteens, workshops and garages. It even had its own brothel. The sawmill further accommodated around 30 large logging trucks that travelled back and forth between the upriver logging camps and the sawmill heavily loaded with timber. Apheng made a profit estimated to be approximately Rp 400 billion (US$45 million) per year from his logging business in the borderland (*Sinar Harapan* 2004d).

The presence of the sawmill also provided access to sought-after Malaysian consumer goods at discount prices.[41] After having delivered their cargo, the company timber trucks returning from Sarawak loaded up with Malaysian consumer goods that were brought back to the sawmill in Indonesia and sold at discount to the workers. That way many

---

[40] Apheng ran four sawmills in the Batang Lupar district: 'Koperasi Segala Burung', 'Guntul Mandiri', 'Bunsu Bahtera' and 'Telaga Betung'.

[41] The trade in endangered wildlife for pets (such as infant orangutans) and medicines (such as bear claws and gallbladders) was also expanding as was trade in rare orchids (*Pontianak Post* 2004c). These export items were usually acquired by loggers working in the forest and passed across the border through the sawmill operator.

Iban men working in these sawmills could supply most of their families' everyday necessities from the company at a favourable price instead of buying these products at a higher rate in Lanjak town.

SMALL BORDER ELITES

Although he operated in close tandem with district officials, Apheng would never have obtained his high level of success as a local patron without the consent and protection of the local elites and communities. In the case of cooperative logging in the Ulu Leboyan there were two groups of local brokers: those who maintained the day-to-day dealings with the *tukei* foremen, in this case the five longhouse heads, and those who initiated contact with the *tukei* through their large networks. The latter group of brokers consisted of a local businessman, an *adat* leader and two district civil servants, all Iban and originating from the Ulu Leboyan but resident in Lanjak, Badau and the district capital Putussibau. Some of the brokers, as portrayed in the following examples, fit into both of the above categories. In order to provide a better picture of the ambivalent character of these brokers, I will briefly introduce three members of the Iban elite, all of whom have multiple positions as traditional leaders, are active in the creation of a new border district (see Chapter 8), and who, in various ways, have been engaged as brokers in the timber business during and after the New Order period.[42]

Nanang is a middle-aged man in his late fifties who was born in the Ulu Leboyan area but through marriage moved to a longhouse near Lanjak where he holds the position of *adat* elder (*patih*). In the late 1950s and early 1960s Nanang was a promising young student and one of the few Iban to attend senior high school. In 1963, he joined the National Red Cross (Palang Merah Indonesia, PMI) in Badau. All young students were obliged to join the PMI training, which at the time strongly resembled light military training. The students were trained in basic medical care and how best to assist the Indonesian troops and volunteers engaged in fighting along the border. After finishing training, Nanang began teaching in the local schools. During the height of the PARAKU, the young Nanang was appointed an intelligence gatherer

---

[42] The border elite are not to be seen as a homogenous category. There are tensions, squabbles, disagreements, and rival agendas among the elite members themselves

for the Indonesian army under the direct authority of General Soemadi. Forty such intelligence assistants gathering information on the PARAKU movements in the border area were supposedly appointed in the subdistrict of Kecamatan Batang Lupar in the 1960s and 1970s.[43] Nanang's intelligence data resulted in a successful ambush of PARAKU patrols along the Leboyan River. Pleased with his performance, a military officer offered to sponsor Nanang's further education. In return for assisting the army, Nanang, together with several other community leaders (*temenggong*, *patih* and *panglima perang*), were given control of their own timber concession.[44]

The majority of Nanang's close family are Malaysian citizens, and through these long-term cross-border kinship relations, he managed to attract Malaysian investors to the company managing the concession. As co-manager of this concession, whose headquarters were placed in the provincial capital Pontianak, Nanang became acquainted with the intricate web of networks involved in the West Kalimantan timber business. Besides sharing management of this Iban-headed company, Nanang used his military contacts and worked closely with Pontianak-based Chinese timber contractors who worked the Yamaker concessions in the border area. His involvement included the role of broker between the companies and local communities. Nanang further consolidated his authority when, in the late 1980s, he was elected as the local representative for the Golkar party in the district assembly (DPRD II) in Putussibau. Nanang was, for example, the Iban DPRD II mentioned in Chapter 4 who went to Jakarta in the 1990s with two Iban *panglima perang* to lobby for a new border road.

Nanang's position among local communities is dual: on the one hand, he enjoys respect as *adat* elder because of his ability to solve local disputes; on the other hand, his close association with outsiders makes him somewhat suspect. By local standards, Nanang is doing quite well and has managed to send both his son and daughter to university in Pontianak.

Jabak, another prominent local leader engaged in the logging business, is a man in his sixties. In the late 1960s, Jabak was hired as a scout by the Indonesian army to hunt down PARAKU rebels in the

---

[43] Personal interview, Lanjak, 23-3-2007.
[44] Several of the *panglima perang* who were originally given the concession by the military have since passed away, and other local leaders (*patih* and *temenggong*) have taken their place.

upriver forest along the border. His military deeds and outspoken anti-Communist sentiments later earned him the military rank of *panglima perang*. Later, in the mid-1970s he was appointed to the customary rank of *temenggong*, which afforded him considerable advantage in negotiating with military and timber companies on behalf of local communities. Like Nanang, Jabak became involved with the Yamaker concessionaries, such as PT Benua Indah. Jabak further claims to have strong kinship ties with the former paramount chief of the Iban in Sarawak, Tun Jugah. Jabak is a member of the District Assembly for Golkar and an active lobbyist for the border district movement.

Ranting is a village headman in his late thirties from a renowned kinship line of Iban customary leaders. His family's success is largely based on cross-border labour migration, employment in the Sarawak timber industry, and various business relationships with the former Yamaker concessions. His family was economically successful by local standards, which meant that Ranting was one of a lucky few sent off to boarding school in Putussibau. After finishing high school, he was sent to the provincial capital Pontianak on a government scholarship where he obtained a university degree in economics and became one of the few Iban to be college educated. While Ranting was at university in the 1990s, his father, a highly regarded tribal leader, was killed in a logging accident in the Ulu Leboyan while employed by Yamaker.

After returning to the borderland, Ranting took over his father's position of community leader and in early 2003 succeeded in getting a position as civil servant in the *bupati* office in Putussibau. Besides working as a civil servant of the government, Ranting was also the person who was most deeply engaged in negotiating logging agreements with ethnic kin across the border and with Apheng. For Ranting to employ the benefits of being a government civil servant and simultaneously cultivate economic and social relations with kin and friends across the border poses a few contradictions. Ranting, like many other inhabitants in the Ulu Leboyan, acknowledges his strong affiliation with Sarawak and ethnic Iban identity while at the same time he takes strategic advantage of his Indonesian identity when it benefits him and his community. For example, while working in the *bupati* office, Ranting did extensive lobbying to benefit his own community. He succeeded in allocating funds for a new school just next to his longhouse and, paradoxically, he had the Malaysian logging company clear the building area of trees with their bulldozers. Besides negotiating benefits for his own community, Ranting also managed to direct some resources into his own pocket and invested in land, shops, and a new house in Putussibau.

Ranting, like most other local timber brokers, creatively used his relationship with the *tukei*. The local brokers knew that the *tukei* would have immense difficulty operating in the border area without their support. The *tukei* dependency on their authority gave the brokers considerable leverage in negotiating their own benefits; for example, several brokers established small but lucrative trading businesses in the border towns, ordering cheap consumer goods from Lubok Antu across the border in Apheng's name (an arrangement that supposedly offended Apheng). Ranting forged his role as broker between local communities and the *tukei* by continuously negotiating the opportunities brought along by his dual position as government official and local tribal head, which again enhanced his bargaining power over local forest resources.

Finally, conceiving the borderland as a semi-autonomous social field, the authority of the border elite rests upon their capacity to produce or control rules, and to arbitrate and eventually solve conflicts. Being long-time residents on the border between the two politically and economically divergent nation-states of Indonesia and Malaysia and exposed to the special opportunities and semi-autonomy that this location offers, Nanang, Jabak, and Ranting have self-confidently played this historical and economic advantage to their own and their community's benefit. Thus, the actions of these men have not been purely predatory, and they are also regarded as conscientious community leaders. Border elite authority is immensely dependent on the good will of the majority of borderland society. This is especially so as their authority is based on various kinds of local reciprocity, and they need a certain degree of local legitimacy to exercise their authority. Their high status within society was not a fixed given, but a result of constant negotiations and the distribution of favours. All members of the elite had strong kinship ties, responsibilities, and commitments with their birth villages and fellow village members. Local displays of benevolence, such as sponsoring schooling for less well off kin or financing community development projects are intricate tools for maintaining legitimacy. Long-standing personal ties put certain restrictions on the freedom to act; however, these elites were constantly under local pressure to deliver either economic or social benefits.

As traditional leaders, they were obliged to act as mediators in inter village disputes, and as upholders of traditional norms and laws. As prominent local politicians, government officials and entrepreneurs with business ties across the border, they were expected to use their authority to attract jobs and promote prosperity. Self-enrichment was, to a certain degree, locally endorsed if the elite at the same time managed to keep the local economy blossoming. Elite strategies, however, involved balancing their various roles, and thus they not only focussed on personal gain in order to fill their own coffers, but they also played an important role in attracting and distributing wealth within local society. Men like Nanang, Jabak, and Ranting played a critical 'mediating' role in the borderland by connecting different spaces, state and non-state alike.[45]

COOPERATION AND DISPUTES

For Rumah Manah and the four other Iban longhouses situated in the Ulu Leboyan along the border, negotiations with Apheng's company resulted in several advantages for the communities involved. These advantages would have been unthinkable during the New Order concessions. Furthermore, while the former New Order concessions showed little recognition of local *adat* forest rights, Apheng was careful to operate within local norms and largely recognized local forest rights. Having worked in Iban areas elsewhere, Apheng was aware of the importance of getting along and pleasing local communities. As confided by a Sarawak Chinese company supervisor, 'The Iban are rough (*kasar*) and strong minded (*tahan hati*) people, with whom you do not want to have any problems. However, if you treat them respectfully they are very trustworthy'.[46]

Today, as in the past, the borderland Iban have proven themselves quite capable of taking matters into their own hands if they feel that they have been treated unfairly. Not having the direct support of the Indonesian military as earlier concessions in the area had, Grand Atlantic Timber Sdn. Bhd opted for cooperation, although with a mini-

---

[45] The lack of a more detailed characterization of the particular elite members is partly the result of the ethical dilemma of providing a too intimate portrait of certain individuals and thereby compromising their anonymity. Taking the contested character and often-violent borderland setting into consideration, I decided that such shortcomings were unavoidable and opted for full anonymity of my key informants. This unfortunately meant leaving out important details that might help the reader grasp the full complexity of elite strategies.
[46] Personal interview, Lanjak, 05-11-2003.

mum of expenses. Well aware that the Company has no official permits to operate in the area and that all the Sarawak employees work without permits and in general reside in the area illegally, local Iban have used this reality strategically when dealing with the company. On several occasions, I witnessed how local Iban, as a subtle warning, commented on the twilight status of Grand Atlantic Timber Sdn. Bhd when reprimanding the company supervisors if they were too demanding when negotiating fees or other benefits with the communities. Bonds of kinship and friendship were also common among local Iban and Sarawak Iban workers in the companies. This dynamic has contributed greatly to the local loyalty towards the Sarawak companies and the preservation of an atmosphere of fairly peaceful cooperation between the two parties.

Besides the border elites, few Iban held key positions within the company workforce, and in Rumah Manah, most work contracts were short-term. The men were usually hired on a weekly or monthly basis, and the work included tracking down areas with a high percentage of valuable timber, building new feeder roads for heavy machinery to enter the areas. The actual tree felling was generally considered too dangerous by the locals and usually left to outsiders. The duration of work contracts was usually a few weeks to a month. In 2002, a month of tracking paid RM600 (US$158), and people working as gatekeepers at the upriver logging camp were paid a daily wage of RM15 (US$4). The Iban were also hired in teams; for example, six men were hired for a week to build a new logging camp in the Ulu Leboyan. The RM800 remuneration was to be split among the six of them. The examples are numerous, and most men have similar work experiences to report. What is important to note here is that wages are relatively high compared to local standards and can easily compete with those in Sarawak.

In large-scale operations in the Ulu Leboyan, a high percentage of the workers in logging crews consists of Sarawak Iban, brought in by the *tukei*. Even more so than the Kalimantan Iban, these Iban usually have considerable experience working in the Malaysian timber industry and have often learned special skills such as mechanics and driving. Their presence, however, introduces an interesting social dynamic: far away from their families, these men seek company in local longhouses, and their hosts welcome the news, conversation and consumer goods that they bring. One could cite numerous examples of Sarawak Iban forming strong friendships with local Iban and in some cases actually bringing their families from Sarawak to live with local families. In addition, Sarawak Chinese working in the logging operations (many of whom speak fluent Iban) often visit nearby longhouses to socialize after work. A very popular local pastime is cockfighting, and the Sarawak Chinese and Iban workers happily participate in the betting. These cockfights are important arenas for networking and making deals. The district government allows cockfighting in the borderland as it is seen as part of the cultural heritage of the local peoples (Wadley 1998). In Sarawak, on the contrary, cockfights are illegal because of the heavy gambling involved. The booming economy that resulted from increased logging activity gave local men more ready cash resulting in more widespread gambling.[47]

The presence of outsiders in the area presents an interesting contrast that further underscores the importance of local Iban identity. Loggers from Timor and Flores working for the *tukei* routinely visit local Iban longhouses to buy pigs and chickens and socialize with residents, their common Christianity being the culturally salient link.[48] But nowhere do the interpersonal relations and identification run as deep as they do than between the border Iban, Sarawak Iban, and Chinese from the Iban-dominated areas of Sarawak. When asked privately, many Iban felt little commitment towards their own central and provincial governments, and saw no problem with cooperating with the *tukei* and his Sarawak Iban workers despite the fact that such operations were regarded as illegal by the centre. As shown above, their relationship with the *tukei* and his Sarawak Iban workers is characterised by quite a different kind of dedication. The fact that the Sarawak relations are more familiar with local Iban customs and language than most government officials and have shown that they are able to satisfy the immediate economic needs of the Iban seems to play a large role in the placement of local Ibans' loyalty. Both socially and economically, the Iban feel much relaxed and comfortable dealing with their Sarawak relations.

The incentives for cooperation with the company were numerous,

---

[47] The headmaster of one of the schools in Lanjak told me that when school fees had to be paid, fathers complained of the high expenses, while during a cockfight they easily gambled away cash worth several months of school fees.

[48] The presence of the small Sambas Malay logging crews mentioned earlier presents an interesting contrast. Although Sambas are border inhabitants in their own right, they remain cultural outsiders to local Iban; as a result, the Sambas logging crews rarely visited Iban longhouses or socialized with locals in the same way Sarawak Iban and Chinese did. Indeed, the Sambas crews lived apart and generally looked for entertainment in the market towns, where there were other (though more often local) Malays.

and my informants from Rumah Manah emphasized two in particular. First, they spoke of transportation and mobility. Because of timber road construction, one can now visit Lanjak or cross the border at Nanga Badau and return to the longhouse of Rumah Manah in one day. The communities in the Ulu Leboyan had a standing agreement with the *tukei* that any company vehicle passing the cooperative longhouses should take up passengers waiting at the side of the road. On a normal day during the dry season I would count as many as 10 or more fully loaded logging trucks passing the longhouse, not counting the numerous company Jeeps cruising back and forth between the main sawmill and the upriver logging camp. The wide availability of such free transportation has meant an enormous increase in the number of people who commute to and from the area each day. Every day several inhabitants of Rumah Manah travel to sell produce in Lanjak or at the large Sarawak-owned sawmill on the main road, and people often go on a one-day shopping trip across the border to Lubok Antu. Formerly such trips were made on foot and took days or even weeks.

Second, cash commissions are paid based on the amounts of timber harvested in their forest, determined through negotiation with Grand Atlantic Timber Sdn. Bhd. In the case of the Ulu Leboyan (as in many other places in the district), negotiations with the company are largely carried out by local brokers and result in the following type of arrangement: between 2002 and 2003, the *tukei* paid a compensation of approximately Rp 25,000 to 35,000 (US$3-4) per m^3 of timber collected. When the timber crossed the border into Sarawak the value of the timber rose dramatically and the *tukei* received approximately RM1000 (US$270) per m^3.[49] Each month the communities further received Rp 50,000 for each log removed. For the communities in the Ulu Leboyan this means that each household on average receives Rp 1 million to 1,5 million per month (US$100-170). Commissions vary from community to community and depend on the community's ability to negotiate and the distance to the border. Commissions are calculated locally in either Indonesian *rupiah* or Malaysian *ringgit*, but logs are measured in British tons, reflecting the dominance of Malaysian *tukei* as well as the fact that border Iban are more comfortable with British measurements, many having worked for decades in the timber industry of Sarawak and Sabah.

[49] Personal interview, timber broker, Lanjak, 20-11-2003.

To keep track of the amount of logs removed, the communities select representatives who work at the large down-river sawmill, counting each log arriving. In order to know which logs are removed from which community forests, the logs are painted with red numbers indicating their community 'ownership', and the representatives write down the numbers for the later collection of commissions. The commission received was divided among each family in the respective longhouses. In reality, however, the question of commissions is not straightforward, and agreements are continually renegotiated or attempts are made to sidestep certain provisions of them. Instead of paying commissions in cash, the company often tries to pay off the communities in consumer goods such as diesel fuel for their generators or sawn timber for maintaining longhouses. In most cases, the commissions are late or less than agreed upon. (One often-used company excuse for deficient or tardy payment is the ever shifting world price for lumber.).

As the cases above show, transnational ethnic relations play an important role in these logging operations and directly influence local Iban decision-making and strategies. The use of ethnicity as a conscious strategy is twofold: local Iban (elite and non-elite) use the relationship with Sarawak Iban workers to promote their own position and heighten their rewards. Malaysian companies use the same Sarawak Iban as ethnic liaisons when negotiating with local communities in the attempt to win Iban confidence and influence their decision to cooperate.

Local engagement in cooperative logging with the *tukei* is not entirely free of problems and has an effect on relations between communities. Internal disagreement become more common as communities become aware of the stakes at play and the commercial value of their forest. In some instances, disputes are settled by a traditional cockfight, with the winning community gaining possession of the contested forest but leaving the losers embittered. Locals recognize all this as a scramble to make claims on timberland so that local profits from logging might go to them. These cases also represent the confluence of a booming economy and traditional Iban political organization focussed on the longhouse and its autonomy from similar communities. Given the complex ties of kinship and marriage between longhouses, inter-longhouse disputes can feed internal divisions. As I will illustrate in the cases below, the competition over resources and strengthening of community autonomy in some instances superseded former inter-community solidarity, and in its wake,

| *At the edges of states*

new alliances were made in the ever-changing borderland milieu.

In one case during 2000, an Iban community refused to cooperate with logging operations, and the *tukei* intentionally created troubles between it and another Iban community that was cooperating (*Media Indonesia* 2000b). The *tukei* gave shotgun shells to people from the cooperating longhouse in order to intimidate their neighbour. People from the first longhouse became aware of this situation and fired their shotguns at the sawmill camp owned by the *tukei*, located near the cooperating longhouse. Several people from the first community then wrote a letter to local government officials objecting to such foreign intrusions and threatening to act alone if the government did not deal with the problem. The dispute went unsolved and created a fair deal of 'bad blood' between the neighbouring communities.

Another example concerns the planned construction of a Malaysian sawmill close to Rumah Manah in 2003. Ranting, the village head of Rumah Manah, had been contacted by close Iban relatives in Sibu, Sarawak, during a previous search for work. Together with a local Sarawak Chinese entrepreneur, they had proposed to sponsor the opening of a new sawmill near Rumah Manah for the purpose of manufacturing plywood for sale across the border. In the manufacturing of plywood the quality and size of the timber used is less important, and the idea was to enter the areas that already had been logged and harvest the smaller trees left behind. As such, this smaller Timber Company would not be competing with the much larger Grand Atlantic Timber Sdn. Bhd that was only interested in valuable hardwood timber. In order to make the sawmill operation profitable, however, a large forest area had to be included, meaning the involvement of all five Iban longhouses in the area that made up one *desa*. Furthermore, in order to make the operation agreeable to the district government, the sawmill would be run as a *desa* cooperative with timber extracted from the longhouse territories and as such a license for a community cooperative (HPHH) was needed, and that required a signature from all five community heads. Being anxious to begin work, the company pushed hard for an agreement and promised high economic returns. Ranting and his Sarawak relatives agreed that he should use his authority to involve the other four communities and collect the needed signatures. After considerable effort, Ranting succeeded in convincing all four longhouses as well as his own to play along, give their signatures, and begin negotiations with the Malaysians.

After weeks of meetings and long hours of tough negotiation in the roofed communal gallery of Rumah Manah, a provisional agreement was made. The logging and the sawmill operations were to be run as a cooperative between the five Iban longhouses in the area and the company. As part of the agreement the company had to promise that the new jobs created by these operations would primarily be assigned to local Iban and local commissions would be more equally adjusted to the actual profit earned after selling the timber in Sarawak. Furthermore, company obligations included the construction of a new school and a small medical clinic and the installation of running water in each longhouse. Grand Atlantic Timber Sdn. Bhd., still operating in the Ulu Leboyan, initially gave similar promises, but they were only partly fulfilled.

Whether the many promises made by the company were genuine was never put to a test. Before the final agreement was signed, one of the Iban communities had second thoughts and pulled out of the negotiations because of disagreements about where the sawmill should be placed and where the timber was to be extracted. This defection not only made the other longhouse communities very disappointed and angry, but it also frightened the investors away. Members of Rumah Manah who had kinship ties to the smaller Sarawak Timber Company were especially bitter about the collapse of the agreement. Without the full commitment of all communities, the company could not build the sawmill and begin logging, and they therefore left the area. Ranting and his kinship group who had most at stake were enraged at the longhouse community that was responsible for the breakdown of negotiations. Ranting lost credibility and face because he could not keep his part of the agreement with his Sarawak relatives. Like the first case described above, this dispute remained unresolved and has created resentment among the communities.

Another example from Rumah Manah shows disputes take place internally, within longhouses. In 2003, the *tukei* operating in Ulu Leboyan recruited members of several closely related households to build a new logging camp without offering the opportunity to others within the same longhouse. When the deal became public, the others expressed outrage at the distribution of benefits of logging on community territory going to a select few, and some household heads threatened privately to move to other longhouses. Although these threats were never carried out, the case illustrates that internal resentment over how certain individuals use their better-established networks to gain special agreements with and higher commissions from the *tukei* can develop. Knowledge of higher commissions paid to these local liaisons strengthens already present resentment and may exacerbate material inequalities. As mentioned previously the Iban have an anthropological reputation as being 'egalitarian' and, at the ideological level, this is certainly the case, with strong values of personal autonomy and achievement. Because of those values, substantial material and political differences between households within the same longhouse can become the source of resentment and disdain in internal relations.

NON-STATE FORMS OF AUTHORITY

When starting fieldwork, my first impression was that the local claims of regional autonomy and the major timber smuggling taking place along the border were to be understood as a direct outcome of the chaos following recent decentralization processes within the country. After New Order some remote, disadvantaged and subdued regions rebelled and wrested control out of the hands of a central government that long had been ruled by the strong and suppressive central state apparatus of Soeharto's regime. This explanation provided an instant clue to local incentives but left too many questions unanswered. The way in which these so-called illegal practices developed so effectively and smoothly merited further explanation.

One puzzle that was left unanswered was the intimate and very personal relationships between the Malaysian timber barons, Indonesian military officers, district officials, and border elites. Clues to causality began to emerge when local informants began to explain the continuity of current patronage relations by pointing to previous periods of military intervention along the border in the 1960s and 1970s. Several accounts vividly described how some members of the border communities colluded with the military and later received rewards in the form of timber concessions. Decentralization processes thus provide an exceptionally favorable environment for these patronage relations to blossom freely, but it was not the sole explanation for their formation. Instead, what these events showed were the many continuities between current relations and former arrangements of informal networks and coalition-making during the New Order regime.

This chapter has shown how the economic and political changes in the borderland after 1998 have been most dramatically manifested by the heavy involvement of Sarawak timber companies in logging forests under the tenuous control of local elites and communities. I argue that acts of patronage are a plausible coping strategy in a remote borderland milieu where state institutions are weak and state power continuously waxes and wanes. Further, in the cases discussed, patronage relationships become especially potent because of traditionally rooted patterns of respect, strong leadership, and authority.

The basic outline of this activity appears to be similar to that of other places in Indonesia where 'illegal' logging occurs (McCarthy 2000; Casson 2001), and where Malaysian logging enterprises operate in widely removed locations, from West Africa to West Papua. In few other places, however – except possibly other borderlands – has the configuration of the borderland and local community autonomy come together to structure the patterns reported here. The 'CV Munggu Keringit Sdn. Bhd' sign described previously symbolizes not just a willingness among the border Iban to maintain diverse sources of livelihood in the face of great uncertainty, something most subsistence-level peoples practice, but an intimate knowledge and association with the other side of the border, generated by the history of both ethnic partition and border inequalities.

Furthermore, the traditional political autonomy of longhouse communities results in divergent interests between longhouses in the same *desa* or cooperative. Implementation of regional autonomy in the area has weakened what little administrative power the desa system had and strengthened longhouse autonomy. During this period, border communities had the power to manage their resources for and by themselves. However, they too are worried about the future of their natural resources, not only because of competition from timber and oil palm companies that might gain legally binding licenses to their forests but also competition from neighbouring and related communities. These threats appear to be one factor driving locals to allow logging in their forests, though communities are not equally enthusiastic about it. The ecological consequences of the logging boom in the borderland remain unstudied, though various preliminary reports from government and NGOs indicate that the level of logging does not bode well for local forests and thus for local, forest-dependent livelihoods (Kepmenhut 2004; Susanto 2005). Even prior to regional autonomy some worried about severe environmental degradation and greater resource conflict resulting from formal autonomy, not to mention confusion over its implementation and very meaning (*Media Indonesia* 2000a).

These developments underscore the vulnerability of local people in the face of outside interests in their forests: With millions of cubic metres of timber being smuggled into Malaysia annually (from throughout Indonesia), the country loses a substantial amount of taxable profit. Not surprisingly, the national and provincial governments have moved to criminalize 'illegal' logging by making occasional police raids to arrest loggers and confiscate logs (though no 'big operators' have yet been caught), and labelling *tukei* as 'mafia' and 'gangsters' in the media. Although the loss of revenue is an obvious motivation, these manoeuvres may also signal a nationalistic desire to reclaim Indonesian territory and resources, as well as a national and provincial challenge to the autonomy that the districts have enjoyed since regional autonomy was implemented. Nonetheless, it is not as if local communities are caught passively between these forces; local people remain active participants. The boom in 'illegal' logging once again challenged government efforts to control the Indonesian-Malaysian border, and as border inhabitants, the Iban again straddle the line, as they have in the past.

Economic links between West Kalimantan and Sarawak have intensified during the period of *reformasi* (Fariastuti 2002), and this has been especially true in the Kapuas Hulu borderland. Yet those links have always been there, as have strong cultural and social relations. What makes this set of cross-border relations different is not so much the direction of resource flow (still into Sarawak) as it is the physical presence of Sarawak enterprises competing for local resources. From the standpoint of resource extraction and forest habitat, the outcome may not be so different from Indonesian concession logging under the New Order. However, Indonesians appear to be of two minds: away from the border they see foreigners threatening national resource sovereignty, but on the border they see interactions with familiar people, even kin, during a time of enhanced, though tenuous, local empowerment. In the following chapter, I will investigate this apparent paradox by analyzing several cases of vigilantism that illustrate the ambivalent nature of legality and illegality in the borderland and highlight how local communities openly defy the limits of official legality if it collides with local rules and norms.

Fig 33: Jalan Lintas Utara during the rainy season, 2003 (Photograph by author)

Fig 34: Graffiti on a shop in Lanjak displaying local discontent with logging stoppage, 2005 (Photograph by author)

Fig 35: Confiscated logs from up-river logging camps, 2007 (Photograph by author)

Fig 36: Apheng's deserted and burnt down logging camp close to the Sarawak border, 2007 (Photograph by author)

Fig 37: Control post along a timber road, 2002 (Photograph by author)

Fig 38: Police post close to the Sarawak border, 2007 (Photograph by author)

6

Intersecting spheres of legality and illegality

For those living in the borderland, it is a zone unto itself, neither wholly subject to the laws of states nor completely independent of them. Their autonomous practices make border residents and their cross-border cultures a zone of suspicion and surveillance; the visibility of the military and border forces an index of official anxiety (Abraham 2006:4).

Borderland lawlessness, or the 'twilight zone' between state law and authority, often provides fertile ground for activities deemed illicit by one or both states – smuggling, for example. Donnan and Wilson (1999) note how borders can be both 'used' (by trade) and 'abused' (by smuggling) concur with Van Schendel's claim that '[t]he very existence of smuggling undermines the image of the state as a unitary organization enforcing law and order within clearly defined territory' (1993:189). This is especially true along the remote, rugged and porous borders of Southeast Asia where the smuggling of cross-border contraband has a deep-rooted history (Tagliacozzo 2001, 2002, 2005).

As noted in Chapters 3, 4 and 5, illegal trade or smuggling (*semukil*) of various contraband items back and forth across the West Kalimantan-Sarawak border has been a continuous concern of Dutch and Indonesian central governments ever since the establishment of the border. Drawn by the peculiar economic and social geography, several scholars mention how borderlands often attract opportunistic entrepreneurs. They also mention how such border zones may promote the growth of local leadership built on illegal activities and maintained through patronage, violence and collusion.[1] Alfred McCoy asserts that the presence of such local leadership at the edges of Southeast Asian states is a significant

---

[1] Gallant 1999; McCoy 1999; Van Schendel 2005; Sturgeon 2005; Walker 1999.

'manifestation of an ongoing, incomplete process of state formation' (1999:130).

In such situations, border communities often enjoy a fair measure of autonomy from state interference, which may exacerbate their already ambivalent relations with either state. State definitions of what is deemed illegal are often situational and inconsistent, depending on changes in government administrations and policies. In the borderland case, this reality has resulted in much confusion among border communities and a heightened mistrust of state laws and regulations. As one Iban community leader (*temenggong*) formerly employed in the logging business commented:

> In the period of illegal logging, the government and forestry said nothing. They did not declare any prohibition. The police, *bupati*, all of them were working in the logging business. Then suddenly in 2004 the government declared everything illegal. We are confused (*bingung*). What is legal, what is illegal? Who knows (*mana tahu*) what the government plans are, central or local.[2]

In the first place, the term 'illegal' presents a problem of meaning. The word glosses too easily over a complex picture, especially when understood from the point of view of the border population. 'Illegal' implies a sense of wrongdoing or its potential, which may be quite adequate for state-level concerns, but it does not necessarily 'represent the ways in which border residents proudly stake their economic claim in transborder trade movement' (Flynn 1997:324). On the contrary, although aware of being involved in something defined by distant politicians as illicit, the border population may feel no moral qualms and regard such laws as unjust and unreasonable (Abraham 2006:4). Thus, what is illegal as defined by state law is usually clear to government agents (though they too may circumvent their own laws), while border populations may more routinely engage state regulations with flexibility, not feeling as responsible for obeying laws they see as imposed from the outside and against their interests. This is most clearly seen in logging operations carried out in joint ventures between locals and the Sarawak *tukei* in the borderland since 1998 – largely deemed illegal by the central government but

---

[2] Personal interview, Lanjak, 25-3-2007.

6 Intersecting spheres of legality and illegality |

considered legitimate by border communities back in control of their traditional forests. The following cases show how this widespread 'illegal' logging (*penebangan liar*) suddenly came to be designated a problem of national importance.

Recognition of this issue should not be taken to mean that I condone, in any way, the activities described below, nor should the description of such activities imply that all Iban are equally involved. In fact, some individual Iban are actively engaged in various environmental NGOs, and whole communities (although few) strongly resist any involvement with the *tukei*. Finally, to understand such activities only as illegal or subversive is to oversimplify the relationship between locals and government authorities. Donnan and Wilson stress how government agents, whether they are on a national or on a regional level, themselves promote such subversive activities because of the economic benefits they bring (1999:105-6). Pedestrians agree that state power at some borders is more about regulating the flow of people and goods than preventing it (Donnan and Wilson 1999:16). In the case of the West Kalimantan-Sarawak border the traffic of 'illegal' harvested timber has until recently been ignored by local state authorities because of the huge revenue this illegal trade has brought the district government. According to Van Schendel and Abrahams, borderlands are characterised by a complex interplay of power and authority where local norms of what are considered licit practices are deep-rooted in borderland history and often brought into play alongside state laws.[3] Local norms can also be invoked in place of state laws if the latter do not comply with what is considered legitimate in the borderland (Schendel and Abraham 2005:4-7). Such statements fit well with Moore's (1978) understanding of a semi-autonomous social field mentioned previously.

Taking this further, the statements point towards the conceptual and practical difficulty of drawing clear distinctions between the legal and illegal when studying borderland practices. In line with Van Schendel and Abrahams, this book argues that borderlands provide excellent lenses for observing the limitations of these distinctions. Although borderlands provide especially good arenas for viewing the intersections between the state and legality/illegality in Indonesia, it is important to remember that

---

[3] The district government of Kapuas Hulu was quite aware of this long tradition of local autonomy in legal matters, and in order to stay on good terms with the local communities, the *bupati* in 2000 issued a district decree that 'officially' recognized the authority of a number of selected customary leaders in each subdistrict (KepBKH 2000a).

these shadowy practices of governance and government bureaucracy are found throughout Indonesia (Van Klinken 2008b). In order to deal with the problem of 'illegality' without solely resorting to government categories of right and wrong, Van Schendel and Abraham suggest using the distinction 'licit' and 'illicit' when denoting practices which according to local norms or social perceptions are seen as legitimate but otherwise illegal in a formal sense. This further emphasizes the importance of remembering that government authority cannot simply be equated with law and order (Abraham and Van Schendel 2005). Such a distinction between the dichotomies legal/illegal and licit/illicit is helpful for considering the often divergent views of what is deemed legitimate by central government (at least officially) and by borderland inhabitants, and it provides a better understanding of the reason border inhabitants continue to break the law.

As I will illustrate in the following paragraphs, the borderland is an arena in which complex and often illicit practices are negotiated within a triadic relationship between locally based elites, local communities, and representatives of various government institutions. This chapter will engage with these issues of lawlessness and illegality in the borderland with special attention to incidents of 'vigilantism' and 'gangsterism' that occur under the increased autonomy experienced by local communities during the logging boom explored in the previous chapter. 'Vigilantism' refers here to the taking, or advocating the taking, of the law into one's own hands – that is, the circumvention of established channels of law enforcement and justice in the face of the central government authority's apparent failure to deal effectively with criminal matters (Wadley and Eilenberg 2006). According to Abrahams, acts of vigilantism often appear in 'frontier zones' and here constitute a criticism of ineffectual and corrupt state institutions (Abrahams 1998:1-9).

VIGILANTES: THE USNATA KILLING

> The border area is faced with many problems; in order to deal effectively with these problems I was elected as local judge in settling these local matters. People here do not trust the police and government judges. They believe in customary rule (*hukum adat*).[4]

---

4   Personal interview, *temenggong*, Lanjak, 25-3-2007.

6 Intersecting spheres of legality and illegality |

The above quote clearly stresses local suspicion towards external legal authorities, a suspicion that more often than not leads to informal resolutions of local disputes. State laws are only partly recognized as long as they are believed to fit local norms of fairness and justice. As I will describe in the case below, when state laws and local norms collide, border communities are not slow to actively resist encroachment upon their legal rights.

On 13 December 2000, a courtroom in Putussibau, the district capital of Kapuas Hulu, became a murder scene when a group of around 300 to 400 Iban men armed with shotguns and machetes (*parang*) avenged the death of a kinsman. The victim, a 31-year-old Malay man named Usnata, was on trial for the January 2000 murder of a 35-year-old Iban moneychanger (*pedagang valuta asing*) named James Sandak from the border town of Badau. Before proceeding, let us take a step back in time and look into the background of this apparently cold-blooded killing.

The logging boom in the borderland had created welcome opportunities for certain energetic locals to profit from the cross-border trade in timber, resulting in a prospering local economy. Sandak was one such industrious person who immediately saw that the improvement of the local economy meant more cash circulating within the community. In his role as moneychanger, Sandak's financial assets were based on capital input from about 80 families in the Badau area with whom he had a business relationship. Every month he distributed the revenue from his transactions to these families. In January 2000, however, the families waited in vain for their returns. Sandak never appeared and a few months later he was found floating dead in the nearby river.

The courtroom killing of Usnata attracted the attention of the national and international press as the first vigilante killing inside an Indonesian courthouse, and it resulted in a public outcry of condemnation throughout Indonesia. The incident attracted a great deal of public as well as government attention and was portrayed as a sadistic act of the masses, a vivid example of the extreme lawlessness Indonesia was experiencing in the wake of political and economic transition. The president at the time, Abdurahman Wahid, met with the victim's family at a largely staged meeting, and provincial officials in West Kalimantan promised to bring the perpetrators to justice whatever the cost. The incident consequently drew vast media attention.[5] The head of the provincial police (Kapolda) announced in the local media that he took this incident extremely serious and would immediately dispatch a team of special investigators to the scene of the crime along the lawless border (*Pontianak Post* 2000e). Yet despite the eagerness to secure law and order in the months and years afterward, the incident fell 'off the radar screen' of local and national authorities, and out of the several hundred who participated in the killing, no one has ever been, nor will likely be, charged in the murder. District police authorities have felt no pressure to carry out the orders from the head of provincial police and to apprehend the vigilante killers. As described in previous chapters, local authorities have a healthy respect for the Iban capability for armed mobilization, and they know that the apprehension of these vigilantes would definitely lead to violent reprisal, as their actions were locally considered just punishment.

On the surface, this appeared to be another case of *amuk massa* (*Pontianak Post* 2000f, 2001) – the seemingly spontaneous killing of people accused of often petty crime in the context of an ineffective justice system (Colombijn 2002). However, its underlying structure and motivation, something not addressed in the press, reveals the interplay of borderland identity, diminished state power, and official corruption. Sandak, the Iban moneychanger, was in fact related by marriage to Usnata, the latter having married Sandak's cousin. Understandably, Sandak, with his bag filled with RM 85,000 equivalent to approximately US$22,400, from his transactions with various families on the border, would board a speedboat with Usnata for a long boat journey to the bank. On the way Usnata and the driver, a Padang man named Edi Caniago, allegedly killed Sandak, dumped his body overboard, and divided the money between themselves (*Pontianak Post* 2000e; *Tempo* 2001b). Only after five months was Sandak's body discovered in the river, and the police began to suspect Usnata. (Edi had fled to the island of Batam.) Not only was Usnata one of the last people to have been with Sandak, but he had been able to buy expensive consumer goods after Sandak disappeared. According to local media, Usnata was interrogated by the district police (Polres) and confessed to the crime, saying that he and his accomplice Edi had been tempted by the large amount of cash that Sandak carried (*Pontianak Post* 2000e).

---

[5] *Kompas* 2000d; *Kyodo News International* 2000; *Pontianak Post* 2000a, 2000d; *The Straits Times* 2000.

Accustomed to considerable autonomy in dealing with civil and criminal matters (a practice with roots in the Dutch colonial government), Sandak's Iban kin demanded that Usnata pay blood money in accordance with Iban *adat*. When he refused, the case was turned over to the district court for trial. After the first day of the trial, the Iban present in the courthouse decided that Usnata would probably be acquitted; they suspected that he had bribed the presiding judge. Hence they organized the attack, recruiting Iban from both sides of the border that were connected to Sandak in various ways as kin or friends. Several hundred Iban departed Nanga Badau and drove towards Putussibau in five trucks. Arriving at the courthouse in Putussibau where Usnata was detained, the crowd demanded that the presiding judge hand over Usnata to face local judgment. Shortly afterwards the crowd entered the courthouse and ran to the courtroom where they shot Usnata as he hid under the judge's bench[6] The judge, who had been posted in this remote district for five years, recounted in horror how he hid in his office with an armed guard while the crowd ransacked the courtroom.

The 68-man police force who had been on hand to prevent the rumoured attack were greatly outnumbered and retreated when the heavily armed Iban men arrived. Besides being outnumbered, the police force was aware of the speed by which Iban communities could congregate and was afraid that by interfering in the incident they could end up in open battle. Furthermore, the Iban have a reputation for being fierce warriors (and headhunters), which made the non-Iban police less willing to interfere, although the police did negotiate with the vigilantes after the killing and persuaded them not to cut off the victim's head.

Part of the Ibans' rationale for their actions, besides revenge, was that the court was corrupt and justice from the government unattainable; they were also incensed that Usnata had refused to adhere to local norms of conduct in the borderland by paying a fine to Sandak's family. Indeed, had Usnata paid the blood money, he would probably still be alive. Thus, though stemming from common perceptions of an ineffectual and corrupt criminal justice system out of touch with the particularities of borderland life, this vigilante killing is far different from the usual *amuk massa* killings in places like Java, which occur almost spontaneously when someone identifies a thief or similar petty criminal on the street or mar-

---

[6] See also *Kyodo News International* 2000; *Pontianak Post* 2000e.

ketplace. *Amuk massa* killings are rapid and immediate following identification and accusation. Usnata's killing was planned and organized over several days, occurred in a court of justice (which is unique to vigilante killings in Indonesia), and involved direct but non-violent confrontation with police.

In light of the historical ambiguity between border communities, state institutions, and the context of *de facto* governmental decentralization and demoralization of the police and military following the fall of Soeharto in 1998, the revenge killing of Usnata makes much more sense, and a number of historical continuities appear. The strong sense of cultural autonomy – the belief that local customs should supersede national law and that the forceful pursuit of local (Iban) interests is entirely legitimate is particularly apparent in this case. The ability of the Iban to mobilize rapidly also emerges and finds its historical parallel in nineteenth-century raiding expeditions that could number in the hundreds and thousands. Although changes in Indonesian political life provided them additional latitude for exercising extra-legal judgment and punishment even in cases of serious crime after 1998, the Iban involved in the Usnata incident would not have been able or willing to engage in it without these historical precedents.

This case of vigilantism serves as a good starting point for illustrating the creative engagement with government institutions undertaken in the borderland, especially how local norms about what is considered licit often clash with formal government laws. In the following paragraphs I will illustrate this ambiguity further by returning to incidents that demonstrate the intricate patronage relations between the *tukei* and border communities discussed in the previous chapter, namely, how such local institutions of authority work in the twilight between state and society, between public and private (Lund 2006a). Returning to Moore's (1973) concept of a 'semi-autonomous field' the borderland comes to constitute a social field that generates its own rules, norms and regulations that in certain instances and periods prevail over state laws, which become partially obsolete. While the outside legal system penetrates the field, it does not dominate it; there is room for considerable 'judicial' autonomy and the semi-autonomous social fields in which they find themselves largely determine the strategies of local actors.

6 Intersecting spheres of legality and illegality |

'WILD' LOGGING AND 'GANGSTERISM'

> There is a bustling atmosphere in the border town of Badau; crowds of people working the sawmills that line the border mingle with locals at the main market, many of whom carry their shotguns and pistols wide open in public. The town is floating with counterfeit money, drugs and hard liquor, and prostitution is mushrooming in the mould of the rainy season. This is definitely a place without law and without government. Welcome to the world of the tough cowboys (*koboi yang keras*) (*Sinar Harapan* 2004d).

The above quote is taken from a newspaper article written by two Indonesian journalists based on their visit to the borderland in 2004. The article vividly describes their first encounter with the border town of Badau as a typical instance of the popular image of a frontier town, accentuating lawlessness, violence, and underdevelopment. This portrayal of the borderland as a wild frontier inhabited by rough and trigger-happy frontiersmen and lacking in state presence was common in journalistic and government accounts of conditions in the borderland during the local logging adventure from 1998 to 2005.

In the years following the onset of heavy cross-border logging, the provincial and national press reported only sporadically about the logging in the remote Kapuas Hulu.[7] But in the period between 2003 and 2004, the increase in cross-border logging in the remote Kapuas Hulu district and consequent loss of national resources and state revenue began to reach the provincial and national press. Although there are no exact figures on the total value of the smuggled timber, it was estimated at the time that the province each month lost revenues amounting to US$1 million, or approximately Rp 8 billion (*Pontianak Post* 2004d).

Headlines with clearly nationalistic and critical undertones emerged, nearly leading to international disputes between Indonesia and Malaysia. Several incidents over the previous years of border transgression had served to keep things 'hot' in the media as well as in diplomatic circles.[8] For example, in 2000 the Indonesian military command in West

---

[7] *Jakarta Post* 2000a, 2000c; *Kompas* 1999a, 1999b; *Pontianak Post* 2002.

[8] In December 2002 the International Court of Justice in The Hague ruled that the small and long-disputed border islands of Sipadan and Ligitan on the tip of East Kalimantan belonged to Malaysia (*Jakarta Post* 2002a). This ruling resulted in a public demand for the Indonesian government to put more effort into protecting its national borders (*Jakarta Post* 2004c).

Kalimantan accused Malaysia of violating Indonesia's sovereignty by purposely moving the concrete pillars marking the borderline in order to conceal illegal logging carried out on Indonesian territory (*New Straits Times* 2000b). Another case involved local cross-border disputes over farmland. In 2002, a group of Sarawak communities from Sri Aman claimed ownership to 230 ha of land across the border in Kapuas Hulu from which they migrated decades ago (*Kalimantan Review* 2002). Police and military patrols from both sides of the border have several times been close to exchanging fire due to these disputes.[9]

The Indonesian press accused Malaysia of colonizing the border area and exploiting West Kalimantan resources, alleging that large segments of the economy of Sarawak were supported by illegal logging in Kalimantan. Provocative headlines appeared, such as 'Malaysia eats our fruit (*makan buahnya*), while Indonesia swallows the sap (*telan getahnya*)' (*Suara Pembaruan* 2003) and 'When will Malaysian 'colonization' (*penjajahan*) of the Kalbar[10] border end?' (*Suara Pembaruan* 2004a). The media particularly implied that the presence of Malaysian citizens, and their business undertakings, in the border area was a clear sign of Malaysia's expanding sovereignty and its attempts to re-colonize this resource-rich region. The stronger nationalist tone to these later reports also included an explicit criminalization of cross-border activities, especially concerning logging. Sarawak authorities did not deny the allegations that certain individuals from Malaysia were violating the law on Indonesian territory, although they vehemently denied that Malaysia as a whole or its timber industry specifically was involved in any illegal activities. Instead Malaysian spokespersons claimed that the problem lay with corrupt Indonesian authorities who allowed the timber to enter Sarawak in the first place (*Berita Harian* 2003).[11]

The *tukei* and their Malaysian workers came to be portrayed as gangsters armed with guns, looting national resources and intimidating local communities, with '*Gengster Cina Malaysia*' (Chinese Malaysia gangsters) and '*Mafia Kayu*' (timber mafia) becoming common buzz phrases.[12] The

[9] *Jakarta Post* 2000e; *Kompas* 2000b, 2000c; *New Straits Times* 2000a; *Pontianak Post* 2000c; *Suara Pembaruan* 2000.
[10] An acronym for *Kalimantan Barat* or West Kalimantan.
[11] Although rather late, the international community also became aware of the Malaysian timber barons 'illegally' operating on Indonesia territory (*Jakarta Post* 2007a).
[12] *Media Indonesia* 2004; *Pontianak Post* 2004d, 2004f; *Sinar Harapan* 2004a, 2004b; *Suara Pembaruan* 2004b.

disappearance of huge quantities of timber, worth billions of rupiah, across the border stirred Indonesian national emotions (*Pontianak Post* 2003a). The Department of Forestry and Plantations (Dinas Kehutanan dan Perkebunan) in Kapuas Hulu estimated that in 2003 alone the country's losses due to illegal logging in their part of the border area totalled Rp 50 billion (US$6 million), and the Malaysian *tukei* took approximately 273,354 m^3 of timber across the border (*Sinar Harapan* 2005d). Major General Herry Tjahjana from the regional military command[13] responded to these news reports describing clear breaches of national sovereignty by saying, 'We are trying our best (*berupaya sekuat*) to secure the border. However, it is not easy to secure such a long border when facilities and personnel are very limited (*sarana dan personel yang sangat terbatas*)' (*Kompas* 2004h).

Because of this change in political will to stop smuggling, national and provincial politicians in Indonesia demanded that district officials take prompt action. Despite district government assurances about dealing with these 'Malaysian gangsters,' early attempts to crack down on illegal logging in the border area were few and half-hearted, and the people arrested were mostly 'small fry' especially as district officials were in no hurry to end lucrative cross-border connections with the Sarawak *tukei*.[14] District and provincial police attempts to apprehend the notorious *tukei*, Apheng, failed, and it seemed that the 'gangsters' would continue their activities unabated, abetted by district officials and local communities.[15] For example, in 2003 the district forestry department carried out several investigations into alleged illegal logging activities along the border and filed a report to the *bupati* recommending follow-up investigations. The reports were subsequently rejected by the district police as were results of follow-up investigations, the reason being it would have too large a socio-economic impact on the region (*Sinar Harapan* 2004c). Besides these half-hearted initiatives carried out by the district, a team from central government that went under the name of 'Team Wanalaga' visited the border area in early 2004. This team also made no concrete efforts to stop the logging; according to locals, it used its time in the border area to collect under-the-table 'taxes' from the various Malaysian logging companies. I will describe this incident in more detail later in

13 Komando Daerah Militer (Pangdam) VI Tanjungpura.
14 *Kompas* 2003a, 2003c; *Pontianak Post* 2004l.
15 *Kompas* 2004c, 2004d, 2004g; *Sinar Harapan* 2004e.

the chapter. As mentioned in a national newspaper, the only thing to do was to wait for serious and competent politicians who are able to put an end to the 'colonial domination' of the Malaysian forest mafia (*Suara Pembaruan* 2004a).

Because of immense public pressure that accentuated the weakness of national legislation in dealing with these illegal matters, Indonesian President Susilo Bambang Yudhoyono (often called 'President SBY') late in 2004 pledged 'tough action' against illegal loggers throughout Indonesia (*Jakarta Post* 2004d). This statement was followed by a presidential decree directed at eradicating all such 'wild logging' (*penebangan liar*).[16] The decree revoked all previously decrees and permits issued by district governments concerning the logging sector and gave sole authority over forest issues back to the Ministry of Forestry, enabling law enforcement officials to prosecute illegal loggers immediately after apprehension and seize all their equipment (*Inpres* 2005).[17] The above events seemed to have had the desired effect and led to several high-profile Forest Law Enforcement Operations (FLE) throughout the border region.

As examples of border elite collusion with the *tukei* and their continuing ambivalent loyalty towards their own government I will recount here two interrelated borderland incidents that took place immediately after the central government's official announcement about eradicating illegal logging in late 2004 and early 2005.

CONFESSION OF A MALAYSIAN TIMBER BARON

In early December 2004 a team of provincial and district police and military officers, representatives of other government institutions and environmental NGOs, known as the West Kalimantan Consortium on Illegal Logging (Konsorsium Anti-Illegal Logging Kalimantan Barat, or Kail Kalbar), initiated several coordinated raids on illegal logging opera-

---

[16] Within state rhetoric the concept of *liar* or wild is often applied in denoting illegal practices and people (such as border populations) beyond government reach and control.

[17] This decree had been postponed several times under the former president, Megawati, allegedly due to government fears of the possible impact it might have on the social and political stability of the affected regions. Many regions depended heavily on the illegal timber trade (*Jakarta Post* 2004b).

tions along the border, including timber camps and sawmills in the study area. Several Malaysian citizens were apprehended.

On 7 December a raid at a local sawmill, Guntul Mandiri, about 25 km from Lanjak and a upriver logging camp, Camp Sebabai, resulted in the arrest of three Malaysian Chinese (Alok,[18] Ling and Akiong) and the confiscation of both equipment and timber (Dephut 2005; *Kompas* 2004a, 2005g). The camp was emptied of anything of value and burned to the ground by the police and military, while the sawmill along the border road was simply closed down and sealed. Nearby communities prevented the sawmill from being looted and burned, as they claimed that the land on which the sawmill was erected was their property and the buildings under their protection. Government authorities confiscated approximately 22,000 m³ of timber, or 3,000 logs, as evidence. Among the equipment confiscated were seven bulldozers, six land cruisers and one fuel truck and an excavator, all bearing with Malaysian number plates (PMARI 2006). The ringleader and sawmill owner was the notorious Malaysian Chinese *tukei*, Apheng, who escaped. The presence of Apheng in Indonesian territory had been widely known for years, and demands for his apprehension had become more persistent. Apheng controlled at last four large sawmills that operated 24 hours a day in the subdistricts of Badau, Batang Lupar, Embaloh Hulu and Puring Kencana (*Equator News* 2004a; 2004b).

Local media claimed that the three people apprehended were Apheng's henchmen (*kaki tangan*). According to local inhabitants, Apheng was playing badminton in another upriver logging camp during these raids and was not arrested because he was warned beforehand. The police and military were afraid of violent reprisals if they arrested him, as Apheng enjoyed the protection of surrounding, well-armed communities. He subsequently escaped into Malaysia following the old PARAKU trails. The incident is locally known as 'Apheng's great escape'. Many locals often referred to him as a 'brave and generous man' (*berani dan bermurah hati*)', a 'saviour' or 'rescuer' (*dewa penyelamat*) who had made the area prosper in a way the former nationally owned companies and

---

[18] During interviews with senior Iban who took active part in the anti-PARAKU warfare in the 1970s, the name 'Alok' was mentioned several times as a key figure among the former PARAKU rebels in the area.

government operators had failed to do.[19] Meanwhile, the national media portrayed Apheng as a dangerous criminal.

After these initial government raids Apheng became registered in national police (Polri) records as the mastermind behind illegal logging (*otak pembalakan liar*) in the border area and consequently one of the most wanted criminals on the Daftar Pencarian Orang (DPO) in the province of West Kalimantan (*Pontianak Post* 2004b; *Sinar Harapan* 2004a). As early as July 2002, before the government raids, the Kapuas Hulu police had registered Apheng together with 16 other Malaysian citizens on the DPO, but no measures were taken to apprehend them. Several outside commentators believe that this attempt by the district police to apprehend Apheng was just a manoeuvre to demonstrate active enforcement activity and deflect criticism. Apheng was placed on the DPO because he allegedly violated Article 102, Law No. 10/1995 on customs (*kepabeanan*) by bringing heavy equipment across the Badau border (*Sinar Harapan* 2004a, 2005d). Apheng was further accused of entering and operating in West Kalimantan without proper documents such as a passport and working visa. He was said only to be equipped with a short-term visa (*pas sempadan*), valid for 28 days. Immigration officials consequently promised to arrest Apheng the next time he crossed the border (*Pontianak Post* 2004e). In response to these vague attempts by district government to appear committed to upholding the law, a member of the provincial assembly (DPRD II) in Pontianak was quoted as saying, 'This is only a trick (*akal-akalan*). Apheng's situation is unchanged, he can just wander around all the way to Pontianak if he pleases, accompanied by a crowd of corrupt officials (*oknum pejabat*)' (Sinar Harapan 2005d).

Later, in a March 2005 interview with a journalist from the weekly Indonesian news magazine *Tempo*, Apheng declared from his office in Sibu, Sarawak, 'I am not afraid of being arrested (*tidak takut ditangkap*) as I am no villain (*perampok*)' (*Tempo* 2005c). In this and later interviews he defended himself and the 'legality' of his business in the border area by claiming that he had received an operating permit and maps of the border area back in 1998 from the *bupati* office in Putussibau. He was also invited by local community cooperatives (*koperasi*) to build sawmills and help to open up 'their forest' for exploitation and sale. Apheng supposedly worked with and supplied financial input to no less than 15 coopera-

---

[19] Personal interviews, Lanjak, 19-7-2007.

tives, all of which had permits issued by the district government (*Berita Sore* 2007b; *Suara Karya* 2007a). Apheng stated in another newspaper interview, 'Actually at first I did not want to take their timber. But they consistently begged me to buy. What should I do, I really wanted (*ingin bantu*) to help [the communities], therefore (*terpaksa*) I agreed to buy' (*Pontianak Post* 2005b).

Apheng put special emphasis on the question of local forest ownership/rights and that all the cut timber was the property of local communities and came from their traditionally managed forest (*kayu milik masyarakat adat*), not from national parks or other kinds of protected forest (*hutan lindung*) as he often was accused of doing.

Apheng argued that since 1998 he had paid around Rp 1 billion in taxes to the customs office in Pontianak (Kantor Pelayanan Bea dan Cukai) for bringing heavy logging equipment into the Indonesian border area. He did acknowledge not paying any official taxes for bringing out the timber through the Badau border crossing because there was no official border crossing and tax office. Instead he claimed to have paid taxes to the district government and local communities:

> Entrepreneurs [*tukei*] like us certainly want to work in a proper manner (*kerja benar*) and pay our taxes. In Malaysia, all dutiful citizens (*warga patuh*) pay tax. But to work properly in Indonesia is very difficult because regulations change rapidly (*peraturan cepat berubah*) (*Tempo* 2005c).

In the eyes of local Iban brokers, *tukei* involvement as partners in small-scale timber concessions in the border area was not illegal per se, as district government sanctioned it through its policy of regional autonomy. However, what might make it appear as illegal in the eyes of the central government was the subsequent export of timber across the border without proper export permits from the Ministry of Trade. Then again, the timber exporters already had paid export taxes (Pajak Ekspor Barang, PEB) to the District Industry and Trade Office (Dinas Perindustrian dan Perdagangan) in Putussibau (*Pontianak Post* 2003b). This interpretation of the regional autonomy laws was largely overruled by the provincial police authorities who stated that the *tukei* engagement in cooperative logging was by definition a crime because foreign citizens were not entitled to form cooperatives and thereby gain the right to exploit forest on Indonesian territory (*Berita Sore* 2007b).

In response to the allegations, Apheng argued that he had been the sole financial benefactor for border communities and district government in the area during the relevant period. He claimed, for example, to have paid for the erection of a military border post in Nanga Badau and the renovation of the police headquarters in Putussibau, to which he also donated a new patrol car. When confronted with Apheng's claims of having 'donated' millions of rupiah to the police and local government, a highly placed regional police officer made the rather dubious comment that he saw no problem with accepting these donations because Apheng's money was earned by stealing from Indonesia; it was entirely just and proper that this money should be used to develop the region (*Berita Sore* 2007b). Local timber brokers interviewed claimed that Apheng paid a monthly 'operating fee' of approximately Rp 30 million (US$3,500) to the *bupati*, while subdistrict heads (*camat*) and police (Koramil) received between Rp 1 million and Rp 2 million a week.[20]

On the village level, Apheng further developed infrastructure; for example, in the village of Ukit-Ukit he provided a clean water supply and electricity, which was dedicated by the subdistrict administrative head (*camat*) (*Sinar Harapan* 2005a). According to Apheng he had invested more than Rp 1 trillion (US$110 million) in the district during the seven years he operated in the Kapaus Hulu (*Berita Sore* 2007a):

> I am actually very concerned about the border communities, as the Indonesian government does not supply them with decent living conditions. They have not been provided with electricity, roads, water, hospitals, and good job opportunities. We tried to help out by providing these facilities.... These border people greatly need (*sangat butuh*) Malaysia.... Prohibited or not prohibited (*dilarang atau tidak dilarang*), they [local communities] will keep on cutting the trees because that is their only hope for getting something to eat.... For now I have stopped working because the sawmills are shut down. But for now much of my heavy machinery is in the safekeeping (*dimankan*) of the local communities. They have begged me to return, but the situation is too serious at the moment (*lagi gawat*). I am sad that so many people are out of a job and feel sympathy for them (*kasihan mereka*) (*Tempo* 2005c).

[20] Personal interview, Lanjak, 7-11-2003.

Portraying himself as the generous and compassionate patron taking care of his clients' needs, needs, which the Indonesian state is incapable of or unwilling to provide, Apheng downplayed the unequal relationship he himself had with the majority of border communities, whose share of logging revenue was minute compared with what *tukei* gained from the logging boom. Although local benefits were limited, what ostensibly kept the patron-broker-client network running was mutual dependency and respect. In return for the goodwill and protection of border elites and communities, the *tukei* provided various social services, crucial venture capital, expertise, and access to the timber market in Sarawak. By offering services that gave the locals a certain amount of social and material security, Apheng's position as powerful patron was accepted, and he asserted the right to operate freely while locals were willing to relinquish some authority.

Despite mutually beneficial agreements, the *tukei* continuously had to walk the thin line of keeping all parties on whom he depended content. In doing so, he was obliged to renounce some short-term benefits and cultivate a local reputation of being trustworthy, generous, and powerful. One way of obtaining and holding onto local trust and respect was to manipulate the strained relationship border communities had with their own nation state by playing the dual role of local benefactor and 'strong man' or brave 'rebel' against unjust state laws and regulations. Praising Apheng in numerous interviews as a brave and generous patron, a man of wisdom and business acumen, locals not only expressed their gratitude but also recognized and identified strong traditional virtues of independence, bravery, courage, and wealth (Eilenberg 2003; Mashman 1991). To respect and trust the authority of a 'brave man' who at least on the surface appears to 'honour' local norms comes far more naturally than respect for and trust of a distant and contradictory state apparatus often regarded with suspicion.

The personal reputation of Apheng clearly played a vital role in maintaining local support. Such embedded traditional virtues of strong individualism and bravery continually surface in the borderland; for example, when the Iban talk about the colonial period, the name 'Raja Brooke', the label used for the consecutive colonial heads of the Brooke family in Sarawak, enjoys far more respect than does the often-shifting Dutch administration. Local oral narratives do not mention any of the names of the rotating Dutch officials stationed along the border. The

Brookes' more personalized relations with the Iban and their reputation for strong and often violent leadership made them notorious on both sides of the border, but they were also known for respecting Iban norms and protecting Iban culture. In comparison the Dutch, who generally ruled the more or less autonomous Iban from a distance, gained little recognition in the local epics of brave men (Lumenta 2005; Wadley 2001c).

No doubt the many *tukei* operating in the borderland were quite aware that they were operating in the twilight of legality and illegality and were therefore aware that their positions were vulnerable to outside forces such as shifting legislation and politics. Operating under a constant threat, they were forced to rely on the networks of their clients to reinforce their positions. Apheng, for example, acknowledged knowing that the Ministry of Forestry revoked the *bupati* authority to issue HPHH logging permits as early as 2002, but he nevertheless continued his business relationship with these cooperatives and the district government. As he expressed it in a 2005 interview, 'I am still working as usual, because I have a guarantee (*jaminan*) from the Kapuas Hulu District Consultative Forum (Musyawarah Pimpinan Daerah, or MUSPIDA) that I will not be harassed (*diusik*) (*Sinar Harapan* 2005a).

Apheng seemed convinced that he had been made a scapegoat and his name sacrificed (*dikorbankan*) in the struggle over authority between the districts and the provincial/central government. He expressed his frustration by mentioning the hypocrisy of suddenly portraying him as a dangerous criminal or mafia don working without local support. He argued that he at no time during his seven years operating in the borderland had made any effort to hide his operations (*bukan rahasia*), a fact the Indonesian officials and the public already knew (*Tempo* 2005c). As Apheng boldly stated in one of the many newspaper interviews, 'On what basis did I enter the DPO? I am not a hardened criminal. Please arrange a meeting with President Susilo Bambang Yudhoyono so I can explain the real problems' (*Sinar Harapan* 2005a).

Apheng's claim that he did not fear apprehension has a double meaning in this regard. First, as mentioned above, he believes that he operated with the full legal support of local government and secondly, if he were to be apprehended and accused of illegal activities all the government institutions with whom he cooperated (military, police etc.) would be just as accountable and the incompetence of the government revealed. Apheng expressed his stance on the matter through the following Chinese saying: 'If somebody throws a bucket of water (*siram air*), I will certainly not be the only one who gets wet (*saya tidak mau hanya basah sendiri*)' (*Pontianak Post* 2005b).

Only six weeks after the Kail Kalbar operation, yet another government team entered the borderland in order to apprehend Apheng and additional persons engaged in illegal logging who had escaped the earlier raids. As we shall see in the next case, the previous raid seemed to have severely angered local residents, especially in Iban communities that co-operated with the *tukei*.

SHIFTING LOYALTIES

In January 2005, two national Indonesian newspapers published articles describing how a team of 27 government officials and one television journalist was investigating illegal logging in the Ulu Leboyan area in the vicinity of the Betung Kerihun National Park (*Antara* 2005a; *Kompas* 2005f). This team included district forest rangers (Polhut), prosecutors (Kejaksaan Negeri Kapuas Hulu), police (Polres), and military personnel (Kodim), some of them well armed. This new team set out from the district capital of Putussibau hoping to apprehend Apheng, who had escaped the previous raids but still made occasional appearances in the area. They found that their Indonesian Kijang vehicles could not negotiate the bad roads in the hilly border area; they therefore commandeered three of Apheng's previously confiscated Toyota Land Cruisers (with Malaysian license plates) from the district police in Putussibau.

After the team had stopped to make camp for the night at Apheng's upriver logging camp, two pick-ups with Malaysian plates and carrying around 20 to 35 armed men approached. A local Iban man and timber broker, acting as leader of the group, began to interrogate the team, apparently not intimidated by its armed police and military members. Upon discovering the team's purpose and its use of confiscated vehicles, the man grew angry and accused them of being responsible for the loss of local jobs. In the heated atmosphere, he ordered his men to seize the vehicles and to leave the team on foot. In a curious twist to the incident, the team negotiated transport to the local subdistrict police headquarters (Polsek) in Lanjak, to which the local group agreed. Upon arrival in Lanjak, the locals refused to return the vehicles and fled with them across the border before the now-reinforced police could catch them. In the meantime, personnel from the district police had been despatched from Putussibau in response to rumours of the Kail Kalbar team being terrorized and taken hostage by an armed 'mob'. The police attempt to apprehend the local group of men and retake possession of the stolen cars failed as the cars had already entered Malaysia and been returned to their owner, Apheng.

The journalist was dumbfounded by the inability or unwillingness of the police or army to intervene even though they had had several chances to act. They remained passive throughout the whole incident. The journalist reported that the security force members of the team had agreed with the Iban leader to not interfere, perhaps to avoid further conflict with local communities. Indeed, district officials later told him that the incident was a local matter and that there was no need to involve outside parties and no need to make the incident public. The provincial coordinator of Kail Kalbar, however, expressed his lack of understanding of how local Indonesians could be more loyal to a foreigner (Apheng) than to their own government. He suggested that the provincial police (Kapolda) would have to take over from the district police (Kapolres) if the latter were unable to perform their proper duties.

Controversy over the district's lack of action intensified a few days after the Kail Kalbar incident when local media brought news of continued logging carried out by Apheng in the area. After the shutdown of his large sawmill along the Lanjak-Badau road, Apheng had simply moved most heavy sawmill equipment and personnel to another more remote and less visible sawmill away from the main road (*Kompas* 2005c; *Pontianak Post* 2005d). Perhaps the Kail Kalbar coordinator was in possession of some 'inside knowledge', because within two months, provincial and national police had launched yet another wave of raids, codenamed Operation Forest Conversion (Operasi Hutan Lestari), resulting in the arrest of several Malaysians and Indonesians (Chinese, Iban, and Malays) involved in cross-border logging. These raids effectively closed down all logging operations in the district.

The anti-logging raids had aroused the wrath of the border communities who had come to depend economically on cross-border logging. As described in the case above, there were several confrontations between the Kail Kalbar team and locals who were often led by members of the

6 Intersecting spheres of legality and illegality |

Iban elite who previously had functioned as brokers or intermediates between local communities and the *tukei*. Although these confrontations ended peacefully, local emotions ran high as the government team was accused of being responsible for the loss of local jobs. An official from the district forestry department in Putussibau described the situation as follows:

> Going there [Lanjak] these days is a bit risky (*agak rawan*). Because they are still revengeful (*dendam*) toward us [Forestry Department], we have to be careful. After the big sawmill was closed and the Malaysian men were captured, more than 700 people who live around Lanjak lost their only local source of income (*mata pencaharian*). They are extremely displeased (*rasa tidak senang*).[21]

The situation deteriorated even more under Operation Forest Conversion, which besides arrests also resulted in a total ban on transporting already cut timber across the border, a move that upset locals who had derived income from the trade as truck drivers. In response the locals sent a large delegation of around 200 people carrying along 1200 signatures to the district capital, Putussibau, to lobby for a lifting of the ban or at least allowing the sale of already cut timber, arguing that the timber came from community forests (*hutan adat*) and that Indonesians markets were prohibitively distant. While the new Basic Forestry Law (No. 41/1999) released in 1999 recognizes (in principle) the existence of local rights to what is considered customary forest, the legal standing of these rights is still very unclear and largely up to government interpretations as there are no clarifications of the term. Furthermore, the Ministry of Forestry must recognize all claims to customary forest, and ultimately the law states that all forest and forest resources are under state authority.

In front of the district assembly office, the delegation demanded that no further logging raids be carried out and that all confiscated timber be released. As voiced in a complaint by one prominent Iban community leader from Embaloh Hulu, 'We are like living dead (*hidup mati*) [in the borderland], we ask for immediate attention. We are charged (*dituduh*) as perpetrators [in illegal logging] but have never enjoyed the rewards' (*Sinar Harapan* 2005d).

[21] Personal interview, Putussibau, 14-3-2007.

Although the *bupati* and local assembly members expressed their understanding of the difficulty of the situation, they were under immense pressure from the central government to take a stance on the issue. A meeting with representatives of the local communities and the various district departments (forestry, military and law enforcement) was immediately arranged. Local protests were acknowledged, but the head of police announced, 'The police cannot release the timber that has been confiscated. All procedures must be processed in accordance with applicable law (*sesuai hokum*)' (*Kompas* 2005e). The head of the forestry department added, 'The forestry problem (*masalah kehutanan*) from now on is under central authority (*kewenangan pusat*), the region cannot do much (*daerah tak bisa berbuat banyak*)' (*Kompas* 2005e).

The group's efforts proved eventually to be fruitless, with the Indonesian Minister of Forestry, M.S. Kaban, declaring that border communities had no legal right to permit commercial timber harvesting and sell across the border.[22] As indicated previously, more than half (56.51%) of the land area of Kapuas Hulu is designated as protected forest, and according to the decentralization laws all protected forest is under the authority of the central government. Parts of the forest claimed as *hutan adat* by local communities are classified as protected forest. The Minister of Forestry had planned in October 2005 to visit the borderland but later cancelled his visit, to the disappointment of local communities who had hoped to express their concerns and come to an agreement concerning the logging ban with the minister (*Jakarta Post* 2005c). In response to the unwillingness of district and central government to take the necessary steps in overcoming local community hardships, an Iban leader from Badau, cited in the main national newspaper, *Jakarta Post*, replied:

> It is only natural that locals continue to fell trees in the forest. About 90 percent of the people depend on the forest to support themselves. If what they have been doing is considered illegal, then what must be done to make it legal? Unless the government provides an alternative, how can they give up their long-standing activities? (*Jakarta Post* 2005c)

---

[22] *Equator News* 2005g; *Kompas* 2005b; *Media Indonesia* 2005a; *Pontianak Post* 2005c.

6 Intersecting spheres of legality and illegality |

In an attempt to engage in a discussion with the border communities, the Kail Kalbar team in August 2005 invited community leaders and DPRD II representatives from the border subdistricts to a focus group discussion in Putussibau. In a 2007 interview the head of Kail Kalbar described the outcome as follows:

> During the discussions, they presented their perspective on the matter. They talked about their rights as local citizens in using natural resource (*memanfaatkan Sumber Daya Alam*). But finally they seemed to realize the side effects of illegal logging. But their thinking is still very pragmatic (*berfikirnya pragmatis*), and concentrated on immediate needs. After the boom of illegal logging in the area we face many problems to be solved, social, economic, cultural and even political. But since the beginning Kail is not only monitoring the illegal logging but also trying to understand its root (*akar*) causes.[23]

Despite these genuine attempts to engage in dialog, the Kail Kalbar team had no authority or means to deal with current and pressing needs of the border communities. As of 2007, no solution had been found, and the border towns that had boomed from the cross-border timber trade and flow of people and goods have become small ghost towns (*Equator News* 2005b). Concerns about the loss of future income opportunities were widely displayed as graffiti on houses and shops in the town of Lanjak. One local shop house carried the following message written in large letters: 'If the timber business is shut down (*kayu tutup*) the people will be bankrupt (*rakyat bangkrut*).' In January 2007 the Indonesian Ministry of Forestry issued a new regulation that reaffirms the central government's control over forest and leaves the district with little legal authority pertaining to management of these resources (Perdu 2007).

ILLEGAL BUT LICIT: CIRCUMVENTING THE LAW, ENFORCING LOCAL NORMS

What state officials view as illegal and therefore criminal behaviour may be considered well within the bounds of the acceptable by those who dis-

---

[23] Personal interview, Pontianak, 26-2-2007.

play this behaviour and by the communities to which they belong (Abraham and Van Schendel 2005:25).

How have these events and the ban on logging influenced the inhabitants of Rumah Manah and other Iban communities in the Ulu Leboyan? Apheng's company operating in the Ulu Leboyan was shut down and both logging camps and sawmill deserted. Inhabitants from Rumah Manah and surrounding communities who worked in this company have now been deprived of their only nearby source of cash income. Many men who had previously supplemented their household income with cash earned in the local logging industry are now, as they did in the past, taking up labour migration to Malaysia.

The border populations' ambivalent relationship with their own state was clearly expressed in the days after the government crackdown, when local communities went to Apheng's logging camp and sawmill to 'confiscate' machinery and timber, which they regarded as their property; in other words, the machinery was being protected for the future return of the *tukei*. Furthermore, in order to prevent outsiders from entering the upriver logging camps that are still full of cut timber, barriers were put up across logging roads using the locally confiscated bulldozers. During my 2005 fieldwork the large amount of logs that remained in the upriver timber camps had 'BB' written on them in large red letters. The letters meant '*bahan bukti*,' which meant that the timber was being held as government evidence. According to locals more than 10,000 logs were rotting in the camps close to the national park. The 'BB' label had been written by the central government anti-logging teams to indicate that all timber was state property and did not belong to local communities. The battlelines between local residents and central authorities were tightly drawn up, and their conflicting views of the situation were further expressed on a partly burnt timber shack with the following dialog written in black letters: 'Apheng is the one who loots (*merampok*) our country's forest and Apheng's followers become rich while eating Indonesia's future.' As a reply to this allegation, another message was written in half Indonesian and half Iban just above: 'Who is the one not ashamed or embarrassed (*enda pandai malu*) about eating the revenue (*makan hasil*) of this forest, it is the central government (*pusat*). The one who actually robs the communities' traditionally managed forests is the TNBK'. Following this message was a drawing of a man decapitating another man with a traditional war sword (*mandau*).

I discussed the writings on the shack with the group of Iban accompanying me on the trip, and several interpretations seemed possible. First, the local reply points towards the long-term duplicity of the actions of government officials, military and police; it accuses them of double standards when they condemn local community involvement with the *tukei* while they themselves harvest the larger share of the revenues from illegal logging. TNBK is an abbreviation for the Betung Kerihun National Park (Taman Negara Betung Kerihun), which locally is seen as a symbol of state authority. Several of the participants in the government anti-illegal raids were park rangers. The creation of the TNBK has for a long time been disputed, and still is, especially as the park boundaries fall within areas traditionally recognized as community forest, and the issue of local compensation remains unresolved. Many communities see few benefits from the national park, in which all resource exploitation is illegal and no local jobs are generated. Second, the writing conveys the message that the forest is believed to be local property and that there is a growing willingness to enforce local rights.

Disagreement between government and locals about what practices are to be designated illegal has once more resulted in locals taking matters into their own hands. Similar disregard for government decisions is seen in Lanjak where trucks loaded with logs continued to navigate the road between Lanjak and the border town of Nanga Badau in the month after the crackdown, despite the ban on the transport of logs across the border (*Kompas* 2005c). Now, however, the logs were transported at night in order to attract as little attention as possible; in daytime the roads were deserted. But as most sawmills in the area were inoperative, the logs transported were all from before the government raids. Many cut logs had been dumped in the lake area close to Lanjak in order to hide them from confiscation, and it was these logs that now were loaded onto trucks. But as no new logging is in progress, this source was soon exhausted.

The borderland inhabitants are awaiting the outcome of the situation. At the time of fieldwork it was unknown whether there will be any further repercussions for those who had been engaged in illegal logging. Three Malaysian Chinese who formerly worked for Apheng in the Ulu Leboyan have each been sentenced to nine years imprisonment and fined up to Rp 500 million (US$51,500), by the district court in Putussibau and the Indonesian supreme court in Jakarta. Several others are still awaiting trial (*Equator News* 2005d; PMARI 2006; PPNP 2005).[24] In early 2007 during a short trip to the town of Badau, one of my research assistant went shopping in the bazaar just across the border in Lubok Antu; here he saw Apheng having a cup of coffee in a roadside coffee shop. Despite having an arrest warrant hanging over his head in Indonesia, and a agreement for his capture and extradition has been made between the West Kalimantan and Sarawak police, Apheng still seems to move freely in Sarawak (*Berita Sore* 2007b). Several informants claim that Apheng is still following the situation in the borderland with interest, waiting for a chance to return. In June 2007 a team of journalists from the Indonesian television station SCTV (*Surya Citra Televisi*) approached Apheng in a restaurant in Sibu, Sarawak. Working undercover as Indonesian businessmen, the journalists managed to interview Apheng who again claimed that his (former) logging operations were strictly legal (SCTV 2007). Apheng has since left the logging business and is supposedly engaged in the oil palm plantation industry (*Berita Sore* 2007a).

DEFYING THE LIMITS OF LEGALITY

> The line between 'legal' and 'illegal is held to be clear and definitive inside a given state, a hegemonic claim. Yet actual practice is ambiguous and subject to resourceful manipulation. Legality and illegality are thus simultaneously black and white, and shades of gray (Heyman 1999b:11).

Interviews and discussions with local border inhabitants in the period after the large-scale government anti-logging operations reveal widespread sentiments of once again being treated unjustly by the central government. Growing confusion over whose authority should be reckoned with, that of district or central government, convinced many border inhabitants of the government's indifference to their situation and that it was time once again to take things into their own hands.

The issue of illegality in regard to logging was particularly vigorously discussed at community meetings and other local gatherings, where

---

[24] Nationwide (Kalimantan, Sumatra and Papua) more than 178 foreign timber entrepreneurs (mostly Malaysians) have been arrested for their alleged involvement in illegal logging (*Republika* 2005).

6 *Intersecting spheres of legality and illegality* |

people seemed to come to consensus that the legal concepts of central government always ended up working against local practices. As stated by an Iban leader:

> We are justified when taking the timber, as it is our own timber (*Kami disini berhak ambil kayu, kayu kita*). What is illegal? If they believe that the timber is illegal, why do our logging trucks have to pay to pass the border in Badau. Why does the district government make a gate at the border collecting fees? If they think the timber is illegal, they have to stop everything. Who did not know about the logging activities that happened in front of everybody's eyes (*terjadi di depan mata*)? The district officers knew, the *bupati* knew, the police knew, everybody knew about the logging in the border area. They did not declare any prohibitions as they all took part in it.[25]

Not only were the double standards of district government discussed; also the central government logging raids were criticized for not being transparent. For example, a local Iban businessman on a tour around Badau with a group of Malaysian investors in 2004 witnessed how an anti-logging team from the central police command in Jakarta code-named 'Wanalaga' stayed three days in Badau inspecting the cross-border trade in timber. According to the businessman the team members went around the area and collected money from all the timber companies; the money collected was stored in an 'Indomie' (noodle) box and brought along when the team left, and no receipts were given.[26] Such accusations of anti-logging teams led by crooked government officials also appeared in the provincial newspapers, where district assembly members (Iban) from Kapuas Hulu criticized the Wanalaga team for its dubious practices. Included in the criticism were allegations of the Wanalaga team disturbing local communities and receiving money for bypassing and ignoring certain sawmills and timber camps during their inspection tours (*Pontianak Post* 2004k; 2004l; 2004m). Apheng was, for example, accused of bribing the Wanalaga officials with Rp 3 billion (US$300,000) (*Tempo* 2005d).

The confusion concerning the legal standing of forest extraction expressed by locals in the borderland in the wake of the numerous anti-logging operations is also to be found in the inconsistent and contradic-

[25] Personal interview, Lanjak, 30-5-2007.
[26] Personal interview, Pontianak, 22-8-2007.

tory definitions of what is legal and illegal presented by the multi-level actors and the vaguely defined legislation. For example, while the 2005 presidential decree directed at eradicating illegal logging (*Inpres* 2005) mentioned previously put much emphasis on what was considered illegal timber extraction, it presented no clear indication of what then was to be considered legal. There were no clear boundaries between legal and illegal, which meant that these new laws were just as fuzzy and open to the same degree of interpretation as the previous laws on regional autonomy that had inspired the districts to secure revenue from local natural resources in the first place.

SHADES OF GRAY

> The difficulty of distinguishing insider from outsider produces confusion in the minds of state forces that can no longer tell where they themselves are located. This uncertainty is a product of the interplay of the licit and the illegal, an effect produced by the coincidence of the geographic and political limits of the state (Abraham 2006:4).

Several things are at work in the incidents discussed above. First, local district government and border elites have been given more power because of national decentralization processes, and cross-border logging is seen as a good opportunity to develop and promote borderland economy, which has long been neglected by the central government. Additionally, given sharp declines in financial support from the central and provincial governments, district officials have had to find ways to provision their own ranks. Second, as described earlier, many Iban (like some district officials) do not share central and provincial government views on the illegality of current logging activities, and the interference of 'outsiders', such as in the government operation described above, is largely understood as a breach of local autonomy that lacks local legitimacy. As documented in this and previous chapters, the Iban have always shown themselves to be quite capable of taking the law in their own hands and carrying out acts of vigilantism when they feel injustices have been committed. Thus commonly heard remarks like: 'what is the law' and 'for whom is the law' refer to a local recognition that the 'legitimate' state law has little to offer them.

Being well armed and having a reputation for vigilantism, the Iban are seen as a player not to be taken lightly. So when local district police and military in the case above choose the strategy of passivity instead of confrontation the reason is twofold: first, the economic benefits of the logging boom; and second, a sound respect for local Iban ability to take action. Local police and military officials are, by and large, not 'local' themselves but come from a variety of places – elsewhere in the province or well beyond, such as Java and Bali. Given the link between cross-border activities and illegality, it is difficult to assess how or if local officials are involved beyond simply facilitating and collecting fees from such activities on their side of the border. It is widely known in the area that the police and the military are economically dependent upon, and indeed benefit greatly from, the so-called illegal activities, especially as there is so little help given by central command (police/military) to the subdistrict commands. Most of the local units or sub-commands within the area have been encouraged to look for an economically viable way to support their own members. It is most likely they are working together with local communities and the *tukei*. This once again highlights the fact that local state agents and central government do not necessarily share the same interests and that various state agents tactically support acts of illegality. This assertion relates to the point made by Heyman and Smart that intimate case studies of state illegality help to 'transcend the stultifying assumption that states always uphold the law' (Heyman 1999b:1).

As portrayed by the Iban borderland inhabitants, what makes their engagement in cooperative logging illegal in the eyes of the central government is a general government lack of understanding of the special circumstances of life in the borderland. Given the special borderland context and the fact that local government agents themselves for long have participated and profited from these illegal activities, locals have rendered these practices licit. Thus, being situated on the borderline between two nation-states, one wealthier than the other, the search for viable livelihood strategies inevitably means moving back and forth across the border and in and out of intersecting spheres of legality and illegality. This chapter has discussed how the concepts 'legal' and 'illegal' often blur together and how state definitions of legality are highly political and their definitions ever shifting according to state power along these state edges.

Finally, the multi-level networks, nested relationships, and fluid loyalties play a major role for understanding the outcome of the various cases described above. However, in order to comprehend border community actions it is essential to return to the issue of patron-client relationships and their particular formation in the borderland. Despite the inherent inequality within this relationship and the central government's harsh condemnations of the Sarawak entrepreneurs, the larger percentage of the border population has remained remarkably loyal towards the *tukei*. However, the ethos of this relationship, as touched upon in previous chapters, was mainly based on economic cost-benefit calculation. Such economic motivation does not entirely explain this strong sense of loyalty shown the *tukei* patrons vis-à-vis the central state, locally embedded norms of respect, interpersonal obligations and reciprocity nurtured through centuries of shifting borderland life and persistent cross-border relations need to be taken into consideration. When reflecting on these conditions and patterns of solidarity, one might find the question raised earlier by the head of one of the anti-logging teams – 'How could locals be more loyal and cooperative toward a foreigner (Apheng) than to their own government?' – more understandable.

As we shall see in the following chapters, the anti-logging operation initiated by central and provincial government largely altered the previous state of affairs. Indeed, what we may now be seeing is a national and provincial attempt to wrest control of revenue streams and authority from the districts by outlawing locally managed forest extraction, re-militarizing the border and establishing large-scale plantation schemes. On the surface the scale once again seems to have tipped towards increasing state authority in the borderland, as we saw during the period of militarization in the 1960s and 1970s and centrally controlled logging in the 1980s and 1990s. In the next chapter, I will add further layers to my analysis of the borderland by analyzing the rhetoric of central government development programs and grand schemes up to and in the years after the crackdown on illegal logging. I will here put special emphasis on cases that demonstrate state attempts to regain authority over its borders and natural resources and how such attempts are modified on the local-level and have lead to a further strengthening of local desires for increased autonomy.

7

Sovereignty and security

> The territorialized nation-state, in modern state formation, comes hand in hand with the implementation of citizenship, state control over access to and use of national land and resources, and effort to control national space up to international borders (Sturgeon 2004:481).

This analytical statement made by Janet Sturgeon in her study of the ambivalent relationship between state and local village elites in claiming resource access in the Thai-China borderlands largely resembles many dynamics unfolding in the resource-rich border areas of West Kalimantan, especially the stretch of borderland discussed here.

In June 2005, a few months after the large-scale government crackdowns on illegal logging along the border, President Susilo Bambang Yudhoyonn made a two-day visit to the province for a helicopter inspection tour along the international border with Sarawak, making the sudden crackdown on illegal logging seem more than a pure coincidence and part of a larger scheme. Returning to the provincial capital Pontianak, the president praised the enormous potential for development of the province, emphasizing oil palm plantations as a major development possibility along the lightly populated but heavily forested border with Malaysia (PKB 2005a, 2005c). This, he said, was in line with a newly introduced government development plan whose main goal was the creation of large-scale plantations that would run along the entire length of the Kalimantan-Malaysian border (*Jakarta Post* 2005b). In connection with the execution of this master plan, national media revealed how the government was planning the opening of a 2000 km border road and the establishment of several permanent military control posts to secure peace and order and protect the country against external threats (*Jakarta Post* 2005d; *Kompas* 2005a).

| *At the edges of states*

These presidential statements initiated a new era of central state involvement in the borderland. Through large-scale development plans and an increase in military authority, the Indonesian government once again underscored the perceived importance of strengthening state presence and sovereignty along its borders with Malaysia.[1] It was envisaged that the 'lawless' border region should once again be controlled by a strong army presence, and plantation 'development' should be the new security buffer zone facing an expanding neighbour (*Jakarta Post* 2005d). Among border communities, such initiatives were received with scepticism and widely understood to be part of the central government's efforts to regain control of the border region, especially of the lucrative forestry sector, which it had partly lost with the official implementation of regional autonomy in 2001. More widely these new government proclamations seemed to feed into current government efforts to slow down or even re-centralize parts of the decentralization process, especially where local governments' ability to control natural resources like forests were concerned.[2]

Large-scale development projects are elements of what James Scott has called 'state simplification', which is above all concerned with issues of legality and ultimately the enhancement of state control (Scott 1998). I do not here wish to present a picture of 'the state' as all seeing and all powerful; rather, I want to depict how such large state schemes along the border are based on simplistic analyses of the borderland and its population. Such schemes often do not work out as expected as they become part of an ongoing negotiation between higher- and lower-level players (Li 2005).

The borderland is a source of extreme anxiety for the modern Indonesian state that views the border population as unreliable and potentially subversive subjects. In the words of Abraham and Van Schendel,

> Social groups that systematically contest and bypass state control do not simply flout the letter of the law; with repeated transgressions over time, they bring into question the legitimacy of the state itself by questioning the state's ability to control its own territory (Abraham and Van Schendel 2005:14).

[1] President SBY is himself a retired general and former security minister.
[2] Warren 2005; Wollenberg et al. 2006; Yasmi et al. 2006.

7 *Sovereignty and security*

As indicated in the previous chapter, the implementation of regional autonomy in the borderland led to drastic changes in the regulative powers concerned with forest resources. The result has been heightened tension between the central government and the districts. Before venturing into a discussion of how border communities and elites deal with recent intervention from the central state in regaining authority of the borderland, I will discuss a few examples of such top-down government interventions and how they fit into a broader state policy as it applies to the border, the adjacent borderland and its population. I will show how questions of 'border development' and 'security' have regained priority in the thinking of central and provincial legislators and how these processes run parallel with recent local border strategies already discussed in the previous chapters.

Another purpose of the chapter is to emphasize the oscillating character of the border; that is, how central state power waxes and wanes. At times, it appears weak, as during the previous period of community logging, while now state authority appears especially strong due to the increased military presence in the borderland. While this chapter recognizes the profound inequalities of power, uncertainty and risk that permeate life in the borderland, it does not portray state authority as absolute (Chalfin 2001). Rather, as thoroughly illustrated in previous chapters, the Indonesian state is far from the highly centralized state and unitary structure it claims to be, and the recent push to reassert state authority through large top-down government schemes and coercive military force was rapidly reshaped by the realities of everyday life and local-level politics in the borderland.

SECURITY THROUGH DEVELOPMENT

Underdevelopment and poor infrastructure along the border with Malaysia, together with the rise in illegal logging and smuggling, have long been seen by the central state as a national security problem. The central and provincial governments view development and national security as closely connected, and border development has long been named as a main priority by shifting governments. As discussed in chapter four, the focus on border development and security has been a continuous and dominant state discourse since the late 1960s when the forested borderland first became categorized as a green 'safety belt' (*sabuk pengaman*) to be solely managed and 'developed' by the army-owned foundation Yamaker. Development in most instances became an excuse for large-scale resource extraction. Decades later, in 1994, nearly half a century after independence, President Soeharto issued the first official presidential decree on development initiatives in the border areas of Kalimantan (Keppres 1994). According to the decree border development was imperative for national security, and the approach taken should therefore be generated through a system of defence and security (*sistem pertahanan keamanan*). The 1994 decree appointed a special 'Agency for the Implementation and Control of Development in the Border Area, BP3WPK'.[3] This agency involved various ministries but was mainly headed by the Ministry of Defence and Security (Departemen Pertahanan dan Keamanan, Dephankam) that also controlled the Yamaker Foundation.

On 30 July 1994, immediately after the agency's creation, its chairman issued a decree[4] on the formation of a technical team[5] whose main purpose was to initiate joint security and development initiatives along the border. Although grand development plans for the border area were put forward; like opening up the area to transmigration settlements, mining, and plantations, any genuine commitment of the team to the noble cause quickly died away, and from 1996 onwards the team was largely inactive. The only 'development' processes taking place in the borderland were large-scale forest resource extraction. This is not surprising, considerating that genuine development initiatives would have interfered with the timber business of Yamaker. It is widely believed among the border population today that any genuine development efforts were purposely neglected and ignored by powerful sections (military) within the New Order government in order to promote its own business arrangements. The lack of genuine commitment from powerful military players was also declared by border elites as the reason why they initially became engaged in the timber business. As often stated, it was better to cooperate and receive little than to get nothing and see all revenue from local forest resources ending up in the pockets of outsiders.

The 1994 presidential decree was very vague about actual initiatives

---

[3] Badan Pengendali Pelaksanaan Pembangunan Wilayah Perbatasan, BP3WPK.
[4] Keputusan No. Skep/894/VII/1994 Tanggal 30 July.
[5] Tim Teknis Pelaksanaan Pembangunan Wilayah Perbatasan.

and never resulted in any concrete development plan. It was consequently seen as a tool for legitimizing certain groups' exploitation of the border's natural resources. Despite highlighting the discourse of development, what characterised the approach behind this first presidential decree was that more weight was given to security and defence than development. However, one of the accomplishments of the team was to define the actual border zone and thereby the future development corridor along the border. The corridor was defined to be four kilometres wide and about 2000 km long. The border zone has since been defined very differently depending on which government department you ask; the width has been defined as anywhere from 4 to 100 km.

In Chapter 4, I mentioned that President Habibie closed down the Yamaker logging operations in the border area in 1999, a year after the fall of Soeharto. Another outcome of this change of government was the issuance of a new presidential decree revoking the previous decree (No. 44/1994) regarding border development issued by Soeharto (Keppres 1999). This step was part of a larger attempt by the Habibie government to downgrade the role of the military in national politics and other public matters as highlighted in the *dwifungsi* doctrine. The new decree stated that the BP3WPK team headed by Dephankam had been completely ineffective and had not achieved any development goals. Consequently, all of this agency's authority was to be withdrawn and divided among a unspecified wider selection of government agencies. In 2001 under the presidency of Abdurrahman Wahid, government plans for the management of the border areas were specified in yet another new presidential decree creating a special council[6] for development of the eastern part of Indonesia, especially the border areas of Kalimantan (Keppres 2001).[7] In the following years, under President Megawati (2001-2004) and later President Yudhoyono, a series of draft plans, surveys and strategy reports appeared on the border issue that discussed development initiatives and spatial planning, although no real effort was made to implement these; logging was still big business along the border. The security and prosperity approach (*pendekatan keamanan dan kesejahteraan*) as initially introduced by Soeharto was still, post-Soeharto, playing a vital role in government border plans, and was repeatedly mentioned in various reports. However,

---

6   Dewan Pengembangan Kawasan Timur Indonesia.
7   This council later became the Ministry for the Acceleration of Development in Eastern Indonesia, today known as Ministry for the Development of Disadvantaged Regions.

compared to the New Order regime the official rhetoric now seemed to be more focussed on prosperity and development than security and defence.

On 14 October 2003, a meeting was held in East Kalimantan between the Indonesian government and officials from the Malaysian states of Sabah and Sarawak to discuss cross-border trade and development of a spatial plan for the border area between the two countries. A report prepared for the meeting stated that the main spatial policy was: 'To boost the development of [the] border area as an Indonesian 'front line' to Malaysia.' Attached to the report were several maps plotting all 25 subdistricts along the entire length of the border and specifying their development potentials, such as plantation, logging, forestry and mining activities (DJPR 2003). A month later, in November 2003, the National Development Planning Agency, Bappenas[8] released the first official report on a strategy and model for developing the border areas of Kalimantan (Bappenas 2003). In this and several supplemental reports in 2004, 2005 and 2006 it was officially recognized that the border area for too long had been viewed as the 'backyard' (*halaman belakang*) of the country, stressing underdevelopment and lawlessness.[9] Concurrently the Ministry of Forestry released its own decree sketching a strategic plan for forestry development in the border area, highlighting the problem of illegal logging and an urgent need for consistent law enforcement (Kepmenhut 2004).

According to the reports, a new paradigm was to be developed making the borderland into the 'front yard' (*halaman depan*) of the country, calling attention to its potential for prosperity and progress. Reports stated that the merely exploitative character of past development policies, with their emphasis on the need for security in the form of military presence, had resulted in low rate of infrastructure improvement in the border area and between the two neighbouring countries. In a 2007 interview on the Kapuas Hulu borderland, the head of the socio-cultural branch (*social-budaya*) of the Regional Development Planning Agency (Bappeda) supported this new view with the following statement:

> Kapuas Hulu has for too long been left behind compared to other regions. For example if they [the border population] want to go Pontianak,

---

[8] Badan Perencanaan Pembangunan Nasional.
[9] Bappenas 2004, 2005, 2006a, 2006b.

it is too far because of non-existant infrastructure. Yes in this way we have pushed them closer to Sarawak (*dekatkan dia dengan Serawak*). We have raised the need for an overall presidential decree concerning the border with central government but no agreement has been made yet. Border development and planning is a federal or central issue. Districts may not make agreements on their own with Malaysia.[10]

Development initiatives needed to be balanced more evenly between a security approach and a prosperity approach. The ultimate mission, as quoted in a 2006 report on the key management plan of the countries' borders, was to create a: 'Secure, Orderly, and Advanced Territory'. According to the report 'secure' means creating security conditions that can be controlled and are conducive for business and free from illegal activities. 'Orderly' means that all economic, social and cultural activities at the border are based on law and regulation. And finally, 'advanced' refers to the better economic welfare of local communities (Bappenas 2006a:41).

Once again, border development was seen as closely related to the mission of national development and security. In the Middle-Term National Development Plan for 2004 to 2009 (Rencana Pembangunan Jangka Menengah Nasional, RPJM), border development was highlighted as one of the main priorities. This plan, among other things, emphasizes the eradication of cross-border smuggling as a means for securing and maintaining order in border areas of Indonesia. As stated in chapter six, page nine of the RPJM plan on 'Enhancing Security and Order, and Overcoming Crime,' the aim of the government is 'to secure border areas of Indonesia by securing cross-border activities in the state border areas, and to take measures to secure the outermost islands of the nation's borders'. Furthermore, chapter 26, paragraph 3 in 'The Program of Development of Border Areas' aims at

> Maintaining the territorial integrity of the Republic of Indonesia, through the affirmation of the sovereignty of the NKRI (Unitary State of the Republic of Indonesia)... enhance nationalism of the [border] communities; and to ensure the supremacy of law and legal regulations with regard to violations that are occurring in border areas (Perpres 2005b).

[10] Personal interview, Pontianak, 20-2-2007.

In an August 2005 speech at a plenary session of the Regional Representatives Council (DPD-RI) on the issue of regional development policy, President SBY stated that the government was now committed to improving the welfare of the border communities:

> I have much sympathy towards the communities living in the area just in front of the nation's borders. Their patriotism (*rasa kecintaan*) towards our beloved homeland (*tanah air tercinta*) is immense, and we therefore need to continue the development activities in the area (Ketpem 2005:9).

According to this presidential statement the only way to guarantee sovereignty (*keutuhan*), territorial integrity (*kedaulatan wilayah*) and national security (*pertahanan nasional*) was to improve the welfare of people in the border region. Border development was to change its orientation from the backyard of national development to 'outward looking' so the region could be used as a gateway for trade and economic activities with neighbouring countries. The main strategy for attaining this goal, as noted in several reports, was to create a large agricultural region or corridor along the border (*kawasan agropolitan*) (Bappenas 2003, 2004, 2006c)[11] and thereby create local prosperity and minimize the border population's economic dependency on neighbouring Malaysia as well as prevent separatism and illegal activities, especially illegal logging. As stated by the president during an official speech at the House of Representatives in August 2008 quoted in *Tempo* magazine, 'Our border areas should be regarded as the front porch of the Unitary Republic of Indonesia, therefore we need to open up this back yard of the country', here referring to the current underdevelopment along the border – a statement that has been repeated several times since (Agustiar 2008[12]; *Borneo Tribune* 2009a).

The numerous reports on border development further defined the district of utmost concern within the two border provinces of East and West Kalimantan. The five Iban-dominated subdistricts within the

---

[11] The concept of an Indonesian-Malaysian agricultural corridor had already been suggested as a suitable border strategy in a 2001 publication from the National Agency for the Assessment and Application of Technology (Hamid et al. 2001). The concept of an agricultural corridor has since been promoted by various district governments along the border as a means of economic development (Thamrin et al. 2007).

[12] Already during the 2004 presidential election campaign one of Susilo Bambang Yudhoyono's slogans was to make the border region into a shiny 'front porch' (*beranda depan*) of the nation by developing the neglected and under-developed border region.

Kapuas Hulu district were highlighted as first priority, in special need of development and increased national attachment.[13] Additionally, in the spatial planning (*tata ruang*) of the Kalimantan-Sarawak-Sabah border region (KASABA) the central and provincial government selected five border entry points in West Kalimantan that would be developed into economic growth centres and agricultural regions; one of these was to be situated in the borderland at Nanga Badau (Bappenas 2006c:33; *Equator News* 2007a).[14]

For much of the past half-century, the only official border-crossing point (Pos Pemeriksaan Lintas Batas, PPLB) where non-border residents could pass and international trade was allowed was at Entikong (West Kalimantan)-Tebedu (Sarawak), situated far away from the Kapuas Hulu borderland. The Nanga Badau crossing is not yet a designated PPLB although several attempts have been made to open it in the past decade.[15] There are several reasons why this border point has not been officially opened yet, including the lack of funds and the issue of tax. As indicated in Chapters 5 and 6, the Badau border point was the main artery for smuggled logs into Sarawak during the logging boom and the unofficial status of this crossing made it possible for district officials and police to collect their own, unofficial taxes. As plainly stated by an Iban member of the district assembly (DPRD II):

> The reason why the Badau gateway is not opened yet is that now every cross-border transaction can continue to be declared illegal, and when illegal it in the end becomes the game of government institutions for collecting unofficial taxes (*mainan aparat pemerintah untuk sopoi*). Even the security apparatus (*aparat keamanan*) is involved. If the border gates become official, there will be no more unofficial tax (*cukai-cukai dibelakang*). I visited Badau two weeks ago where I was told that every person who went 'shopping' in Sarawak was asked to pay 50 Malaysian Ringgit to various officials [military and police] when they returned. I got very disappointed (*kecewa*) and must say that if this gate is not opened soon it means that central government wishes the border area to remain unlawful.[16]

---

[13] See also Paragraph 1, Article 6 in the draft presidential regulation from 2005 (Perpres 2005a).
[14] Likewise, five economic growth centres were selected in the neighbouring province of East Kalimantan.
[15] *Equator News* 2005c; *Kompas* 2002; *Pontianak Post* 2004i; *Sinar Harapan* 2003b.
[16] Personal interview, Putussibau, 1-3-2007.

As part of the central government plan for 'legalizing border trade', initial steps to open this border point have been taken; customs and immigration buildings have been constructed and a gate erected (*Equator News* 2006b). Ironically, during a 2007 visit to Badau I found that this 'official' gate was still locked and all movement of people and goods across the border still followed a small, unofficial dirt road into Sarawak that had initially been built for smuggling logs during the years of illegal logging. Likewise, Malaysian authorities have been hesitant to develop infrastructure for a similar official border crossing point on their side because of the bad road conditions on the Indonesian side and the huge influx of labour migrants that might result (*Borneo Tribune* 2009b; *Pontianak Post* 2007a). Nevertheless, in anticipation of an impending opening and the new economic boom that might follow, several highly placed officials in Putussibau bought up all the land close to the border gate for erecting shops.

Despite these initiatives and wider attempts to develop a master plan for the border region, the various government bodies involved in this process has been largely crippled as there still is no official law or decree that specifies what exactly makes up the borderland and what the division of labour is between the different levels of government (*Jakarta Post* 2009). In need of a legal umbrella (*payung hukum*), the Indonesian parliament has since the presidency of Megawati Sukarnoputri discussed the content of a coming border law draft (Rancangan Undang-undang Perbatasan, RUU) to determine the levels of government and departments that will be responsible for the future management of Indonesia's border regions.[17] Both the governments of Megawati Sukarnoputri and SBY have previously had draft laws made up on the spatial planning of the Kalimantan border area that stipulated the main priorities for the border. However, these drafts have never been signed by the president and therefore have not taken effect as formal laws (Keppres 2003; Perpres 2005c). Local speculation in the border districts interprets this slow progress of legalizing border activities as a central government excuse for strengthening its authority over the 'lawless' border through re-militarization of the borderland.

In order to speed up the process of creating border legislation, the previous governor H. Usman Ja'far (2003-2007) put together a special

---

[17] *Equator News* 2006e, 2007c; *Tempo* 2006.

provincially headed 'Agency for the Preparation of Special Border Area Development' (Badan Persiapan Pengembangan Kawasan Khusus Perbatasan, BP2KKP) (Pergub 2005). The BP2KKP works under the Regional Development Planning agency in Pontianak, and its main objective is to survey and collect socio-economic data on the border that later is to feed into the overall presidential master plan. Head of the BP2KKP, Nyoman Sudana, stated in a 2005 interview that the most urgent problem in the border area is related to national sovereignty, and he was worried that the relative poverty of the border people would cause a decrease in nationalism:

> Until now there is no clear agreement on the borderline between the two countries and many border poles are damaged or removed. The border area has not yet been properly socialized into the nation. The dominant merchant trading is carried in foreign currency (*mata uang asing*) and moreover, our citizens at the border are more familiar with the leaders of our neighbours (*mengenal pemimpin di Negara tetangga*) compared to those of their own country (*dibandingkan dengan negara sendiri*) (*Equator News* 2005c).

On the provincial level, border development was seen as a major future economic asset, which could enhance the lucrative cross-border trade with Malaysia. The slow pace of the centre caused several provincial and district level commentators to accuse the central government of being inconsistent and uncommitted in its effort to develop the border area, as it repeatedly has postponed the implementation of official legislation. Provincial and district assembly representatives express an increasing bewilderment about central government's main goals. The demand for immediate action has become increasingly pronounced and made headlines in provincial newspapers.[18] This general perplexity over the unclear signals from Jakarta was clearly expressed in an interview with provincial assembly (DPRD I) members in 2007:

> Our main problem is that every decision concerning the border has to be taken by central government; everything must go to Jakarta first. This means that compared to our neighbour Sarawak who does not have to wait for central Malaysian decisions we are much slower in making deci-

---

[18] *Equator News* 2005e, 2005f, 2006c, 2006f; *Pontianak Post* 2006a.

sions, and are lagging behind. Therefore, we ask the president to promptly create an official border law. We have asked the president for special treatment (*perlakuan khusus*)that could enable us it to improve the social economic development in the border area. However, our pleas have not yet been answered by the central government, a sign especially for us as the people's representative here that the central government is indifferent (*setengah hati*) about giving special treatment on particular issues that have been requested by West Kalimantan. We fear (*pesimislah*) that we will have to wait another 20 years for the planning of central government and again are going to be left behind (*tertinggal*). When our president visited the border post at Entikong [SBY's visit to the province in June 2005], he said that the border should become the front window (*jadikan jendela depan*) of West Kalimantan. But how is this to be realized? For now it is only rhetoric (*retorika saja*). I am worried that if we get a new president; this law is not going to be created. The point is that now there is a rising willingness (*keinginan*) from the border districts to take action, but they have only limited capacity, financially and legally, to take care of these matters.[19]

The head of the provincial assembly was even quoted as saying that the whole border area was like a 'time bomb' just waiting to explode if central government did not soon create a clear set of guidelines and subsequent legislation for developing the area (*Sinar Harapan* 2007).

GRAND SCHEMES

Following the numerous and vaguely defined border plans previously outlined by central government, and despite the lack of an overall legal framework, Minister of Agriculture Anton Apriantono publically announced in May 2005 the formation of a plantation corridor to span the entire length of the border with Malaysia (about 2000 km). The initial goal of this grand plan was the creation of the world's largest oil palm plantation (1.8 million hectares) (*Pontianak Post* 2005a). Quoted in the *Jakarta Post*, the Minister claimed that the plantation would create more than half-a million jobs and attract foreign exchange to the country. Besides creating jobs for local populations the government ex-

[19] Personal interview, Pontianak, 21-2-2007.

pected to move unemployed workers from densely populated provinces of Indonesia into the sparsely populated border area as part of a large transmigration project. The main investors in the plantation were to be the Chinese government and Malaysian companies, with Rp 5.5 trillion (US$567 million) in projected initial capital over the next five years. The minister stated, 'The project is aimed at strengthening our border against our neighbour Malaysia, as well as reducing the prosperity gap between our people living along the border and those in Malaysia' (*Jakarta Post* 2005b). These statements on border security concerning Malaysia sounded rather hollow considering that some of the main investors were to be Malaysian companies.

In a public speech to the provincial government in Pontianak during his visit in June 2005, President SBY supported the plan announced by his Agricultural Minister and said that plantation development was crucial for the overall development of the border area. President SBY expected that jobs created through plantation development would help the local border population become less dependent on wage labour in Malaysia and more attached to their own country. Furthermore, the development of infrastructure such as roads along the border would strengthen the country's border against so-called illegal practices like cross-border timber smuggling and undocumented labour migration. President SBY stated:

> In order for this [plantation plan] to develop, we also have to develop a road running parallel to the border. We must close down all the mouse roads (*jalan-jalan tikus*) that frequently are employed for the undertaking of illegal activities [smuggling of timber into Malaysia]. If this plantation plan goes well, tens or even hundreds of thousands of people could be employed in the border area (PKB 2005c).

The president further elaborated on this grand plan to *Tempo*:

> Our plan is to develop the areas alongside the border for palm oil plantations, forestry, and tourism centres. If we can develop this from the West to the East, security and stability will be better. Palm oil and agricultural cultivation will raise incomes, absorb the workforce, and increase regional taxes. Meanwhile, we will be able to keep on nurturing the sense of nationhood and being Indonesian (*Tempo* 2005a).

In July 2005 the government-owned plantation cooperative PT Perkebunan Pusantara (PTPN) informally released a rather hasty and not well thought out report showing that the proposed palm oil plantation scheme would run straight through and overlap with two large national parks, one of which was the Betung Kerihun National Park in the borderland (Persero 2005). That extensive planning proposal was quickly turned down by the central government when Minister of Forestry Malam S. Kaban said that his ministry would stop any new conversion of forest into plantations and instead use abandoned and deforested land in the border area for such developments (*Jakarta Post* 2005a). In August 2005, Kaban addressed a letter to the minister of agriculture concerning oil palm plantations in the border area and requested that the agricultural ministry remember that large parts of the border area were set aside for conservation purposes and forestry cultivation.[20] The minister of agriculture later (October 2005) acknowledged that only 180,000 hectares rather than 1.8 million hectares along the border were actually suitable for oil palm plantations (Wakker 2006), and in December the Directorate General of Spatial Planning acknowledged the need to consider the environmental impact when developing spatial planning for the Kalimantan border (DJPR 2005).

At the time of writing, the status of the 'world's largest' plantation is unclear. The overall plantation plan has received major attention from national and worldwide media.[21] The plan drew strong criticism from various national and international NGOs for its immense effect on the natural and human environment (*Down to Earth* 2005; Lorens 2006; Wakker 2006). The World Wildlife Foundation (WWF) in particular lobbied intensively against the government plan, as it was afraid that the plan would destroy its 'Heart of Borneo' initiative, an initiative that sought to establish 225,000 km^2 of conservation area along the Indonesia-Malaysia border. WWF, like many local communities, saw the plantation plan as an excuse to cut the remaining forest along the border, especially as there was more than enough 'sleeping' (fallow) land (*lahan tidur*) or 'empty' land (*tanah kosong*) that had been deforested and abandoned and could be developed into plantations.[22] Furthermore,

[20] Surat 476/Menhut-IV/2005 Tanggal 16 Agustus.
[21] *Antara* 2005b; *Jakarta Post* 2005b, 2005e; *Sinar Harapan* 2005e; *Tempo* 2005b; *The Wall Street Journal* 2005.
[22] *Jakarta Post* 2005f; Lorens 2006; *Media Indonesia* 2005b; Susanto 2005.

large stretches of the border are unsuitable for oil palm production as the proposed land is very hilly and highly vulnerable to soil erosion (Lorens 2006).

In response to the widespread and mostly negative international attention, Indonesian authorities have begun downsizing and modifying the plan. Despite not being implemented in its original grand form, an Indonesian-Malaysian agricultural corridor along the border is still on the government agenda and could be readily implemented. The vast territory is now split up into smaller segments and being developed on a lower and less conspicuous level; for example, plantation (logging) companies are negotiating directly with local communities and district governments. (Departemen Pertanian 2009).

RE-MILITARIZING THE BORDER

As discussed in previous chapters, the military presence and authority in the border area has waxed and waned over time, from being extremely conspicuous during the Soeharto era to less noticeable in the nearly ten years of decentralization as a consequence of shifting reform government's attempts to diminish military authority. The political role of the military was greatly reduced after the fall of Soeharto when the new reform governments initiated a restructuring of the institution. In 1999, the Habibie government banned any army participation in national elections and required the army to cut all ties with the Golkar party and remain neutral. Subsequently, military factions within the different levels of government and civil politics were steadily reduced. The Indonesian military changed its name from the Indonesian Armed Forces (ABRI) to the Indonesian National Army (TNI) and was separated from the National Police (Polri). However, the military has always had a powerful role in shaping the borderland even at times it has been less obvious. Despite losing ground within civil politics, the military seems to have largely maintained their role within the business sector (Human Rights Watch 2006).

During the post-Soeharto 'illegal' logging boom in the borderland, the military, although less visible, was engaged in the timber business, mostly receiving benefits for keeping their eyes shut and providing protection to various companies (*Kompas* 2004h). The prosperity and

| At the edges of states

security approach reintroduced by recent central government border development plans have come as a highly welcomed and long awaited opportunity for the military to regain visibility along (and access to) the resource-rich border and to reclaim its past glory as protectors of territorial sovereignty and security.[23] Some of the more cynical spectators among the border population even speculate that the discourse of national sovereignty and border security is manufactured in order to justify larger budgets for the military. It is locally argued that the military requires a good cause in order to prove the need for a strong military establishment in post-Soeharto Indonesia.[24]

Immediately after the government presented the plan for a large-scale, mostly oil palm plantation corridor along the border, high-ranking military spokespersons were quick to express their strong support for the plan. Riding high on the central government rhetoric of security and a general public demand for stronger territorial defence against Malaysia, the establishment of several permanent military control posts was proposed in order to secure the border area and protect the country against external threats such as cross-border illegal logging and trade.[25] The porous border and lawless borderland were further seen as an obvious entry point for foreign terrorists and therefore in dire need of military and police protection. Some even suggested that a unit of the police special anti-terror corps (Detasemen Khusus, Densus 88 Anti-Terror) should help patrol the border (*Equator News* 2005a).

In December 2005 Major General Erwin Sudjono from the Kalimantan regional command in Pontianak[26] expressed the military's views on large-scale plantations in a daily provincial newspaper under the title 'The Army supports oil palm on the border,' where he was quoted saying, 'Why should we [the army] not open up the border area

---

[23] The focus on border militarization and national sovereignty has recently been sharpened by the latest controversy involving accusations made by Indonesian military that a Malaysian paramilitary force (Askar Wathaniyah) deployed to safeguard the Sarawak border has recruited members of the Indonesian border populations (*Antara* 2008). Another ongoing controversy is the issue of the border poles. Indonesian news media and military spokespersons have occasionally accused Malaysian plantation companies of moving border poles several meters into Indonesian territory in order to gain access to more land and timber. The Indonesian military even claim that 50 poles have gone missing altogether (*Equator News* 2005c; *Berita Sore* 2009, *Jakarta Globe* 2009). For example in July 2009, the military command in Pontianak exterminated several Malaysian oil palm plots on the border that supposedly were 'illegally' encroaching on Indonesian territory (*Sinar Harapan* 2009).
[24] Personal interviews, Badau, 21-3-2007.
[25] *Jakarta Post* 2005d; *Kompas* 2005d; *Pontianak Post* 2005f; *Sinar Harapan* 2005c.
[26] Panglima Komando Daerah Militer, Pangdam VI/Tanjungpura,

[for oil palm]? The army controls this area. The border area is the sole property of the army (*milik TNI*) (*Pontianak Post* 2005e).

Later, in March 2006, on a inspection tour to the East Kalimantan part of the border, Commander-in-Chief of the National Armed Forces (TNI) Djoko Suyanto, accompanied by Major General Erwin Sudjono, announced that he was strongly in favour of plans to develop the border using agribusiness, especially oil palm plantations. He stated:

> We support the development of border areas in the aim to improve the welfare of the people (*kesejahteraan rakyat*); in addition to this there are strategic goals (*tujuan strategis*) related to aspects of security to be considered. This [development] program has actually been planned for tens of years.... There is no reason to reject the development of the border because the main purpose is the welfare of the people in the area as well as the security aspects (*aspek keamanan*).... We will continue to build defence posts (*pos penjagaan*) along the border in the years 2006, 2007, 2008, and 2009 until the issue of [economic] disparity in the border area is completely solved (*Berita TNI* 2006).

Djoko Suyanto was further quoted as saying, '[T]he border between Kalimantan and Malaysia was a region in special need of being strictly guarded (*diwaspadai*) as the area was exposed to many illegal activities, like illegal logging, illegal mining and illegal fishing (*Suara Karya* 2006).

Concerning the environmental impact of the plantation corridor Major General Erwin Sudjono from the regional command denied that it would cause any major problems, as he himself had noticed during many helicopter inspection tours along the border that large tracts of the forest were already damaged due to illegal logging (*Berita TNI* 2006).

Besides introducing large-scale and top-down plantation development to replace the subversive economy of illegal logging, the wake of the anti-logging campaign discussed in the previous two chapters brought a large increase in military personnel stationed along the border (*Pontianak Post* 2006b). Starting in late 2006, several hundred soldiers were dispatched to the area, and control posts or camps were erected in the borderland with barbed wire and a shooting range. Each camp was manned by one heavily armed company locally known as the LIBAS border soldiers (Tentara Lintas Batas). Furthermore, just a few kilometres away from the district capital Putussibau a large military camp with room for one battalion (Battalion Infanteri 644 Walet Sakti) was erected and additionally a large military airbase planned (*pangkalan udara* or *lanud*) (*Equator News* 2008). The large military camp was supposedly constructed farther away from the immediate border area in order not to provoke the Malaysians to counter the move and begin reinforcing the army presence on their side of the border.[27] In spite of this effort to avoid provoking the Malaysians, however, the Indonesians' increased military presence was quickly countered across the border (*The Sunday Post* 2007).

This sudden show of force reminded many locals of the period of militarization in the 1960s and 1970s, although now the supposed enemy was not Chinese Malaysian communists but Chinese Malaysian capitalists (the *tukei*) and their local associates. Therefore, the army was welcomed to the borderland with mixed emotions and suspicion. The main objective of the LIBAS soldiers was to secure the area by patrolling the road between Putussibau and Badau and thereby prevent further attempts to smuggle logs across the border. Permanent camps were erected at strategic points along this stretch of border; Three camps were built in the borderland discussed: one at the Badau border, one in Puring Kencana and one along the Leboyan River in the vicinity of the community of Rumah Manah. Ironically, this camp was erected in the same location as a former Yamaker logging camp and previous army camps of the 1960s and 1970s, so it is not surprising that local communities felt that the past was repeating itself. Placed strategically beside the logging road leading up to Apheng's now abandoned logging camps in the Ulu Leboyan, the LIBAS was able to monitor all traffic going in and out of this still heavily forested area along the border.

Signs of tension between local residents and LIBAS quickly emerged, usually triggered by LIBAS soldiers' lack of sympathy towards local norms of conduct and general interference in local activities. LIBAS soldiers were generally very young and usually from outside the province, and they were only stationed for three months at a time in the camps before being replaced by fresh recruits. One outcome of this was that they felt little commitment towards local communities and little understanding of local grievances. Furthermore, meagre salaries and boredom resulted in many LIBAS soldiers becoming deeply involved in different forms of illegal trade and extortion. When they appeared in public they

[27] *Antara* 2007; *Equator News* 2007g; *Pontianak Post* 2007d.

were heavily armed and entered villages without local approval; this superior attitude was very provocative for local youths especially and did not fit well with the local sense of autonomy. The LIBAS stationed in the vicinity of Rumah Manah, for example, stripped Apheng's large logging camp in the Ulu Leboyan of anything of value and sold the items for their own personal gain, an act that generated a fair amount of local disapproval and anger as these items were considered local property after the flight of Apheng.

During my fieldwork in 2007, several minor clashes between young soldiers and young Iban men occurred; one incident nearly led to a local uprising. On 30 May 2007, a quarrel broke out between a group of young Iban men and a group of LIBAS soldiers in a small roadside coffee shop in Lanjak. The fight had been ignited a few hours before during a cockfight in a nearby village. The betting on cocks involved large amounts of cash and the consumption of liquor; consequently emotions were running high when suddenly one of the attending soldiers grabbed one of the fighting cocks before the fight was declared finished, which was considered a major offence. The soldier supposedly grabbed the cock on which he was betting because it was mortally wounded and destined to lose. The soldiers immediately left the village, but Iban men remained and began discussing the many grievances they had experienced since the arrival of the LIBAS. Later, in Lanjak, the same soldiers ran into some of the Iban from the cockfight and a fight broke out. One of the soldiers pulled a knife and stabbed one of the Iban men several times. The surrounding Iban immediately struck down the offending soldier. The local police arrived and brought all involved parties to the station in order to find a solution. Compared to the LIBAS army patrols (on short term contracts) the local subdistrict police (Polsek) and small army commands (Koramil) are, due to their long-term presence in the area, deeply entrenched in local society, and the personnel are often locally married. These ties enabled them to mediate between the youth and LIBAS.

In accordance with local customary law, the Iban community demanded that the LIBAS pay a fine of Rp 30 million (US$3,300) if the victim died and Rp 15 million if not. The LIBAS refused to pay any compensation, and because it is out of the jurisdiction of the police to deal with matters involving the army the soldiers were released. The following day a large group of LIBAS soldiers arrived in Lanjak to avenge their friend who had been severely beaten during the incident.

They cruised the town threatening locals and ended up hitting two men with the barrels of their rifles. This disregard of local norms and rules provoked strict condemnations from local *patih* and *temenggong*, who demanded that just action be taken to punish these soldiers; they also threatened that if the military did not pursue this it would be dealt with locally. Immediately afterwards the head of the local military command reprimanded the soldiers, who quickly were assigned to another part of the border. The tension was partly settled by the LIBAS paying a symbolic fine of Rp 1 million. Although not pleased with the size of the fine, the symbolic token and the fact that the young Iban victim survived prevented the locals from taking more drastic actions. However a majority of the Iban mentioned that they still preferred that the LIBAS leave the area completely.

With state authority becoming more conspicuous in the borderland, border communities were once again forced to adjust to the changing power configurations. The border communities had enjoyed a fair amount of autonomy in the years of increased administrative decentralization. Hence the arrival of new 'outside' players exercising state authority inevitably increased tensions. Statements by high ranking military generals, as well as the military's past and current business interests, indicate that there is more at stake for the military than security issues. Several commentators claim that the military build-up in the border area is more about reclaiming a share of the revenues from further timber harvesting and oil palm plantations than about dealing with illegal activities threatening national security (Wakker 2006; WALHI 2007). One local rumour goes that besides valuable timber resources the army is interested in the possibly large gold and coal reserves to be found in the hills along the border.

CONTESTING LARGE-SCALE SCHEMES

The border elite quickly linked concurrent attempts to stop illegal logging and timber smuggling along the border to central government's large-scale development projects and subsequent attempts to strengthen border security through militarization. However, as noted by *temenggong* Jabak during a 2005 interview, rather than curbing the degradation of forest resources and opening plantations, these new government plans are likely to mean that even more forest is cleared and more timber is provided for trade. This time, however, control will be back in the hands of central and provincial level players, as was the case in the Soeharto days. Such proclamations from border elite might sound rather hollow taking into account that segments of the border elite themselves colluded with powerful state players during Soeharto's New Order. As further indicated by an Iban District Assembly member,

> It is important to remember history. Nearly all previous attempts to promote top-down plantation development in the borderland like oil palm have failed as the centrally based companies usually left the area as soon as they had cut all valuable timber on the forest plots allocated for such plantations.[28]

This DPRD was referring particularly to an incident in the late 1990s when the company PT Plantana Razindo (partially military owned) attempted to cut down community forest in the Badau area under the pretence of clearing land for an oil palm plantation (see Chapter 5). A similar example was a plantation company headed by the Rokan Group Holding Company that in the early 1990s opened up community lands for oil palm production and Javanese transmigrants in the subdistricts of Badau and Empanang (150,000 ha). This company later abandoned its concessions, having logged the area and rendered it unproductive.[29]

Among other concerns, local communities fear that locally claimed land along the border is in danger of being forcefully converted into oil palm or rubber plantations (*Media Indonesia* 2005b). A presidential regulation dated 3 May 2005 stated that the government could force the release of land when this is in the public interest (Perpres 2005a). This regulation restates the Agrarian Land Law (Agrarische Wet) of the Dutch from 1870 which stipulated that all uncultivated land was state property that could be leased out to companies for plantation development on a long-term basis. After independence, this law, a kind of authority for eminent domain, was incorporated into the 1960s Indonesian legislation enabling the commandeering of land in the national interest. The justification of 'public interest' (national security and development) for the current development plan led to fears on the part of the local community that the

[28] Personal interview, Putussibau, 14-6-2005.
[29] Personal interview, Iban *patih*, Badau, 19-3-2007.

government would apply this regulation in order to revoke their newly gained authority over local forestlands (*Suara Bekakak* 2006). As noted earlier, in the heyday of decentralization reforms local communities experienced a degree of regional autonomy that created authority to deal with local forest resources without interference from the central government. But now, as power relations between the centre and the districts once again seem to be changing, locals are concerned about how those changes will affect the status of their land. Most border communities lack official certificates showing legal ownership of their land and therefore are vulnerable to encroachment from plantation companies backed by state power and regulations (*Borneo Tribune* 2008).

Centuries of engagement in kinship relations and labour migration across the border into Sarawak have made local communities aware of the way Iban in Sarawak have experienced a major loss of customary lands as a consequence of state-initiated oil palm development. Consequently, a majority of local communities along the border have a healthy suspicion of large-scale plantation projects. Border elites and communities were not opposed to plantations as such and many are quite favourably disposed towards small-scale plantations as long as the local people retain control of their land and engage in cooperation with outside investors, like Malaysian companies.[30] The main fear is that government will forcibly allocate their land to plantation companies and provide these companies with legally binding licenses, meaning that local communities will have to work as common workers on their own land.

Although local plantation development within the borderland was seen as a way out of the economic depression and a possible road towards prosperity, the announcement of government controlled large-scale plantations was locally received with caution and suspicion. Several members of the border elite announced that they would not allow any outside companies to enter local forestlands without prior agreements with local communities. As stipulated by an Iban *temenggong* in a 2007 interview:

> Many companies want to enter the area and open oil palm plantations, but we have not yet given our consent (*belum terima*). We will wait until we have gained official authority over the area.... For too many years,

---

[30] The border communities have a long history of small-scale rubber cultivation while the cultivation of oil palm is unfamiliar to most.

we have been controlled and managed by others, and still our lives are the same as they were 50 years ago. Nothing has changed. We intend to manage our own region *(ngurus daerah kita sendiri)*. We will only get the maximum benefits if we manage things ourselves. Government promises and programs never 'touch the ground' *(tidak menyentuh)*, as they are all top-down. [31]

The *temenggong* is here referring to the Iban's long-time borderland aspiration of separating from the Kapuas Hulu district and creating their own administrative district along the border. A new district would help them gain control of their own natural resources and revenues derived from these. These and similar statements clearly reflect long-standing dissatisfaction with the central government's past lack of commitment to integrating the borderland into the broader national economy beyond extracting its natural resources.

TIGHTENING BORDER REGIMES

Since the Habibie government downgraded the role of the military in politics and the economy in 1999, the military have been searching for alternative ways to make their services more necessary. The above chapter about the tightening border regimes indicates that the military are trying to conjure up an imminent need for military protection of national sovereignty along international borders. Moving from a role as protectors of internal unity by eradiating attempts of separatism during Soeharto, they now seek a lucrative role as protectors of national sovereignty against outside threats like Malaysian timber gangsters. The re-militarization of the borderland could thus indicate the beginning of another chapter in the waxing and waning of state power on the border. Through its ability to provide concrete acts of 'development', the central government anticipate a strengthening of the experience of inclusion in the state project among their border citizens and at the same time assertion of its sovereignty along the border.

The case of the world's largest oil palm plantation and its consequent failure to materialize in its envisioned form shows how grand schemes

---

[31] Personal interview, Lanjak, 28-3-2007.

often are undermined by the numerous, and at times contradictory, agendas of various state agents and agencies. In the following chapter, I will demonstrate how these contradictory interests open up room for manoeuvring and negotiation by local-level actors through their various networks. I will specifically focus on how the rhetoric of development and security – which was proclaimed as the main reasons for implementing these large state schemes – is used by border elites to negotiate increased local autonomy.

Since the crackdown on logging activities in 2005, the borderland has been in a state of economic depression. The anger generated within local communities has been immense and appears to be both economic and cultural – based on the central government's usurpation of 'traditional rights'. The central and provincial government is perceived as the catalyst and direct cause of recent economic hardship. Although ordinary community members only received a small share of profit from the harvested forest during the logging boom taking place between 2000 and 2005, benefits to them had still been much larger than under the centralized political system of the New Order when the local economy had prospered greatly. The central government's subsequent crackdown on what was perceived as 'illegal' logging severely angered local communities who had viewed the logging in the spirit of regional autonomy. By taking things into their own hands and circumventing the higher levels of government, the border population experienced the possibilities of greater autonomy. This feeds into a more general local disillusionment with the slow pace of genuine border development that seems to nurture a local sense of borderland solidarity and a drive for more autonomy (*Kalimantan Review* 2005). As indicated by a Badau community spokesman, 'Officially, we now have regional autonomy (*autonomy daerah*), but central government keeps pulling the strings and only approaches the issue of autonomy half-heartedly' (*setengah-setengah hati*).[32]

In the wake of the above-mentioned events, the idea of a new autonomous border district emerged among the local elite. The same elite had gained authority and useful political networks through past and present engagement in the lucrative timber business. However, lessons learned from the subsequent state ban on logging accentuated the importance of accommodating state laws and regulations, and thus re-asserting

---

[32] Personal interview, Badau, 20-3-2007.

themselves as good citizens of an imaginary unitary nation-state – for their efforts to succeed. These local struggles over forest and the shifting and overlapping spheres of authority between border elites and district and central governments form the basis for contemporary political manoeuvres designed to create a new autonomous border district in West Kalimantan.

8

Borderland autonomy and local politics

> The national border itself emerges as a site where various forms of power, agency and constraints creatively (and often unequally) interact, rather than a place where state power stands opposed to local aspirations (Walker 2006b:5).

In the previous chapters I discussed how border elites mediated access to resources through long-term patronage relations that involved collaborations with different state authorities (such as the military and district officials) and cross-border associates (Malaysian timber barons). I examined how border elite strategies and networks that have been used during the post-Soeharto period of increased autonomy can be related to the period of border militarization in the 1960s, and, once again, seem to challenge the sovereignty of the Indonesian-Malaysian border. Adding to the complexities of these processes are the ongoing attempts of central government to reclaim authority along the border through large-scheme development programs that, as I will show in this chapter, are yet again met with amplified local claims for increased autonomy. After the logging ban in 2005, the struggle over access to resources has taken a new political turn. While earlier local attempts to claim authority over forest occurred in the twilight between legality and illegality, such claims are now made through intricate political manoeuvring within the legal but ambiguous framework of recent government reform and through state rhetoric of development and security.

In this final chapter, I give further consideration to the unfolding of this dyadic relationship between border elites, border communities and government institutions and their different strategies for negotiating and claiming authority over forest by tracking the fate of a political movement for a new district in this resource-rich border region. This 'border

| *At the edges of states*

movement' directly links to the cases discussed in previous chapters and is the latest attempt to claim border autonomy. The case of re-districting or district splitting (*pemekaran*) discussed here provides an excellent view of the intricate web of alliances and networks that form the basis of the new and evolving relationship between local actors and the Indonesian government along the border. The chapter further addresses some of the wider implications of these claims for border autonomy.

PROMOTION OF A 'NORTH BORDER DISTRICT'

Since the early 1990s, an Iban-initiated movement in the border area has pushed for border development and increased local autonomy. Already during the New Order regime border elites had begun formulating ideas about approaches to dealing with the chronic underdevelopment of the border area. However, until after the fall of Soeharto, this movement remained rather quiescent, as efforts to increase local autonomy were not given much leeway to effect change under the highly authoritarian New Order regime. The rhetoric of this emerging movement was therefore mostly centred on practical questions of development while issues of increased autonomy were largely downplayed (Kuyah 1992).

Post New Order, this movement has gained momentum and re-emerged as a local response or counter-movement against the increase in outside involvement in what are perceived as local matters. By creating their own district, the border elite expects to boost local autonomy and strengthen their control of local forestlands (*Equator News* 2006d). They further anticipate that controlling border access will become an important political and economic resource in the near future, as enhanced commercial exchange is expected to develop between the two bordering regions of West Kalimantan and Sarawak (*Equator News* 2005h).

One unintended outcome of the early decentralization laws was the sudden rise of many new districts throughout the nation. Law No. 22/1999 on regional autonomy opened up the possibility of dividing existing districts into smaller ones. As stipulated in Government Regulation No. 129/2000, proposals for new districts must be able to demonstrate a capacity for regional autonomy.[1] The viability of a new

---

[1] The procedures and criteria in Regulation No. 129/2000 are being amended in parliament.

district is measured in terms of its economic capacity, regional potential, population size and land area. The government's justification for creating new districts assumes that such processes reflect the genuine aspirations of the people, and that the smaller administrative units will bring the government closer to the people and create new economic opportunities (Fitrani et al. 2005). These expectations have led to a rush to create new districts in Kalimantan and all over Indonesia. Portrayed as a bottom-up process in which common people can gain a larger degree of empowerment and transparency in local government matters, district-splitting became immensely popular in Indonesia. The numbers of new districts rose dramatically from 292 in 1998 to 483 in early 2007 (ICG 2007). Law No. 22/1999, which was hastily drawn up in the early days of decentralization, has since been revised and superseded by the more restrictive Law No. 32/2004, which, among other things, raised the minimum number of subdistricts to be included in a new district from three to five. This tightening was an attempt to slow down the process of re-districting. Since 1999, several large Kalimantan districts bordering Malaysia have been subdivided. The establishment of these new, often Dayak-dominated districts has largely been dictated by ethnic politics and greater access to local resources. For example, in 1999 in West Kalimantan, the large border district of Sambas was split into Sambas and Bengkayang district; and in East Kalimantan, the resource-rich district of Bulungan was split into the districts of Bulungan, Malinau and Nunukan (Tanasaldy 2007; Wollenberg et al. 2006).

Officially, the process is known as *pemekaran*, or 'blossoming', but in reality the *pemekaran* process is a complex affair involving intricate political manoeuvrings.[2] Successful re-districting has largely been dependent on the ability to draw on a broad network ranging across all administrative levels of government and considerable financial backing (Vel 2007:93). More often than not, the driving force behind *pemekaran* is the urge to gain authority over various resources rather than the establishment of more accountable local governments (Roth 2007:146). The economic incentives of large financial transfers from the central government to support new districts, and lucrative positions in the new administration, have undoubtedly been an important motivator for local elites. The

---

[2] *Pemekaran* not only refers to the splitting of districts but also to other levels of administrative fragmentation like the creation of new provinces, subdistricts, villages, and hamlets (Kimura 2007; Roth 2007).

decentralization laws (No. 22/1999 and No. 32/2004) stipulate that new districts will receive subsidies in form of both general allocation funds (*dana alokasi umum*) and special allocation funds (*dana alokasi khusus*) from the central government. In the case discussed here, the prime motivator has been the struggle for a larger share of benefits from forest resources and future border trade.

In 2000, in the heyday of decentralization, the Iban elite initiated the first preliminary and official steps in the creation of a new district. A group lobbying for the creation of a new district was set up, but progress was quickly disrupted by the booming timber business and consequent growth in the local economy. Only several years later, after the logging adventure came to an abrupt end and the region was once again plunged into economic depression, was there renewed interest in the possible formation of a new district.

The overall goals have been to develop and ensure the common good of the border communities. Although virtually everyone I interviewed in the five subdistricts in 2007 passively supported the idea of a new district, there was also widely expressed concern about the question of whether the border elite would work to benefit all levels of society if a new district were created. The border elites' history of conspicuous consumption and individual enrichment, coupled with collusion with various government agents, is the prime reason for these reservations. Compared to the elite and their multiple networks, most non-elite Iban are largely tied to life in the border hills and dependent on the remaining forest resources and cross-border labour migration. Moreover, that same elite had acted as brokers between local communities, the district government, and the Malaysian timber barons during the recent logging boom.

This is not to say that all members among the border elite necessarily approach the *pemekaran* process and its future possible benefits solely with their own enrichment in mind. Since the major crackdown on logging activities, which has plunged the area into economic depression affecting all layers of local society, the importance of a genuine bottom-up process and local unity in the interests of full development of the area has been continually emphasized. Despite past efforts of the elite to monopolize access to resources, the overall benefits of a new district would certainly trickle down and affect the life of ordinary people. Without the personal networks and political expertise of the elite, it would be impossible to bring the new district into existence.

The leading members of the movement are primarily ethnic Iban; the two other ethnic groups that inhabit the area, the Maloh and Melayu, also support the movement, but their minority status makes them less influential.[3] The core members are all part of the small but prominent 'traditional' elite discussed in the previous chapter: traditional Iban leaders like *temenggong, patih, panglima perang*, and village headmen (*tuai rumah*). Besides these, the movement includes members of the district assembly (Dewan Perwakilan Rakyat Daerah, DPRD II), district government officials, and a small handful of Jakarta-based supporters.[4] The movement further draws on the support of a group of young, educated but unemployed men, who dream of the many new jobs to be created by a new district administration.

Due to the historical processes discussed in the previous chapters, members of this elite have managed to strengthen their power by gaining access to various political networks within the government administration and powerful business alliances. With the assistance of these networks, some of these traditional leaders have themselves become local business figures. Others have pursued influence through involvement in local politics as party politicians or local government officials. For example, a small handful of prominent local figures have become elected members of the district assembly in Putussibau, giving them a front row position from which to influence decisions made on the district level concerning their own constituencies along the border. The border movement is learning from the experience of other border district splits in the province, especially the subdivision of Sambas district into Bengkayang and Sambas districts in 1999.[5] The head of the border district movement is a highly educated Iban (originally from the study area) who now holds an influential government position as head of a district-level office (*kepala dinas*) in one of these recently created districts mentioned above. Having a good vantage point from which to observe the success of these new districts and the complicated political processes involved with *pemekaran*,

---

3 Issues of interethnic distrust between the Maloh and Melayu and the dominant Iban group play into the dynamics of this movement and will be discussed below.
4 The Jakarta supporters include a few researchers from University of Indonesia and civil servants from central state ministries like the Ministry of Agriculture (Departemen Pertanian) and Ministry of National Education (Departemen Pendidikan). The West Kalimantan representatives of the Regional Representative Council have also promised their support for the new district (*Equator News* 2006d).
5 Law No. 10/1999.

he initiated the border movement together with a small group of other well-educated Iban men.

The movement further feeds into a larger alliance of border communities known as the 'Forum for Border Community Care' positioned in the provincial capital, Pontianak. This forum was created in 2004 with the purpose of lobbying for and promoting the overall development of the border regions of West Kalimantan; its members are from all the ethnic groups living along entire length of the border.[6] The head of this forum is also a prominent Iban from one of the five border subdistricts. So far, the forum has mainly been used by the border movement as a meeting place for consolidating new alliances, especially with provincial government officials and politicians. All the founding members of the movement originate from the border area, but they live and work in or near the provincial capital and only seldom visit the border area. One prominent Pontianak-based supporter of the movement is the former *bupati* of Kapuas Hulu, Jacobus Layang, mentioned previously. In 2006, Layang published a book (his MA thesis) on the implications of underdevelopment in the border area, criticizing the lack of central government commitment in developing the border communities (Layang 2006). Layang was also one of actors who had a stake in the plantation company PT Plantana Razindo operating along the border in early 2000. As I will detail below, all core players in the border movement have complex positions in relation to each other and within their own communities.

After numerous meetings and discussions, in early March 2007 representatives and supporters from the five subdistricts (approximately 400 people) met with the *bupati* at an official gathering in the district office in Putussibau. A committee known as the 'Committee for the Establishment of the North Border District' (Panitia Pembentukan Kabupaten Perbatasan Utara, PPKPU), which was the main organization pursuing the formation of the new district, boldly proclaimed the new district name as 'The North Border District' (Kabupaten Perbatasan Utara). At the same time, they presented a final report of several hundred pages containing the legally stipulated requirements for a new district and signatures of all local (elite) supporters (*Equator News* 2007e). This report, which emphasized the considerable potential of the border area and its current underdevelopment, was the outcome of an unof-

---

[6] Forum Peduli Masyarakat Perbatasan Kalimantan Barat (FPMP).

ficial feasibility study carried out by the committee in cooperation with a Jakarta-based NGO (PPKPU 2007).

In the period between 2004 and 2007, the movement had carried out an extensive lobbying campaign. In February 2006, it sent out its first formal letter of aspiration (*surat aspirasi masyarakat*) to the *bupati*, presenting the plan for a new district. To give the letter an extra touch of formality, the name of the proposed district was stamped on the letterhead in large black type. Then, in late 2007, the committee attempted to precipitate the *pemekaran* process (*Equator News* 2007f). It was well aware that rapid progress on the establishment of the new district was imperative, given the looming national election and the new government border act mentioned earlier. The outcome of the general elections in 2009 could mean that the movement would have to begin the lobbying process and alliance-making all over again, as old parliamentary allies might be replaced and a new president elected. Furthermore, from the middle of 2008, members of parliament would be too busy campaigning for their respective parties to push for the subdivision of the district.

With the disappointments of failed efforts of the past in mind, the border movement has been eager to push on. Early in the presidency of Megawati (2001-2004), the same border elite had applied to the central government to be recognized as a special authority region (*otorita daerah khusus*) and thereby receive favourable conditions such as free border trade and a higher degree of political autonomy (in line with the status of Batam). According to leading movement members, a letter of decree (*surat keputusan*) that would have granted special authority to the border area (*otorita perbatasan*) was being prepared, but then in 2004 a new president was elected and the decree was supposedly postponed. A few days before President Megawati left office in October 2004, she signed the revised decentralization legislation, Law No. 32/2004, that replaced the former law from 1999. This new law states the requirements for creating a special administrative zone (*kawasan khusus*) in an area within a district or province of special importance for national interest. This autonomous zone would enjoy the status of a free trade zone (Law No. 32/2004, chapter II, part 2, article 9). During the Megawati presidency the government prepared a development strategy for the Kalimantan border region, and according to the members of the movement the change in the central administration turned out to be a significant setback for the lobbying efforts of the border movement at the time (Bappenas 2003).

In a 2007 statement outlining the urgency of the current campaign, a Badau-based committee member said,

> We need to push forward now and keep going (*jalan terus*). We cannot wait for official approval from the district office. Government regulations as they look today may be different tomorrow so we need to act while there is still an opportunity (*peluang*).[7]

However, the most crucial task is to forestall the possible government suspension of all district-splitting discussed in parliament. This moratorium was proposed by the president in 2007 and was based on his strong criticism of the general lack of fiscal capacity of new regions to look after themselves (*Jakarta Post* 2007b, 2007c). The huge popularity of *pemekaran* throughout Indonesia has put immense strain on the central government's resources and budget, while outcomes in the form of improved services for the majority of people have so far been meagre. Meanwhile, corruption and nepotism have reportedly increased, a development that the central government is largely blaming on self-interested regional elites. Such accusations have fostered widespread protest from provincial and district assembly members who accuse the central government of being arrogant and not committed to the development of the outer regions and the re-allocation of promised economic benefits from the centre to its margins (*Pontianak Post* 2007b).

JUSTIFICATION FOR A NEW DISTRICT

The first step in the *pemekaran* process as stipulated in the government laws and regulations is a demonstration of the viability of a proposed new district and justification of the need for its creation. As indicated by the name 'The North Border District', the PPKPU committee clearly specified the common ground and key resources of the five subdistricts involved. Despite its vast natural resources, the border area, after more than 60 years of Indonesian independence, is still categorized as a region of extreme poverty (*daerah tertinggal*) with insufficient infrastructure, health services and education facilities (KNPDT 2007). As proclaimed

---

[7] Personal interview, Badau, 20-3-2007.

by participants during an August 2006 borderland 'awareness-raising' meeting (*rapat sosialisasi perbatasan*) in Badau that was held to discuss the advantages of redistricting:

> It has now been 63 years since we became an independent nation (*63 tahun kita sudah merdeka*) but our roads are still yellow [dirt] and at night, our lamps are still dark. Is this the result of independence (*apakah ini hasil kemerdekaan*)?' [A chorus of voices from the crowd replied], 'We still live in misery and poverty. Development has left us behind' (PPKPU 2007).

The main argument put forward for splitting the Kapuas Hulu district was its sheer size and lack of capacity to develop its outer subdistricts. The 'mother' district (*kabupaten induk*) consists of no less than 23 subdistricts spread over 29,842 km^2 (20.33 percent of West Kalimantan) with a population of only 209,860 (*Kabupaten Kapuas Hulu* 2006). As Nanang, an ex-DPRD member and one of the spokesmen of the committee, stated:

> Geographically the district is too large. It is like a piece of bread we break here and there (*kita pecah sini, pecah sana*). In the end, each subdistrict only gets a little piece. Eventually it will starve.... Nothing has changed in the border area since independence; there is no meaningful advancement (*tidak ada suatu kemajuan yang sangat berarti*). The roads are still those gravel roads made by Apheng. There is no other development planning; there is nothing. Well, seeing things like that, some people then have gathered together and encouraged the promotion of a new border district.[8]

Members of the border committee stressed the fact that past and current district administrations had not succeeded in developing the border area compared to other areas in the district. As a result, they said, the border people were forced to act by themselves if any changes were to take place:

> Until now the border communities have just been a tool (*dijadikan alat saja bagi pemerintah*) of the government in extracting natural resources, that is why the community wants their own autonomy (*otonomi sendiri*), to take

---

8 Personal interview, Lanjak, 2-3-2007.

control by themselves, and at least have their own district. Because the natural resources are abundant (*sumberdaya alam melimpah*).[9]

As leading members of the committee announced to a local newspaper, a new border district would come to reflect the true aspirations of local border communities (Akcaya 2007b).

Applying the government rhetoric of defence, security and development, and emphasizing the role of border inhabitants as loyal citizens, were another conscious strategy among the movement members in attaining government good will for their cause. The members proclaimed that the creation of a new border district was a local effort to maintain a unitary state of the Republic of Indonesia (NKRI); as enhanced political and economic autonomy would prevent acts of separatism among the border communities. Furthermore, the border district would become the new, bright, outward face of Indonesia towards Malaysia and, most importantly, would improve national defence and guarantee security (*Equator News* 2006a). The movement members were quick to disavow in public past so-called 'illegal' activities in the border area and to claim that such activities were the act of desperate people and solely in response to a long-standing economic disparity along border. The only way to prevent any further illegal activities and enhance national loyalty was to involve border communities in developing the area through engagement in local-level politics and economic affairs. As stated by an Iban district assembly member on the motives behind a new district,

> We do not want the central government to think 'danger'; what are the politics of the border people in creating a district. We are Indonesian. We continue to love Indonesia (*cinta Indonesia*). However, what we want is a change and advancement of the border area. That is our argument and motivation behind a new Border District.[10]

Numerous news reports touching upon the issue of national loyalty among the West Kalimantan borderland population have appeared in the national press, expressed in headlines such as: 'Communities living along the Kalimantan-Sarawak border are still isolated within their

9   Personal interview, Lanjak, 1-3-2007.
10 Personal interview, Putussibau, 13-3-2007.

own country' (*Masyarakat perbatasan Kalimantan-Sarawak terasing di Negerinya sendiri*) (*Kompas* 2000f). More often than not, the Iban population is presented as a vivid case of this borderland dilemma. Such a depiction highlights isolation, underdevelopment and cross-border ethnicity as the main reasons for cross-border solidarity and subsequent lack of national consciousness. As expressed in the headlines of the main provincial newspaper: 'The border citizens still rely on Malaysia' (*Warga perbatasan masih harapkan Malaysia*) (*Pontianak Post* 2005g). The border communities are still seen as a national security threat because of their strong cross-border ties.

SEPARATISM: PLAYING THE BORDER CARD

Movement members may have officially proclaimed their strong national loyalty in local news media, but during the heated debates in local meetings, becoming part of Malaysia was often mentioned as a final option. The Iban generally accepted their status as Indonesian citizens, and everybody knew that secession was impossible, but the threat clearly indicated the preparedness of the committee to play the 'border card' in political negotiations with the district and central governments. Even fears of local Iban separatism have been expressed as a possible future outcome of such special borderland circumstances.[11] As an excited Iban supporter from Badau announced,

> We will just join (*bergabung*) Malaysia. We will organize training over there and rebel (*berontak saja*). We will still try the nice way first (*cara-cara bagus*) but if official procedures turn out to be unworkable, well, what can we do? We will get help from smart people in Malaysia, [from the] Iban people there.[12]

During the Dutch colonial period in Indonesia, Raja Brooke, the Sarawak ruler at the time, offered the Iban border population the opportunity to join the much larger Iban population across the border in Sarawak, al-

---

[11] *Kompas* 2000e, 2001b, 2003b.
[12] Personal interview, Lanjak, 21-3-2007.

though such offers never resulted in concrete action.[13] 'We are all related *(kami semoa kaban)*' is a common statement made when talking about the 'Iban cousins' on the other side of the border. The historical cross-border relations and ongoing, mostly rhetorical support from small segments of the Iban population in Sarawak definitely boost local Iban confidence. As one committee member commented during a local meeting, 'We can make things very difficult for them (district and provincial officials)', referring to former acts of vigilantism and close ethnic ties to the Iban in Sarawak. Despite these statements, the speakers always stressed that everything they did would have to conform to the law (Law No. 32/2004), and that they should not attempt to win some sort of independence like Aceh. No attempt should be made to disturb the stability of the border *(stabilitas perbatasan)*.[14] On the question of what would possibly happen if the border communities were not given increased autonomy and their own district, an Iban *temenggong* answered:

> If the border area *(daerah perbatasan)* is not allowed to emerge as a new district by the central or local government, I am afraid that many of the communities would lose the faith *(kepercayaan)* in the unity of NKRI and want to separate themselves or break away *(berpisah)* to Malaysia. If you ask the community, 99 percent would prefer to be under the political control of Malaysia, and that would put the unity of NKRI in danger. Well, older people like us try to protect the unity of the Indonesian nation by suggesting the creation of a new district instead of separatism.[15]

ETHNIC SENTIMENTS

United we are strong *(bersama kita teguh)*, as one we struggle for the development of the border region in Kapuas Hulu, West Kalimantan. In numbers, we will actualize the formation of the Northern Border District that we jointly desire *(inginkan bersama)* (PPKPU 2007:213).

---

[13] See Letter to Nederlands-Indie Governor-General s'Jacob from Charles Brooke, 25-9-1882, Mailrapport No. 1066, Ministerie van Koloniën, ARA [TransRW].
[14] By promoting district autonomy, the founders of the decentralization process hoped to prevent acts of separatism that eventually could break up the country (Aspinall and Fealy 2003a:4).
[15] Personal interview, Embaloh Hulu, 13-6-2007.

The above quotation taken from the PPKPU charter is the official motto of the movement and clearly shows the importance of unity among the various ethnic groups inhabiting the borderland. The promotion of a common border identity, as a medium for popular mobilization of the local communities, is clearly an attempt to downplay the question of ethnicity, which could end up becoming a major source of conflict and split the movement. In other parts of Indonesia, *pemekaran* is often carried out along ethnic lines, which in many cases has resulted in violent conflicts (Duncan 2007). Yet, despite these attempts to ignore ethnicity, the issue is definitely an important one. For example, during local meetings some Iban members made jokes about the movement being called the Free Iban Movement (Gerakan Iban Merdeka, GIM), seeing it primarily as a movement for Iban revitalization. The reference here is to the Free Aceh Movement (Gerakan Aceh Merdeka, GAM) in North Sumatra. Among some members, such jokes express the dreams of promoting Iban *adat* authority and reclaiming control of what they perceive as their traditional territory, now claimed by other ethnic groups. Later, during the same meeting, Iban members changed the acronym GIM to GBM (Gerakan Bersama Maju) or Together We Prosper Movement and thereby downplayed the issue of ethnicity.

Although they do not express their concerns openly within the movement, the much smaller groups of Maloh and Melayu certainly have their reservations about these aspirations on the part of the Iban. The prospect of a large local Iban majority has profound implications for them, especially with regard to competition over political power and resources. In fact, there is a long history of confrontation between Maloh and Iban communities, going back to pre-colonial times of tribal warfare (King 1976a, 1976b). As both groups have moved around extensively in the last several hundred years, community boundaries have blurred and are continually being renegotiated (Wadley 2002b). Today Maloh communities have generally become isolated in small pockets surrounded by the much larger Iban communities, usually with little opportunity for expansion. Furthermore, since independece, in contrast to the Iban, the Maloh have embraced formal education on a much larger scale, resulting in a generally higher level of education and greater access to jobs in government administration. The Iban communities were traditionally very resistant to the preaching of the early Christian Capuchin missionaries and, compared to the Maloh, they felt no need to convert. Therefore they forfeited the benefit of missionary schooling.

These factors make both sides fearful of each other. The Maloh are afraid that the Iban majority will outmanoeuvre them by force of numbers, while the Iban fear that being less educated and holding fewer government positions, they will be subject to Maloh encroachment on land where they claim customary rights of access as Maloh officials channel benefits towards their own kin and communities. Despite this interethnic rivalry, the various groups realize that for the movement to succeed, the five subdistricts must at least officially appear as one 'border community'. Therefore, such concerns remain veiled, even as tension continues to build along accentuated ethnic lines. During fieldwork in 2007, there were several cases of land disputes, mainly between the Iban and the Maloh. These cases were largely triggered by the existing climate of uncertainty regarding central government plans for the border area, in particular the potentially lucrative outcomes of land ownership in the immediate border area, were it to become a centre of official cross-border commerce between the two countries.

MULTIPLE LEVELS OF POWER STRUGGLE

After popular mobilization, the next step in the *pemekaran* process is to secure the approval of all government administrative levels. Approval is needed from the district assembly, the *bupati*, the provincial assembly, the governor, the Ministry of Home Affairs, the Indonesian national parliament, and finally the president. This part of the process can be extremely expensive and time-consuming, and extensive lobbying is required. The *pemekaran* process requires the ability to draw on multiple networks at all levels of government. During an interview, a member of the border committee emphasized that large bribes have to be paid in order to gain support from provincial and central parliamentarians. One of the committee members' main activities has been raising the needed cash for lobbying and for transport back and forth between the different levels of government administration. Committee members have used their own savings to keep the process running.

The movement quickly experienced its first problems when approaching the district office, despite the initial go-ahead from the district assembly following a successful lobbying campaign the previous year.

On 20 April 2006, approximately 100 people representing the five subdistricts met with members of the district assembly in Putussibau. The representatives were greeted positively, and the assembly subsequently issued a letter of decree supporting the formation of a new district in the border area (KepDPRD 2006). Before issuing this decree a handful of district assembly members originating from the border area had carried out intensive lobbying within the assembly.

On the surface, the *bupati* of Kapuas Hulu, Abang Tambul Husin, also initially appeared to be supportive of the idea of a new district, attending meetings and personally donating funds to the border committee.[16] Nevertheless, he also seemed to be deliberately stalling the process. Like the *bupati* in other resource-rich districts, he has, since the outset of decentralization, become a 'small king' (*raja kecil*) who has consolidated his power and support through income from natural resources.[17] Informal interviews with district government officials in Putussibau produce a picture of a general, although not publicly expressed, worry within the *bupati* office that the existing district risks losing major income from strategic resources such as timber and the future lucrative border trade if it is split. In the budget for the period 2008-2009 the district Department of Plantations and Forestry in Kapuas Hulu planned to use no less than Rp 41.3 billion to development of the forestry and plantation sector in the border area (*Perhut Kapuas Hulu* 2007). The law further requires the mother district to support the new district economically for the first few years before the new district receives its own fiscal transfers from the central government. The creation of the 'North Border District' could further end up isolating the mother district, which is already the most remote district in the province. Besides the five border subdistrics studied, an additional nine subdistricts in Kapuas Hulu are planning to make their own district, to be known as Kabupaten Sentarum.[18] If these two new districts are created, the mother district will be geographically

---

[16] During a previous gathering, the *bupati* personally donated Rp 20 million (US$2,200) to the border committee (Akcaya 2007a).
[17] Tambul Husin faces several allegations of corruption. During the logging boom, the Provincial Forestry Agency accused the *bupati* of withholding Forest Resource Provision funds (Provisi Sumber Daya Hutan, PSDH) and Reforestation Funds (Dana Reboisasi, DR) amounting to Rp 150 billion (US$17 million). District courts have not yet found enough convincing evidence of these allegations to push the issue further, despite charges filed by the provincial prosecutor's office back in 2004. Husin allegedly did not deposit PSDH/DR fees in the minister of forestry's account but directly transferred the fees to regional accounts and later to a personal account (Rinaldi et al. 2007).
[18] 'Sentarum' refers to the shallow lakes at the base of the border hills.

and possibly economically isolated in the most northern corner of the province. The sheer distance to the provincial capital, more than 700 km away, makes border access highly important for the local economy, as Sarawak economic centres across the border are much closer than the provincial capital.

There are numerous reasons why the *bupati* office may seek to stall the *pemekaran* process. However, the core issue, according to an Iban committee member, is to maintain control of the resource-rich border region:

> Now we are actually able to fulfil the requirements for creating a new district put forward by central government, but the mother district seems to be hesitant about letting us go. It keeps holding on to our tail (*ekor dipegang*). There is too much potential so they cannot let go and let the new district emerge. For example, the territorial boundary of the five subdistricts still encompasses an abundance of valuable timber, as well as two large national parks (Betung Kerihun and Danau Sentarum) and the north-bound national highway (Jalan Lintas Utara), which connects the district to the border post in Badau. It will be difficult for the mother district to let the five subdistricts go; it needs our rich natural resources to cover its expenses. I think if Putussibau lets the border area become a district, Putussibau will die. If the head of the district refuses to give his recommendation, then the Governor will not either, and that is it.[19]

However, during the campaign for the 2005 district election (Pilkada), the *bupati* was re-elected for a five-year period (2005-2010) by promising the five border subdistricts larger autonomy on local forest issues and general infrastructure development. Since the revision of the law on regional autonomy in 2004, district heads have been voted into office by direct popular elections and not by the district legislative assembly as was done previously. District heads are therefore more dependent on popular sentiment for re-election than before (Buehler 2007). An outright rejection of a new border district could make dealings along the border more difficult and possibly mean loss of support from the border population on whom the *bupati* is partly dependent for maintaining his authority in this remote part of the district. Until now, however, the *bupati* office has managed to keep the most critical voices at bay by contributing minor funding for the

---

[19] Personal interview, Badau, 19-3-2007.

border movement while at the same time prolonging the bureaucratic process involved in the proposed split. Several Iban and Maloh inhabitants interviewed in the border subdistricts further expressed their lack of confidence in the *bupati*; they believed that he, being a Malayu, was more accommodating towards the needs of the Melayu than towards that of the other ethnic groups in the district. When Tambul Husin initially was elected *bupati* in 2000, his election met with local protest. He was accused of bribing certain district assembly members to cast their votes for him (*Jakarta Post* 2000d).

NATIONAL AND TRANSNATIONAL NETWORKS OF INFLUENCE

In her research on *pemekaran* processes in West Sumba, Jacqueline Vel shows how multiple networks link the regions with the centre and demonstrates the importance of these networks in border elite projects (Vel 2007:93).[20] These often very personalized networks that link the border movement to regional networks at the district and province level appear much stronger than those with the centre in Jakarta. For example, the district office is required to carry out an official feasibility study of the border area, which is to be handed over to the governor's office before the pemekaran process can proceed to the Ministry of Home Affairs in Jakarta. The finalising of this study has been postponed several times. The slow progress on the study has made the border movement impatient, and it has led them to present their own feasibility report directly to members of parliament without the blessing of the district or the province. By circumventing the lower levels of government and lobbying directly with national parliamentarians, they hope to speed up the entire process.

Such acts of defiance have only been possible with the help of a small group of supporters in Jakarta (various academics, former military officers and NGOs) who in preceding years had established contacts with various national parliament members. However, several committee members were somewhat sceptical about the prospects for success of such an endeavour because they saw these Jakarta networks as the

[20] See also Ehito Kimura and his discussion of elite politics within *pemekaran* processes in Sulawesi, where what he refers to as vertical coalitions, or elite alliances, span different administrative levels and connect centre and periphery (Kimura 2006).

weakest link in the campaign. None of the Jakarta supporters possessed the necessary power or capital for effective lobbying. The former allies among the military officers stationed along the border in the 1970s were now pensioners and less powerful in the current political climate. The chronic lack of funding also put an effective constraint on the movement's negotiating power among national parliamentarians. Although old military alliances in Jakarta may be dwindling, the regional military command has, according to movement members, expressed its support of a new district. Several movement meetings were attended, although passively by military officers. According to a movement member, military interest in the new district is dual. First, if a new district is realized it would be entitled to erect a new district military command (Kodim) and thereby the military would be able to further consolidate its presence in the area. Second, the new district would become one of the main trade zones with Malaysia or, as stated in the interview, the door to the border (*pintu perbatasan*).[21]

In fact, one leading member of the movement declared that a more effective step in lobbying would be to send a delegation of border community leaders to Jakarta in order to allow them to present their cause directly to the national parliament and the president and to display their military decorations as proof of their loyal service to the republic. This suggestion was inspired by the strategy and success of the Papuans, who appeared before the parliament and openly stated their demands for regional autonomy. An Iban member of the border movement commented, 'We fought during the communist era to defend the new republic. Many people suffered and died. Now we are left behind, forgotten (*ditinggalkan, dilupakan*) just like that. That is how we feel'.[22]

Transnational networks add to the complexity of this case. During the many local meetings about the new border district several Malaysian 'investors' from across the border attended, along with some Malaysian Chinese and Iban. Many of these 'investors' were also involved in the logging boom that ended in 2005. Economic support from wealthy Malaysians could end up being a key factor in realizing the establishment of the new district. Even more importantly, cross-border resources may make the new district less dependent on central government politics and financial support. As indicated by an Iban businessman from Lanjak,

[21] Personal interview, Badau, 19-3-2007.
[22] Personal interview, Putussibau, 13-3-2007.

'If we already had a new district here, many smart [Iban] people from Malaysia would come and invest their money in plantations and so on. There are plenty of them waiting across the border. But for now, they do not want to come, as they do not trust the government'.[23]

These comments are symptomatic of widespread mistrust of government authorities and of the conviction that they (the border communities) would be better off handling things themselves. During fieldwork, I often confronted the general assumption that distant provincial and national centres do not comprehend the special circumstances of life in the borderland.

By the very act of inviting Malaysian businessmen to their meetings the movement put subtle pressure on the central government to disclose its plans for the border area, particularly its forest resources. Negotiating directly with cross-border business connections as they had done in the past, local communities once again showed their ability to take things into their own hands. The current uncertainty about the central government's plans has made both Indonesian and Malaysian investors hesitant about investing in the area, exacerbating the economic depression that has existed since the logging stopped. Local communities and elites are eager to get the economy up and running. One way of venting their frustration over the lack of clear commitment from the centre is to push forward independently by calling on their own long-term connections to Malaysian entrepreneurs.

At the time of writing, the border movement was still awaiting a formal response to their request for a new district. When I left the borderland in August 2007 the outcomes seemed as uncertain as ever and highly dependent on rapid political changes taking place locally and nationally and on the readiness of higher-level authorities to take action. The future of the *pemekaran* process very much depended on the good will of key politicians in Jakarta and of local government administrative heads like the *bupati* and governor, who have their own, often divergent, agendas for the border area. The *bupati* of Kapuas Hulu, together with four other district heads, is involved in yet another *pemekaran* process. These five district heads wish to split from the current province of West Kalimantan and create a new province, Kapuas Raya'. What effects this plan may have on the future of the border district was still too early

---

[23] Personal interview, Lanjak, 1-8-2007.

| *At the edges of states*

to forecast, but all available district resources seemed directed towards carrying out this grand plan for some kind of new province (*Kalimantan Review* 2008).

Although it is still too early to draw conclusions, I envisage several possible outcomes of the *pemekaran* process and the more general struggle over forest resources discussed in this chapter. First, in late November 2007 a new governor was elected in West Kalimantan. The new governor, Cornelis-Christiandy Sanjaya, former *bupati* of Landak, is himself a Dayak or 'son of the soil' (*putra daerah*) as he often proclaimed during his campaign for a the governorship. [24] Before the election, and as part of his campaign, Cornelis attended meetings in Pontianak and showed his support for the border movement, in return expecting that the border population would send their votes his way. During a highly publicized April 2007 seminar initiated by the 'Forum for Border Community Care', primarily led by the Iban elite, Cornelis announced publicly that if elected governor he would do his utmost to develop the economy of the border area (*Equator News* 2007d). This strong new ally in the highest administrative post in the province may put the needed pressure on the district head in Kapuas Hulu to take the *pemekaran* process to the next level. However, such strong support from the governor might have come too late, given the proposed national moratorium on district splitting. During an interview in late 2007, the head of the provincial legislative assembly (Ketua Komisi A, DPRD) in Pontianak expressed strong doubts as to whether a new border district would have any chance of being approved at the central level. According to him, one of the major hurdles is the low population density. With only about 30,000 inhabitants, the proposed border district would be too sparsely populated to survive on its own. He estimated that it might take another five to ten years before that border population could be ready to manage its own district.

In the heated debate about the viability of many new districts in recent years, some commentators, national and regional, have suggested that the central government should prioritize the establishment of new districts and provinces in regions with special needs such as underdeveloped and sensitive state border areas. This, they argue, would be in line with one of the original ideas behind decentralization, namely that of facilitating and ensuring national unity.[25] Already in 2004 the National

[24] Sanjaya is the second Dayak governor to take office since 1960.
[25] *Equator News* 2007b; *Jakarta Post* 2007c; *Kompas* 2007; *Sinar Harapan* 2006.

Development Planning Agency suggested that district splitting might be a sensible way to make the development effort more efficient in the thinly populated border region (Bappenas 2004:76). In addition, the central government has been hesitant and vague regarding its plans for the border regions. As indicated in reports in several news media, the central government's plans to introduce a border law will not necessarily involve an increase in local autonomy, but more likely would foster the reclaiming of central authority over these resource-rich peripheral regions. In recent years, the central government has expressed reservations about the rapidity with which authority and funds are being transferred to the districts, arguing that the results are mixed and often lead to communal conflict and rampant rent-seeking among political elites, while the benefits for ordinary citizens are less obvious.[26] As indicated in this study, these reservations about central authority have been most obvious in the borderland through an increase in militarization and strict control over the utilization of the border's extensive natural resources.

The *pemekaran* case discussed in this final chapter once again demonstrates the complexity of relations between local communities and the various levels of government bureaucracy. It constitutes a concrete example of how border elites over time have attempted to negotiate authority over resources along the border. Furthermore, the chapter argues that such negotiations are carried out through the appropriation of the state rhetoric of development for local purposes and (personal) interests, while at the same time cross-border connections and trade are used to resist government authority, thus challenging its sovereignty and power.

Although it is uncertain whether the border movement discussed in this chapter will succeed, the border elite will continue to exploit opportunities presented by decentralization and the duality of life along the border in order to negotiate authority and attempt to strengthen their position. The alliances formed or renewed during the *pemekaran* process will, despite the process' uncertain outcome, feed into local elite networks of influence. The struggle over access to resources will be waged between such border elite movements, district officials and central government agencies in the borderland in the years to come. An authority such as the *pemekaran* phenomenon suggests a complex relationship between state and local control that helps shed light on the often ambivalent relation-

[26] *Jakarta Post* 2007b; *Pontianak Post* 2007b, 2007c; *Suara Karya* 2007b.

ship between border populations in Kapuas Hulu and their state as well as the more general processes of state formation taking place along the edges of the Indonesian nation-state. Honest attempts are being made by certain resourceful segments of the border population to attract the attention of highly placed politicians to the chronic underdevelopment experienced by the majority of the inhabitants of the immediate border area. However, despite such good intentions, behind the scenes a mounting struggle for access to resources is exposing old sentiments and alliances often consolidated along ethnic lines.

9

Conclusion

This book set out to explore how authority is constituted in the interrelation between state formation and local politics in the borderlands of West Kalimantan, Indonesia. The special borderland features and the shifting extent of state authority along these state edges, it is argued, have created novel opportunities for upward political and economic mobility for some resourceful elite members of the border communities. Through their often intricate and historically complex networks of patronage with state agents and wider cross-border relations, these border elites have positioned themselves as both patrons and brokers, controlling access to valuable natural resources and becoming guardians of regional autonomy. Such acts of self-determination or 'semi-autonomy' are most evident in the borderland occupied by the ethnic Iban, who have enjoyed a large degree of autonomy based on local traditional rules and customs.

The book rests on the premises that territorial borders, such as that between West Kalimantan (Indonesia) and Sarawak (Malaysia), offer an exciting study arena, on which to view, the diffuse dynamics that shape and foster processes of state formation. Hence, borders and adjacent borderlands can tell us important things about how marginal citizens relate to their nation-state and in particular, how alliances, with their competing and multiple loyalties, are managed on a daily basis. In addition, whereas border populations often have been portrayed as more or less passive victims of state power, this book has challenged this view by showing that these power relationships are not so clear-cut.

The book argues for a more benign approach in understanding the relationship between state and society along borders than has generally been the case. While acknowledging that some of these relationships played out on the border are similar to that of other marginal peoples, it argues that the special political and economic circumstances along borders make them 'extreme' places to observe state-society relations. The borderland dynamics presented in the book provide vivid evidence of the fragmented character of the Indonesian state and how it is both 'a part of and apart from society' as phrased by Migdal (2001). This perspective reminds us that the Indonesian state is non-monolithic and multifaceted – even disaggregated, as it is constituted through an ongoing negotiation with various levels of society. As suggested by Barker and Van Klinken, 'institutional patchiness' might be a more accurate term in describing the institutional arrangement of the modern Indonesian state (Barker and Van Klinken 2009).

This patchiness or disaggregation is particularly evident when the nation is viewed from its spatial limits – its geographical borders – where the imagined unitary state is repeatedly challenged through the existence of competing non-state forms of authority. In this case, these non-state forms of authority take the form of small border elites, men of ability operating in the twilight of legality and illegality, and whose multifaceted networks span the border. Here these non-state forms of authority defy the constraints of strict territorial boundaries. They have historically negotiated the value of these artificial lines in the landscape, and formed small zones of semi-autonomy in adjacent borderland zones where state authority is under siege and manipulated.

FLUID BORDERS AND FLUCTUATING BORDERLANDS

To conclude, I will return to the question I posed in the introductory chapter: If the border is to be understood as a productive site for studying state formation and the everyday and often mundane bureaucratic practices of governance, then what can we learn about 'the state' from local perceptions of the border? Answering this question, I have argued that in their role as key symbols of state sovereignty and makers of statehood, borders and borderlands become places where states often are most eager to govern and exercise their power. Borders become the raison d'être of state sovereignty. Yet as illustrated throughout this book, borders and borderlands are also places where state authority is most likely to be challenged, questioned and manipulated as border communities often have multiple loyalties that transcend state borders and contradict state concepts of sovereignty, territory and citizenship.

9 *Conclusion* |

State strengths and weaknesses are thus especially apparent along these edges of the nation. Further, because of the suspicion with which central government has often viewed the border communities and because of these communities' marginal status as rebellious frontier dwellers, there is a paradoxical shifting allegiance to the nation-state, which appears to be accentuated by the dual character of borders.

At times, local strategies involve the evocation of strong national loyalties and the use of government rhetoric of development and security, while in other circumstances, or simultaneously, questions of autonomy and separatism towards neighbouring Malaysia are evoked. Thus, borders and adjacent borderlands provide a context where the dynamics between state and society become explicit. While former approaches to understanding state and society relations along territorial borders have portrayed state authority as nearly complete, and border populations as strongly resistant to its presence, this book has sought to widen our understanding of these dynamics by adding the level of mutual interaction (although often unequal). That is, I show how those local everyday strategies are not necessarily opposed to central state aspirations or attempts to counter its authority. On the contrary, they are to a large degree complementary, occurring in the intersection of interests between state authorities and local communities. As insightfully noted by Migdal,

> The two boundaries of the state, the territorial and the state-society divide, are not inviolable, no matter how much state officials claim to the contrary. Other practices, many of which are incorporated into the state by its own agents and officials, blur, erase, or diminish these boundaries, boundaries that the state image portrays as sacrosanct. Through manifold alliances, state officials and other social actors engage in practices that reduce the importance of the line separating the state from other social groupings – collectively, society – as well as that separating it from other states (Migdal 2004:22).

In order to understand the effects of future negotiations over border resources, and the power relations entangled in these negotiations, the book argues, we need to look at the larger historical and political context of state formation along the border. By applying a process-oriented approach and by investigating local negotiations of autonomy I have illustrated the 'hidden' connections between what, at first glance, seem to be disjoined events. When viewed in a historical and extra-local context, these events become linked and provide great insight into how local border agents have maintained an active role in shaping the borderland and the adjacent border over time. I have argued that in order to understand contemporary socio-economic processes taking place in the borderland, we need to look at the overall borderland experience and take into account dynamic historic processes and long-term patronage networks. This is done by documenting how border elites in the remote border district of Kapuas Hulu have actively responded to past and present political transformations. By unravelling their engagement with various levels of government bureaucracy I have attempted to fill empirical gaps in our understanding of the processes of collaborative state and community formation that take place along international borders.

Based on an historical account of the Dutch and British colonial partitioning of the border in the mid-twentieth century, Chapter 3 discussed the deep anxieties of the Dutch colonial state about the border population and how attempts to subdue these recalcitrant subjects and extend the colonial administrative discipline to the unruly border areas resulted in a pronounced local suspicion of state authority among the majority of the border population. Moreover, colonial events illustrate how local border strategies were shaped in response to conflicting state discourses on either side of the border. One major contributing factor to these Iban and colonial skirmishes was a long history of movement, particularly for trade and warfare, that did not recognize arbitrary state borders.

These first colonial encounters further show how the border population took advantage of the artificial line dividing Dutch and British territories and the anxiety experienced by the colonial rulers concerning the shifting national loyalties of their border subjects. As demonstrated, the border population never became the loyal 'taxable' state subjects envisioned by the colonial administrators. On the contrary, the border population continued its economic, social and political interactions with communities on the other side of the border and still do so. Post-independence, the border population once again was pulled into the macro politics of territoriality and state formation, now under the new authoritarian Indonesian state.

Chapter 4 explains how the border population became tangled up in highly militarized international disputes with neighbouring Malaysia and military cooperative 'counter-insurgency' efforts by the two states. Under great pressure from both sides in the conflicts, the border population chose the flexible strategy of betting on both sides, which often meant compromising their loyalty to the Indonesian state. The degree of national loyalty among the majority of the border population was continually questioned, resulting in severe punishment, violence, and forced national indoctrination.

However, a small border elite, through its active involvement in the fighting, managed to establish powerful alliances with high-ranking military officers, which was no small achievement at the time, considering the highly authoritarian regime at the centre. Although collusion with the military created some internal resentment towards members of the border elite, it also meant that the border communities were given a fair amount of autonomy in dealing with local matters. Moreover, this elite, made up of various traditional leaders, strengthened its own authority by acting as brokers between the local and central level in negotiating access to the borderland's immense forest resources.

By exploring the historical connections between past and present borderland strategies, the book has thus illustrated how the foundation for present elite authority and the quest for increased autonomy was forged in negotiations with first the Dutch colonial state and later the changing regimes of the modern Indonesian state. It has shown how traditional institutions of leadership officially became recognized as institutions of authority by the colonial and postcolonial state, resulting in increased power of negotiation by these leadership figures. Consideration of these historical borderland dynamics when examining recent processes of decentralization and regional autonomy renders the continuity of borderland strategies most evident. Here the book emphasizes the importance of regional historical context for understanding the interrelatedness of seemingly unconnected events.

CLAIMING AUTHORITY, NEGOTIATING AUTONOMY

In Chapters 5 and 6 the linkages between border elites, local government and cross-border entrepreneurs are examined in the context of administrative decentralization. These chapters demonstrate that the decentralization processes in Indonesia has created mass incentives for some segments of local society to capitalize on their newfound authority, especially those with an already existing and long-term network of influence reaching beyond the immediate local level. In this case, such networks not only pointed towards the centre of governance in Jakarta but also breached its territorial borders. The dynamics involved in the intricate patronage relations between the Iban border population and Malaysian Chinese timber barons/gangsters (*tukei*) demonstrate the special advantages of being located between two economically divergent nation-states.

On the surface, these relations seem to be purely anarchic and ad hoc, perpetuated by mere 'gangsters', but in reality, non-state forms of authority, built on long-term trust and strong cross-border interconnections, facilitate them. Local socio-economic involvement with the various Malaysian *tukei* was thus part of a locally accepted survival strategy among borderland populations. The strength of these non-state forms of authority is a clear indicator of the weak presence of government rule during this period of increased regional autonomy.

The book discusses how these borderland strategies, carried out in the intersection between legality and illegality, too easily are condemned as mere criminal acts. It considers such views insufficient as they fail to take into account how borderland people themselves define their actions and give meaning to their lives. What is actually happening to these inhabitants of the edges on the Indonesian nation-state? The book argues that state definitions of what is deemed legal and illegal are situational and inconsistent. They depend on changes in state strategies and policies that do not necessarily coincide with local borderland definitions of legality. Local claims of legitimacy, in this case, are expressed by emphasizing a deep identification with the borderland and with perceived rights to take part in and profit from border advantages. Here certain illegal activities are locally rendered licit practice and understood as reasonable and rational behaviour.

The book argues for a more nuanced understanding of so-called 'illegal activities' in the West Kalimantan borderlands and elsewhere along Southeast Asian borders that moves beyond rigid categories of 'legal' and 'illegal'. Such absolute categories do little justice to local realities where these distinctions are less clearly disaggregated or outright impossible to make. The book suggests that borderlands provide us with an especially good locale for observing the shortcomings of these official distinctions. Additionally, the borderland traits described in this study seem applicable throughout Southeast Asian borderlands – regions often situated along similar resource-rich and politically contested borders. Conclusions derived from the Indonesian case could raise interesting questions in advancing our understanding of Southeast Asian borderlands in general.

Moreover, as pointed out by Schulte Norholdt and Van Klinken, the rise of localism or regionalism contrasted with decentralization 'made certain hidden aspects of the state more explicit as it revealed the extent to which local actors used the state for their own interests' (2007a:24). Ultimately the borderland can be viewed as a critical site for exemplifying the changing dynamics of state authority that Indonesia is experiencing in the wake of decentralization. The insights to be drawn from these borderland cases suggest that although lines of authority have to a certain degree been rearranged during the decentralization processes, considerable continuities with former arrangements of informal networks and alliances remain.

Border elites who colluded with the Soeharto regime have largely maintained their networks and remain active players in local politics in the post-Soeharto period, often with enhanced authority as a result of increased regional autonomy and the ability to bypass central state authorities. Thus, this study shows the continuity in informal networks and that the reshuffling of authority since decentralization has sharpened the struggle over resources on the local level. However, the benefits of this new political era of 'regionalism', implemented for nearly a decade in the Kapuas Hulu borderland, are still enjoyed mainly by a small, politically adept elite. In taking the vantage point of the border population, this study does not attempt to romanticize local agency and thereby downplay the highly unequal power relations at the border.

On the contrary, the study shows how various state institutions are constantly and often forcefully engaged in reclaiming authority over borderland resources in tandem with border elite actors, leaving the non-elite community highly vulnerable and increasingly marginalized. The book has shown how past and present large-scale resource exploitation has been justified by both state and local elite actors as a means to obtain border development and security.

| *At the edges of states*

ZONES OF SEMI-AUTONOMY

In Chapters 7 and 8, the book examines two cases that in various ways show the overlapping strategies of the central government and border elites. The central government's attempts to regain authority through re-militarization of the border and promotion of large- scale development schemes are countered and accommodated locally through the use of government's own development rhetoric in promoting a new administrative district that would lead to increased regional autonomy.

Chapter 7 shows how the borderlands are once again becoming a battleground for national politics of sovereignty. It seems that this return to the rhetoric of defence and security has a dual purpose, as it did during the New Order regime of Soeharto. First, it reclaims the image of a strong unified state whose power is solidified at the border, thereby countering strong media criticism of the central government for its weakness and inability to police its territorial borders. Second, besides being a territorial delimiter the border is also perceived as a natural frontier in the sense that the adjoining borderlands are still widely forested. The borderland contains large patches of what in government policy narratives are designated 'waste' or 'idle' lands to be readily exploited for agricultural development. The chapter points out how the re-emergence of state interests in the West Kalimantan borderlands, both politically and economically, are met with local suspicion, as such top-down development initiatives are perceived as central government attempts to reclaim authority over resources, territory and people along the supposedly lawless border.

In Chapter 8, this tension is spelled out through the case of district splitting (*pemekaran*) favoured by border elites. By promoting the formation of a new border district, the border elite attempts to ensure increased regional autonomy over local political and economic matters attained during the early period of the Indonesian decentralization program. The local strategy of maintaining local authority through *pemekaran* should not be analyzed as a mere act of resistance towards any outside involvement; on the contrary, government development initiatives are largely welcomed if they can be altered to enhance local advantage. How the larger non-elite community in the borderland stands to gain from the new top-down, state- driven development plans and border elite political manoeuvres of *pemekaran* are still unclear. It is, however, evident that the scramble over border access will continue and become an even more contentious issue when the pendulum swings and the border region once again becomes a highly strategic political and economic resource.

In other words, what the cases demonstrate is that central state authority in the borderland has never been absolute, but waxes and wanes. State rules and laws have always been open to local interpretation, manipulation and negotiation, although the degree of such negotiation also changes depending on the strength of the central state. For although 'the state' appears fragmented, individual agents within the state apparatus still possess significant power and ability to induce immense change in the border region even from a distance.

One effect of the renewed interest in the border issue might be a new era of top-down border development. One could speculate that these large-scale attempts at domesticating the border region would lead to a progressive growth of central state authority in the borderland. In the future, this might develop into a good example of the 'border effect' mentioned by Gallant (1999), the manner in which freely roaming timber 'gangsters' and other 'military entrepreneurs' working the border have openly challenged formal law and hence compelled the central government to take action by forcefully eradicating these 'illegal' practices.

In sum, this book has engaged with a wide range of scholarly writings about states, borders, and borderlands. What these studies remind us of are the processual character of state formation, and especially how states are multifaceted and government agents deeply entangled in local webs of reciprocity. In particular, they show how 'the state' is a construct that has local manifestations and effects.

Conclusions drawn from this study on the West Kalimantan borderland show that state agents and border populations alike are embedded and enmeshed in everyday forms of state formation on the border – often constituted through practices carried out in the grey zone of legality and illegality. Consequently, the West Kalimantan borderland has never been an isolated and static margin as government rhetoric has portrayed it. Instead, throughout history it has been deeply integrated with regional political and economic centres across the border in Sarawak, Malaysia, and simultaneously maintained patronage relations with the central Indonesian state. As an effect of the oscillating character of the border, and the possibilities and constraints it entails, a constant flux of people and ideas has entered the borderland. Complex interdependencies have been established, which largely have blurred the division between 'formal' and 'informal', 'legal' and 'illegal', 'state' and 'society'.

Appendix

TIMELINE OF IMPORTANT EVENTS

1850s	First Dutch encounter with the border Iban
1920s	Iban pacification
1962	*Konfrontasi* with Malaysia
1966	The beginning of Soeharto's New Order regime
1968	'Operation Destruction' and PARAKU uprooting
1997	Commencement of the economic crisis in Indonesia
1998	Collapse of Soeharto's authoritarian regime
1999	De-facto regional autonomy in the border area
2000	Initial ideas behind special autonomy in the border region emerge
2001	Official implementation of regional autonomy
2000-2005	Cooperative (illegal) logging between local elites, Malaysian entrepreneurs, and district government
2005	Operation Everlasting Forest (central government crackdown on illegal logging in the border region)
2005	Central government presentation of border development plans: large-scale plantations and increased military control
2006	Local lobbying for new border district formally initiated
2007	'Border District' committee officially declared

Acronyms and abbreviations

ABRI	Angktan Bersenjata Republic Indonesia (Armed Forces of Indonesia, name applied before 1999)
ARA	Algemeen Rijksarchief (Central State Archives)
BAPPEDA	Badan Perencanaan Pembangunan Daerah (Regional Development Planning Agency)
BAPPENAS	Badan Perencanaan Pembangunan Nasional (National Development Planning Agency)
BKTRN	Badan Koordinasi Tata Ruang Nasional (National Coordination Body for Spatial Planning)
BP2KKP	Badan Persiapan Pengembangan Kawasan Khusus Perbatasan (Agency for the Preparation of Special Border Area Development)
DOM	Daerah Operasi Militer (Area under strict military control)
DPD RI	Dewan Perwakilan Daerah (Regional Representative Council)
DPR RI	Dewan Perwakilan Rakyat Republik Indonesia (the National Parliament)
DPRD I	Dewan Perwakilan Rakyat Daerah Tingkat I (Provincial Parliament)
DPRD II	Dewan Perwakilan Rakyat Daerah Tingkat II (District Parliament)
DSNP	Danau Sentarum National Park
FPMP	Forum Peduli Masyarakat Perbatasan Kalimantan Barat (Forum for Border Community Care)
GGNI	Governor General of the Netherlands East Indies
GMT	Greenwich Mean Time
Golkar	Golongan Karya (Group of Functionaries. The dominant political party of former President Soeharto)

HPH	Hak Pengusahaan Hutan (Commercial Forest Concession)
HPHH	Hak Pemungutan Hasil Hutan (Permit to Harvest Forest Products)
Inpres	Instruksi Presiden (Presidential Instruction)
Kalbar	Kalimantan Barat (West Kalimantan)
Kemenhut	Keputusan Meneteri Kehutanan (Ministry of Forestry Decree)
Keppres	Keputusan President (Presidential Decree)
Kodam	Komando Daerah Militer (Regional Military Command)
Kodim	Komando Distrik Militer (District Military Command)
Kopassus	Komando Pasukan Khusus (Army Special Forces)
Koramil	Komando Rayon Militer (Subdistrict Military Command)
Krismon	Krisis moneter (Monetary crisis)
LIPI	Lembaga Ilmu Pengetahuan Indonesia (The Indonesian National Institute of Sciences)
LSM	Lembaga Swadaya Masyarakat (Community Self-Help Organization)
MYT	Malaysia standard time (GMT + 8)
NKRI	Negara Kesatuan Republik Indonesia (Unitary State of the Republic of Indonesia)
PAD	Pendapatan Asli Daerah (District tax)
PARAKU	Pasukan Rayakat Kalimantan Utara (North Kalimantan People's Force)
PEMDA	Pemerintah Daerah (Local government)
Perda	Peraturan Daerah (Local government regulation)
Perdu	Peraturan Pemerintah (Government regulation)
Perpres	Peraturan President (Presidential regulation)
Pilkada	Pemilihan Kepala Daerah (direct election of district head)
PGRS	Pasukan Gerilya Rakyat Sarawak (Sarawak People's Guerrilla Force)
PKI	Partai Komunis Indonesia (Indonesian Communist Party)
PLB	Pos Lintas Batas (Border Crossing Post)

Polri	Kepolisian Republik Indonesia (Central Indonesian Police)
Polda	Kepolisian Daerah (Provincial Police)
Polhut	Kepolisian Kehutanan (Forest Police/rangers)
Polres	Kepolisian Resort (District Police Command)
Polsek	Kepolisian Sektor (Subdistrict Police Command)
PPKPU	Panitia Pembentukan Kabupaten Perbatasan Utara (Committee for the Establishment of the North Border District)
PPLB	Pos Pemeriksaan Lintas Batas (Border Crossing Inspection Post)
PMARI	Putusan Mahkamah Agung Republik Indonesia (Indonesian Supreme Court Verdict)
PPNP	Putusan Pengadilan Negeri Putussibau (Putussibau District Court Verdict)
PT	Perseroan Terbatas (Designation for a privately held corporation)
RM	Ringgit Malaysia (Malaysian currency)
Rp	Rupiah (Indonesian currency)
RPKAD	Resimen Para Komando Angkatan Darat (Army Para Commando Regiment)
RUU	Rancangan Undang-Undang (Law Act Draft)
Skep	Surat Keputusan (Decision letter)
SBY	President Susilo Bambang Yudhoyono
SCO	Sarawak Communist Organization
TNI	Tentara Nasional Indonesia (Indonesian Armed Forces name applied since 1999)
TNKU	Tentara Nasional Kalimantan Utara (North Kalimantan National Army)
Yamaker	PT Yajasan Maju Kerja (Foundation run by the Indonesian Armed Forces)
UU	Undang-undang (National Law)
WANRA	Perlawanan Rakyat (The people's resistance units)
WIB	Western Indonesian standard time (GMT + 7)

Glossary

(I) DENOTES STRICTLY IBAN TERMS; UNMARKED TERMS ARE INDONESIAN OR DUTCH

Adat	Local customary law and practices
Afdeling	Division
Nanga Badau	West Kalimantan border town
Balok	Beam of wood
Batang Lupar River	Key river in Sarawak. The upper course runs parallel to the border with West Kalimantan.
Batang-Loepars	The Dutch name for the Iban population residing along the border
Berani	Brave
Bilik	A room, family living quarters
Controleur	Dutch government controller
Dayak	Native ethnic groups of Kalimantan (such as Iban Dayaks)
Dinas	District agency reporting to the Bupati
Duit	Money, cash
Dwifungsi	Dual function of the Indonesian military
Emparan	Hills south of the border and north and east of the Kapuas Lakes
Hutan	Forest
Jalan Lintas Utara	Main government road connecting the border town of Badau with the district capital of Putussibau
Jalan Tikus	Illegal roads across the border (literally, mouse trails)
Kaban (I)	Relatives/kin
Kabupaten	District administration
Kapuas Lakes	Several shallow lakes in the subdistrict of Batang Lupar
Kayu	Wood, timber
Kecamatan	Subdistrict administration
Kedang Range	Range of hills along the border.

Ketinggalan	Lagging behind (development)
Konfrontasi	The 1960s confrontation between Indonesia and Malaysia
Lanjak	Administrative town in the subdistrict of Batang Lupar
Leboyan River	One of the main rivers in the subdistrict of Batang Lupar and northern tributary of the Kapuas River.
Lubok Antu	Sarawak border town
Melayu	Malay
Masyarakat	Society
New Order	The 32-year regime of former President Soeharto (1966-1998)
Ngayap (I)	Courtship
Onderafdeling	District
Pembangunan	Development
Pemekaran	District splitting (literally to blossom)
Perbatasan	Border
Pindah	Immigrate
Pontianak	Provincial capital in West Kalimantan
Putussibau	District capital of Kapuas Hulu
Tembawai (I)	Old longhouse settlements
Terasing	Isolated
Terbelakang	Backward
Tukei (I)	Malaysian Chinese timber entrepreneur
Ulu (I)	Up-river
Urang	Iban spelling for orang (man)
Yayasan	Foundation

Bibliography

Abraham, Itty
2006   'Illegal but licit', *International Institute for Asian Studies, IIAS Newsletter* 42:1-4.
Abraham, Itty and Willem van Schendel
2005   'Introduction: The making of illicitness', in: Willem van Schendel and Itty Abraham (eds), *Illicit flows and criminal things*, pp. 1-37. Bloomington, IN: Indiana University Press.
Abrahams, Ray
1998   *Vigilant citizens: Vigilantism and the state*. Cambridge, MA: Polity.
Abrams, Philip
1988   'Notes on the difficulty of studying the state', *Journal of Historical Sociology* 1:58-89.
Agustiar, Dwi Riyanto
2008   'Presiden anggap perbatasan beranda depan negara. *Tempo Interaktif* 15 August.
Agustiar, Memet
2000   'Indonesian workers in Sarawak: The direction of the daily commuting workers via the Entikong-Tebedu border post', in: M. Leigh, *Language, management and tourism. Borneo 2000. Proceedings of the Sixth Biennial Borneo Research Conference*, pp. 235-44. Kuching: Universiti Malaysia Sarawak (UNIMAS).
Akcaya Kalimantan Barat
2007a   'Bupati dukung pemekaran Kabupaten Perbatasan Utara Kapuas Hulu'. 9 March.
2007b   'Pemekaran perbatasan utara murni aspirasi masyarakat', 9 March.
Alqadrie, S.I., T. Ngusmanto Budiarto and Erdi
2003   *Kebijakan desentralisasi sektor kehutanan dan dampaknya terhadap kelestarian hutan dan kesejahteraan penduduk di Kabupaten Kapuas Hulu, Provinsi Kalimantan Barat, Indonesia*. Bogor, Indonesia: Center for International Forestry Research.

Alvarez, Robert R.
1995   'The Mexican-US Border: The making of an Anthropology of Borderlands', *Annual Reviews in Anthropology* 24:447-70.
Alvarez, Robert R. and George A. Collier
1994   'The long haul in Mexican trucking: Traversing the borderlands of north and south, *American Ethnologist* 21:606-27.
Amster, Matthew
2005a   'Cross-border marriage in the Kelabit highlands of Borneo', *Anthropological Forum* 15: 131-50.
2005b   'The rhetoric of the state: Dependency and control in a Malaysian-Indonesian borderland', *Identities: Global Studies in Culture and Power* 12:23-43.
2006   'Narrating the border: Perspectives from the Kelabit Highlands of Borneo', in: A. Horstmann and R.L. Wadley (eds), *Centering the margin; Agency and narrative in Southeast Asian borderlands*, pp. 205-28. New York: Berghahn.
Anderson, Benedict
1991   *Imagined communities: Reflections on the origin and spread of nationalism.* London: Verso.
Anderson, James and Liam O'Dowd
1999   'Borders, border regions and territoriality: Contradictory meanings, changing significance', *Regional Studies* 33:593-604.
Anonymous
1921   'Apostolisch Vicariaat van Borneo: De school te Landjah gesloten', *Onze Missiën in Oost- en West-Indië: Tijdschrift der Indische Missie-Vereeniging* 5.
Antara News Agency
2005a   'Kail sesali pembiaran perampasan mobil bukti illegal logging', 15 January.
2005b   'Mentan: Pengembangan sawit di perbatasan terbuka lagi investor', 28 June.
2007   'Indonesia-Malaysia bangun 40 pos perbatasan', 15 June.
2008   'Mixed reactions loom over Malaysia's Askar Wathaniah', 16 February.
Ardhana, I. Ketut, Jayl Langub and Daniel Chew
2004   'Borders of kinship and ethnicity: Cross-border relations between the Kelalan Valley, Sarawak, and the Bawan Valley, East Kalimantan', *Borneo Research Bulletin* 35:144-79.

Asiwaju, A. I.
1985   *Partitioned Africans: Ethnic relations across Africa's international boundaries, 1884-1984.* New York: St. Martin's.
1990   *Artificial boundaries.* New York: Civiletis International.
1993   *Development of border regions: Proceedings of the Nigerian National Planning Conference, Durbar Hotel, Lagos, 10-12 August, 1989.* Lagos, Nigeria: National Boundary Commission.

Aspinall, Edward and Greg Fealy
2003a   'Introduction: Decentralisation, democratisation and the rise of the local', in: E. Aspinall and G. Fealy (eds), *Local power and politics in Indonesia; Decentralisation and democratisation*, pp. 1-11. Singapore: Institute of Southeast Asian Studies.

Aspinall, Edward and Greg Fealy (eds)
2003b   *Local power and politics in Indonesia: Decentralisation and democrotisation.* Singapore: Institute of Southeast Asian Studies.

Bala, Poline
2001   'Interethnic ties along the Kalimantan-Sarawak border: The Kelabit and Lun Berian in the Kelabit-Kerayan highlands', *Borneo Research Bulletin* 32:103-11.
2002   *Changing borders and identities in the Kelabit Highlands: Anthropological reflections on growing up near an international border.* Kota Samarahan, Sarawak, Malaysia: Unit Penerbitan. Kuching, Sarawak: Universiti Malaysia.

Badan Perencanaan Pembangunan Nasional
2003   *Strategi dan model pengembangan wilayah perbatasan Kalimantan.* Jakarta: Kementerian Perencanaan Pembangunan Nasional, Bappenas.
2004   *Kawasan perbatasan: Kebijakan dan strategi nasional pengelolaan kawasan perbatasan antarnegara di Indonesia.* Jakarta: Kementerian Perencanaan Pembangunan Nasional, Bappenas.
2005   *Rencana induk pengelolaan perbatasan Negara: Buku rinci di Provinsi Kalimantan Barat (Draft Akhir).* Jakarta: Kementerian Perencanaan Pembangunan Nasional, Bappenas.
2006a   *Buku utama rencana induk pengelolaan perbatasan negara.* Jakarta: Kementerian Perencanaan Pembangunan Nasional, Bappenas.
2006b   *Laporan akir: Evaluasi kebijiakan perencanaan program pengembangan wilayah perbatasan.* Jakarta: Kementerian Perencanaan Pembangunan Nasional, Bappenas.

2006c *Rencana induk pengelolaan perbatasan negara: Buku rinci di Provinsi Kalimantan Barat (Draft Akhir)*. Jakarta: Kementerian Perencanaan Pembangunan Nasional.

Badan Pusat Statistik-Propinsi Kalimantan Barat

2006 *Propinsi Kalimantan Barat dalam angka*. Pontianak, KB: BPS-KB.

Badan Pusat Statistik-Kabupaten Kapuas Hulu

2002 *Kabupaten Kapuas Hulu dalam angka 2001*. Putussibau, KB: BPS-KH.

2003 *Kabupaten Kapuas Hulu dalam angka 2002*. Putussibau, KB: BPS-KH.

2006 *Kabupaten Kapuas Hulu dalam angka 2006*. Putussibau, KB: BPS-KH.

Barker, Joshua and Gerry van Klinken

2009 'Reflections on the state in Indonesia', in: Gerry van Klinken and Joshua Barker (eds), *State of Authority: The state in society in Indonesia*, pp. 17-46. Ithaca, NY: Southeast Asia Program, Cornell University.

Barr, Christopher, Ida Resosudarmo, Ahmad Dermawan and John McCarthy (eds)

2006 *Decentralization of forest administratation in Indonesia*. Bogor, Indonesia: Center for International Forestry Research (Cifor).

Bath, C. Richard

1976 'The status of borderland studies: Political sciences', *The Social Sciences Journal* 13:55-67.

Baud, Michiel and Willem van Schendel

1997 'Toward a comparative history of borderlands', *Journal of World History* 8:211-42.

Berita Harian

2003 'Balak Kalimantan Barat masuk ikut peraturan', 3 September.

Berita Sore

2007a 'DPO illegal logging alih profesi jadi pengusaha sawit', 15 June.

2007b 'Polda Kalba-PDRM kerjasama tangkap cukong pembalak liar Apeng', 16 June.

2009 'Malaysia moves border poles into RI's land for oil palm plantations', 4 March.

Berita Tentara National Indonesia

2006 'Panglima TNI: Tidak ada alasan tolak pembangunan perbatasan', 23 March.

Borneo Bulletin, The
1962   'Mission: "Liberation"', 26 May.
Borneo Tribune
2008   'Tanah di perbatasan belum bersertifikat', 25 September.
2009a   'Jadikan perbatasan beranda depan', 11 February.
2009b   'Malaysia ingkari kesepakatan pembukaan PPLB Badau', 7 November.
Bouman, M.A.
1924   'Ethnografische aanteekeningen omtrent de Gouvernement-slanden in de boven-Kapoeas, Westerafdeeling van Borneo', *Tijdschrift voor Indische Taal- Land- en Volkenkunde* 8:173-95.
1952   'Gegevens uit Semitau en Bowen-Kapoeas (1922)', *Adatrechtbundels* 44:7-86.
Brackman, Arnold C.
1966   *Southeast Asia's second front*. London: Pall Mall.
Brooke, Charles
1990   *Ten years in Sarawak*. Singapore: Oxford University Press. [Original 1866.]
Brown, David W.
1999   *Addicted to rent: Corporate and spatial distribution of forest resources in Indonesia: Implications for forest sustainability and government policy*. Indonesia-UK Tropical Forestry Management Programme.
Budiman, Arif
1990   *State and civil society in Indonesia*. Clayton, VIC: Monash University Press.
Buehler, Michael
2007   'Local elite reconfiguration in post-New Order Indonesia: The 2005 elections of district government heads in South Sulawesi', *Review of Indonesian and Malaysian Affairs* 41:119-47.
Buil, Gonzales
1921   'De geschiedenis van Landjah', *Borneo-Almanak* 11, 69-74.
Burgemeestre, J.E.L.
1934   *Memorie van Overgave van den Gezaghebber van Semitau, 2 Maart 1930-14 September 1934*. Den Haag, Netherlands: Memorie van Overgave. KIT 999, Nationaal Archief.
Campbell, Howard and Josiah Heyman
2007   'Slantwise: Beyond domination and resistance on the border', *Journal of Contemporary Ethnography* 36:3-30.

Casson, Anne
2001 'Decentralisation of policymaking and administration of policies affecting forests and estate crops in Kotawaringin Timur District, Central Kalimantan. CIFOR Reports on decentralisation and forests in Indonesia, Case Study 5. Bogor, Indonesia: Center for International Forestry Research.

Casson, Anne and Krystof Obidzinski
2002 'From New Order to regional autonomy: Shifting dynamics of "illegal" logging in Kalimantan, Indonesia', *World Development* 30:2133-51.

Central Intelligence Agency (CIA)
1970 *Highland peoples of Southeast Asia's borderland with China: Their potential for subversive insurgency*. Washington, DC: Central Intelligence Agency. [Report CIA/BCI50.]
1973 *Peking's support of insurgencies in Southeast Asia*. Washington, DC: Central Intelligence Agency. [Report CIA/POLO LIII.]

Chalfin, Brenda
2001 'Working the Border: Constructing sovereignty in the context of liberalization', *Political and Legal Anthropology Review* 24:129-48.

Colfer, C.J.P., R.L.Wadley, A. Salim and R.G. Deudley
2000 'Understanding patterns of resource use and consumption: A prelude to co-management', *Borneo Research Bulletin* 32:29-88.

Colombijn, Freek
2002 'Maling, maling! The lynching of petty criminals', in: Freek Colombijn and J. Thomas Lindblad (eds), *Roots of Violence in Indonesia*, pp. 299-329. Leiden: KITLV Press.

Conboy, Kenneth J.
2003 *KOPASSUS: Inside Indonesia's special forces*. Jakarta/Singapore: Equinox.

Cooke, Fadzilah Majid
2009 'Border crossings in the Asia Pacific: Metaphoric and jurisdictional', *Asia Pacific Viewpoint* 50:24-8.

Corbridge, Stuart, Glyn Williams, Manoj Srivastava and Rene Veron (eds)
2005 *Seeing the state: Governance and governmentality in India*. Cambridge: Cambridge University Press.

Das, Veena and Deborah Poole (eds)
2004a *Anthropology in the margins of the state*. Santa Fe, NM: School of American Research Press.

Das, Veena and Deborah Poole
2004b	'State and its margins: Comparative ethnographies', in: Veena Das and Deborah Poole (eds), *Anthropology in the margins of the state*, pp. 3-33. Santa Fe, NM: School of American Research Press.
Davidson, Jamie S.
2002	Violence and politics in West Kalimantan, Indonesia. PhD thesis, Department of Political Science, University of Washington.
2003a	'The politics of violence on the Indonesian periphery', *South East Asia Research* 11:59-89.
2003b	'Primitive politics: The rise and fall of the Dayak Unity Party in West Kalimantan, Indonesia', *Asia Research Institute, Working Paper Series* 9.
Davidson, Jamie S. and Douglas Kammen
2002	'Indonesia's unknown war and the lineages of violence in West Kalimantan, Indonesia'. *Indonesia* 73:1-36.
Dennis, Peter and Jeffrey Grey
1996	*Emergency and confrontation: Australian military operations in Malaya and Borneo 1950-1966*. Departemen Pertanian. St Leonards, NSW: Allen & Unwin.
2009	*Pedoman teknis pengendalian lahan pertanian di wilayah perbatasan*. Direktorat Jenderal Pengelolaan Lahan Dan Air, Departemen Pertanian. Jakarta: Direktorat Pen-gelolaan Lahan.
Department Kehutanan Republik Indonesia
2005	'Tiga warga negara Malaysia tersangka pelaku illegal logging segara disidangkan'. Jakarta: Dephut. [No. S. 210/II/PIK-1/2005 23 March.]
Dermawan, Ahmad
2004	Has the big bang hit the trees and people? The impacts of Indonesia's decentralization on forest conservation and the livelihood of communities. MSc thesis, Department of Economics and Resource Management, Agricultural University of Norway (Aas).
DetikNews
2004	'Cerita dari perbatasan RI-Malaysia (4): Lagu lama yang sudah usang', *DetikNews* 22 June.
Dickens, Peter
1991	*SAS The jungle frontier: 22 Special Air Service Regiment in the Borneo campaign 1963-1966*. London: Arms and Armour.

Dinas Kehutanan Kalimantan Barat
2004	*Laporan tahunan 2003*. Pontianak: Dinas Kehutanan Kalimantan Barat.

Direktorat Jenderal Penataan Ruang (DJPR)
2003	*Spatial policy and development of Kalimantan-Sarawak-Sabah border area*. Departmen Pemukian dan Prasana Wilayah (14 October).
2005	*Strategi perwujudan rencana tata ruang pulau Kalimantan dalam rangka menunjang pelaksanaan progaam Heart of Borneo*. Departmen Pemukian dan Prasana Wilayah. [7 December.]

Donnan, Hastings and Dieter Haller
2000	'Liminal no more: The relevance of borderland studies', *Ethnologia Europea/Journal of European Ethnology* 30:7-22.

Donnan, Hastings and Thomas M. Wilson (eds)
1994	*Border approaches: Anthropological perspectives on frontiers*. Lanham, MD: University Press of America.

Donnan, Hastings and Thomas M. Wilson
1999	*Borders: Frontiers of identity, nation and state*. Oxford: Berg.
2003	'Territoriality, anthropology, and the interstitial: Subversions and support in European borderlands', *Focaal: European Journal of Anthropology* 41:9-20.

Dove, Michael R.
1982	'The myth of the "communal" longhouse in rural development: The Kantu of Kalimantan', in: C. MacAndrews and Lin S Chia (eds), *Too rapid rural development: Perceptions and perspectives from Southeast Asia*, pp. 14-78. Athens, OH: Ohio University Press.

Down to Earth
2005	'Oil palm expansion will bring more conflict', *Down to Earth Newsletter* 66, pp. 1-16

Driessen, Henk
1999	'Smuggling as a border way of life: A Mediterranean case', in: M. Rösler and T. Wendl (eds), *Frontiers and borderlands: Anthropological perspectives*, pp. 117-27. Frankfurt am Main, Germany: Peter Lang.

Duncan, Christopher R.
2007	'Mixed outcomes: The impact of regional autonomy and decentralization on indigenous ethnic minorities in Indonesia', *Development and Change* 38:711-33.

Easter, David
2005 '"Keep the Indonesian pot boiling": Western covert intervention in Indonesia, October 1965-March 1966', *Cold War History* 5:55-73.

Edward, Churchill
2007 'Security posts proposed for border villages', *The Sunday Post* 7 February.

Effendy, Machrus
1995 *Penghancuran PGRS-PARAKU dan PKI di Kalimantan Barat*. Jakarta: PT Dian Kemilau.

Eghenter, Cristina
1999 'Migrants' practical reasonings: The social, political, and environmental determinants of long-distance migrations among the Kayan and Kenyah of the interior of Borneo', *Sojourn* 14:1-33.
2007 'Of negotiable boundaries and fixed lines in Borneo: Practices and views of the border in the Apo Kayan Region of East Kalimantan', *Moussons* 11:133-50.

Eilenberg, Michael
2003 'An anthropological study of children and childhood among the Iban in West Kalimantan, Indonesia'. Aarhus, Denmark: Department of Ethnography and Social Anthropology, University of Aarhus. [Unpub. field report in Danish.]
2005 'Paradoxical outcomes of national schooling in the borderland of West Kalimantan, Indonesia: The case of the Iban', *Borneo Research Bulletin* 36:163-84.

Eilenberg, Michael and Reed Lee Wadley
2009 'Borderland livelihood strategies: The socio-economic significance of ethnicity in cross-border labour migration, West Kalimantan, Indonesia', *Asia Pacific Viewpoint* 50:58-73.

Eisenstadt, S. N. and Luis Roniger
1980 'Patron-client relations as a model of structuring social exchange', *Comparative Studies in Society and History* 22:42-77.
1984 *Patrons, clients and friends: Interpersonal relations and the structure of trust in society*. Cambridge: Cambridge University Press.

Enthoven, J.J.K.
1903 *Bijdragen tot de geographie van Borneo's Wester-afdeeling*. Leiden: Brill.

Environmental Investigation Agency (EIA)
2001 'Illegal timber trade in the ASEAN region', in: *A briefing document*

> for the Forestry Law Enforcement Conference Preparatory Meeting, pp. 1-8. Jakarta: EIA.

Environmental Investigation Agency/Telepak

2004   *Profiting from plunder: How Malaysia smuggles endangered wood.* Jakarta: EIA/Telepak February.

Equator News

2004a	'Tangkap Apeng, kenapa baru sekarang', 9 August.
2004b	'Tangkap Apheng: Masyarakat masih tunggu janji Kapolda', 14 September.
2005a	'Jalan tikus perbatasan pun diintai Densus 88', 15 November.
2005b	'Lanjak kini telah menjadi kota matiPasca penertiban illegal logging', 13 December.
2005c	'Membangun perbatasan, mensejahterakan masyarakat lokal', 6 December.
2005d	'Pembalak kayu TNBK divonis 9 tahun', 19 July.
2005e	'Pengelolaan wilayah perbatasan masih setengah hati', 24 September.
2005f	'Perbatasan perlu otoritas', 8 June.
2005g	'Perkerja kayu kembali datangi Dewan: Sordorkan 1.200 tanda tangan', 23 August.
2005h	'Sempadan Badau-Lubuk, pembangunan masa depan!', 7 October.
2006a	'Kabupaten perbatasan, upaya pertahankan NKRI', 28 July.
2006b	'M'Sia masih ogah buka PLB Badau', 18 September.
2006c	'Pembangunan perbatasan jangan hanya angin segar', 22 March.
2006d	'Perjuangkan kabupaten perbatasan', 22 April.
2006e	'Perpres perbatasan masih persiapan', 3 January.
2006f	'Soal perbatasan, pemerintah pusat tak konsekuen', 10 February.
2007a	'Badau dipersiapkan jadi kawasan agropolitan', 20 November.
2007b	'Dua kabupaten di Kapuas Hulu layak dimekarkan', 15 November.'
2007c	'Keppres perbatasan masih dibahas', 25 February.
2007d	'Kesenjangan masyarakat di perbatasan masih tinggi', 30 April.
2007e	'Masyarakat sepakati nama Kabupaten Perbatasan Utara', 10 March.
2007f	'Pemekaran kabupaten upaya menyerap aspirasi masyarakat', 13 November.

2007g   'Perbatasan dijaga 500 personel TNI', 19 February.
2008   'Kesepakatan pembangunan lanud Putussibau diteken', 7 August.

Fariastuti
2002   'Mobility of people and goods across the border of West Kalimantan and Sarawak', *Antropologi Indonesia* 67:94-104.

Ferguson, James and Akhil Gupta
2002   'Spatializing states: Toward an ethnography of neoliberal governmentality', *American Ethnologist* 29:981-1002.

Fernanda, Pirie
2006   'Legal Autonomy as political engagement: The Ladakhi village in the wider world', *Law & Society Review* 40:77-104.

Fitrani, Fitria, Bert Hofman and Kai Kaiser
2005   'Unity in Diversity? The creation of new local governments in a decentralising Indonesia', *Bulletin of Indonesian Economic Studies* 41:57-79.

Flynn, Donna K.
1997   '"We are the border": Identity, exchange, and the state along the Benin-Nigeria border', *American Ethnologist* 24:311-30.

Forbes, Mark
2005   'Truth still a casualty of our secret war', *The Age*, 23 March.

Fox, James J., Dedi Supriadi Adhuri and Ida Aju Pradnja
2005   'Unfinished edifice or pandora's box? Decentralisation and reseource management in Indonesia', in: B.P. Resosudarmo (ed.), *The politics and economics of Indonesia's natural resources*, pp. 92-108. Singapore: Institute of Southeast Asian Studies (ISEAS).

Freeman, J. Derek
1970   *Report on the Iban*. London: Athlone.

Galemba, Rebecca B.
2008   'Informal and illicit entrepreneurs: Fighting for a place in the neoliberal economic order', *Anthropology of Work Review* 29:19-25.

Gallant, Thomas
1999   'Brigandage, piracy, capitalism, and state formation: Transnational crime from a historical world-system perspective', in: J. Heyman (ed.), *States and illegal practices*, pp. 25-62. Oxford: Berg.

Gellner, Ernest
1977   'Patrons and clients', in: E. Gellner and J. Waterbury (eds), *Patrons and clients in Mediterranean societies*, pp. 1-6. London: Duck-

worth, in association with the Center for Mediterranean Studies of the American Universities Field Staff.

Gregorian, Raffi
1991 'CLARET operations and confrontation, 1964-66', *Conflict Quarterly* XI:48-62.

Grundy-Warr, C. (ed.)
1990 *International boundaries and boundary conflict resolution*. Durham, England: International Boundaries Research Unit, University of Durham.

Gupta, Akhil
1995 'Blurred boundaries: The discourse of corruption, the culture of politics, and the imagined state', *American Ethnologist* 22:375-407.

Gurr, Robert
1995 *Voices from a border war: A history of 1 Royal New Zealand Infantry Regiment 1963 to 1965*. Melbourne, VIC: R.M. Gurr.

Haller, Dieter and Hastings Donnan
2000 'Borders and borderlands: An anthropological perspective', *Journal of European Ethnology* 30-2:126.

Hamid, Sri Handoyo Mukti and Tien Widianto
2001 *Kawasan perbatasan Kalimantan: Permasalahan dan konsep pengembangan*. Jakarta: Pusat Pengkajian Kebijakan Teknologi Pengembangan Wilayah (BPPT).

Hann, Chris and Elisabeth Dunn (eds)
1996 *Civil society: Challenging Western models*. London: Routledge.

Hansen, Thomas Blom and Finn Stepputat
2001 *States of imagination: Ethnographic explorations of the postcolonial state*. Durham, NC: Duke University Press.

Hara, Fujio
2005 'The North Kalimantan Communist Party and the People's Republic of China', *The Developing Economies* XLIII:489-513.

Harold, James and Denis Sheil-Small
1971 *The undeclared war*. London: Leo Cooper.

Harwell, Emily
1997 *Law and culture in resource management: An analysis of local systems for resource management in the Danau Sentarum Wildlife Reserve, West Kalimantan, Indonesia*. Consultant's report for Indonesia-UK Tropical Forest Management Programme Project 5: Conservation International -Indonesia Programme (21 February).

2000a   'Remote sensibilities: Discourses of technology and the making of Indonesia's natural disaster', *Development and Change* 31:307-40.
2000b   The un-natural history of culture: Ethnicity, tradition and territorial conflict in West Kalimantan, Indonesia, 1800-1997. PhD thesis, Yale University, New Haven, CT.

Heidhues, Mary Somers
2003   *Golddiggers, farmers, and traders in the 'Chinese district' of West Kalimantan, Indonesia*. Ithaca, NY: Cornell University.

Heyman, Josiah McC. (ed.)
1999a   *States and illegal practices*. Oxford/New York: Berg.

Heyman, Josiah McC. and Alan Smart
1999b   'States and illegal practices: An overview', in: Josiah McC. Heyman (ed.), *States and illegal practices*, pp. 1-24. Oxford/New York: Berg.

Horstmann, Alexander
2002   *Incorporation and resistance: Borderlands, transnational communities and social change in Southeast Asia*. Oxford: ESRC Transnational Communities Program. [Working Paper WPTC-02-04.]

Horstmann, Alexander and Reed L. Wadley
2006a   'Centering the margin in Southeast Asia', in: Alexander Horstmann and Reed L. Wadley (eds), *Centering the margin: Agency and narrative in Southeast Asian borderlands*. New York: Berghahn.

Horstmann, Alexander, and Reed L. Wadley (eds)
2006b   *Centering the margin: Agency and narrative in Southeast Asian borderlands*. New York: Berghahn.

Hugo, Graeme
2003   'Information, exploitation and empowerment: The case of Indonesian overseas workers', *Asian and Pacific Migration Journal* 12:439-466.

Human Rights Watch
2006   'Too high a price: The human rights cost of Indonesian military's economic activities', *Human Rights Watch* 18:1-136.

Indonesian Observer
2000   'Minister warns of bad consequences of autonomy', 7 December.

Istruksi Presiden Republik Indonesia (Inpres)
2005   'Pemberantasan penebangan kayu secara illegal di kawasan hu-

tan dan peredarannya di seluruh wilayah Republik Indonesia', *Inpres* 4 (18 March).

International Crisis Group (ICG)
2007 'Indonesia: Decentralisation and local power struggles in Maluku', *Asia Briefing* 64 (22 May).

Irwin, Graham
1955 *Nineteenth-century Borneo: A study in diplomatic rivalry.* The Hague: Martinus Nijhoff.

Ishikawa, Noboru
2010 *Between frontiers: Nation and identity in a Southeast Asian borderland.* Athens, OH: Ohio University Press.

Jakarta Globe
2009 'Lost border markers investigated', 28 January.

Jakarta Post
1999 'Perhutani takes over Yamaker's forest areas', 27 May.
2000a 'Crackdown a letdown as illegal loggers fly the coop', 28 May.
2000b 'Forests "endangered" by regional autonomy', 23 December.
2000c 'Illegal logging rampant along Indonesian-Malaysian border', 23 May.
2000d 'Locals protest elected regent', 18 March.
2000e 'Malaysia commits serious border violations: Widodo', 14 June.
2002a 'Govt told to settle border with neighbors', 31 December.
2002b 'Loggers head for heart of Betung Kerihun National Park', 26 November.
2003 'West Kalimantan unable to halt illegal logging', 18 March.
2004a '15 Malaysians detained for illegal logging', 30 January.
2004b 'Govt delays endorsing logging edict', 8 September.
2004c 'Mega asks country's borders marked', 3 August.
2004d 'Susilo pledges stern action against illegal logging', 12 December.
2005a 'Forest conversion on Kalimantan border halted', 12 September.
2005b 'Government plans world's largest oil palm plantation', 18 June.
2005c 'Illegal logging crackdown adds to problems of border dwellers', 11 July.
2005d 'Military wants battalions in border areas', 8 August.
2005e 'Planned giant plantations threatens Borneo forests'. 24 October.

2005f   'WWF warns govt over new plantation areas', 15 October.
2007a   'EU, U.S. report Malaysian businessmen in illegal logging in Indonesia', 5 June.
2007b   'SBY slams self-interested new regions', 24 August.
2007c   'The limit of creating new regions in Indonesia', 28 August.
2009   'Development stalls along border areas as govt offices struggle with management', 29 May.

Japari, H.A.M.
1989   *Buku I: Pembangunan jalan darat di kabupaten dati II Kapuas Hulu sebagai upaya membuka isolasi daerah*. Pemerintah Kabupaten Daerah Tingkat II Kapuas Hulu. Putussibau, Kalimantan Barat.

Jawan, Jayum A.
1994   *Iban politics and economic development*. Bangi, Malaysia: Penerbit Universiti Kebangsaan Malaysia.

Jones, Matthews
2002   *Conflict and confrontation in South East Asia, 1961-1965*. Cambridge: Cambridge University Press.

Kabupaten Kapuas Hulu
2006   *Data pokok-Kabupaten Kapuas Hulu*. Putussibau: Kantor Penelitian, Pengem-bangan dan Informatika.

Kahn, Joel S.
1999   'Culturalising the Indonesian Uplands', in: Tania Murray Li, *Transforming the Indonesian Uplands: Marginality, Power and Production*, pp. 79-101. Amsterdam: Harwood Academic.

Kalimantan Review
2001   '100 hectare concessions of forest product extraction (HPHH 100 Ha)': West Kalimantan's forest destroyer', (English edition) 6:19-21.
2002   'Malaysia kembalikan tanah Indonesia', (Indonesian edition) 86.
2005   'Kemerdekaan warga perbatasan', (Indonesian edition) 121/ Th.XIV:9-12.
2008   'Pembentukan Provinsi Kapuas Raya', 7 March.

Kartodihardjo, Hariadi and Haryanto R. Putro
2004   *Analysis of Kapuas Hulu district policies*. Jakarta: WWF Indonesia.

Kater, C.
1883   'Iets over de Batang Loepar Dajakhs in de "Westerafdeeling van Borneo"', *De Indische Gids* 5:114.

Kementerian Negara Pembangunan Daerah Tertinggal (KNPDT)
2007 *Rencana aksi nasional pembangunan daerah tertinggal tahun 2007-2009*, Jakarta.

Kementerian Penerangan Malaysia (KPM)
1965 *Indonesian aggression against Malaysia*. Kuala Lumpur.

Keputusan
1994 *Badan Pengendali Pelaksanaan Pembangunan Wilayah Perbatasan, Jakarta.*]BP3WPK, Keputusan No. Skep/894/VII/1994 Tanggal 30 July.]

Keputusan Bupati Kabupaten Kapuas Hulu (KepBKH)
2000a *Penetapan nama-nama kepala adat difintif se Kabupaten Kapuas Hulu*, No.130. Putussibau, Kalimantan Barat.
2000b *Petunjuk pelaksanaan tata cara pemberian ijin hak pemungutan hasil hutan melalui permohonan dengan luas maksimal 100 Ha*, No. 2. Putussibau, Kalimantan Barat:
2001 *Prosedur tetap permohonan ijin hak pemungutan hasil hutan dengan luas maksimal 100 Ha*, No. 8. Putussibau, Kalimantan Barat.

Keputusan Dewan Perwakilan Rakyat Daerah Kabupaten Kapuas Hulu (Kep-DPRD)
2006 *Persetujuan pembentukan Kabupaten Sentarum dan Kabupaten di Wilayah Perbatasan Kabupaten Kapuas Hulu*, No. 8. Putussibau, Kalimantan Barat.

Keputusan Menteri Kehutanan (Kepmenhut)
2004 *Rencana stratejik pengelolaan kawasan hutan wilayah perbatasan RI-Malaysia di Kalimantan*, No. SK.55.

Keputusan Presiden Republik Indonesia (Keppres)
1994 *Badan pengendali pembangunan kawasan perbatasan*, No. 44.
1999 *Cabutan keputusan presiden nomor 44 tahun 1994 tentang badan pengendali pelaksanaan pembangunan wilayah perbatasan di Kalimantan*, No. 63.
2001 *Dewan pengembangan kawasan timur Indonesia*, No. 55 (25 April).
2003 *Penataan ruang kawasan perbatasan Kalimantan, Sarawak dan Sabah*. Draft Ke-7, Direktorat Jenderal Penataan Ruang (16 October).

Kessel, O. van
1850 'Statistieke aanteekeningen omtrent het stroomgebied der rivier Kapoeas (Westerafdeeling van Borneo)', *Indisch Archief* 1:165-2004.

Keterangan pemerintah (Ketpem)
2005   *Kebijakan pembangunan daerah di depan sidang paripurna dewan perwakilan daerah republik Indonesia* (23 August).

Kielstra, E. B.
1890   'Bijdragen tot de geschiedenis van Borneo's Westerafdelingen', *De Indische gids* 12:1090-1112, 1482-1501.

Kimura, Ehito
2006   Provincial proliferation: Vertical coalitions and the politics of territoriality in post-authoritarian Indonesia. PhD thesis, University of Wisconsin, Madison, WI.
2007   'Marginality and opportunity in the periphery: The emergence of Gorontalo Province in North Sulawesi', *Indonesia* 84:71-95.

King, Victor T.
1976a   'Migration, warfare, and cultural contact in Borneo: A critique of ecological analysis', *Oceania* 46: 306-27.
1976b   'Some aspects of Iban-Maloh contact in West Kalimantan', *Indonesia* 21:85-114.
1990   'Why is Sarawak peripheral?' in: Victor T. King and Michael J.G. Parnwell (eds), *Margins and minorities: The peripheral areas and peoples of Malaysia*, pp. 110-129. Hull, England: Hull University Press.
2001   "A question of identity: Names, societies, and ethnic groups in interior Kalimantan and Brunei Darussalam', *Sojourn* 16:1-36.

King, Victor T. and Jayum A. Jawan
1996   'The Ibans of Sarawak, Malaysia: Ethnicity, marginalization and development', in: D. Dwyer and D. Drakakis-Smith (eds), *Ethnicity and development: Geographical perspectives*, pp. 195-214. Chichester, England: John Wiley.

Klinken, Gerry van
2001   'The coming crisis in Indonesian area studies', *Journal of Southeast Asian Studies* 32:263-8.
2004   'Dayak ethnogenesis and conservative politics in Indonesia's outer islands', in: Henk Schulte Nordholt and H. Samuel (eds), *Indonesia in Transition: Rethinking "civil society", "region" and "crisis"*, pp. 107-28. Yogyakarta: Pustaka Pelajar.
2008a   'Blood, timber, and the state in West Kalimantan, Indonesia', *Asia Pacific Viewpoint* 49:35-47.

2008b	'The state and illegality in indonesia', *South East Asia Research* 16:157-63.

Kompas

1999a	'Badau, kompleks di perbatasan Kalbar dan Sarawak: Masing raba-raba dan muluk-muluk', 18 August.
1999b	'Warga Malaysia ditahan', 23 June.
2000a	'Hutan jadi korban tarik-menarik pusat-daerah', 23 November.
2000b	'Kejar pencuri kayu, Indonesia dituduh langgar batas Malaysia', 1 July.
2000c	'Malaysia belum tanggapi soal pencurian kayu', 4 July.
2000d	'Terdakwa tewas dihakimi massa', 14 December.
2000e	'Warga perbatasan terhimpit isolasi', 16 August.
2000f	'Masyarakat perbatasan Kalimantan-Sarawak terasing di negerinya sendiri', 7 August.
2001	'Jalan rusak, isolasi fisik makin parah', 8 June.
2002	'Pos Lintas Batas Badau dibangun', 22 April.
2003a	'Cukong kayu illegal asal Malaysia belum tertangkap', 23 July.
2003b	'Indonesia bangsaku, ringgit uangku', 21 March.
2003c	'Operasi Wanalaga II tahan 116 pelaku penebangan liar', 17 June.
2003d	'Seribu truk bawa kayu curian ke Malaysia', 16 June.
2003e	'Warga Malaysia gunakan KTP Kapuas Hulu dalam penebangan ilegal', 1 October.
2004a	'Babat hutan, 3 WN Malaysia ditangkap', 9 December.
2004b	'Cukong kayu asal Malaysia menjadi "Raja"', 24 August.
2004c	'Dukung Kapolda tuntaskan illegal logging', 11 August.
2004d	'Hutan makin rusak, industri kayu makin sulit', 25 September.
2004e	'Lima bupati di Kalbar tahan Dana PSDH/DR hingga 302.6 miliar', 13 January.
2004f	'Mobil ilegal semakin marak di Kalbar', 18 May.
2004g	'Pengiriman kayu illegal ke Malaysia masih terjadi', 28 July.
2004h	'Rebutan kayu di perbatasan Malaysia', 13 January.
2005a	'2.000 km jalan dibangun di perbatasan Kalimantan', June 24.
2005b	'Menhut: Masyrakat adapt dilarang terbitkan izin penebangan hutan', 29 March.
2005c	'Penyelundupan kayu ke Malaysia marak lagi', 2 July.
2005d	'TNI tambah 30 pos perbatasan RI-Malaysia', 17 March.
2005e	'Warga protes Operasi Hutan Lestari', 23 March.

2005f	'Wartawan TV5 dan tim olah TKP digelandang massa di Pontianak', 15 January.
2005g	'WN Malaysia ditangkap', 21 March.
2007	'Pemekaran wilayah perbatasan jadi prioritas', 11 September.

Kroef, Justus M. van der
1963	'Indonesia, Malaya, and the North Borneo crisis', *Asian Survey* 3:173-81.
1970	'Indonesian communism since the 1965 coup', *Pacific Affairs* 43:34-60.
1968	'The Sarawak-Indonesia border insurgency', *Modern Asian Studies* 2:245-65.

Kuyah, Fredrik
1992	*Pengaruh pembangunan terhadap peningkatan masyarakat perbatasan kabupaten Kapuas Hulu*. Lokaraya Hukum dan Pembangunan Masyarakat Perbatasan Kabupaten Kapuas Hulu, Lanjak 5-8 December.

Kyodo News International
2000	'Indonesian mob kills suspect under judge's table', 13 December.

Layang, Jacobus Frans
2006	*Implikasi ketertinggalan pembangunan kawasan perbatasan terhadap ketahanan nasional*. Pontianak, 3 Kalbar: Romeo Grafika Pontianak.

Leimgrubber, W.
1991	'Boundary, values and identity: The Swiss-Italian transborder region', in: D. Rumley and J.V. Minghi (eds), *The geography of border landscapes*, pp. 43-62. London: Routledge.

Li, Tania Murray
2005	'Beyond "the state" and failed schemes', *American Anthropologist* 107:383-94.

Lijnden, D.W.C. van and J. Groll.
1851	'Aanteekeningen over de landen van het stroomgebied der Kapoeas', *Natuurkundig Tijdschrift voor Nederlansche-Indie* 2:537-636.

Lorens
2006	*Kelapa sawit sang primadona: Suatu analysis pembangunan perkebunan kelapa sawit di kabupaten wilayah perbatasan Indonesia-Malaysia, provinsi Kalimantan Barat*. Jakarta: WWF Indonesia, Forest Conversion Initiative Program (May).

LKPDPI *see* PPKPU 2007
Lumenta, Dave
2001 'Reconstructing Iban identities over a glass of tuak: Notes from a field trip to the Batang Kanyau Iban in West Kalimantan', *Antropologi Indonesia* 66:110-3.
2005 'Borderland identity construction within a market place of narrative: Preliminary notes on the Batang Kanyau Iban in West Kalimantan', *Masyarakat Indonesia-Majalah Ilmu-Ilmu Social Indonesia* 30:1-26.
Lund, Christian
2006a 'Twilight institutions: An introduction', *Development and Change* 37:673-84.
2006b 'Twilight institutions: Public authority and local politics in Africa', *Development and Change* 37:685-705.
2007 *Twilight institutions. Public authority and local politics in Africa.* London: Blackwell.
Mackie, J.A.C.
1974 *Konfrontasi: The Indonesia-Malaysia dispute 1963-1966.* Kuala Lumpur: Oxford University Press.
Majid, Harun Abdul
2007 *Rebellion in Brunei: The 1962 revolt, imperialism, confrontation and oil.* London/New York: I.B.Tauris.
Martínez, Oscar J.
1994a *Border people: Life and society in the U.S.-Mexico borderlands.* Tucson/London: The University of Arizona Press.
1994b 'The dynamics of border interaction: New approaches to border analysis', in: Clive H. Schofield (ed.), *Global boundaries: World boundaries,* Vol. 1, pp. 1-15. London: Routledge.
Mashman, Valerie
1991 *Warriors and weavers: A study of gender relations among the Iban of Sarawak.* Williamsburg, VA: The College of William and Mary.
McCarthy, John F.
2000 *"Wild logging": The rise and fall of logging networks and biodiversity conservation projects on Sumatra's rainforest frontier.* Bogor, Indonesia: Center for International Forestry Research.
2002 'Power and interest on Sumatra's rainforest frontier: Clientelist coalitions, illegal logging and conservation in the Alas Valley', *Journal of Southeast Asian Studies* 33:77-106.

2004	'Changing to gray: Decentralization and the emergence of volatile socio-legal configurations in Central Kalimantan, Indonesia', *World Development* 32:1199-223.
2006	*The fourth circle: A political ecology of Sumatra's rainforest frontier*. Stanford, CA: Stanford University Press.
2007	'Sold down the river: Renegotiating public power over nature in central Kalimantan', in: Henk Schulte Nordholt and Gerry van Klinken (eds), *Renegotiating boundaries: Local politics in post-Suharto Indonesia*, pp. 152-76. Leiden: KITLV Press.

McCoy, Alfred W.

1999	'Requiem for a drug lord: State and commodity in the career of Khun Sa', in: J.M. Heyman (ed.), *States and illegal practices*, pp. 129-67. Oxford: Berg.

McKeown, Francis

1983	The Merakai Iban: An ethnographic account with special reference to dispute settlement. PhD thesis, Monash University, Clayton, VIC.

McMichael, Scott R.

1987	*A historical perspective on light infantry*. Fort Leavenworth, KS: Research survey, Combat Studies Institute 6.

Media Indonesia

2000a	'Otonomi daerah dan konflik lingkungan', 26 September.
2000b	'Peneliti asing di Kalbar tinggalkan taman nasional: Cukong kayu paksa ubah peta', 18 August.
2004	'Belum ada fakta gangster Malaysia kuasai perbatasan', 25 April.
2005a	'Masyarakat Kapuas minta polisi tidak segal kayu hutan adat', 29 March.
2005b	'Pembangunan perbatasan: Eksplotasi tanpa pertimbangan ekonomi', 1 November.

Merry, Sally Engle

1988	'Legal pluralism', *Law & Society Review* 22:869-96.

Migdal, J.S.

1994	'The state in society: An approach to struggles for domination', in J.S. Migdal, A. Kohli and V. Shue (eds), *State power and social forces: Domination and transformation in the Third World*, pp. 7-36. Cambridge: Cambridge University Press.

2001 *State in society: Studying how states and societies transform and constitute one another*. Cambridge: Cambridge University Press

2004 'Mental maps and virtual checkpoints: Struggles to construct and maintain state and social boundaries', in: J.S. Migdal (ed.), *Boundaries and belonging: States and societies in struggle to shape identities and local practices*, pp. 3-26. Cambridge: Cambridge University Press.

Milne, R.S.

1973 'Patrons, clients and ethnicity: The case of Sarawak and Sabah in Malaysia', *Asian Survey* 13:891-907.

Minghi, J.V.

1963 'Boundary studies in political geography', *Annals of the Association of American Geographers* 53:407-28.

Moore, S.F.

1973 'Law and social change: The semi-autonomous social field as an appropriate subject of study', *Law & Society Review* 7:719-46.

1975 'Epilogue: Uncertainties in situations, indeterminacies in culture', in: S.F. Moore and B.G. Myerhoff (eds), *Symbol and politics in communal ideology: Cases and questions*, pp. 210-39. Ithaca, NY: Cornell University Press.

1978 *Law as process: An anthropological approach*. London: Routledge & Kegan Paul.

Morishita, Akiko

2008 'Contesting power in Indonesia's resource-rich regions in the era of decentralization: New strategy for central control over the regions', *Indonesia* 86:81-107.

New Straits Times

2000a 'Bordermarkers: Probe under way', 17 June.

2000b 'Indonesia insists all four were logging in its territory', 12 July.

2005 'Cops, soldiers in car ring banished', 31 October.

Niclou, H.A.A.

1887 'Batang-Loepars-Verdelging-oorlog: Europeesch-Dajaksche sneltocht', *Tijdschrift voor Nederlandsch-Indie* 16:29-67.

Nugent, Paul and A.I. Asiwaju

1996 *African boundaries: Barriers, conduits, and opportunities*. London/New York: Pinter.

O'Dowd, Liam and Thomas M. Wilson (eds)

1996 *Borders, nations and states*. Aldershot, England: Avebury.

Obidzinski, Krystof
2003   Logging in East Kalimantan, Indonesia: The historical expedience of illegality. PhD thesis Universiteit van Amsterdam.
Obidzinski, Krystof, Agus Andrianto and Chandra Wijaya
2006   *Timber smuggling in Indonesia: Critical or overstated problem? Forest governance lessons from Kalimantan.* Bogor, Indonesia: Center for International Forestry Research.
2007   'Cross-border timber trade in Indonesia: critical or overstated problem? Forest governance lessons from Kalimantan', *International Forestry Review* 9:526-35.
Ominiyi, T.
1997   *My blood, my nation: Ethnicity and nationality as alternative and hierarchical identities in African borderlands.* Leuven, Belgium: ITL.
Ormeling, F.J.
1996   'J.J.K. Enthoven (1851-1925): Inspirerend promotor van de kartering in voormalig Nederlands-Indie' *Kartografisch Tijdschrift* XXII-2:7-14
Padoch, Christine
1982   *Migration and its alternatives among the Ibans of Sarawak.* The Hague: Martinus Nijhoff.
Peluso, Nancy Lee
1992   *Rich forests, poor people: Resource control and resistance in Java.* Berkeley, CA: University of California Press.
2005   'Passing the red bowl: Creating community identity through violence in West Kalimantan, 1967-1997', in: C.A. Coppel (ed.), *Violent conflicts in Indonesia: Analysis, representation, resolution,* pp. 83-116. New York: Routledge.
2008   'A political ecology of violence and territory in West Kalimantan', *Asia Pacific Viewpoint* 49:48-67.
Peluso, Nancy Lee and Emily Harwell
2001   'Territory, custom and the cultural politics of ethnic war in West Kalimantan, Indonesia', in: M. Watts and N.L. Peluso (eds),*Violent Environments,* pp. 106-128. Ithaca, NY: Cornell University Press.
Peraturan Presiden Republik Indonesia (Perpres)
2005a   *Pengadaan tanah bagi pelaksaan pembangunan untuk kepentingan umum.* [Perpres 36.]
2005b   *Rencana pembangunan janka menengah 2005-2009.* [Perpres 7.]

2005c *Rencana tata ruang kawasan perbatasan negara di kalimantan*. Draft KE-14, Direktorat Jenderal Penataan Ruang (18 August).

Perdu

1999 *Pengusahaan hutan dan pemungutan hutan pada hutan produksi*. Peraturan Pemerintah Republik Indonesia 6.

2002 *Tata hutan dan penyusunan rencana pengelolaan hutan, pemanfaatan hutan dan pengunaan kawasan hutan*. Peraturan Pemerintah Republik Indonesia 32

2007 *Tata hutan dan penyusunan rencana pengelolaan hutan, serta pemanfaatan hutan*. Peraturan Pemerintah Republik Indonesia 6.

Pergub

2005 *Pembentukan badan persiapan pengembangan kawasan khusus provinsi Kalimantan Barat*. Peraturan Gubernur Provinsi Kalimantan Barat, Pergub 161.

Perhut Kapuas Hulu

2007 *Rencana anggaran biaya kegiatan pengelolaan perbatasan RI-Malaysia di Kabupaten Kapuas Hulu, tahun 2008-2009*. Dinas perkebunan dan kehutanan, Kabupaten Kapuas Hulu (February).

Persero

2005 *Pembangunan kawasan perbatasan melalui pembangunan perkebunan kelapa sawit di propinsi Kalimantan Barat*. PT Perkebunan Nusantara 1-14.

Pirous, Iwan Meulia

2002 'Life on the border: Iban between two nations'. *Latitudes Magazine* 20:1-8.

PKB

2005a 'Jumpa pers bersama president RI, Susilo Bambang Yudhoyono', *Berita Pemerintah Kalimantan Barat* (24 June).

2005b 'Menteri pembangunan daerah tertinggal adakan kunjungan kerja kalbar', *Berita Pemerintah Kalimantan Barat*

2005c 'Presiden SBY: Kalbar sangat potensial untuk maju'. *Berita Pemerintah Kalimantan Barat* (23 June).

PMARI

2006 'Demi keadilan berdasarkan ketuhanan yang maha esa – Perkara tentang: illegal logging, penyelundupan, izin imigrasi'. *Putusan Mahkamah Agung Republik Indonesia*, No.50 PK/Pid/2006 (24 July).

Pontianak Post

2000a	'400 massa bersenjata serang PN Kapuas Hulu', 14 December.
2000b	'Andi: Daerah terancam chaos', 21 December.
2000c	'Kalbar terancam kehilangan arealny'a, 16 November.
2000d	'Keluarga Usnata lapor ke president', 19 December.
2000e	'Pembunuh Usnata diminta serahkan diri', 24 December.
2000f	'Tak dipercaya', 19 December.
2001	'Perlu kehatian-hatian penegak hukum', 4 October.
2002	'West Kalimantan-Sarawak border wall could prevent illegal logging', 15 February.
2003a	'Sepekan, ratusan truk kayu keluar masuk Badau', 16 September.
2003b	'Tak ada kewenangan', 16 October.
2003c	'Tambul: Tak berpihak ke rakyat kecil, SK HPH 100 Ha dicabut, 34 ribu pekerja nganggur', 4 October.
2004a	'150 truk/hari dicuri lewat Badau', 15 June.
2004b	'Apheng, DPO illegal logging no.1 Kalbar', 28 July.
2004c	'Banyak satwa liar diselundupkan lewat perbatasan', 31 May.
2004d	'"Gangster" cina dari Malaysia jarah hutan: Setiap bulan, Kalbar rugi Rp 8 M', 24 April.
2004e	'Imigrasi janji tankap Apheng: Penjarah kayu perbatasan Kalbar', 15 September.
2004f	'Isu gangster di perbatasan, razia digelar', 22 May.
2004g	'Lalulintas truk kayu kembali normal', 20 April.
2004h	'Pemerintah setuju badan otonomi perbatasan perjuangan panjang menggolkan status border Entikong', 7 August.
2004i	'PLB dibuka, illegal logging kian menggila difalitasi oleh pengusha Malaysia', 24 June.
2004j	'Tanggapan bupati atas illegal logging: Bupati Kapuas Hulu, Abang Tambul Husin', 11 August.
2004k	'Tim Wanalaga berdatangan ke perbatasan', 6 March.
2004l	'Tim wanalaga sita kayu illegal di perbatasan', 16 March.
2004m	'Tim Wanalaga tak trasparan: Peras pengusaha kayu perbatasan', 28 July.
2005a	'Buka lahan sawit sepanjang perbatasan: Strategi baru amankan batas Malaysia-Kalimantan', 10 May.
2005b	'Jika terkena air, tak mau basah sendiri-Pengakuan Apeng; Buron Polda Kalbar terkait illegal logging', 11 October.

| 2005c | 'Masyarakat perbatasan minta solusi illegal logging', 4 April.
| 2005d | 'Pasca razia, penjarahan kayu berlanjut', 10 February.
| 2005e | 'TNI AD Dukung sawit perbatasan', 1 December.
| 2005f | 'TNI tambah 7 pos perbatasan-Bambang: Pecat oknum TNI terlibat illegal log-ging', 4 May.
| 2005g | 'Warga perbatasan masih harapkan Malaysia', 24 May.
| 2006a | 'Bangun kawasan perbatasan, segera terbitkan Peppres', 6 November.
| 2006b | 'TNI tempatkan 600 personil: Jaga sepanjang perbatasan Kalbar', 2 August.
| 2007a | 'Aznoor: Malaysia belum tentukan PPLB prioritas', 26 February.
| 2007b | 'Diprotes, moratorium daerah', 15 November.
| 2007c | 'Kalla desak hentikan pemekaran daerah', 14 November.
| 2007d | 'TNI AD kaji skuadron heli di perbatasan', 7 March.

Porritt, Vernon L.
| 2004 | *The rise and fall of communism in Sarawak 1940-1990.* Clayton, VIC: Monash University Press.
| 2006 | 'Tim Hardy: Special Branch, Sarawak, December 1961-March 1968', *Borneo Research Bulletin* 37:69-85.

PPKPU
| 2007 | *Gambaran umum kelayakan pemekaran pembentukan Kabupaten Perbatasan Utara di Kapuas Hulu, Kalimantan Barat.* Panitia Pembentukan Kabupaten Perbatasan Utara (PPKPU) dengan Lembaga Kajian Pemerintahan Daerah dan Pembangunan Indonesia (LKP-DPI).

PPNP
| 2005 | Pekara tentang: Illegal logging, penyelundupan, izin imigrasi. *Putusan Pengadilan Negeri Putussibau, No. 10/PID.B/2005/P.N.PTSB* (18 Juli).

Prescott, J.R.W.
| 1987 | *Political frontiers and boundaries.* London: Allen and Unwin.

Pringle, R.
| 1970 | *Rajahs and rebels: The Ibans of Sarawak under Brooke rule 1871-1941.* London: Macmillan.

Pugsley, Christopher
| 2003 | *From emergency to confrontation: The New Zealand armed forces in Malaya and Borneo 1949-1966.* Oxford: Oxford University Press.

Rachman, Ansar, Ahmad Mansjur, Lettu Salijo and Staff Semdam XII Tanjungpura
1970 *Tanjungpura Berdjuang-Sejarah Kodam XII/Tanjungpura, Kalimantan Barat*. Ponti-anak: Kodam Tanjungpura, Kalimantan Barat

Rahman, Mohd Daud Bin Abdul
1972 *The threat of armed communism in Sarawak*. Kuala Lumpur: Penchetak Kerajaan.

Razzaz, Omar M.
1994 'Contestation and mutual adjustment: The process of controlling land in Yajouz, Jordan', *Law & Society Review* 28:7-39.

Republika
2005 "Sebanyak 178 cukong kayu WNA ditangkap", 27 July.

Resosudarmo, Ida Aju Pradnja
2003 'Shifting power to the periphery: The impact of decentralization on forest and forest people', in: E. Aspinall and G. Fealy (eds), *Local power and politics in Indonesia*, pp. 230-44. Singapore: Institute of Southeast Asian Studies (ISEAS).

Rinaldi, Taufik, Marini Purnomo and Dewi Damayanti
2007 'Fighting corruption in decentralized Indonesia', *The local government corruption study (LGCS)*. [Jakarta]: The World Bank.

Riwanto, Tirtosudarmo
2002 'West Kalimantan as "border area": A political-demography perspective', *Antropologi Indonesia Special Issue*, pp. 1-14.

Rösler, Michael and Tobias Wendl
1999 *Frontiers and borderlands: Anthropological perspectives*. Frankfurt am Main, Germany: Peter Lang.

Roniger, L., J. Smelser Neil and B. Baltes Paul
2001 'Patron-client relationships, Anthropology of.' in: *International Encyclopedia of the Social & Behavioral Sciences*, pp. 11118-20. Oxford: Pergamon.

Roth, Dik
2007 'Many governors, no province: The struggle for a province in the Luwu-Tana Toraja area in South Sulawesi', in: Henk Schulte Nordholt and Gerry van Klinken (eds), *Renegotiating Boundaries: Local politics in post-Suharto Indonesia*, pp. 121-47. Leiden: KITLV Press.

Sandin , Benedict
1967 *The Sea Dayaks of Borneo before White Rajah rule.* London: Macmillan.
1994 'Sources of Iban traditional history', *The Sarawak Museum Journal, Special Monograph* 7.
Sarawak Tribune
1990 'Armed Communist units to leave Sarawak jungles', 18 October.
Sather, Clifford
1996 'All threads are white: Iban egalitarianism reconsiderd', in: J. Fox and C. Sather (eds), *Orgins, ancestry and alliance,* pp. 70-110. Canberra, ACT: Research School of Pacific and Asian Studies, The Australian National University.
2004 'Iban', in: O.K. Gin (ed.), *Southeast Asia: A historical encyclopedia from Angkor Wat to East Timor. Vol. 2,* pp. 623-6. Santa Barbara, CA: ABC-Clio.
Schendel, Willem van
1993 'Easy come, easy go: Smugglers on the Ganges', *Journal of Contemporary Asia* 23:189-213.
2005a 'Spaces of engagement: How borderlands, illicit flows, and territorial states interlock', in: Willem van Schendel and Itty Abraham (eds), *Illicit flows and criminal things: States, borders, and the other side of globalization,* pp. 38-68. Bloomington and Indianapolis: Indiana University Press.
2005b *The Bengal borderland: Beyond state and nation in South Asia.* London: Anthem.
Schendel, Willem van and Itty Abraham (eds)
2005 *Illicit flows and criminal things: States, borders, and the other side of globalization.* Bloomington and Indianapolis: Indiana University Press.
Schmidt, Steffen W., Laura Guasti, Carl H. Landé and James C. Scott (eds)
1977 *Friends, followers, and factions: A reader in political clientelism.* Berkeley, CA: University of California Press.
Schoenberger, Laura and Sarah Turner
2008 'Negotiating remote borderland access: Small-scale trade on the Vietnam-China border', *Development and Change* 39:667-96.
Schulte Nordholt, Henk and Gerry van Klinken
2007a 'Introduction', in: Henk Schulte Nordholt and Gerry van Klinken (eds), *Renegotiating boundaries: Local politics in post-Suharto Indonesia,* pp. 1-29. Leiden: KITLV Press.

2007b	*Renegotiating boundaries: Local politics in post-Suharto Indonesia.* Leiden: KITLV Press.

Scott, James C.

1972	'The erosion of patron-client bonds and social change in rural Southeast Asia', *The Journal of Asian Studies* 32:5-37.
1977	'Patron-client politics and political change in Southeast Asia', in: S.W. Schmidt, L. Guasti, C.H. Landé and J.C. Scott (eds), *Friends, followers, and factions: A reader in political clientelism*, pp. 123-46. Berkeley, CA: University of California Press.
1985	*Weapons of the weak: Everyday forms of peasant resistance.* New Haven, CT: Yale University Press.
1998	*Seeing like a state: How certain schemes to improve the human condition have failed.* New Haven, CT: Yale University Press.
2008	'"Stilled to silence at 500 metres": Making sense of historical change in Southeast Asia', *IIAS Newsletter* 49:12-13.
2009	*The art of not being governed: An anarchist history of upland Southeast Asia.* New Haven, CT: Yale University Press.

Sharma, Aradhana and Akhil Gupta

2006	*The anthropology of the state: A reader.* Malden, MA: Blackwell.

Siburian, Robert

2002	'Entikong: Daerah tanpa krisis ekonomi di perbatasan Kalimantan Barat-Sarawak', *Antropologi Indonesia* 67:87-93.

Sinar Harapan

2001	'Kawasan HPH dirambah penebang bercukong', 24 July.
2003a	'Dana tak terbatas untuk tumpas penyelundup kayu di Kalbar', 18 June.
2003b	'PPLB Badau dirampungkan tahun 2004', 12 May.
2004a	'Cukong kayu Malaysia masuk daftar buronan', 29 October.
2004b	'"Gangster" bersenjata Malaysia dilarporkan kuasai perbatasan'. 22 April.
2004c	'Mabes Polri didesak buru 16 penjarah hutan Kalbar', 26 April.
2004d	'Pembalakan liar di perbatasan Indonesia-Malaysia (2): Korupsi, judi dan nar-koba jadi pemicu konflik', 6 May.
2004e	'Pembalakan liar di perbatasan Indonesia-Malaysia (3-habis): Hukum lemah, hutan pun hilang', 7 May.
2005a	'Cerita tentang cukong kayu DPO Mabes Polri', 8 October.

2005b	'Dephan tolak bertanggung jawab tunggakan Yamaker', 26 March.
2005c	'Malaysia lebih unggul dalam strategi pertahanan darat', 8 March.
2005d	'Pembalakan liar di perbatasan Indonesia-Malaysia (1) Miliaran rupiah menguap ke negara tetangga', 5 May.
2005e	'Perkebunan kelapa sawit di perbatasan: Menjaga batas atau menjarah hutan?' 29 November.
2006	'Wilayah perbatasan jadi prioritas pemekaran', 18 March.
2007	'40 tahun rujuk Malaysia-Indonesia: Malaysia lebih leluasa nikmati perbatasan (1)', 9 August.
2008	'Hutan adat Sungai Utik dipertahankan puluhan tahun', 8 August.
2009	'TNI babat kelapa sawit Malaysia di Perbatasan', 3 July.

Skeldon, Ronald
1999   'Migration in Asia after the economic crisi', *Asia Pacific Population Journal* 14:3-24.

Smart, Alan
1999   'Predatory rule and illegal economic practices', in: J.M. Heyman (ed.), *States and illegal practices*, pp. 99-128. Oxford: Berg.

Smith, Neil
1999   *Nothing short of war: With the Australian army in Borneo 1962-66.* Brighton, VIC: Citadel.

Sodhy, Pamela
1988   'Malaysian-American relations during Indonesia's confrontation against Malaysia, 1963-66', *Journal of Southeast Asian Studies* 19:111-36.

Soemadi
1974   *Peranan Kalimantan Barat dalam menghadapi subversi komunis Asia Tenggara: Suatu tinjauan internasional terhadap gerakan komunis dari sudut pertahanan wilayah khususnya Kalimantan Barat.* Pontianak, Kalbar: Yayasan Tanjungpura.

Stockwell, A.J.
2004   'Britain and Brunei, 1945-1963: Imperial retreat and royal ascendancy', *Modern Asian Studies* 38:785-819.

The Straits Times
2000   '"Killer" lynched by mob in court', 15 December.

Strassoldo, Raimondo
1989 'Border studies', in: A.I. Asiwaju and P.O. Adeniyi (eds), *Borderlands in Africa: A multidisciplinary and comparative focus on Nigeria and West Africa*, pp. 383-95. Lagos, NG: University of Lagos Press.

Sturgeon, Janet C.
1997 'Claiming and naming resources on the border of the state: Akha strategies in China and Thailand', *Asia Pacific Viewpoint* 38:131-44.
2004 'Border practices, boundaries, and the control of resource access: A case from China, Thailand and Burma', *Development and Change* 35:463-84.
2005 *Border landscapes: The politics of Akha land use in China and Thailand*. Seattle and London: University of Washington Press.

Suara Bekakak
2006 'Kawasan perbatasan bukan untuk sawit, masyarakat berdaulat atas pengelolaan sumber daya', in: *Berita triwulan Taman Nasional Danau Sentarum*.15/Th.6. [July-September.]

Surya Citra Televisi (SCTV)
2007 'Apeng, buron pembalakan liar yang masih bebas', *Liputan 6* (23 June).

Suara Karya
2006 'Pengamanan wilayah perbatasan diperketat', 19 May.
2007a 'Kapolda: Tak ada "jalan tikus" di Kalbar', 7 August.
2007b 'Mendagri: Pemekaran belum sejahterakan rakyat', 19 September.

Suara Pembaruan
2000 'Sengketa perbatasan yang berawal dari berebut hasil hutan', 11 September.
2003 'Lika-liku praktik illegal logging di Kalbar: Malaysia makan buahnya, Indonesian telan getahnya', 9 May.
2004a 'Kapan "penjajahan" Malaysia di perbatasan Kalbar berakhir?', 22 December.
2004b 'Mafia Malaysia babat hutan di perbatasan Kalbar', 22 April.

Subritzky, John
2000 *Confronting Sukarno*. New York: St. Martin's.

Sulistyorini, Pembayun
2004 'Pemberontakan PGRS/PARAKU di Kalimantan Barat', *Jurnal Sejarah dan Budaya Kalimantan* 3:39-79.

The Sunday Post
2007 'Security posts proposed for border villages', 4 February.
Sundhausen, Ulf
1982 *The road to power: Indonesian military politics 1945-1967*. Kuala Lumpur: Oxford University Press.
Susanto, Purwo
2005 *Survey kawasan perbatasan Indonesia-Malaysia wilayah Kalimantan Barat: Dari beranda belakang menuju ke serambi depan*. Jakarta: WWF Indonesia -Forest Conversion Initiaive Program (October).
Sutlive, Vinson
1988 *The Iban of Sarawak*. Arlington Heights, IL: AHM Publishing.
1989 'The Iban in Historical Perspective', *The Sarawak Museum Journal* 40-61:33-43.
Tagliacozzo, Eric
1999 Secret trades of the straits: Smuggling and state-formation along a Southeast Asian frontier, 1870-1910. PhD thesis, Yale University, New Haven, CT.
2001 'Border permeability and the state in Southeast Asia: Contraband and regional security', *Contemporary Southeast Asia: A Journal of International & Strategic Affairs* 23:254.
2002 'Smuggling in Southeast Asia: History and its contemporary vectors in an unbound region', *Critical Asian Studies* 34:193-220.
2005 *Secret trades, porous borders: Smuggling and states along a Southeast Asian frontier, 1865-1915*. New Haven, CT: Yale University Press.
Tan, Gabriel
2008 *Indonesian confrontation and Sarawak Communist insurgency 1963-1966*. Kuching, Sarawak: Penerbitan Sehati Sdn. Bhd.
Tanasaldy, Taufiq
2007 'Ethnic identity politics in West Kalimantan', in: Henk Schulte Nordholt and Gerry van Klinken (eds), *Renegotiating boundaries: Local politics in post-Suharto Indonesia*, pp. 349-71. Leiden: KITLV Press.
Tempo
1971a 'Sepucuk telegram dari gerombolan: Cerita di balik kamp PGRS', Edisi 33-01 16 October.
1971b 'Siapakah Kie Chok', Edisi 33-01, 16 October.
1974a '166.129 orang itu mau kemana; Dari WNA ke WNI', Edisi 24-04, 17 August.

1974b	'Agama and perut', Edisi 34-04, 26 October.
1974c	'Bedil Serawak', Edisi 27-04, 7 September.
1974d	'Membenahi perbatasan', Edisi 17-04, 29 June.
1974e	'Warga Negara Asing', Edisi 24-04, 17 August.
1987	'Vonis Datuk Hiew Ming Yun', Edisi 01-17, 7 March.
1989	'Paru-paru bumi koyak', Edisi 34-19, 21 October.
2001a	'All in the hands of the regents', (English edition) 30 July.
2001b	'Keadilan jalanan makin menakutkan', *Tempo Interaktif,* 8 January.
2005a	'Border integrity', (English edition) 50-5, 16-22 August.
2005b	'Pemerintah akan buka kebun sawit perbatasan', *Tempo Interaktif,* 28 June.
2005c	'Saya tidak takut ditangkap', *Tempo Interaktif,* 21 March.
2005d	'Tak kuasa menghadang penebang', *Tempo Interaktif,* 31 January.
2006	'Department Dalam Negeri susun RUU perbatasan', *Tempo Interaktif,* 20 January.
2008	'Presiden anggap perbatasan beranda depan negara. *Tempo Interaktif,* 15 August.

Thamrin, Surjono H. Sutjahjo, Catur Herison and Supiandi Sabiham
2007   'Sustainability analysis of West Kalimantan-Malaysian border for the development of agropolitan region', *Journal Agro Ekonomi* 25:103-24.

Thung, Ju-Lan, Yekti Maunati and Peter Mulok Kedit
2004   *The (re) construction of the 'Pan Dayak' identity in Kalimantan and Sarawak: A study on minority's identity, ethnicity and nationality.* Jakarta: Pusat Penelitian Kemasyarakatan dan Kebudayaan (PMB), The Indonesian Institute of Sciences (LIPI).

Tirtosudarmo, Riwanto
2002   'West Kalimantan as "Border area": A political-demography perspective', *Antropologi Indonesia*: XXVI, Special Volume:1-14.

Toyoda, Norioko
2002   'The troubled state of Kalimantan's forest: Local autonomy and Malaysian investments drive illegal logging in Indonesian Borneo', *The Borneo Project: Borneo Wire Newsletter* (Summer).

Trocki, Carl
2000   'Borders and the mapping of the Malay world'. Paper. Annual Meeting, Association of Asian Studies, San Diego, CA.

Tsing, Anna Lowenhaupt
1994   'From the Margins', *Cultural Anthropology* 9-3:279-97.

Tuck, Christopher
2004   'Borneo 1963-66: Counter-insurgency operations and war termination', *Small Wars and Insurgencies* 15:89-111.

Ung-Ho, Chin
1996   *Chinese politics in Sarawak: A study of the Sarawak United People's Party.* Oxford: Oxford University Press.

Utrechts Nieuwsblad
1912   'Koppensnellers', 9 March.

Vandergeest, Peter and Nancy Lee Peluso
2006   'Empires of forestry: Professional forestry and state power in Southeast Asia, Part 1', *Environment and History* 12:31-64.

Vel, Jacqueline
2007   'Campaigning for a new district in West Sumba', in: Henk Schulte Nordholt and Gerry van Klinken (eds), *Renegotiating Boundaries: Local politics in post-Suharto Indonesia.* pp. 91-119. Leiden: KITLV Press.

Veth, P.J.
1854   *Borneo's Wester-afdeeling, geographisch, statistisch, historisch,voorafgegaan door eene algemeene schets des ganschen eilands.* Zaltbommel, NL: Joh. Noman en Zoon.

Wadley, Reed L.
1997   Circular labor migration and subsistence agriculture: a case of the Iban in West Kalimantan, Indonesia. PhD thesis, Department of Anthropology, Arizona State University.
1997   'Variation and changing tradition in Iban land tenure', *Borneo Research Bulletin* 28: 98-108.
1998   'The road to change in the Kapuas Hulu borderlands: Jalan Lintas Utara', *Borneo Research Bulletin* 29:71-94.
2000a   'Reconsidering an ethnic label in Borneo: The Maloh of West Kalimantan, Indonesia', *Bijdragen tot de Taal-, Land- en Volkenkunde* 156:83-101.
2000b   'Transnational circular labour migration in northwestern Borneo', *Revue Européenne des Migrations Internationales* 16:127-49.
2000c   'Warfare, pacification, and environment: Population dynamics in the West Borneo borderlands, 1823-1934', *Moussons* 1:41166.
2001a   'Frontiers of death: Iban expansion and inter-ethnic relations in West Borneo', *International Institute for Asian Studies Newsletter* 24:14.

2001b	'Temenggong Jemat Rentap', in: V. Sutlive and J. Sutlive (eds), *The Encyclopaedia of Iban Studies*, 3:1844. Kuching, Malaysia: Tun Jugah Foundation.
2001c	'Trouble on the frontier: Dutch-Brooke relations and Iban rebellion in West Borneo borderlands (1841-1886), *Modern Asian Studies* 35:623-44.
2002a	'Border studies beyond Indonesia: A comparative perspective', *Antropologi Indonesia* 67:1-11.
2002b	'The history of displacement and forced settlement in West Kalimantan, Indonesia', in: D. Chatty and M. Colchester (eds), *Conservation and indigenous mobile peoples: Displacement, forced settlement and sustainable development*, pp. 313-328. Oxford: Berghahn.
2003	'Lines in the forest: Internal territorialization and local accommodation in West Kalimantan, Indonesia (1865-1979)', *South East Asia Research* 1:91-112.
2004	'Punitive expeditions and divine revenge: Oral and colonial histories of rebellion and pacification in western Borneo, 1886-1902', *Ethnohistory* 51:609-36.
2006	'Community cooperatives, "illegal" logging and regional autonomy in the borderlands of West Kalimantan', in: F.M. Cooke, *State, communities and forests in contemporary Borneo*, pp. 111-32. Canberra, ACT: ANU E Press.
2007	'Slashed and burned: War, environment, and resource insecurity in West Borneo during the late nineteenth and early twentieth centuries', *Journal of the Royal Anthropological Institute* (N.S.) 3:109-28.

Wadley, Reed L. and Michael Eilenberg
2005	'Autonomy, identity, and "illegal" logging in the borderland of West Kalimantan, Indonesia', *The Asia Pacific Journal of Anthropology* 6:19-34.
2006	'Vigilantes and gangsters in the borderland of West Kalimantan, Indonesia', in: A. Horstmann (ed.), *States, Peoples and Borders in Southeast Asia* (A Special Issue of the *Kyoto Review of Southeast Asia*) 7:1-24

Wadley, Reed L. and F. Kuyah
2001	'Iban communities in West Kalimantan', in V. Sutlive and J. Sutlive (eds), *The Encyclopaedia of Iban* 2:716-34,. Kuching, Malaysia: Tun Jugah Foundation.

Wadley, Reed L., R. Dennis, E. Meijaard, A. Erman, H. Valentinus, W. Giesen and A. Casson
2000 'After the conservation project: Danau Sentarum National Park and its vicinity: conditions and prospects', *Borneo Research Bulletin* 31:385-401.

Wagner, U.
1972 *Colonialism and Iban warfare*. Stockholm: OBE-Tryck Sthim.

Wahana Lingkungan Hidup *Indonesia* (WALHI)
2007 'There is still military in the forest', *Indonesian Forum for Environment* (27 June).

Wakker, Eric
2006 *The Kalimantan border oil palm mega-project*. AIDEnvironment (April).

Walker, Andrew
1996 'Borders, frontier communities and the state: Cross-river boat operators in Chiang Khong, Northern Thailand', *Canberra Anthropology* 19:1-28.
1999 *The legend of the golden boat: Regulation, trade and traders in the borderlands of Laos, Thailand, Burma and China*. Surrey, England: Curzon.
2006a 'Beyond hills and plains: Rethinking trade, state and society in the upper Mekong borderlands', in Willem van Schendel (ed.), *Underworlds and Borderlands*. Vol. 42: IIAS Newsletter 42 Special Issue (September).
2006b 'Beyond hills and plains: Rethinking trade, state and society in the upper Mekong borderlands', *International Institute for Asian Studies, IIAS Newsletter* 42:5.
2009 'Conclusion: Are the Mekong frontiers sites of exception?, in: M. Gainsborough (ed.), *On the border of state power: Frontiers in the Greater Mekong Sub-Region*, pp. 101-11. London and New York: Routledge.

The Wall Street Journal
2005 'Jobs vs. jungle in Borneo', 4-6 November.

Warren, Carol
2005 'Mapping common futures: Customary communities, NGOs and the state in Indonesia's reform era', *Development and Change* 36:49-73.

Weingrod, Alex
1977 'Patrons, patronage, and political parties', in: S.W. Schmidt, L. Guasti, C.H. Landé and J.C. Scott (eds), *Friends, followers, and factions: a reader in political clientelism*, pp. 323-36. Berkeley, CA: University of California Press.

Weinstein, Franklin B.
1969 *Indonesia abandons confrontation: An inquiry into the functions of Indonesian foreign policy*. Interim Report Series, Southeast Asia Program, Cornell University, Ithaca, NY.

Wilson, T.M.
2005 'Europe without borders: Remapping territory, citizenship, and identity in a transnational age', *JCMS: Journal of Common Market Studies* 43:414-5.

Wilson, Thomas and Hastings Donnan (eds)
1998a *Border identities: Nation and state at international frontiers*. Cambridge/New York: Cambridge University Press.
1998b 'Nation, state and identity at international borders', in: Thomas Wilson and Hastings Donnan (eds), *Border identities: Nation and state at international frontiers*. Cambridge/New York: Cambridge University Press.
2005a 'Territory, identity and the places in-between: Culture and power in European borderlands', in: Thomas Wilson and Hastings Donnan (eds), *Culture and power at the edges of the state*, pp. 1-29. Münster, Germany: LIT Verlag.
2005b *Culture and power at the edges of the state*. Münster, Germany: LIT Verlag.

Wollenberg, Eva, Moira Moeliono, Godwin Limberg, Ramses Iwan, Steve Rhee and Made Sudana
2006 'Between state and society: Local governance of forests in Malinau, Indonesia', *Forest Policy and Economics* 8:421-33.

Yasmi, Yurdi, Gusti Z. Anshari, Heru Komarudin and Syarif Alqadri
2006 'Stakeholder conflicts and forest decentralization policies in West Kalimantan: Their dynamics and implications for furture forest management', *Forests, Trees and Livelihoods* 16:167-80.

Yong, Kee Howe
2006 'Silences in history and nation-state: Reluctant accounts of the Cold War in Sarawak', *American Ethnologist* 33:462-73.

Index

Abrams, Philip 52
accounts, oral 78, 96, 101
actors 5, 51, 57, 65, 67, 69, 266
adat elders 14, 187-8
advancement 66, 95, 269-70
African borders 85
agency 6, 29, 238, 245, 258, 261
  local 33, 43-4, 53, 55, 59, 289
Agency for the Preparation of Special Border Area Development *see* Badan Persiapan Pengembangan Kawasan Khusus Perbatasan (BP2KKP)
agents 5-6, 23, 56, 121, 285, 291
  local border 286
Agrarian Land Law 255
agreement 149, 157, 176-7, 182, 195-7, 221, 226, 230, 241
agriculture, subsistence 30 *see also* swidden
ai Belanda 92
alliances 29, 53, 59-60, 78, 115, 182, 262, 266, 281-3, 287, 289
Amoy 133
amuk massa 210

Angkatan Bersenjata Republik Indonesia (ABRI) 132-3, 136, 141, 249, 297
Anglo-Dutch treaty 83
Apheng 164, 182-7, 189-91, 202, 215, 217-24, 228-31, 234, 252-3, 269
  apprehend 218, 223
  family clan 184
  patron 185
Apriantono, Anton 246
army 125, 127, 135, 188, 224, 249-54
Army Para-Commando Regiment *see* Resimen Para Komando Angkatan Darat (RPKAD)
Asian economic crisis 23, 161
Asiwaju 50, 85
assembly, provincial 218, 245-6, 274
Aswin, Aspar 147, 182
authority 5-7, 27-9, 54-5, 57-60, 75-8, 89-90, 167-70, 190-1, 221-2, 255-6, 281, 283-5
  central 226, 228, 281
  increased 169-70
  non-state forms of 54, 198, 284, 288

public 13-4, 54
autonomy 7, 34, 68, 105, 132, 159, 167, 172, 195, 200, 258, 285
Azahari, A.M. 116

Badan Pengendali Pelaksanaan Pembangunan Wilayah Perbatasan (BP3WPK) 238
Badan Perencanaan Pembangunan Daerah (Bappeda) 240
Badan Perencanaan Pembangunan Nasional (Bappenas) 128, 240-3, 267, 281
Badan Persiapan Pengembangan Kawasan Khusus Perbatasan (BP2KKP) 245
Badau 2, 13, 18, 142-3, 168, 173-4, 183, 185-7, 230-1, 243-4, 268-9, 276
  border point 243
  border town of 35, 209, 213, 218-9, 252, 299
bandits 66-7, 106
Bantin 98-101, 103, 157
bargaining power 61
Basic Forestry Law 151
Batang Lupar, subdistrict of 17
Batang Lupar Dayaks 88-9
Batang Lupars 17-8, 30, 70-2, 89-90, 94, 100, 104, 131, 186, 217
Batavia 84, 87
Batu Bankai 102
Batu Lintang 117, 121
Belanda 92
Bengkayang 263
Betung Kerihun National Park *see* Taman Negara Betung Kerihun
bonds, cross-border ethnic 25

border
  access 262, 276, 291
  advantage 24, 31
  the anthropology of 45
  area 7, 21-2, 26-7, 128, 136-7, 214-5, 218-9, 238-43, 245-52, 266-70, 274-7, 279-80
  autonomy 34, 262
  Basic Agreement 1967 21, 124
  boom economy 169, 193, 195
  checkpoint 175
  chiefs 56, 148
  colonial Borneo 85
  committee 269, 274-5
  conceptualizing 49
  confrontation 76
  contested 34, 289
  Dayaks 78
  demarcations 45
  development 3, 129, 237, 239, 241-2, 245, 262, 289
  development plans 3, 293
  district committee 293
  districts 3, 127, 168, 180, 244, 246, 270, 279-80
  formation 33
  gates 243-4
  guards 106
  hills 2, 39-40, 105, 123, 133, 264, 275
  Iban 91, 95, 126, 193-4, 199, 293
  infrastructure 12, 19, 220, 237, 244, 247
  law draft 244
  lawless 210, 244, 290
  militarization 76, 250, 261
  movement 265-7, 277-81
  outlaws 98-9, 101, 105

patrols 94, 121
poles 245, 250
posts 21, 52, 96, 246, 276 *see also* Pos Lintas Batas (PLB)
provinces 242
rebels 66
road 13, 147, 166, 186, 217
security 247, 250
studies 43-5, 56
subdistricts 18, 181, 227, 277
towns 179, 190, 227
zones 205, 239
Border Community Care 295
Border Crossing Post *see* Pos Lintas Batas (PLB)
border districts
  new autonomous 258-9
  semi-autonomous 24
border dwelling Malay communities 32
border economy 142
  booming 185
border effect 60, 66, 291
border elite 4-6, 56, 64-5, 155-6, 178, 254-6, 258-9, 261-2, 264, 281, 286-7, 289-90
  act 65
  actors 289
  authority 60, 190
  collusion 76, 216
  members of 15, 63, 77
  movements 281
  power base 24, 76, 114
  strategies 261
border law official 246
border regions 3, 6, 15, 44-5, 48, 77, 128, 133, 153, 242, 291, 293
  lawless 6, 236

populated 281
remote 11, 22, 66
resource-rich 261, 276
under-developed 242
borderland 12-6, 23-8, 31-4, 43-50, 53-60, 75-8, 147-51, 165-71, 205-9, 211-3, 233-8, 286-92
  adjacent 5, 17, 33, 43, 46, 237, 283, 285
  adjoining 43, 290
  the anthropology of 45
  autonomy 261, 263, 265, 267, 269, 271, 273, 275, 277, 279, 281
  communities 21, 57, 126
  dynamics 6, 52, 69, 284
  experience 11, 159, 286
  fluctuating 284
  forested 114, 238
  history 4, 55, 75, 77, 207
  identity 210
  lawless 3, 250
  lawlessness 205
  livelihood strategies 53
  narratives 160
  population 4, 34, 160, 288
  patriotic 114
  practices 159, 207
  solidarity 258
  strategies 287-8
borderlines 9-10, 76, 83-4, 214, 233, 245
  exact 84, 124
  invisible 8
  new 92
  physical 8
  populated 97
  territorial 159
Boven-Kapoeas 88, 105

Index

bravery 123, 133, 221
Brigade Mobil (BRIMOB) 118
British Crown Colonies of Sarawak and North Borneo 115-6
British North Borneo 114
brokers 62-5, 177, 179-80, 187-8, 190, 225, 264, 283, 287
Brooke 86-7, 92-103, 120, 222
  administration of 87, 89, 92-8, 100
Brooke, Charles 91, 93-6, 184, 272
Brooke, James 86-7
brothels 2, 186
brothers, blood 65, 140
Brunei 87, 114-6
Brunei Rebellion 115-6
bupati 169-70, 172-4, 181-5, 206-7, 215, 220, 226, 231, 266-7, 274-7, 279
  Kapuas Hulu 119, 149, 172, 174, 181, 275, 279
  office 171, 189, 218, 275-6

Cambodia 184
Cameroon 184
Central Kalimantan 90
China 134
Chinese communities 127
  ethnic 114, 127-8, 177, 184
Chinese government 247
Chinese Malaysian 183, 252
citizens
  good 130, 259
  marginal 160, 283
citizenship 5, 24-5, 34, 114, 235, 284
class 28, 56, 62
clientelism 64
clients 61-2, 64-5, 180, 221-2
coal reserves 254

coalition-making 198
coalitions 53, 61
cockfights 193, 253
collusion 9, 55, 67, 165, 175, 205, 264, 287
colonial
  administrations 88, 92, 94
  Africa 85
  borders 30, 85, 92
  artificial 85
  expedition 83, 94, 96-7, 100
    punitative 91-2, 98, 101, 141
  extermination-war 96
  powers 79, 97, 102, 106
commander 94, 140, 145-7, 150
commissions 176, 178-9, 194-5, 198
Committee for the Establishment of the North Border District *see* Panitia Pembentukan Kabupaten Perbatasan Utara (PPKPU)
  members 272, 274, 277
Commonwealth forces 120-1, 123
  New Zealand 123
  troops 9, 124
communism 113, 115, 126-7
Communist 20, 126-7, 132-3, 135-6, 139, 146, 148, 153
  coup Indonesia 147
  infiltration 27, 113, 126-8, 154
  insurgency 9, 16, 33, 128
  insurgents 114, 125
  sympathizers 179
community leaders 2-3, 14, 77, 154, 188-9, 227
companies 118, 123, 138, 153, 155-8, 169, 173, 175-6, 180-3, 187-8, 191-7, 255-6

342

compensation 20, 155-7, 176, 184, 194, 253
conflict 14, 28, 48-9, 67, 96-8, 115, 120-1, 133, 167, 172, 181, 190
Confrontation (*see also* Konfrontasi) 10, 76, 102, 113, 119-20, 122, 124, 133, 142, 165, 224-5, 233
Congo 184
connections, cross-border business 279
contestations 52-3
contraband, cross-border 205
contracts 61, 157-8
controversy 94, 224, 250
counter-insurgency 113, 129, 144, 160, 287
countries, *batang lupar* 82
courage 122, 221
courtroom 209, 211
  killing 209
criminals 98, 218
cross-border 47
  activities 47, 92, 214, 233
    securing 241
  associates 261
  commerce, official 274
  connections 6, 120, 215, 281
    maintaining 148
  cultures 205
  interaction 11, 21, 25, 46, 48
  interests 175
  logging 175, 177, 213, 224, 232
  relations 33, 200, 283
    historical 272
  ties 47
  timber commerce 2
  trading 22, 46

Crush Malaysia campaign 118
cukong *see* tukei

Daftar Pencarian Orang (DPO) 218, 222
Dana Reboisasi (DR) 158, 167, 275
Danau Sentarum National Park 20, 295
Dayak Adat Assembly 181
Dayaks 78, 93, 96-7, 117, 119, 121, 123, 127, 131, 133, 142, 181
  border-dwelling 87, 120
  free 78
decentralization 4, 7, 58-9, 63-4, 66, 165-9, 249, 263-4, 275, 280-1, 287, 289
  processes 33, 58-60, 172, 198, 236, 272, 287, 289
decrees 152-3, 158, 170-1, 216, 238, 244, 267, 275, 296
  border development 238
defence 151-2, 182, 238-40, 270, 290
delegation, community 157, 225, 278
Delok River 98
development 6, 14, 20, 22-3, 48-9, 147, 235-41, 247-8, 251, 257-8, 261-2, 268-70
  economic 246
  initiatives 128, 238, 241
  national 4, 23, 160, 241-2
  plans, recent central government border 250
Dewan Perwakilan Daerah Republik Indonesia (DPD-RI) 242
Dewan Perwakilan Rakyat Daerah (DPRD) 245, 255, 280, 295
Dewan Perwakilan Rakyat Daerah (DPRD) II 179, 188, 218, 243, 265

| *Index*

Dinas Perindustrian dan Perdagangan 219
disputes, inter-longhouse 195
district 9
  assembly 5, 147, 170, 188, 243, 265, 274-5
  assembly members 231, 268, 275, 277
  capital 209, 223, 225
  decrees 171, 207
  election 181, 277, 280
  government 22, 28, 33, 167-70, 172-3, 178-80, 183, 193, 196, 207, 218-20, 231
    officials 265, 275
  heads 1, 3, 150, 152, 276, 279-80, 296
  legislative assembly 276
  office 174, 266, 268, 274, 277
  police 210, 215-6, 218, 223-4
  splitting 262-3, 280-1, 290 *see also* pemekaran
District Military Command *see* Komando Distrik Militer (Kodim)
District Industry and Trade Office *see* Dinas Perindustrian dan Perdagangan
Dutch 6, 33, 62, 76, 78, 83-4, 86-98, 101-6, 116, 123, 129, 146
  authorities 87, 90, 98, 101
  colonial state 286-7
  efforts 88, 90, 104
  frustrations 9
  government 83, 131
Dutch territories 84, 87, 96, 99, 101, 103
Dutch West Borneo 74, 84, 86-7, 104-6

dwifungsi doctrine 150
dwikora sukarelawan 117, 181 *see also* volunteers

East Kalimantan 32, 61, 64, 152, 175, 213, 240, 251, 263
education, mental 130
egalitarian 28, 61, 198
egalitarianism 28
elites, regional 59-60, 148
Embaloh Hulu 18, 145, 149, 225, 272
Embaloh River 89
Emergency campaign 120
Empanang 18, 27, 137, 255
Emparan 26, 299
Enthoven 79, 83
Entikong 243, 246 *see also* Pos Pemeriksaan Lintas Batas (PPLB)
entrepreneurs 59, 64, 144, 152, 154, 168, 171, 173, 176, 183, 191, 219
  cross-border 15, 65, 165, 287
ethnic, liaisons 195
ethnic groups 18, 77-9, 85, 88, 92, 141, 265-6, 273, 277, 299
ethnicity 24-5, 56, 195, 273
  cross-border 271
European colonialism 83

factions 61, 144, 149
Fast Mobile Force *see* Pasukan Gerah Tjepat (PGT)
Federation of Malaya 114
fieldwork 10, 14-5, 23, 77, 90, 122, 173, 184-5, 198, 228-9, 253, 274
gatekeepers 15, 62, 178, 192
informants 13, 15-6, 140-1, 154-5, 193

Flores 2, 193
followers 62, 64, 98-101, 103, 141, 146
foreign ideologies 126, 132
forest 23-4, 30, 133, 140-1, 148-9, 151-2, 154-6, 170-1, 175-7, 179-80, 199-200, 225-9
  customary 225
  local 155, 199
  logged 162, 164, 184
  old-growth 19-20, 180, 183
  protected 19-20, 172, 219, 226
  resources 24, 33, 60, 151, 153, 168, 171-2, 175, 225, 237, 264, 279-80
  local 24, 172, 176, 190, 238, 256
Forest Concession Liaison Fee *see* Iuran Hak Pemungutan Hasil Hutan (IHPHH)
Forest Law Enforcement Operations 216
Forest Resource Provision Funds *see* Provisi Sumber Daya Hutan (PSDH)
Forestry Department 215, 225-6
Forum for Border Community Care 266, 280, 295
Free Iban Movement *see* Gerakan Iban Merdeka (GIM)
frontier 12, 83-4, 95, 98-9
  town 213

Gallant 66-7, 106, 205, 291
gangsterism 34, 208, 213
gangsters 3, 66, 200, 214-5, 288, 291
Gerakan Bersama Maju (GBM) 273
Gerakan Iban Merdeka (GIM) 273
Golongan Karya (Golkar) 150
  party 147, 181, 188, 249

government
  administration 105, 206, 265, 273-4
  agents 206-7, 291
  authorities 4, 7, 13, 24, 34, 75, 125, 207-8, 217, 279
  bureaucracy 45, 148, 208, 281, 286
  central 23-4, 167-70, 172-4, 205-6, 215-6, 226, 230-4, 245-6, 256-8, 267-8, 279-81, 290-1
  levels of 150, 244, 249, 258, 274
  monopolies 151-2
  opinion 16
governor, West Kalimantan 2-3, 38, 119, 129, 150, 152, 274, 276, 279-80
Grand Atlantic Timber Sindirian Berhad 168, 180, 183-4, 191-2, 194, 196-7
Gross Regional Domestic Product, Kapuas Hulu 19
guerrilla warfare 7, 113, 115, 117, 119, 121, 123, 125, 127, 133-5, 145-7, 149
Guntul Mandiri 186, 217 *see also* sawmill
Gunung Cemaru 77
Gurkhas 116

Habibie, Bacharuddin Jusuf 157, 167, 239, 249, 257
Hak Pengusaha Hutan (HPH) 151-3, 155, 170, 184
Hak Pemungutan Hasil Hutan (HPHH) 169-70, 172, 180, 196 *see also* timber, community cooperatives
  concessions 170-1, 183
Hard Wood Sendirian Berhads 175

| Index

Harseno, Kentot 134, 146-7
headhunters 120
headhunting 79, 89, 91, 94, 127
   raids 90
Heart of Borneo initiative 248

Iban 24-32, 77-9, 88-95, 97-8, 100-6, 120-2, 125-46, 175-7, 191-3, 211-2, 231-3, 271-4
   adat 103, 211
   border communities 10, 62, 104-5
   border-dwelling 105
   border elites 54
   border population 24, 159, 271
   and Chinese communities 127
   communities, pre-colonial 62
   concession 154
   conservative 129-30
   and Dutch confrontations 102
   elite 62, 65-6, 154, 156, 180, 187, 225, 264, 280
   identity, ethnic 189
   longhouse communities 17, 27
   longhouses 29, 96, 122, 140, 191, 193
   and Maloh communities 129
   mercenaries 93, 95-6
   migrations 79, 89
   military confrontations 144
   pacification 7, 293
   panglima perang 145-6, 188
   patih 123, 134, 255
   rebellions 102, 106
   rebels 95, 102-3, 106
   temenggong 256, 272
   trackers 120-1
   transborder 30
Iban culture, exotic 31

Iban population 18, 25, 29, 31, 54, 76, 86, 92, 271, 299
Iban raiding parties 92
identity 25-6, 32, 105, 123
   common border 273
   ethnic 25, 32
illegal logging 2-3, 7, 63-4, 166, 199-200, 206-7, 214-6, 223, 227, 229-30, 234-5, 251
   crackdown 2, 229, 234-5, 258, 264
illegality 14, 33, 69, 169, 200, 205, 207-9, 211, 213, 215, 221-3, 229-33
illicit 6, 13-4, 16, 22, 48, 66, 205-6, 208
incursions 118-21, 124, 142
   low-impact cross-border 124
indoctrination, nationalist 160
Indonesian 9, 26, 33, 46, 85, 105, 116-8, 121, 123, 130, 152, 182-3
   army 122-3, 125, 127, 134, 136, 139, 146, 149, 187-8
   independence 76, 119, 268
   military 9, 121-2, 124, 126, 132, 136, 154, 157, 191, 249-50
   state formation 4, 7, 66, 77, 114, 160
   territory 120, 214, 219, 250
Indonesian Armed Forces *see* Angakatan Bersenjata Republik Indonesia (ABRI)
Indonesian Border Terrorists 117
Indonesian Communist Party *see* Partai Komunis Indonesia (PKI)
Indonesian National Army *see* Tentara Nasional Indonesia (TNI)
Indonesian National Citizen *see* Warga Negara Indonesia (WNI)
informal networks 59, 63, 166, 289

insurgency 113, 139
insurgents 125-7, 129, 132, 135-7, 140, 142, 149
intelligence 121, 127, 139-40, 142
  assistants 145
  gatherers 136, 187
interethnic
  distrust 265
  feuding 95
international borders 1, 4, 8, 18, 26, 45, 50, 56, 70, 79, 103, 235
investment, cross-border 11
Iuran Hak Pemungutan Hasil Hutan (IHPHH) 171
Izin Usaha Pemanfaatan Hasil Hutan Kayu (IUPHHK) 170

Jakarta 2, 53, 87, 124, 139, 146-7, 153-5, 178, 188, 230-1, 245, 277-9
jalan tikus 10, 19
Japanese occupation 104
Java 60, 86, 117, 146-7, 155, 211, 233
journalists 218, 224, 230
jungle 115, 117, 135, 138
  warfare 160
justice 208-9, 211-3

Kaban, Malam S. 226, 248, 299
Kabupaten Perbatasan Utara 262, 266, 268, 275, 297
Kadarusno, governor 129
Kail Kalbar 216, 224, 227
Kalimantan 10, 21, 25, 27, 31-2, 47, 78, 115-6, 118-22, 126-7, 214, 250-1
Kalimantan Iban 22, 31-2, 47, 75, 95, 120, 122, 128, 177, 184, 192

Kantoek tribe 91 *see also* Kantu
Kantu 78, 95
Kapuas Hulu (*see also* district) 17-9, 124-5, 149-50, 168, 170-4, 181, 184-5, 214-5, 240, 243, 275, 279-80
  district of 10, 170, 174
Kapuas River 88, 300
Kartu Tana Penduduk (KTP) 174
Kater, Cornelis 88, 94, 97, 102
Kawasan Hutan 169
Kedang Expedition 95, 98
Kedang Range 95-6
kin 10, 32, 46-7, 79, 86, 90, 103, 189-90, 211, 274, 299
kings, small border 29
kinship 9, 30, 165, 192, 195
  bonds 16, 192
  relations, long-term cross-border 188
Komando Distrik Militer (Kodim) 139, 296
Konfrontasi (*see also* Confrontation) 9, 114, 119, 122, 132, 134, 138, 147, 155, 160, 293, 300
Koperasi Serba Usaha (KSU) 171, 173
koppensnellen see headhunting
Korps Komando Operasi (KKO) 118
Kuching 12, 98

labour migration, cross-border 10, 189, 264
land conversion permit 182
land disputes 274
land ownership 62, 78, 274
landlords 61-2

Lanjak
  area 104, 120-1, 129, 135, 137-8, 147, 149, 155, 185
  border towns of 2, 179
  incident 4
laws 52-3, 68-9, 167-8, 170, 205-6, 208, 213-4, 218, 232-3, 241, 262-3, 267
Layang 105, 181, 266
Leboyan River 17, 95, 101-2, 139, 157, 188, 252
Legal Pluralism 68
legality 5, 14, 69, 105, 169, 200, 205, 207, 217-9, 229-31, 233, 288
licit 34, 49, 208, 212, 227, 232
Lintas Batas (LIBAS) 252-4
local autonomy 34, 207, 232, 262, 281
local economy 2, 20, 23, 169, 209, 258, 264, 276
local leaders 6, 146, 154, 156, 188
local military commands 146, 179, 254
local norms 65
loggers 166, 185-6, 193
logging 2, 152-6, 169, 171, 173-4, 183, 197, 199, 213-5, 230-1, 239-40, 258
  business 172, 178, 186, 188, 206, 230
  companies 76, 152, 175, 177
  crews 2, 180, 192
  licences 152, 182
  operations 153, 155-8, 172, 175-7, 179-80, 193, 195-6, 206, 224, 230
    cross-border 33
longhouse communities 17, 27-9, 79, 90, 123, 139, 197

Lubok Antu 19, 21, 100, 120-1, 139, 144, 175, 177, 190, 194, 230
lumber 174, 176, 186, 195

McCarthy, John 59, 63-4, 168, 173, 199
Mahmud Subarkah, General 147
Malaysia 11, 21-2, 30-2, 124-5, 176-8, 213-4, 219-20, 235-7, 240-1, 245-7, 250-1, 270-2
Malaysian
  paramilitary forces 250
  state of Sarawak 8, 18, 26
  timber barons 23-4, 33, 65, 168, 198, 214, 216, 261, 264
Malaysian Chinese 19, 153, 158, 168, 170, 176-7, 182, 217, 229, 300
Malaysian Federation 114-5, 117, 119
Malaysian Government White Paper 118
Malaysian peninsula 120
Malaysian Ringgit 174, 194, 243
Maloh 18, 77-8, 95, 131, 265, 273-4
  and Iban communities 273
Maphilindo 115
marginalization 57
margins 50-1, 70, 268
Marine Commandos see Korps Komando Operasi (KKO)
Martínez, Oscar J. 23, 46
massacres, Chinese 127
meetings, awareness-raising 269
Megawati Sukarnoputri 216, 244, 267
Melayu 18, 77-8, 265, 273, 277
  kingdoms 62, 78-9
Memet, Yogie S. 147

mercenaries 94
Middle-Term National Development Plan *see* Rencana Pembangunan Jangka Menengah Nasional (RPJM)
Migdal 1, 43, 50, 52-4, 75, 284-5
migration 76-9, 84, 89, 92, 97, 103
militarization 76-7, 114, 132, 134, 142, 147-8, 150, 234, 252, 254, 281
military 2, 13-4, 122-3, 125-32, 138-47, 149-52, 181-2, 233, 238-40, 249-50, 254-5, 257
  authority 154, 236, 249
  battalion 108, 117-8, 132, 138, 146, 252
  battalions 117, 132, 138, 146, 252
  border post 220
  camp, large 251-2
  command, regional 129, 215, 278
  control post, permanent 235, 250
  entrepreneurs 66, 291
  officers 150, 152, 154, 188, 216, 278
  operations 125-6, 136
  patrols 105, 214
  punishment 139
  veterans 154-5
military certificate 107-8, 138
Ministry of Defence and Security 152, 238
Ministry of Forestry 158, 167, 170, 216, 222, 225, 227, 240, 296
Ministry of Home Affairs 274, 277
Ministry of Trade 219
missionaries 130-2, 273
  Capuchin 131, 273
Moore, Sally Falk 67-9, 165, 207, 212

movement 14, 68, 79, 92, 101, 122, 128, 262, 265-7, 273-4, 278-9
  border autonomy 7, 24
  border district 189, 265
  cross-border 5
  members 267, 270-1, 278
  transborder trade 206
Musyawarah Pimpinan Daerah (MUSPIDA) 222
Musyawarah Pimpinan Kecamatan (MUSPIKA) 146

Nanga Badau 19, 21, 23, 71, 94, 96, 118, 134, 194, 220, 243
  border town of 146, 229
Nanga Kantuk 27
Nasution, Muslimin 158
nation-states, unified 130
national
  consciousness 128, 160, 271
  heartland 12, 47
  loyalties 34, 123, 130, 146, 270, 286-7
national parks 172, 219, 228-9
National Red Cross 187
nationalism 83, 114, 130, 160, 241, 245
nationhood 35, 70, 83, 247
natural, resources, local 172, 232
natural resources 3, 7, 11, 33, 57, 83, 86, 88, 151, 169, 257, 275-6
Negara Kesatuan Kalimantan Utara (NKKU) 116
negotiations 24, 52-3, 57, 61, 67, 69, 175-6, 194, 196-7, 284-5, 287, 291
neocolonialism 115
Netherlands East Indies 86-7

networks 5, 15, 53, 55-6, 59, 61-2, 65-6, 68, 70, 147-8, 261-2, 288-9
  cross-border 6, 32, 57, 60
  cross-border smuggling 84
New Order 10, 51, 150-2, 160, 178, 181, 191, 198, 200, 238, 240, 255
  authoritarian regime 114, 262
  period 16, 154, 176, 178, 187
NGO 159, 199, 207, 216, 248, 267, 277
norms and rules 67-9, 200, 212
North Border District *see* Kabupaten Perbatasan Utara
North Kalimantan National Army *see* Tentara Nasional Kalimantan Utara (TNKU)
North Kalimantan Unitary State *see* Negara Kesatuan Kalimantan Utara (NKKU)

Oevang Oeray 119
oil palm 250-1, 255-6
  plantations 173, 235, 248, 251, 254-5
Operasi Hutan Lestari 224
Operasi Sapu Bersih 125
Operation Claret 120
Operation Clean Sweep *see* Operasi Sapu Bersih
Operation Forest Conversion *see* Operasi Hutan Lestari
Operation Judas 177
operations, anti-PARAKU 147, 155, 184
otonomi daerah *see* regional autonomy
otorita perbatasan 267

Pan-Dayak 119
Pancasila 130, 151
panglima perang 145-7, 149, 155-6, 188, 265
Panitia Pembentukan Kabupaten Perbatasan Utara (PPKPU) 266-8, 273, 297
Partai Demokrasi Indonesia (PDI) 150
Partai Komunis Indonesia (PKI) 117, 147, 150
Pasukan Gerah Tjepat (PGT) 118
Pasukan Rakyat Kalimantan Utara (PARAKU) 133-46, 148-50, 153-4, 177, 187
  rebels 111, 133-5, 141, 149
  Unit Satuan 135
patih 29, 90-1, 104, 143, 156, 179, 187-8, 265
patron-client relationships 60-2, 64, 234
patronage 5, 54, 60-1, 63-6, 165, 167, 169, 171, 173, 175, 177, 199
  networks 54, 60, 62-3, 65, 165
  predatory 57
  relations 33, 61, 63, 177, 180, 198
  patrons 33, 61-5, 180, 185, 221, 283
peace agreement 98, 149
pemekaran 262-3, 265, 268, 273, 281, 290
  process 263-4, 267-8, 274, 276-7, 279-81
Pemilihan Kepala Daerah (Pilkada) 276 *see also* district election
Pendapatan Asli Daerah (PAD) 168, 171
Peng, General 134, 141
penghulu 91

Perlawanan Rakyat (WANRA) 141-2
Philippines 115
plantation (*see also* oil palm) 158, 215, 236, 238, 240, 246-9, 254-6, 275, 279
  companies 255-6
  corridor 246, 251
  development 183, 247, 255
  plan 247-8
Police Mobile Brigade *see* Brigade Mobil (BRIMOB)
Pontianak 12, 20, 26, 94, 99-100, 102-3, 174-5, 218-9, 240-1, 246-7, 250, 280
Pos Lintas Batas (PLB) 21, 35, 296
Pos Pemeriksaan Lintas Batas (PPLB) 243
poverty 23, 57, 245, 268-9
presidential election campaign 242
presidential decrees 141, 216, 232, 238, 241, 296
Pringle, R. 98
processes of situational adjustment 67-8
Program for Development of Border Areas 241
province, new 263, 279-80
provincial capital 76, 178, 266, 276
  Pontianak 18, 152, 188-9, 235
Provincial Forestry Agency 275
provincial governments 2, 172, 177, 193, 200, 232, 234, 237, 243, 247, 258
provincial police 210, 215, 224, 297
Provisi Sumber Daya Hutan (PSDH) 158, 275
PT Benua Indah 152, 189
PT Lanjak Deras 158

PT Perhutani 158
PT Perkebunan Pusantara (PTPN) 248
PT Plantana Razindo Company 182
PT Yamaker 152-9, 178, 180, 189, 238
Puring Kencana 18, 26, 128, 252
Putussibau 23, 147, 174, 181, 188-90, 209, 211, 218-20, 223-5, 243-4, 265-6, 275-6

Rachman 125-7, 130
raiding 77-9, 84, 93, 97-8, 101, 103, 141, 149
raids 10, 91, 93, 101, 118, 217, 223-4
  cross-border 94-5, 122, 128
Raja Brooke 91, 98-9, 221, 271 *see also* Brooke
Rajah of Sarawak 91, 96
Ranting 189-91, 196-7
re-militarization 244, 257
rebellion 87, 97, 116
rebels 66, 98, 100, 116, 118, 125, 133, 140, 146, 157, 221, 271
Reforestation Funds *see* Dana Reboisasi (DR)
reform governments 58
regional autonomy 23, 58, 167-9, 172, 178, 183, 198-200, 219, 236-7, 258, 262, 293
  increased 4, 167, 288-90
  legislation 58
Papuans 278
Regional Representatives Council *see* Dewan Perwakilan Daerah Republik Indonesia (DPD-RI)
regionalism 58, 289

regulations 6, 53, 56, 68-9, 168, 170-1, 173-4, 206, 212, 221, 241, 256
regulative border policies 75
relations, landlord-tenant 61
religion 126, 130, 132
Rencana Pembangunan Jangka Menengah Nasional (RPJM) 241
Rentap 90
Republic of Indonesia 114, 124, 241, 270, 296
Resimen Para Komando Angkatan Darat (RPKAD) 117, 134-5, 146
resistance 44, 55, 61, 68, 70, 101, 290
resource extraction 10, 33, 113, 115, 117, 119, 121, 123, 125, 149-51, 155, 159-61
revenues 155, 167, 172, 174, 200, 207, 209, 228-9, 238, 254, 257
rights 27, 30, 88, 103, 159, 219, 225, 227
  customary 274
road, North Bound 22
roads 1, 22-3, 147, 157, 185, 194, 220, 229, 247, 252, 256, 269
  main border 19
Rokan Group Holding Company 255
royalties 23, 168
rules 14, 29, 45, 48, 52-4, 64, 67-9, 165, 212, 254
Rumah Manah 17, 90, 101-3, 122-3, 139, 191-4, 196-7, 228, 253
Ra'ayat Party 116

Sabah 114
safety belt 151, 238
Sambas 193
Sambas-Lundu border area 84
Sanggau 125, 127, 168
Sanjaya, Cornelis-Christiandy, Governor West Kalimantan 280
Sarawak 9-10, 21-3, 30-2, 86-7, 89-98, 103-4, 116-24, 126-7, 133-5, 173-7, 183-6, 192-4
  authorities 177, 214
  border 10, 175, 181, 202, 204, 250
  border officials 21
  border region 121
  companies 173-6, 192
  Dayaks 98, 100
  entrepreneurs 173, 180, 234
  government 26, 95, 125, 127-8, 149
  relatives 196-7
  ruler 95, 271
  territories 9, 100
  timber industry 183, 189, 194
Sarawak, Iban 31-2, 47, 93, 120, 127, 133, 192-3, 195
Sarawak Border Scouts 120, 142
Sarawak Chinese 133-4, 173, 179, 183, 191, 193
Sarawak Chinese and Iban workers 193
Sarawak Communist Organization (SCO) 133, 137, 177
Sarawak Gazette 97, 99-100
Sarawak Museum Library (SML) 99-100
Sarawak Nationalist Party (SNAP) 122
Sarawak Special Branch 127
sawmills 18, 180, 185-7, 194, 196-7, 213, 217-8, 220, 224-5, 228, 231
schemes, grand 234, 246, 257

Schendel, Willem van vii, 54, 60, 90, 148, 205, 207-8, 236
schooling 26, 30, 130-1, 146, 148, 190, 274
Scott, James 49, 61-2, 65, 79, 85, 105, 236
scouts 120-1, 136, 138, 188
security 22, 34, 97, 145, 152, 158, 224, 237-41, 247, 249-51, 257-9, 289-90
  national 3, 20, 153, 237-8, 242, 254-5
semi-autonomous social fields 67-9, 165, 190, 207, 212
separatism 119, 242, 257, 270-2, 285
settlements, transmigration 238
shotgun 22, 143-4, 196, 209, 213
  shells 22, 196
Sibu 154, 177, 183, 196, 218, 230
  area 180, 184
Simanggang 99-100, 149 *see also* Sri Aman
Simanggang Monthly Reports 99-100
Sintang 127, 168
situational adjustment 67-8
smuggling 10, 21-2, 46, 48, 84, 89-90, 185, 205, 237
social sciences 44-5, 49-50
society 6-7, 28-9, 44, 50-1, 53-4, 59, 66, 190, 212, 264, 283-5, 292
Soeharto, President 13, 23, 51, 58-60, 75-6, 124-5, 135, 150-2, 167-70, 238-9, 249-50, 289-90
Soeharto, regime 76, 124, 289-90
Soekarno, President 115-8, 122, 124-5, 147, 150, 155
Soemadi, Colonel 119, 147

Soemadi, General 128, 135, 141, 145, 147, 188
soldiers 73, 96, 117-8, 123, 130, 134, 138, 140-1, 143-4, 253-4
  regular 93, 121, 125, 142
solidarity, cross-border 271
South China Sea 86
Southeast Asia 33, 43, 46, 50, 55, 57, 61, 83, 113, 184, 205, 288-9
sovereignty 5, 49, 200, 235-7, 239, 241, 243, 245, 247, 249, 251, 257
  national 6, 215, 245, 250, 257
spaces of exception 51
Sri Aman 149, 177, 214
state
  authorities 4, 6, 33-4, 43-4, 46, 52, 54, 56-7, 105-6, 132, 254, 283-6
  central 59, 67, 156, 165, 289, 291
  formation 4, 6-7, 45, 49, 51-2, 54-5, 57, 67, 113, 206, 282-6, 291
  ideal 50
  illegality 233
  laws 53, 68-9, 205-7, 209, 212, 221
  simplification 236
  theory of the 5, 7, 43, 50-2, 160, 236, 284, 291
state-society 51, 285
  relations 4, 7, 51, 59, 61, 67, 165, 284
Stephen Kalong Ningkam 122
Strait of Melaka 83
strategies
  cross-border 11, 49, 103
  local 4, 33-4, 57, 165, 285, 290
strong man 221
subdistricts 15, 17-8, 27, 145, 173, 181, 188, 207, 220, 263, 269, 299-300

five Iban-dominated 18, 242
Sudirman, Mohamad Basofi 146
sukarelawan 117
Sultanate of Brunei 26
Suyanto, TNI Comander-in-Chief 251
swidden 10, 19, 30, 39, 128-9, 143

Taman Negara Betung Kerihun (TNBK) 20, 180, 223, 228-9, 248, 276
Tambul Husin 275, 277 *see also bupati*
Tanjungpura, military command 117, 126, 175, 181, 215, 250
Tanjungpura, University 175, 181
Tanzania 67
taxes 23, 78, 83-4, 90, 97-8, 104, 174, 215, 219, 243
  door 97
  unofficial 3, 243
team, anti-logging 231, 234
Team Wanalaga 215
Tebedu 118, 243
tembawai 9, 101
temenggong 29, 73, 90-1, 104, 143, 146, 155-7, 179, 188-9, 206, 208, 254
Tentara Nasional Indonesia (TNI) 249, 251
Tentara Nasional Kalimantan Utara (TNKU) 115-8, 120, 122, 125, 133-4
territorial borders 6, 70, 83, 88, 106, 151, 283, 285, 288, 290
Thai-Burma-China borderlands 30
Thailand 55-6, 184
Thailand and China border 148

threats, neo-imperialistic 115
timber 173-6, 178-81, 194, 196-7, 214-5, 217, 219, 225-6, 228, 231, 255, 275-6
  barons 2, 14, 64, 66 *see also* tukei
  broker 169, 194, 223
  business 169, 187, 227, 238, 249
  camps 177, 185-6, 217, 231
  community cooperatives 170-1, 173, 178, 222
  companies 28, 155-6, 189, 231
  concessions 146, 152, 154, 158, 170-1, 182-3, 188, 191, 255, 296
  contractors 184
  sawn 2, 163, 195
  smuggling 2, 48, 174, 198, 247, 254
timber mafia 214
Timor 2, 193
Together We Prosper Movement *see* Gerakan Bersama Maju (GBM)
trade
  cross-border 20, 142, 209, 231, 240, 245
  forced 79
trails, cross-border 10
transmigration 247
treaties 83-4
troops 101, 116, 119, 121
trust 13-4, 64-5, 208, 221, 279
tukei 173-80, 183, 187, 190, 192-8, 207, 212, 214, 216, 221-3, 228-9, 233-4 *see also* Apheng
Tun Jugah Anak Barieng 122
tusut 77
twilight
  character 34
  institutions 54

Ulu Ai 100
Ulu Leboyan 101-3, 130, 156-7, 176-7, 180, 186-7, 189, 191-2, 194, 197, 228-9, 252-3
underdevelopment, border 20, 26, 128, 213, 237, 240, 242, 262, 266, 271, 282
upriver logging camps 186, 192, 194, 217, 228
Urang Emparan 26
Urang Kampar 92 *see also* warriors
Usnata 209-12

Vietnam 184
vigilante killings 211-2
vigilantism 7, 14, 34, 54, 157, 200, 208, 212, 232-3, 272
village 28, 63, 65, 132, 135-6, 142, 184, 220, 253, 263
  heads 14-5, 28, 56, 65, 142, 148, 171, 196
violence 15, 127, 140, 205, 213, 287
volunteers 109, 117-8, 125, 134-5, 187

Wahid, Abdurrahman 209, 239
Wanalaga team 231
  units 142

war
  time of (musim kayau) 96
  undeclared border 33
warfare 79, 89, 92, 286
Warga Negara Indonesia (WNI) 127
warriors 92, 101, 211
weapons of the weak 55
Weber, Max 50
West Borneo 77, 83, 90, 93, 104, 151
West Kalimantan 4, 10-1, 31, 76-7, 124-5, 134, 146-7, 152, 167-70, 182-4, 242-3, 290-1
  borderlands of 166, 283
  Iban 25, 30, 104
  province of 26, 150-2, 218
West Kalimantan Army Command 135
West Papua 183-4
West Sumba 277
Western Borneo 86, 88-9, 92
White Paper 137
White Rajah 86 *see also* Brooke
World War II 76, 87, 104, 116
World Wildlife Foundation (WWF) 248

Yudhoyono, Susilo Bambang (SBY), President 216, 222, 236, 239, 242, 247, 297